Software Reusability

Volume I
Concepts and Models

ACM PRESS

Editor-in-Chief:

Peter Wegner, *Brown University*

ACM Press books represent a collaboration between the Association for Computing Machinery (ACM) and Addison-Wesley Publishing Company to develop and publish a broad range of new works. These works generally fall into one of four series.

Frontier Series. Books focused on novel and exploratory material at the leading edge of computer science and practice.

Anthology Series. Collected works of general interest to computer professionals and/or society at large.

Tutorial Series. Introductory books to help nonspecialists quickly grasp either the general concepts or the needed details of some specific topic.

History Series. Books documenting past developments in the field and linking them to the present.

In addition, ACM Press books include selected conference and workshop proceedings.

Software Reusability

Volume I
Concepts and Models

Edited by

Ted J. Biggerstaff

Microelectronics and Computer Technology Corporation (MCC)

Alan J. Perlis

Yale University

ACM Press
New York, New York

Addison-Wesley Publishing Company

Reading, Massachusetts • Menlo Park, California • New York
Don Mills, Ontario • Wokingham, England • Amsterdam • Bonn
Sydney • Singapore • Tokyo • Madrid • San Juan

ACM Press Frontier Series

Library of Congress Cataloging-in-Publication Data

Biggerstaff, Ted J.
    Software reusability / Ted J. Biggerstaff, Alan J. Perlis.
       p. cm.
    Contents: V. 1. Comcepts and models — v. 2. Applications and experience.
    Bibliography: v. 1, p.
    Includes index.
    ISBN 0-201-08017-6 (v. 1). — ISBN 0-201-50018-3 (v. 2)
    1. Computer software—Reusability. I. Perlis, Alan J.
II. Title.
QA76.76.R47B543   1989
005—dc19

88-34280
CIP

ABCDEFGHIJ-AL-89

CONTENTS

FOREWORD

This is a handbook of modern software reusability. I find it hard to imagine any aspect missing—whether viewed by a computer scientist or the software practitioner. This is no surprise: Rarely does one see a book on a single subject by authors with such a variety of backgrounds.

Whence is this breadth? For a moment I thought that the usual had happened again: As a new buzzword emerges, much ongoing work is re-presented in a new light in order to attract attention. But this is not the case here. Each chapter is relevant and the volume spans the entire spectrum of reusability well. The real reason for the breadth is that reusability is the best manifestation of software engineering industrialized, and that the software engineer is becoming less the programmer and more the system designer.

Ultimately, a program is a fiction, not made of matter that wears and tears; it is closer to encapsulated human thought than to physical artifact. Yet software in the form of physical pattern, captured for instance by magnetics, becomes an increasingly important part of an increasingly large number of products and processes, from washing machines to space ships to computerized enterprises. As a result of this trend, software people become exposed to the traditional engineering culture. At the same time, engineers in industry recognize software as the glue that tightens hardware components into system products and information-based processes.

Only the recent edition of an unabridged dictionary contains the word *reuse* and its derivatives, yet traditional engineering survived centuries without explicitly "reusing." Accumulation of experience (reuse of design?), reduction of variety by standardization (reuse of parameterized programs?), and well-defined interfaces for interchangeability and reduced complexity (information hiding?) have always been considered fundamental to engineering and in no need of an explicit term: They are the lifeblood of good design practice.

Introducing all these time-proven concepts to software in a single volume and by such distinguished authors is a huge and welcome step toward further maturing the engineering of software. We need these books now as we must solve problems of increasing complexity. Islands of computer applications gradually become integrated into networks of programs; the hardware vehicle carrying these applications becomes less of a monolith and more of a network of microprocessor-based workstations; and after decades of serving individuals—scientists, accountants, teachers, secretaries—the computer in the network will soon coordinate human cooperative efforts.[1] This requires the design of large, distributed, asynchronous systems of great complexity. We have no choice but to base the design on cumulative wisdom through reuse.

Given this tall order, we cannot focus only on programming in the small, but must pay increasing attention to the upstream (i.e., system design) portion of the software development process. We have been passing on ever more tasks to the machine, the first step being the delegation of code generation and optimization to the compiler. Now we must learn how to step on fellow software engineers' shoulders and not only on their toes, by absorbing and putting to practical use as much of these books' wisdom as our engineering instinct suggests.

L. A. BELADY

Vice President and Program Director
Software Technology Program
MCC

[1] *Proceedings: CSCW '86: Conference on Computer-Supported Cooperative Work*, December 3–5, 1986, Austin, Texas. Sponsored by Microelectronics & Computer Technology Corporation, in cooperation with the Association for Computing Machinery *et al*.

PREFACE

Software Reusability: Concepts and Models, with its accompanying volume, *Software Reusability: Applications and Experience*, is aimed at describing an emerging technical area. In the books, we have tried

- ☐ to present a technological framework or context for understanding software reuse,
- ☐ to present a representative spectrum of the technologies that may be applied to the reuse problem so that the reader who wants to exploit software reuse may start by standing on the shoulders of others,
- ☐ to present a spectrum of viewpoints so that the book will be of value to both the researcher and the working software engineer, and finally,
- ☐ to provide a sense of what works in reuse and what does not.

This book will be of value to a variety of readers:

- ☐ the graduate student grappling with the issues of software development and how to improve it through technology,
- ☐ the industrial manager or senior scientist of a software research, advanced planning, or advanced development organization who is looking for ways to guide his company to improvements in productivity and quality, and
- ☐ the industrial application manager or senior scientist who is tracking advanced technology to keep his department on the leading edge of software development.

Graduate students may be especially interested in papers on component classification and search, on the theory of specification, on knowledge bases and reuse, and on the role of languages and environments in reuse. Each of these papers presents a context of completed work but opens up a number of areas for further research. These papers will provide ample material for a one-term discussion seminar and will suggest a rich list of topics for master's projects and Ph.D. dissertations.

Managers or senior scientists from advanced development or planning departments, will find some early data on quantitative results of reuse, case studies of reuse in both academic and company environments, and some descriptions of various technical approaches to reuse. These papers should provide a rich set of material to aid in the planning and establishment of reuse projects within industrial settings.

Of particular interest to the applications manager or senior scientist are several overview papers that provide both a technical and political context for reuse. These papers serve to inform the reader not only about the technology that can be applied to realize reuse, but also about the forces that foster or impede the application of reuse in software development.

The Introduction is for all readers, in that it attempts to place each paper in a context and to explain the contributions of that paper in the overall framework of reuse research and application. The Introduction goes a bit farther by providing some editorial comment on the adoption of reuse, the risks of ignoring it, and its successes and failures, where we feel that such comment may help the reader to better appreciate a given paper or better understand and foster reuse in his or her environment.

We have resisted the temptation to cast reuse into a strictly language paradigm. That is, we have not taken the position that some language, say Ada, is the answer to all or most reuse issues. Such a position implies that there are no further problems to be solved, or if there are, they are trivially simple. Some people do take a position that is almost as radical as this, but we believe that such an approach misses all of the deep issues and hard problems in reuse and in the end will exploit very little of the significant productivity and quality opportunities that reuse can provide. Yes, the reuse problem does indeed have representational aspects (read that "language aspects," if you like), but these are only a very small part of the problem. Choosing a target programming language is barely a start because programming languages provide so little of the structure necessary for powerful reuse—Ada packages, generics, and parameterization notwithstanding.

There is no consensus about what technical approaches are best for various kinds of reuse problems and little understanding of the nature of reuse opportunities, let alone the constraints, difficulties, and shortcomings of reuse. In this book, we have tried to present a balanced picture of reuse, dispensing with hype and being conservative in promises. We have tried to focus upon the most promising, robust, and well-tested results—those theories that have been well worked out, those technologies that have been tested over some period of time or have been used in a real world environment, and those concepts that grapple with important issues in reuse. We have tried to avoid the "yet another" syndrome of presenting a credible result, but one that is not really distinguished along any of the lines mentioned above. In summary, we have tried to present results that are unique, that stand out, and that will endure.

Acknowledgments

We would like to thank a number of people who have helped to bring this book into existence. First, the authors. They have been cooperative, understanding, and helpful in a project whose scale necessitated such cooperation. Second, the reviewers. We would like to acknowledge the valuable suggestions of the referees who reviewed the manuscript for this book, Dr. John Knight, Professor Marvin Zelkowitz, and Professor C. V. Ramamoorthy. Their comments changed the shape of the book and improved it significantly. Thirdly, the Addison-Wesley editors and representatives, including Peter Gordon and Helen Goldstein, who all labored to help solve problems when they arose, took on tasks the editors could not find the time to do, and generally worked to eliminate road blocks that would have slowed us down. Fourth, Jane Carlton of the ACM, who helped with reprint permissions. Fifth, Gloria Gutierrez, who helped with the early administration, correspondence, and organization of the materials in the book. And finally, Jeanne Kintner has been responsible more recently for administration, organization, correspondence, some text entry, and editing of a few papers, and a myriad of other tasks. Without Jeanne's hard work, commitment, and organizational ability in the face of chaos, the books would have taken far longer.

Ted J. Biggerstaff
Alan Perlis

CONTRIBUTORS

Ted Biggerstaff
*Microelectronics and Computer
Technology Corporation (MCC)*

James M. Boyle
Argonne National Laboratory

Thomas E. Cheatham, Jr.
Harvard University

Paul C. Clements
Naval Research Laboratory

Ed Dubinsky
Clarkson College

Martin S. Feather
University of Southern California

Stephan Freudenberger
Multiflow Computer, Inc.

Joseph A. Goguen
*University of Oxford
SRI International*

Ellis Horowitz
University of Southern California

Shmuel Katz
The Technion

Richard B. Kieburtz
Oregon Graduate Center

Steven D. Litvintchouk
Mitre Corporation

Allen S. Matsumoto
Cimflex Teknowledge

John B. Munson
Unisys Corporation

James M. Neighbors
*System Analysis, Design,
and Assessment*

David L. Parnas
Queen's University

Rubén Prieto-Díaz
CONTEL Technology Center

John Rice
Purdue University

Charles A. Richter
*Microelectronics and Computer
Technology Corporation (MCC)*

Edith Schonberg
New York University

J.T. Schwartz
New York University

Herb Schwetman
*Microelectronics and Computer
Technology Corporation (MCC)*

Khe-Sing The
University of Texas at Austin

Peter Wegner
Brown University

David M. Weiss
Software Productivity Consortium

Dennis M. Volpano
Cornell University

INTRODUCTION

Software reuse is the reapplication of a variety of kinds of knowledge about one system to another similar system in order to reduce the effort of development and maintenance of that other system. This reused knowledge includes artifacts such as domain knowledge, development experience, design decisions, architectural structures, requirements, designs, code, documentation, and so forth. We have tried to be "expansive"—to borrow a term from Horowitz and Munson—in this definition of reuse.

THE VERY LARGE SCALE REUSE PROBLEM

Why do we take this expansive view of reuse? The simple answer is that the more narrowly defined views of reuse have not shown a very large return on investment.[1] Examples of narrow views of reuse are "Reuse is the reapplication of code," "Reuse is the use of subroutine or object libraries," or "Reuse of the use of Ada packages." All of these views center around the reapplication of code components, and because source code languages induce a high degree of specificity on the reusable components, the most highly reusable components tend to be small. Building systems out of small components leaves a lot of work to be done in building the architectural superstructure that binds the components into a whole system, and the cost

---

[1]There are exceptions to this statement, but they tend to occur in very narrowly defined problem domains. See Lanergan *et al.* in Volume 2 of this book for an example of such an exception.

to build this superstructure is typically very much larger than the savings afforded by reusing a set of small components.

Well then, why not just make the code components larger? Unfortunately, this approach produces its own set of problems. As the code components are made larger and larger, they become less and less likely to be reused. Their specificity reduces the likelihood that exactly the same set of requirements will arise again. Therefore, while the potential payoff for any single reuse may be high, it is mitigated both by the low likelihood of reuse and the significant effort that may be required to understand and adapt large components to the new system. This is the crux of what we have dubbed the Very Large Scale Reuse (or VLSR) problem.

Understand that we are not saying code-oriented reuse is bad and should not be done—quite the opposite. We expect code-oriented reuse as a matter of course, but if we are to realize the full potential of reuse, we must look beyond code-oriented reuse to a Very Large Scale Reuse.

VLSR introduces a whole new set of research problems centered around the issue of making the component representation sufficiently general to allow reuse over a broad range of target systems. That is, VLSR requires that we eliminate some of the specificity necessitated by a source code–oriented specification. We must seek representations that allow the large-grain component structure to be described precisely while leaving many of the small, relatively unimportant details uncommitted. Such representations must allow a broader range of information to be specified than source code can accommodate—for example, design structures, domain knowledge, design decision, and so forth. Therefore, with the VLSR problem in mind, these volumes will examine a much broader range of representations and technologies than if we had taken a narrow code-oriented viewpoint.

Reuse today

By our broad definition of reuse, we are already reusing software to a limited extent today. Perhaps we do this unconsciously, informally, and inefficiently, but the seeds of reusability already lurk in our current methods of software development and maintenance. Unfortunately, over the broad range of software developments, we have not been very successful at software reuse today. Of course there are a few exceptions to this picture, and we will focus on these exceptions in order to suggest how to improve the success rate.

How does reuse happen today, to the extent that it does? During initial system development, reuse may be totally absent, but more often it manifests itself as the informal reuse of in-head knowledge about older, similar systems. Sometimes reuse is as simple as the sharing of a set of routines in a run-time library that is designed to be common to both an existing and a planned system. Similarly, two object-oriented systems may share a set of common objects. Occasionally the system to be developed may be a member of a "system family"—that is, a set of systems that have highly similar functionality and architectures. In this case, reuse may involve the adaptation of working modules (ideally, large-scale modules) from existing systems in the family. Of course during maintenance, reuse is a fact of life because the maintenance engineer is continually reusing the whole infrastructure associated with the system being maintained. In this case, reuse is often formalized through a number of project specific support tools.

Thus, over the broad span of systems, reuse is exploited today but to a very limited extent. On the other hand, we see exceptions where reuse is being used far more effectively than today's norm, and these suggest that there is a good deal of room for improvement. To this end, this book will describe those tools, representations, and organizing principles that allow us to more fully exploit software reuse and thereby improve the overall productivity and quality of the software development process. The following sections will introduce papers that provide a variety of concepts and models of software reuse.

▌ OVERVIEW AND ASSESSMENT

The papers in this section develop several different perspectives on the subject of reusability. The Biggerstaff and Richter paper is aimed at providing a contextual framework for the overall volume of papers. Specifically, it establishes a framework for organizing the reuse technologies based on their key properties. It also describes the dilemmas that reuse presents to the practitioner, and looks at some of the factors that affect the acceptance and evolution of the technology. Finally, the paper identifies some problem areas where research is likely to provide results of significant value.

The Horowitz and Munson paper describes several abstract architectures that, in one way or another, reuse elements of previous systems. This paper is important because of its expansive viewpoint. The authors recognize that limiting one's view of reuse to the code component paradigm is procrustean and seriously limits the kinds of inventions that can arise, given the broad range of tools and models that are available to attack the problem. For example, it may be quite advantageous to add a bit of generation technology to a strict component reuse system. This expansive view suggests the breadth of the issues underlying reusability.

The issues of reuse are broader than just the creation of reusable, executable components that will be assembled into a target program. For example, one must recognize the need for standards that transcend any single component or set of components. These standards apply to the data that is interchanged among programs as well as the architectures that impose the broad structural patterns on systems.

Indeed, in every widely successful reuse system, and especially those that are focused on the reuse of code, broad domain standards are essential for the overall coordination of the component sets so that components can truly be assembled based only on their function, inputs, and outputs. There is a strong relationship between such standards and the notion of an architecture that transcends single components. Such standards are much like the standards that hardware component manufacturers establish so that they can plug their components together. At the chip level there are certain kinds of standard signals (e.g., enable, address lines, data lines, interrupt signal lines, and so forth). At the board level there are similar standards (e.g., the S-100, VME, and Multibus bus standards). Chips and boards that adhere to such architectural standards can easily be assembled into high-level structures, and those that do not, cannot.

Herein lies a rule for those who would create libraries of reusable code components. The library should be based on a standard for the domain-specific types of the data consumed and produced by the components in that library. If there is not such an architectural standard that applies across all components in the library, then the level of reuse will be very much less than it could be and very much less than one would like. This observation militates against just finding and throwing together a set of components that have functions more or less covering the needs of the using organization. A library of components that are to be (re)used together needs to be designed according to a common architectural guideline that reflects both the nature of the problem domain (e.g., real-time process control software) as well as the computational needs of the organization.

Wegner provides a certain historical perspective to reuse and, more broadly, to software technology. From this point of view, there are parallels between the role of capitalization in the industrial revolution and the role of capitalization in software technology.

It has often been observed that in our current state of evolution of the software culture, industry has largely failed to capitalize software technology sufficiently. This may result from three factors. First, the financial infrastructure of companies have not yet adapted to the necessity of high capitalization of software development. Second, many companies do not yet understand the degree to which they will depend upon software for their future products and profits. And third, it takes a long time for existing technology successes (e.g., workstations and powerful development environments) to be reflected in company policies, let alone for advanced technologies (e.g., reuse) to be incorporated.

It is likely that the consequences of these policies and attitudes will be much the same as in the steel industry. In short, those companies that recognize the growing role of software in their competitive position and capitalize it aggressively are more likely to survive than those that do not.

Although many American industries are in a denial phase with respect to the competitive role of the Japanese, the fact remains that the Japanese are heavily committed to and are heavily capitalizing software development (with special emphasis on reuse). This is the face of the competition, and survival of many of our industries depends upon similar commitment and capitalization. Time will not be kind to nonaggressive companies and industries.

Capitalization is vitally important to reuse because without such a commitment reuse is just a hollow promise. The lack of sufficient management commitment and capitalization can make reuse fail. With such commitment and capitalization, reuse technology can (even today) make significant improvements in productivity and quality of software. See Lanergan *et al.*, Y. Matsumoto, Cavaliere, and Selby.

Wegner's contribution is an insightful analysis of the role of capitalization in software technology and reuse.

II   COMPOSITION-BASED SYSTEMS

This section examines systems, models, and theories of reuse that are based on composing components. Of course, few systems are entirely composition based or entirely generation based. Most are a mixture of the two ideas. It is a judgment call whether any particular paper should go in this section or some other. In several cases, papers that could have been placed in this section were placed elsewhere because we felt that other aspects of the approach were more predominant than the fact that the system was based on composition technology. For example, we felt that the knowledge-based aspects of the Rich and Waters paper were more predominant than the composition-based aspects, and therefore we included it in the section on knowledge-based systems.

A. Emphasis on Practice

This section includes those composition-based approaches that have a strong emphasis on putting their ideas into practice.

Prieto-Díaz has attacked the "finding" problem—that is, how does one locate a component (assuming that one exists) if one only has an inexact description of the desired component? Prieto-Díaz borrows notions from library science to develop a multidimension description framework of facets for classifying components. His system also provides an estimate of the amount of work required to adapt a given component to a new situation.

Rice and Schwetman focus upon the problem of providing a user interface for a composition system that truly uses the components as black boxes. The chosen domain is numerical computation. Their objective is to let the user choose the (abstract) computations to be performed and the (abstract) types upon which the computations will operate, and let the system provide the interconnection regime.

One can look at what they are proposing from two different points of view. On the one hand, they are establishing a set of standards for expressing the computations and the types—albeit very high-level and flexible standards. On the other hand, they are developing a domain- (or problem-) specific language for numerical computation. Regardless of how one views their proposal, it should be noted that they labor to hide most of the implementation details within the system, invisible to the user. While not ever discussed as such, this kind of analysis is what Neighbors would refer to as domain analysis, and it is an important step in virtually all reuse systems.

Parnas was one of the earliest proponents of design using organizational principles that have become quite popular lately and are loosely grouped under the rubric of "object-oriented systems." There are a number of flavors of object-oriented systems, and we are justified in grouping them together only at the highest level of abstraction, as their details differ significantly.[2] In object-oriented systems according to Parnas, the key design principle used to form modules (or objects, if you like) is "information hiding," which in other object-oriented systems goes by the name of "encapsulation." This design principle enhances the reusability of components because of the isolating effect of information hiding. It allows the components to be reused in more of a black box mode, and even if modifications must be made, they are easier to make because all of the information pertaining to a specific module is organized (i.e., hidden) in that module rather than being randomly scattered about the overall design.

One important aspect of this work is that it has carried a theoretical proposal into large-scale practice—an accomplishment that few other researchers can claim. Parnas and his colleagues have spent the better part of a decade redesigning the avionics software for the A-7E fighter aircraft according to the principles of information hiding. Considering the fact that such a system would generally be developed by a team of tens of designers and programmers, this must be seen to be a daunting task to say the least. Those who must deal with reuse of large-scale components would do well to carefully study this work.

B. Emphasis on Theory

The two papers by Goguen and by Litvintchouk and Matsumoto are both aimed at the problem of developing programs from formal specifications. Their two approaches are closely related. Goguen uses a language called

---

[2]Strictly speaking, we are justified in calling a language or method object-oriented only if it includes the concept of "inheritance." Languages or methods that provide only encapsulation but not inheritance are more commonly classified as "abstract data type" languages or methods.

OBJ to specify "objects" that encapsulate both the code of modules and the theories that are the specifications of the target modules. The paper is rich with examples of module specifications and contains a discussion of how this approach can be used in program design and development.

Litvintchouk and Matsumoto develop the notion of using category theory as the basis of an Ada design technique. The specification language chosen by the authors is Clear, and the authors provide a description of how to use Clear operators to form new theories from old ones. Thus the purpose of various specifications can be specialized or extended in direct ways.

In both papers, the entities that are most reused are abstractions of modules rather than the modules themselves. Because the abstractions contain only the critical concepts without extensive commitment to implementation details, the abstractions lend themselves to greater reuse than one can get from code alone.

Both of these papers are fairly theoretical and expect some mathematical background on the part of the reader.

The paper by Volpano and Kieburtz is related to the work of Goguen and Litvintchouk and Matsumoto. It develops the notion of specifying functions by software templates. Software templates are abstract algorithms defined on abstract data types and containing no commitment to implementation details. Once the software designer commits to specific implementations of the abstract data types (e.g., commits to a file as the representation of the abstract data type *sequence*), the software templates system generates a version of the abstract algorithm customized for the chosen implementation (e.g., files). The generation process may perform a significant amount of reorganization of the abstract algorithm. Thus this process is a good deal more than just macroexpansion of the abstract data types.

Katz and Richter discuss the Paris system for reusing partially instantiated schemas. This system exploits the idea that many different distributed programs, while differing in their details, are fundamentally the same program in the abstract. The Paris system captures this commonality as a program schema in which some portions are concrete and specific and some portions are abstracted. The abstracted portions are specified by a set of assertions. Both the search for applicable schemas to solve a specific problem and the instantiation of the abstracted portions of a particular schema are handled by the Boyer-Moore theorem prover.

III GENERATION-BASED SYSTEMS

In generation-based systems, it is much more difficult to identify a particular component that is being reused, since much of the reused structure is encoded within a program that generates programs. Nevertheless, we are reusing architectural structures, and we can see the patterns of these architectural structures in the structure of the programs generated. We distinguish three subclasses of generation-based systems based on the properties that are emphasized. Language-based systems emphasize their specification language and therefore look a great deal like compilers. Transformation systems emphasize formalization of the process that generates a target program by applying a series of transformations to the specification of the target program. Finally, the application generators category is somewhat of a default category: We put generation systems in this category if they do not fall into one of the other two. In other words, application generators span a broad spectrum of approaches and architectures and are not easily characterized by a single point of emphasis.

A. Language-Based Systems

Language-based generation systems are systems in which the specification language is well defined, truly represents a problem domain (not just a set of inputs to drive the generator), and hides the details of implementation from its user. Reuse is enhanced by such languages specifically because they do hide the details of implementation and raise the level of discourse to the problem domain level rather than the implementation level.

Representative of this class of generation systems is SETL, a language based on the notion of representing computations as operations on mathematical sets. For many problems, this significantly simplifies the expression of the computation, although it often makes the generation of efficient code a challenge. The paper by Dubinsky *et al.* describes using the SETL language to specify a large program, the 15,000-line SETL optimizer, and then transforming that specification into an efficient implementation.

B. Application Generators

Application generators embed in their design the architectural pattern that will be reused in the course of generating specific instances of target systems. Thus the instances generated have that architectural pattern in common. Such patterns are not as clear-cut as the structure of components in composition-based systems, but they are nevertheless the thread of commonality that ties together instances of the generated target systems.

We have chosen the paper by Neighbors on his Draco system to represent this class. Draco could be put in any one of the three generation categories. It requires the development of a domain-specific language in which the user can specify his or her problem, it generates target programs from domain-specific specifications, and it uses a set of user-defined transformations to accomplish this generation.

Perhaps the most valuable service that Neighbors has performed is to raise the collective consciousness of the research community as to the importance of domain knowledge in reuse. It is conventional, when one starts to think about reuse, to think about all of the common, general, and widely applicable (i.e., small- to medium-sized) components, for example, sorts, searches, and string operations. However, as Neighbors has pointed out, these components account for only a very small percent of the size of typical application systems. The bulk of most application systems is in that part of the system that incorporates knowledge for dealing with the domain. For example, radar interpretation systems incorporate more knowledge about the processing of radar signals than anything else. Airline reservation systems incorporate more knowledge about processing airline reservations than about table searches or string operations.

In Neighbors' more recent work, he has begun to analyze large-scale systems and ask questions about how to organize them for improved maintenance, which in some sense is highly focused reuse. Several of us, including one of the editors of this book, are researching the question of reusing large-scale components, where the payoff can be quite large. Many of the issues that must be addressed for the reuse of large-scale components are much the same as the issues that must be addressed for program maintenance within an environment that is forcing slow but inexorable change to the architecture of large, existing systems. Those who have the job of improving the lot of the developers and maintainers of large, complex systems would do well to emphasize the role of problem domain analysis and to follow the work of Neighbors and related work carefully.

C. Transformational-Based Systems

Transformational-based systems focus upon the role, structure, and operation of transformations in the evolution of high-level specifications into operational programs. Cheatham was one of the pioneers of this approach.

Transformation work may provide some guidance for those seeking portability in their programs. Cheatham's ECL experiment used the transformational approach to generate versions of the ECL system for several different target environments. Porting the system to a new environment is claimed to be simpler because the generation of the system the second time is much the same as the first. That is, the scenario of transformations applied in the first generation can be used to guide the transformations of the second generation, with only some of the transformations replaced by new transformations. It is said that the first transformational sequence is "replayed" with appropriate alterations. Of course, this is nòt fully automatic, and there is ample room left for further research. Nevertheless, Cheatham's system is a rich system that provides a number of tools to help the designer develop new transformations and guide the generation of target systems.

One should not overlook the importance of support tools in the application of this technology (or any reuse technology, for that matter). A theory about how to accomplish reuse is only the start. Until one has a fully populated environment of tools and components, one will not be able to truly exploit software reuse.

A second relatively mature reuse effort that uses transformations is the effort that has been under way at ISI for a number of years. In this effort, both the specifications that they are developing and the associated transformations are intended to be reused. This work has focused heavily upon the specification language GIST and in that context, the paper by Feather might just as well have been included in the section on language-based systems.

GIST is interesting in that it is both descriptive, with a style and structure that parallels partially informal specifications, and yet formal and precise in its application. Many of the interesting characteristics of GIST arise out of its use in formalizing natural language specification of target systems. This is probably also the property that has made it so difficult to automatically transform GIST specifications into executable programs.

The reader of this paper will begin to appreciate why natural language specifications are so difficult to understand and lend themselves to such ambiguity. Of course, natural language specifications are not alone in this regard. Formal specifications have their own set of problems that are in many ways worse. As one might expect, there is no easy answer to the specification problem.

Boyle probably holds the record for the largest target system generated, as well as the most successful and most "industrial strength" transformation system. In his paper, he describes a system for translating a pure LISP specification into a variety of efficient implementations on a number of different kinds of machines, including machines with parallel architectures. In each case, the transformations used are tailored to the architecture of the target machine, with the objective of getting the greatest amount of computational parallelism out of the machines that allow such parallelism.

This paper should be valuable not only to those interested in reuse based on transformations, but to those who are wrestling with the difficult problem of how to develop code to exploit highly parallel architectures without investing too much of one's life in developing the target program. In some cases where such tools are not available, the software designer may spend weeks of time preparing a one-shot program that may run only a few minutes or a few hours on a highly parallel architecture. Boyle's experience will be valuable to these designers also.

Volume II

The second volume of this set focuses upon the applications of reuse and the experience derived from such applications. More specifically, it contains a number of papers that look at reuse from the viewpoint of the technologies supporting it (i.e., languages and environments supporting reuse), as well as a number of case studies where reuse has been applied on real development projects. In addition, this volume contains papers that define some of the quantitative benefits that one might realize when applying reuse. Finally, this volume analyzes some of the cognitive aspects of software engineers to see if they are mentally employing some kind of reuse, and if they are, to propose models of how they are doing it.

PART I

OVERVIEW
AND ASSESSMENT

CHAPTER 1

REUSABILITY FRAMEWORK, ASSESSMENT, AND DIRECTIONS

TED J. BIGGERSTAFF *and* **CHARLES RICHTER**
Microelectronics and Computer Technology Corporation (MCC)

1.1 INTRODUCTION

Reusability is widely believed to be a key to improving software development productivity and quality. The reuse of software components amplifies the software developer's capabilities. It allows him or her to write fewer total symbols in the development of a system, and to spend less time in the process of organizing those symbols.

However, while reusability is a strategy of great promise, it is one whose promise has been largely unfulfilled. We will try to explain why we believe this, and we will describe what can be done to allow reusability to fulfill that promise.

This paper is intended to provide a short overview of the reuse of software and then assess the current state of reusability technology. In the sections that follow we will:

☐ describe the problems that must be solved in order to fulfill the promise of reuse;

☐ describe and categorize some of the technologies that can be brought to bear on the reusability problem;

☐ describe some of the dilemmas presented by the reusability problem;

☐ discuss the reuse of code versus the reuse of design;

☐ describe the factors that inhibit reuse, as well as those that activate reuse;

☐ speculate about the evolution of reusability technology; and

☐ describe some important research issues.

1.2 A REUSABILITY FRAMEWORK

One can address the question of reusability from a variety of viewpoints; here we consider it from the technology viewpoint. That is, what technologies, either mature or emerging, are available to advance reusability? How do they work, and how do they differ? If we can answer these questions, we can provide a basis for judging many other facets of reusability. (A more in-depth look at results in these technological areas may be found in [Biggerstaff, 1983] and [Biggerstaff and Perlis, 1984].)

The technologies that are applied to the reusability problem can be divided into two major groups depending upon the nature of the components being reused. These groups are composition technologies and generation technologies. Figure 1.1 shows a framework for classifying the available technologies.

In composition technologies, the components to be reused are largely atomic and, ideally, are unchanged in the course of their reuse. Of course, the ideal is not always achieved, and the components may be modified or changed in order to better fit the computational purposes of the reuser. However, in the ideal case, they are passive elements operated upon (i.e., composed) by an external agent. Examples of such items are code skeletons [Lanergan and Grasso, 1989; Cavaliere, 1989], subroutines [Lanergan and Grasso, 1989; Cavaliere, 1989; Rice and Schwetman, 1989], functions, programs, and Smalltalk-style objects [Goldberg and Robson, 1983].

Deriving new programs from building blocks is a matter of composition: A few well-defined composition principles are applied to the components. The UNIX pipe mechanism [Kernighan, 1984] is a good example: Constructing more complex programs from simpler ones requires the connection of one program's output to another program's inputs. Another example is Smalltalk, in which the two principles of component composition are message

FIGURE 1.1
A FRAMEWORK FOR REUSABILITY TECHNOLOGIES

FEATURES	APPROACHES TO REUSABILITY				
COMPONENT REUSED	BUILDING BLOCKS		PATTERNS		
NATURE OF COMPONENT	ATOMIC AND IMMUTABLE PASSIVE		DIFFUSE AND MALLEABLE ACTIVE		
PRINCIPLE OF REUSE	COMPOSITION		GENERATION		
EMPHASIS	APPLICATION COMPONENT LIBRARIES	ORGANIZATION & COMPOSITION PRINCIPLES	LANGUAGE BASED GENERATORS	APPLICATION GENERATORS	TRANS- FORMATION SYSTEMS
TYPICAL SYSTEMS	– LIBRARIES OF SUBROUTINES	– OBJ ORIENTED – PIPE ARCHS	– VHLLs – POLs	– CRT FMTRS – FILE MGMT	– LANGUAGE TRANSFORM- ERS

passing and inheritance. The former is a generalization of function calls, a static binding of caller to callee. The latter, inheritance, permits a dynamic determination of the method (callee) to be invoked.

Generation technologies are not as easy to characterize as composition technologies, because the components that are reused are not concrete, self-contained entities. In the composition group, we could point at a building block both before and after its use. It was immutable in the sense that, for the most part, it kept its form and identity after use. However, in the generation group, the components being reused are often patterns woven into the fabric of a generator program. The resultant structures often bear only distant relations to the patterns of the programs that generated them. Further, each resulting instance of such a pattern may be highly individualistic, bearing only scant resemblance to other instances generated from the same seed code. In this case, reuse is less a matter of composition (of components) than of execution (of component generators).

Reusable patterns take at least two different forms: patterns of code and patterns within transformation rules. The former are used in application generation, where reusable patterns of code exist within the generator itself. Transformation systems use the latter. In both cases, the effects of the individual reusable components within the target program tend to be more global and diffuse than the effects of building blocks. We cannot easily characterize the principle whereby patterns are reused, except to say that it is a kind of reactivation of the patterns. Neighbors' Draco system (see [Neighbors, 1989]) is an example of both an application generator and a transformation-based system.

1.3 ASSESSMENT

Dilemmas of Reusability

Reusability presents us with a number of dilemmas. The general form of the dilemma is that a positive change in one parameter often leads to a negative change in another.

Generality of Applicability versus Payoff.   The first dilemma is illustrated in Fig. 1.2. Technologies that are very general, in that they can be applied to a broad range of application domains, tend to have a much lower payoff than systems that are narrowly focused on one or two application domains. For example, if a given application generator has facilities for generating both screen and database interfaces for the user, it amplifies the user's capabilities much more than does a straight high-level language. That is, the number of keystrokes is smaller and the number of compositions of architectural pieces is smaller for the process of building the screen and data interfaces. In other parts of the application, there is no noticeable increase in productivity.

Figure 1.2 is not based on rigorous data but rather reflects the authors' opinion about the relative characteristics of the various technologies.

FIGURE 1.2
CHARACTERIZATION OF REUSABILITY TECHNOLOGIES

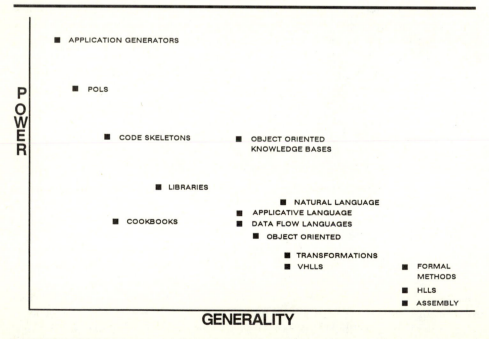

Nevertheless, there is a discernible grouping along a curve from the upper left to the lower right. Even though the placement of individual points may be debatable, we believe that the general shape of the curve is intuitively correct and that most readers would concur with it.

It is unclear whether the curve is hyperbolic or linear, but its exact form is not as important as the general relationship between the axis variables. As you maximize the parameter on one axis, you minimize the parameter on the other axis. To make reusability radically productive, it is important to break away from the restrictions implied by this figure.

Component Size (and Payoff) versus Reuse Potential.   The second dilemma of reusability is based on the mean size of components. As a component grows in size, the payoff involved in reusing that component increases more than linearly. However, as the component grows in size it also becomes more and more specific, which reduces the possibility of its reuse and increases the cost of reusing it when modifications are required.

This dilemma is amplified when we try to reuse code, because code, by its very nature, requires great specificity.

The Cost of Library Population.   The third dilemma is that we must invest a great deal of intellectual capital, real capital, and time before reuse begins to pay off in a significant way. The organizational structure of most companies precludes such large initial capital investment regardless of the potential long-term payoff, and therein lies the dilemma. Generally, such organizational structures consist of teams of people who are working on specific projects, and those specific projects are budgeted to meet a specific set of goals. Those goals generally do not include any extra work to generalize and capture the project results for reuse by other groups. Developing a viable reusability system is a nontrivial investment that does not have an early payoff. Therefore, the activity of populating the library is a large impediment to developing a working reusability system.

The Operational Problems of Reusability

In order to operate successfully, a reusability system must address four fundamental problems:

- ☐ finding components,
- ☐ understanding components,
- ☐ modifying components, and
- ☐ composing components.

The finding process is more than just locating an exact match. It includes locating "highly similar" components, because even if a target component must be partially redeveloped, an example similar to the ideal component can serve to reduce the effort and eliminate many defects.

Several approaches to this problem have been proposed. Rubén Prieto-Díaz has developed a classification scheme for a component library [Prieto-Díaz, 1989], and William Jones [Jones, 1986] has proposed the use of a spreading activation search paradigm in his Memory Extender system to accomplish much the same purpose. A rather different approach was taken in the PARIS system for reusing partially interpreted schemas [Katz, Richter, and The, 1989]. In PARIS, the finding operation used pre- and postconditions plus assertions about component properties to form clauses to be proved using the Boyer-Moore theorem prover. The resulting proof developed a list of candidate components.

The importance of the finding function is closely related to the size-versus-reuse-potential dilemma. Size is a metric that closely correlates with specificity and specificity is the factor that really affects reusability. So we might better have labeled the dilemma as the Specificity versus Reuse Potential dilemma. The more specific modules become, the more difficult it gets to find an exact (or even close) match. Modules subtly encode very specific information about a variety of things: the operating system, the run-time library, the hardware equipment available, the packaging of data, the packaging of interfaces, and so forth. Thus, if we have highly specialized modules, we can expect to need a very large number of them in order to make reuse work. In this circumstance, the finding problem takes on added importance.

If, on the other hand, there are ways to factor out specificity while still providing reasonably large components, the importance of the finding problem is diminished. In fact, if the components are sufficiently abstract and each captures only one aspect or principle of an algorithm, we may end up with a relatively small search space, and the finding problem may be only a minor operation. The search for such an abstraction scheme is being carried out at MCC and is discussed further in the section on research issues.

The understanding process is required in any case, but especially if the component is to be modified. The component user needs to have a mental model of the computation performed by the component in order to use it properly, and such a mental model takes some effort to acquire. This is probably the fundamental problem in the development of any system of reuse, regardless of the underlying technology chosen for its implementation.

One approach to this problem is represented by hypertext systems such as Neptune [Delisle and Schwarz, 1986], NoteCards [Halasz *et al.*, 1987], and PlaneText [Gullichsen *et al.*, 1988]. Hypertext systems are tools for building a web of information that smoothly integrates text, graphics diagrams, and other information, such as existing code. Each element of the web is a node of information that can be examined by the user. A node can be annotated with pointers to other nodes, which can contain descriptions, diagrams, explanations of decisions, invariant equations, and all manner of design information that is often lost in the course of designing a system. Happily, systems such as

PlaneText allow existing files to be annotated without altering them. Thus an existing code file can be annotated for hypertext purposes without affecting its use as a compilable file.

Figure 1.3 shows a small hypertext web. In the figure, we have a node containing the requirements for a product. Some requirements are linked (by "defn" links) to definitions of those requirements, while others contain links to the code that realizes them. One requirement is also annotated with a figure, a piece of which is further refined.

These systems provide the user of the component with instant access to a variety of supporting information. Decisions associated with some portion of the component can be called up to the screen with two or three keystrokes or the touch of a mouse. While such systems are not a panacea, they represent a start at taming the understanding problem.

The modifying process is the lifeblood of reusability. It changes a static library of rocklike building blocks to a living system of components that spawn or evolve new components as the requirements of the environment change. It is overly optimistic to think that we can build a reusability system that allows significant reuse without modifying some portion of the components. Unfortunately, modification is largely a human domain, and there are few tools that provide any measure of help. Some possible exceptions will be discussed in relation to the composing problem.

The composing process imposes the most challenging requirements on the representation used to specify components. The representation must have

FIGURE 1.3
A HYPERTEXT EXAMPLE

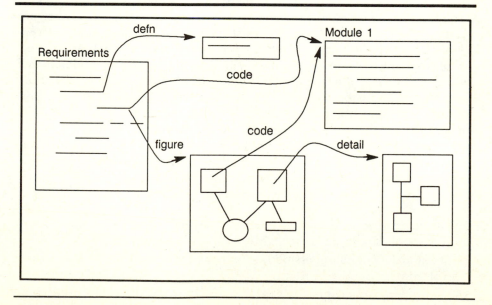

a dual character. It must represent composite structures as independent entities with well-defined computational characteristics, and it must make it possible for these composite structures to be further composed into new computational structures with different computational characteristics. To some extent, these two goals are mutually antagonistic.

The notions of functional composition drawn from mathematical theory are largely inadequate. Mathematical compositions produce their results through straightforward combination of the local effects of individual components. That is, the whole is simply the sum of the parts. Unfortunately, such composition systems are too limited. Human designers produce compositions of components having both global and local effects, and this leads to more powerful, flexible, and practical modes of reuse.

An interesting approach to the problem of composition is Dennis Volpano's "software templates" [Volpano and Kieburtz, 1989]. This approach divides the component information into two parts: the essential algorithm and the data implementation. By separately choosing an algorithm and its implementation, the system generates a customized implementation of the algorithm, often producing a significant code expansion. It remains to be seen how far this work can be pushed.

The four processes of finding, understanding, modifying, and composing components have typically been an informal part of design. A focus on reusability requires that they be formalized, so that automated support structures can be engineered.

The Reuse of Code versus the Reuse of Design

The obvious first approach to reusability is to use components expressed in some programming language and to form them into libraries. There are several problems with this strategy. First, the payoff quickly reaches a ceiling that is difficult to surpass. Our experience has been that either the portion of a system that can be formed from reused components is small (well under half the system) or the target system does not perform to specification. Typically, programs built completely out of reused components have performance problems. At the very least, they have problems of inappropriate functionality.

There are some limited success stories with reuse of code, however. The classic example is the reuse of numerical computation routines. But the numerical computation domain is unique in several ways that allow for this success:

- [ ] The domain is very narrow in the sense that it contains only a small number of data types.
- [ ] The domain is well understood, with a mathematical framework that has evolved over hundreds of years.
- [ ] The underlying technology is quite static. It grows and evolves only very

slowly, and importantly, it evolves in such a way that existing parts of the technology remain unchanged (i.e., there is upward compatibility of the technology).

These three characteristics allow for the establishment of standards within the domain, and these standards lead to the success of reusability in this domain. The narrowness of the domain makes the reuse of code manageable. The cost of developing the reusable parts is small, and because there are only a few data types, components in the library have a high probability of reuse.

The fact that the domain is well understood reduces the amount of investment that one has to make in creating a reusable library. Also, lots of people understand the domain and therefore readily understand a component's function with only the barest description.

The fact that the domain is largely static means that the library of parts can be quite stable, allowing the using organization to amortize the investment over a long period of time. The worst kind of domain for reusability is one where the underlying technology is rapidly changing. An example is the personal computer and workstation domain. Systems software for this domain has a very short half-life and is therefore not very reusable.

Having now claimed that rapidly changing domains do not lend themselves to reuse, we will back off from that position a bit. Even when the code itself is not reusable, the general design ideas are often quite reusable. This observation has led to the notion of reusing design information. The idea is good in principle but has problems in practice, centered around the question of how one represents the design information. Code has well-defined representation schemes, as realized in today's high-level programming languages. However, there is no such representation system for designs. Each potential choice suffers some fatal flaw. Many machine-processible design languages are too close to programming languages and therefore too specific, leading to the same problems that arise with the reuse of code. Languages that are not overly specific are often only processible by machines in very limited ways. The large amount of manual activity required for reuse in these cases reduces the payoff.

The payoff potential is high for reuse of design, and we must do research to attempt to realize that potential. Reuse of design is the only way we can come even close to an order of magnitude increase in either productivity or quality. Reuse and design are really facets of the same activity. When we watch power designers, we are struck by the fact that the same patterns occur again and again in their designs. They will say something like, "Oh that structure is very similar to a widget, and typically you handle widgets in this way." They bring a large amount of prestructured information (i.e., partially specified architectures) to bear on the problem. Very few designers, except total novices, start from scratch. The difference in their productivity can be directly correlated with their experience, as modulated by their basic intelligence.

Unfortunately, in order to put that kind of experience on machines in useful forms and subsequently to entice designers to take advantage of it, we must overcome some factors that inhibit reuse. We discuss those factors in the next section.

Inhibiting Factors

changing base for gen e.g. c → c++

Several factors inhibit the advancement of reusability technology: inadequate representation technology, lack of a clear and obvious direction, the NIH (Not Invented Here) factor, and high initial capitalization.

The first and most important inhibitor of reuse of design across a wide range of domains is the current lack of a representation for design that fosters reusability. We will discuss this problem in detail in the section on research issues.

The second inhibitor is that it is not clear exactly what strategy represents the optimum approach to reusability. Management will generally not take positive steps until it has a strong notion of what seems like the best path. Technologists often lead the way, but in this case the nature of the problem prevents that from working. The technologists are confounded because (1) reusability is a multiorganization problem and (2) it requires a critical mass of components before it really begins to pay off. These facts prevent the technology from arising spontaneously out of the ranks of the technologists.

The NIH factor among the program developers is a strong inhibitor. Nevertheless, this problem is largely cultural and is easily curable compared to some of the technical problems (e.g., the representation problem). The cure is largely a matter of management's establishing the proper culture, one that makes a point of rewarding reuse. Once management establishes the proper culture, the developers rapidly learn that reuse does not hinder their creativity after all—they are now freed up to attack more challenging problems. Once this is realized, resistance to reuse disappears. This has certainly been the case at Hartford Insurance [Cavaliere, 1989] and in Japanese experience [Matsumoto, 1989].

We already mentioned the fourth inhibiting factor, that of initial capitalization, when discussing the cost of library population (under "Dilemmas of Reusability"). Effective reuse requires a very large initial commitment: Libraries of reusable parts must be stocked. We have also noted that the need for a critical mass of components prevents reuse technology from arising spontaneously.

Activating Factors

The factors that will foster the evolution of reusability technology are largely economic. While other technological improvements can provide marginal benefits, those improvements are reaching a point of diminishing returns. For example, providing sufficient personal computing power by means of workstations or shared computer time has provided some improvement, but there is a limit to this improvement. In the end, if the compiler requires a string of several million characters to produce the target system, there is a minimum amount of people-time required to produce and organize those several million characters, and you cannot get below that minimum without a fundamental change in technology.

Another primary activator will likely be the successful application of reuse by competitors. The Japanese have been emphasizing reuse for some time now and have been having some success with it. Initially, U.S. developers will deny that the Japanese are having any success, but when the competitive pressures make it obvious, they will grudgingly admit that maybe the Japanese have made some progress. Once this happens, U.S. software developers will put more emphasis on reuse.

Speculations

We do not expect much immediate progress in generally applicable systems for reuse because of the high initial capitalization required, management indifference, and the lack of a mature technology base.

A few special cases of high-redundancy domains (e.g., COBOL development environments) will show good payoffs just by using simple tools that eliminate much of the redundancy (e.g., shortform tools) and allow storage of common system specification information in one place (e.g., data dictionaries and their progeny).

Several parallel approaches and their associated technologies will evolve:

General Reuse, Ad Hoc.   This approach uses existing technology and just accumulates parts (including both design and code) in an ad hoc way. It is not based on any theory nor dependent upon any technology breakthroughs. The Japanese are likely to work this avenue and achieve a very credible but modest payoff with it. The payoffs will probably be less than a 25 percent increase in productivity, where this 25 percent is a part of (not in addition to) other increases due to other improvements (e.g., design tools). This approach will pay off in two to five years from the start time.

Program Generators Reuse.   Growth in program generators will occur in narrowly defined application domains. The main activity here will be seen in the personal computer market, with somewhat less activity in the workstation market. Today and in the near future, we see very little reusability activity on maxis and minis, except for the porting of facilities developed in the small-machine market. The time to payoff with this approach is very short—less than a year to two years. The narrower the domain, the faster the payoff. Further, the payoff with this approach will be very large, between 60 percent and 90 percent, depending upon how stereotyped the application architecture is. If a fair amount of logic must be developed outside of the application generator, which often happens, then the payoff will be closer to 60 percent.

If not, it will be close to 90 percent. However, the domain of application of these generators is very narrow, and they are aimed largely at the end user, not the professional programmer.

General Reuse, Theory Based.   Representation breakthroughs are necessary for payoffs approaching or exceeding an order of magnitude. These representations must allow factored forms of design information. That is, designers must be able to store and deal with separate aspects (or factors) of a design (e.g., function, implementation data structures, interfaces, etc.) separately. These factors will be woven together to generate an implementation of the design. Such a breakthrough will allow reusability to be applied to a wide set of application domains with the expectation of an order of magnitude (or greater) increase in productivity and quality. Of course, a significant amount of preinvestment is necessary in order to populate the domains of interest before any payoff at all can be expected. The preinvestment will be an inhibitor, at least until some corporation has demonstrated the commercial viability of the technology. The time to payoff is in the five- to ten-year range.

The foregoing figures for percentage improvement in productivity and for time to payoff are based largely upon the authors' intuition and experience. We do not have any scientifically derived data that pin these numbers down.

We are most interested in the third area, a theory of general reuse of design information. The problem of representation, which we mentioned earlier, is important in the development of such a theory. We will now discuss several research issues associated with the representation problem.

General Reuse: Research Issues

The fundamental problem preventing the successful reuse of design information is that of finding the right representation of that design information, a representation that captures designs in a richly machine-processable form. The need for rich machine processing eliminates English language text and most of the block-and-connector styles of graphical representations; these forms allow only relatively superficial forms of machine processing. The representation we are looking for must exhibit the following properties:

- ☐ the ability to represent knowledge about implementation structures in factored form;
- ☐ the ability to create partial specifications of design information that can be incrementally extended,
- ☐ the ability to allow flexible couplings between instances of designs and the various interpretations they can have, and
- ☐ the ability to express controlled degrees of abstraction and precision (i.e., degrees of ambiguity).

Factored Forms.   Code components represent a variety of information in
unfactored form. Information about many domains is woven into a code
component in subtle and nonobvious ways. For example, the control structure
of a code component often takes a particular form due to the structure of the
data that it is to operate upon. If we wished to loop through a list of items,
we would probably use a *for* loop if the list was an array; if it was a linked
list, however, we'd more likely choose a *while* or *repeat until* loop. By the time
we have created code, a variety of requirements and design structures have
been thoroughly mixed together, so that their individual structures may not be
at all apparent.

design decision

   Such a form is not optimal for reuse, as it is difficult to separate the
individual design factors in order to understand the component, modify the
component, and so on. People deal well with the individual design factors but
not with the integrated whole. Therefore, a representation of design must
allow the designer to edit individual factors and to combine several factors,
obtaining a new component. For example, suppose that a designer must design
a process table for a multitasking system—a table containing the description
of each process running under the system. The designer will deal with this
process table from at least two points of view: an application domain view,
which arises out of the fact that it is a process table, and a data structure
view, which arises out of the fact that it is an indexed table. These two
points of view focus on two distinct design factors of a process table, and
the representation must allow the designer to deal with these two factors
separately. Future designers may want to reuse the concept of, say, a process
table without the accompanying notion of an indexed table.

Partial Specifications.   The need for the second property arises because
people, and designers in particular, evolve their notions of design incrementally. First, they express the broad framework of the design, specifying only the
major structures. Then over a period of time they fill in the details, probably
reorganizing the broad framework in the process. The broad structures
(i.e., partial architectures) are highly reusable; the details typically are not.
Inclusion of too much detail—that is, inclusion of too many interrelated detail
commitments—significantly reduces reusability of the overall component.

   The broad structures need to be precisely described, whereas the details
need to be left incomplete and partly ambiguous. That is, the details are
constrained, but only minimally so. The requirement for *partial* constraints
on the details makes the problem difficult. Specification languages usually
insist upon specifying the details precisely or not at all. But we cannot specify
the details too precisely, else we reduce the reuse potential. On the other
hand, if we leave too many of the details completely unconstrained, we
have significantly fewer hooks for automation, and the payoff of reusing the
component is reduced because so much manual labor is involved. Without a
representation that allows a mixture of precision and fuzziness, we lose much
of the advantage of reuse.

The ideal representation must allow the specification and storage of such partial architectures, and it must allow incremental completion of the details over time. No representations exist today that allow this kind of flexibility while still providing the other properties that we desire.

Couplings between Instances and Their Interpretations.　The need for the next property is a consequence of the need for factored representations. Once we have individual factors, we want to create component instances incorporating several factors. For example, suppose again that we are designing a process table. From the point of view of the process table domain, we will want to choose a "process identifier," that is, a method for uniquely identifying or naming the process represented by a specific entry in the table. We will probably want the capability to search for any particular entry in the table using this identifier. Similarly, from the data structure point of view, we need to talk about the "table index," that is, the conceptual entity that identifies an entry in the table. The process identifier and the table index will refer to the same objects, viewed from two separate points of view. Most design languages require us to choose a single name for the field that contains the process identifier (a.k.a. the table index). This means that either we have to foresee all possible intersections of viewpoints and choose a single name for such a field, or we have to find a way to defer this naming decision until design time and allow the designer to indicate that these two different interpretations (or points of view) really apply to the same design structure.

The first option is not only undesirable, but impossible. It essentially requires that we use a global name space—a name space that is self-consistent over all possible intersections of factors. But some factor intersections chosen for one particular design may be inconsistent with factor intersections chosen for some other design. Therefore, a global naming convention that is totally consistent within the infinite number of possible factor combinations is impossible. The second option presents a very difficult research problem, but we believe it is solvable.

Controlled Degrees of Abstraction.　The last property is more fundamental than the previous three, and we believe its existence implies the existence of the other three. Simply stated, it requires that design specifications in the early phases of software development have many of the same characteristics as natural language: abstraction to the point of ambiguity, although carefully controlled ambiguity. That is, the designer must be able to define conceptual structures that initially are largely free of details. These conceptual structures must be rigorous in the following sense: If information can be known based on completed design decisions, that information must be capturable by the representation scheme. For example, suppose that the designer has decided to use a binary search on a data structure. We do not yet know the exact control structure of that algorithm, but we do know that it will have three distinct parts: a section of code that searches the left portion of the search space, a section of code that searches the right portion of the search space, and a section of code that tests the search item against the left-right boundary item to eliminate either the left or the right portion of the search space from the search, and concurrently redefines the left and right portions of the new, smaller search space. The fact that these three distinct areas of the control structure exist must be captured by the design representation even before the details of the control structure are worked out. Indeed, we will insist that the ideal representation must give us a way to refer to these three portions of the target algorithm, even though they are quite fuzzy.

1.4 SEMANTIC BINDING

We advocate a representation system that permits *semantic binding*. We want to represent the essence of a design component (factor) rather than just its details, so that we can apply concepts taken from one domain to structures within an entirely different context. But in order to move a component from one domain to another, the component must have great referential flexibility. It must refer to items it expects in its context, and since it cannot know a priori the specific names of those items, it must be able to refer to them semantically, that is, by their semantic nature rather than their syntactic name. Drawing on our earlier example, a multitasking scheduler will expect to find a target system data item that is simultaneously a table index and a process identifier.

As a further example, suppose that we intend to create a reusable component to suspend a process and that this component will be referring to items in a yet-to-be-defined process table. This component must have a form something like the following (we will use pseudocode to avoid a lengthy discussion of the actual representational form):

```
if (state of process is suspended)
   then return error;
   else {remove process from ready queue if there;
         set state of process to be suspended;
         relinquish control to the scheduler;}
```

This example references the "state of the process." This must eventually be resolved into a reference to an instance variable that names the process state field of a process entry (or to a local variable that has acquired the value of this instance variable). Similarly, the example references one value that the process state can have, "suspended." This value will eventually be resolved into one of several implementation values (probably integers) decided upon during the design.

Now if we had a method by which such a reference could be easily associated with (i.e., bound to) any design entity within a given context that represented the state of the process, we could use the given specification in a variety of contexts where the details (e.g., data structure implementations and names) might differ but the essential intent was the same. Then, as the design process proceeds, the component could be evolved to include the details specific to the emerging design. A reference structure of this level of flexibility can be adapted to most process table organizations and process state value sets that the designer might dream up.

A method of representation with such a reference mechanism is said to allow semantic binding of its objects and operations. We believe that this abstraction mechanism is fundamental to effective and highly productive reuse of designs.

1.5 CONCLUSIONS

We have considered what approaches to reusability have the greatest payoff, what approaches have lesser payoffs, why they produce such varying results, and how they might be improved.

The reuse of code is a reasonable first step toward reuse, but the implementor must be aware that the leverage gained has a rather low upper limit. On the positive side, that leverage limit is strongly coupled to the width of the domain: By narrowing the domain, the payoff can be significantly increased.

The reuse of design has greater potential leverage but will require significant representational breakthroughs to realize its full potential in a largely automated way. Some potion of this leverage may be realized with a mostly manual system, but the overhead of the manual processing will significantly reduce the overall leverage of design reuse.

We strongly believe that the representational breakthroughs with the greatest potential payoff will be those that solve the problems of factored forms, partial specification, the coupling of instances and their interpretations, and controlled degrees of abstraction. We believe that the central mechanism to solving these four problems is the notion of semantic binding, or, in a sense, binding by analogy. This form of binding—applying a design from one context to a new and different context—will provide the most general method for reuse.

REFERENCES

Biggerstaff, Ted, ed. *Proceedings of the Workshop on Reusability in Programming*. ITT, 1983.

Biggerstaff, Ted, and Perlis, Alan, eds. Special issue of *IEEE Transactions on Software Engineering* on software reusability, SE-10(5) 1984.

Cavaliere, Michael J. Reusable code at the Hartford Insurance Group. In *Software Reusability*. Vol. 2, *Applications and Experience*. To be published by Addison-Wesley, 1989.

Delisle, Norman, and Schwarz, Mayer. Neptune: A hypertext system for CAD applications. Tektronix Laboratories technical report no. CR-85-50. 1986.

Goldberg, Adele, and Robson, David. *Smalltalk-80: The Language and Its Implementation*. Addison-Wesley, 1983.

Gullichsen, Eric; D'Souza, Dilip; Lincoln, Patrick; and The, Khe-Sing. The PlaneTextBook. MCC technical report STP-333-86, 1986, Republished as MCC technical report STP-206-88, 1988.

Halasz, F. G.; Moran, T. P.; and Trigg, R. H. NoteCards in a nutshell. In *Proceedings of the 1987 ACM Conference on Human Factors in Computer Systems* (CHI + GI '87). Toronto, Ont., April 1987.

Jones, W. P. On the applied use of human memory models: The memory extender personal filing system. *Int. Journal Man-Machine Studies*, Vol. 25, pp. 191–228 (1986).

Katz, Schmuel; Richter, Charlie; and The, Khe-Sing. PARIS: A System for Reusing Partially Interpreted Schemas. In this volume. 1989.

Kernighan, Brian. The Unix system and software reusability. *IEEE Transactions on Software Engineering* SE-10(5):513, 1984.

Lanergan, Robert G., and Grasso, Charles A. Software engineering with reusable designs and code. In *Software Reusability*. Vol. 2, *Applications and Experience*. To be published by Addison-Wesley, 1989.

Masumoto, Yoshihiro. Some experience in promoting reusable software: Presentation in higher abstract levels. In *Software Reusability*. Vol. 2, *Applications and Experience*. To be published by Addison-Wesley, 1989.

Neighbors, James M. Draco: A method for engineering reusable software systems. In this volume. 1989.

Prieto-Díaz, Rubén. Classification of reusable modules. In this volume. 1989.

Rice, John R., and Schwetman, Herbert D. Interface issues in a software parts technology. In this volume. 1989.

Volpano, Dennis M., and Kieburtz, Richard B. The templates programming methodology. In this volume. 1989.

CHAPTER **2**

An EXPANSIVE VIEW
OF REUSABLE SOFTWARE

ELLIS HOROWITZ
University of Southern California

JOHN B. MUNSON
Unisys Corporation

2.1 DEFINING THE PROBLEM

By now it is hard to imagine that any computer professional has not become aware of the bottleneck in software development. For both commercial and government applications, the annual bill for software is rising at a rapid pace. For example, the U.S. Department of Defense (DOD) spent over $3 billion on software in 1980 and their expenses are projected to grow to $30 billion per year by 1990 (DOD Annual report FY '81). Moreover, these costs are only the tip of the iceberg, as the impact of faulty software, delayed software, and continuing maintenance costs drive the real costs even higher.

We might well ask, why this phenomenal growth in the cost of software? There are several major reasons. One is the fact that the requirements for new software systems are more complex than ever before. For example, military embedded computer systems must often operate in hostile and unpredictable environments. These systems have severe performance requirements that tax even the most powerful of today's computers. Moreover, the software they require interacts in so many ways that correcting any failures may be

©1984 IEEE. Reprinted, with permission, from *IEEE Transactions on Software Engineering*, Vol. SE-10, #5, September, 1984

very expensive or even impossible to do. A second reason for the rising cost
of software is the increased demand for qualified software professionals. A
critical labor shortage now exists, making it impossible for many organizations
to get all of their work done and, with rising salaries, making the cost of
any software development expensive. A third reason, and the one we intend
to address in this paper, is the fact that our software development tools
and methodologies have not continued to dramatically improve our ability to
develop software. Although in the field of computer hardware fabrication new
methods continue to raise productivity, in software we have not experienced
even an order of magnitude improvement over the past decade. For example,
in [Morrissey and Wu, 1979] it is claimed that productivity of the software
creation process has only increased by 3–8 percent per year over the last 20
years. Yet the installed processing capacity has increased at the rate of 40
percent or better per year. Thus we need to take a close and careful look at
the way we create software to see if we can make substantial gains over the
next decade.

In this paper we address ourselves to one concept, which we believe has
the potential for increasing software productivity by an order of magnitude or
more. That concept has come to be known by the phrase *reusable software*. Our
essential purpose is to show that reusability actually comes in many forms and
to analyze its various instantiations. It has for a long time been recognized
that one fundamental weakness of software creation is the fact that an entirely
new software system is usually constructed "from scratch." Input and output
routines, report-generating routines, and computational and processing routines are all designed and written by the staff of analysts and programmers
on the project. This is clearly an unfortunate situation, as studies have shown
that much of the code of one system is virtually identical to previously written
code. For example, a study done at the Missile Systems Division of Raytheon
Company observed that 40–60 percent of actual program code was repeated
in more than one application [Frank, 1981a]. Therefore, the idea of reusability would seem to hold one answer to increasing software productivity. And
yet the simple notion of reusability (i.e., code reusability) has been considered
by computer professionals over the years (e.g., [Read and Harmon, 1981]) but
has never been entirely successful. It is the purpose of this paper to examine reusability in its many forms and to discuss their merits and demerits,
primarily in the domain of programming customized software systems.

There exist three distinct computer scenarios calling for different kinds
of software solutions. The first is when a standard software application is
desired. The obvious solution is to purchase an existing software package.
The second is when an unusual combination of standard data processing
tasks is required. One of two possibilities would be appropriate here: either
the purchase and subsequent customization of an existing software package
or else the hiring of a computer services firm. Either choice is an economical
one and also has the advantage of speed. Third is the case where a totally
distinct computerized system, tailored to the end user, is wanted. This is the
type of software scenario we will be considering in this paper.

TABLE 2.1
POTENTIAL PRODUCTIVITY IMPROVEMENT SOFTWARE/ LIFE CYCLE

	Current Cost	% Improvement	Net Cost
System Requirements	2	0	2
Hardware Requirements	8	25%	6
Software Requirements	10	20%	8
Software Design	12	40%	7
Coding	13	75%	3
Unit Test	24	50%	12
Integration Test	13	30%	9
Documentation	6	30%	4
System Test	12	25%	9
	100	40%	60

If we are to develop methods to improve the software creation process, then we need to be able to define and measure productivity improvement. We can define productivity as the ratio of output to input, where input includes labor, capital, material, and energy. Output is a difficult thing to measure and may only be measured indirectly in the form of unit cost of the product, response time, quality of the information delivered, computer uptime, average time per request, and so on. One measure that has often been used is the number of lines of code produced. This measure has the advantage of being easily trackable, but it is only indirectly related to output.

In Table 2.1 we see the basic life cycle phases of a computerized project. The first column gives the percentage of effort typically consumed by each activity. We see that unit testing requires the largest amount of time, while identification of system requirements requires the least amount. In the second column we see some guesses as to the extent of improvement we can hope to see in the near future. The continued spread of new and powerful languages such as Pascal and (possibly) Ada leads us to hypothesize a 75 percent improvement in coding efficiency. The last column reflects the proportion of effort each task would consume given that the projected level of improvement is achieved. We see that unit testing is still the single largest activity. More importantly, we see that the overall improvement is only 40 percent. Observe that we are not considering the fact that an improvement in one stage may materially affect another stage. Thus this approach is somewhat oversimplified.

Another view of the development cycle is to include *total* life cycle costs, in particular, maintenance. That gives us Table 2.2. Here we see that maintenance takes approximately three times the cost of the original system development. The 40 percent improvement derived earlier is reflected here in development time. Once again we see that the overall effect of this improvement is not very great when entire cycle costs are considered [Frank, 1981b; Prywes, 1977].

TABLE 2.2
POTENTIAL PRODUCTIVITY IMPROVEMENT/TOTAL LIFE CYCLE

System Development	100	40%	60
Installation	15	20%	12
Maintenance			
Defect removal	60	75%	15
Environmental changes	60	30%	42
Enhancements	180	40%	108
	415	43%	237

The major conclusion is that a large improvement in any one of the
categories of Table 2.1 will not substantially improve total productivity. For
example, attempts to improve the coding phase by designing more reliable
languages or improving the design phase by using a program design language
(PDL) are very limited in the extent to which they can affect the entire process.

Now we wish to outline some of the potential ways we see in which
productivity may be improved by an order of magnitude or more in the near
future.

☐ New computer software environments that aid software development.
One recent successful example is the development of the Programmer's
Work Bench on the PDP-11 series of computers. A versatile and efficient
operating system tailored to writing systems programs is coupled with a
powerful language, C, to yield an impressive new tool. The Programmer's
Work Bench provides a range of capabilities that aid software development while the operating system supplies a uniform means of access to
each tool; see [Ivie, 1977].

☐ New computer hardware environments of the future will create substantially different modes of computer access. One possibility is the net-
working together of powerful personal computers. Each staff member
will have his own machine upon which he prepares and tests programs.
The network will permit data sharing and provide access to a large-scale
computer. Mail between computer sites will be supported. This configuration will reduce the competition for CPU cycles and will allow programmers a degree of freedom not possible when they all had to share the
same machine and its software.

☐ The use of careful management approaches to computer development
will improve productivity.

☐ New programming languages such as Pascal and Ada will help. However,
there are no statistics purporting to show that these shorten even the
coding phase of the life cycle process. It is likely that their use will not
double productivity.

☐ The decreased cost of graphics is spurring the development of more
sophisticated man-machine interfaces. The use of a mouse for pointing

is one good example. The use of color will soon begin to be exploited in a much larger way than heretofore.

☐ Prototyping. The "let's build it twice" idea has long been recognized as a useful one, but is too expensive to implement in practice. Now there is increased research on the use of certain languages to form a prototype, followed by interaction with the customer to finalize requirements, followed by incremental builds that successively transform the prototype into a production system.

☐ Perhaps the simplest instance of reusability (and the one with the highest leverage) is the purchase of an existing software package. The purchasing organization pays very little compared to building an equivalent capability inhouse, and it is up and running in a short time. Even if a limited amount of customization is necessary, this is often small compared to the cost of building an entirely new system. If organizations will come to the point of accepting such prepackaged systems, then a major step forward will have been achieved.

☐ Reusable code has for a long time been an attractive idea. Likened to the concept of standard building components such as screws, nails, timber, and so on, this idea has yet to be formed into a practical solution for software creation in the large. More about its strengths and weaknesses in a later section.

☐ Reusable design. This approach, as recently advocated by Neighbors [1980], Rice [1981], and others, consists of performing an analysis of a given domain. This produces a set of concepts and terms that are used when a specific system is to be designed for this domain. The idea of reusing domain analysis has great merit and needs to be explored further.

☐ Application generators. An application generator is a software package designed to help end users build applications in a given domain, such as financial ledger systems. Compared to the previous category, these packages have very specific knowledge about the area of application in which programs are to be written. This permits the specification language to be very precise. Also, they are designed with a naive end user in mind. One could view an application generator as the output of a domain analysis. As the domain becomes more tightly constrained, the efficient use of these systems is easier to achieve.

☐ Formal specification and transformation systems. Here we have a formal specification language in which a system design is expressed. This language can be in predicate calculus form, algebraic form, relational form (inefficient but executable), program form, or declaration form. The specification is automatically checked for consistency and completeness. Then it is transformed into an (efficient) executable program either by automatic means or by interaction with the designer. We will say more about the similarities and differences between these directions in Section 2.3.

Thus we see reusability can come in many forms. To recapitulate, we have prototyping, reusable code, reusable design, application generators, formal specification and transformation systems, and off-the-shelf commercial packages. In Section 2.3, we will examine all but the last of these carefully and analyze their merits and demerits for custom software production.

2.2 EXISTING FORMS OF SOFTWARE REUSABILITY

Before plunging into an analysis of the just-mentioned means of improving reusability, we prefer to stop briefly and examine some existing ways in which software reusability has proved to be successful.

☐ Subroutine libraries. They come in two different forms. One is the library provided by the computing center, which contains a set of functions (or procedures) deemed to be of general utility by the computing community. The second form is the subroutine library all of whose functional elements combine to solve problems in a single application area; examples of such libraries are linear programming packages, statistics libraries (BMD or SPSS), and numerical analysis libraries (IMSL). These two cases have several points in common that account for their success. The need for each module was clear from the application. The purpose of each module is usually definable in a concise way using English. Each routine is fixed except for a few parameters, which affect its operation in a well-defined manner. The routines may be inserted into a user's program and used by that program no matter what language is being used. In short, the definition, cataloging, and interfacing of elements of a subroutine library is a straightforward task. The most common form of the concept of reusable code comes from a desire to scale up on the success of the subroutine library.

☐ Compilers. When an application is of great importance, we often see tools and techniques being developed to support that activity. One primary example of this is in compiler development. The specification language for compiler writing is BNF, which, of course, is used to describe the syntax of the language. Once the BNF formalism is assumed, a parser generator can be built. This digests a BNF specification of a language and automatically produces parsing tables. These tables, coupled with a simple algorithm, allow for the syntactic analysis of sentences. The final tool is the compiler-compiler. This allows for the specification of the source language, the object language, translations of source language into object language, and various optimizations. When the user has provided complete details to the compiler-compiler, the compiler is produced.

From the point of view of a software production environment, there is a valuable lesson to be learned from this example. The formalism of BNF is simple to create and to comprehend. Its use has been universally adopted. Parser generators, viewed as a straightforward extension, have also been adopted, though with somewhat less success. This is due to two factors. One is that hand coding of the parser yields greater efficiency, and the other is that hand coding is required to treat error handling. The compiler-compiler is the culmination of the formal specification of a compiler. But as a practical tool, we observe its use only in rare circumstances. Although we have not done a formal study of why this is so, we do not believe it is due to lack of knowledge or availability. Instead, we feel the reason is that the complete specification effort is tedious. Also, the final output must be optimized, and as it was not created by the programmer, it is difficult to get the programmer to deal with it.

☐ Simulation. Another example of reusability comes from the domain of simulation. Simulation has for a long time been recognized as a major type of generic application for computers. That has caused many people to define the essential elements common to all simulations. These include a mechanism for defining events and relationships between events in the context of simulated clock time. These concepts have been incorporated into programming languages. Whether that language is GPSS (an extension of Fortran) or Simula (an extension of of ALGOL-60), the idea is the same: to gracefully extend a general-purpose programming language with simulation concepts so that any new simulation application can reuse these concepts rather than recreate them.

☐ Parameterized systems. Another attempt at reusability started with the idea that a single all-encompassing system could be constructed for some domain. In addition, a questionnaire is devised that essentially represents each possible option that one can select from the parameterized program. The results of the questionnaire for a specific application are transformed into choices for a preprocessing program. This preprocessor then specializes the large system for the application.

Perhaps the best example of this approach was IBM's effort in the late 1960s on a system they called Application Customizer Service. A questionnaire permitted the user to include or omit various functions, define field sizes, and lay out report formats. According to [Gordon, 1980], experience with this product revealed that being tied to a single comprehensive questionnaire was not a good idea. Since applications contain great variety, the questionnaire quickly became too unwieldy. Also, the variety of systems that could be produced made it difficult to write adequate documentation. Also, it was observed that over the life of any application program certain functions get removed and others need to be added. This is not suitable with the questionnaire approach. Thus product evolution is not handled nicely. Over the short term, the problem is flexibility and control, which is also not adequately addressed by a single parameterized system. In a later version called MACS, and described in [Gordon, 1980], ACS was transformed into an application generator similar in concept to the one we will describe in the next section. For our purposes here it is sufficient to conclude that reusability in the form of a highly parameterized system has been tried and found to be unsuitable for applications development on a broad scale.

The earlier examples cited in this section are instances of the successful use of reusability. The subroutine library is an instance of reusable code. BNF is an example of the reuse of a domain analysis. The compiler-compiler is the result of the complete automation of a domain analysis. Simulation languages show how once a domain analysis is successful, the resulting concepts can be brought together and adjoined to a general-purpose programming language. To this extent reusability has contributed to productivity increases. In the next section we intend to examine various extensions of reusability.

2.3 THE WIDENING SPECTRUM OF REUSABILITY

In this section we examine several newer approaches to reusability and the extent to which they may improve the productivity of large-scale customized software development. Almost all of these approaches are in an early stage of research and development, so we do not intend to criticize them for a lack of experience with practical applications. What we hope to do is to put this work in perspective for the working software engineer and to indicate various avenues that we feel have yet to be pursued before these approaches can be used in practice.

First we examine from a modern perspective the question of reusable code. The other approaches to reusability all rely upon a sophisticated processor that aids the systems analyst in the development process. Such processors are usually minimally capable of understanding a definition of a computer software system, which is expressed in its so-called specification language. Some of these processors work entirely on their own, while others are designed to interact with the systems analyst. We have grouped these approaches together in Section 2.3.2.

2.3.1 Reusable Code

We begin our discussion with an investigation of the notion of reusable code. As we mentioned before, this concept was advocated over 10 years ago by D. McIlroy. It is instructive to review his comments and the comments of his listeners, which were reported in [McIlroy, 1976]. McIlroy advocated what he called a component manufacturing facility. A components factory would first identify techniques for creating a parameterized family of routines for some familiar purposes, for example, a sine routine or I/O. Then it would worry about distribution of the routines, cataloging, and the mix of software products it offered.

Criticism of the concept by the attendees followed. Their comments are summarized in three points. First, it is impossible to create a parameterized system that is efficient, reliable, and convenient for all systems, and where the nature of the package does not impose itself on the user. Second, we will never get around machine dependencies such as fixed numerical representations. Third, regarding cataloging of the components, we do not know how to create descriptors that would permit someone to search for the proper routine. To summarize, our methods for defining components are weak, it is difficult to describe a component to a user, and there are no tools to catalog, refine, and compose components in an efficient manner.

In order for the concept of reusable software to become a reality, the following problems must be successfully addressed:

☐ Mechanisms for identifying components. How can one determine what components are generally useful and adaptable to many different projects? The effort to identify such components without restricting oneself to a specific domain seems doomed to failure.

☐ Method for specifying components. Once a functional component is decided upon, in what way does one write its description so that others can understand it? One might consider any one of the various specification formalisms which are in use, recognizing that they are not terribly perspicuous.

☐ The form of the components. Should they be implemented in some programming language or described by a program design language that permits one to intermix programming constructs with natural language?

☐ How are the components to be cataloged? Since there will likely be many, there needs to be a meta–description language to group similar components.

Note that if the work required to combine components becomes very time-consuming or requires great sophistication, then the potential advantages of reusable code will in large measure be mitigated. Also, recalling the tables in Section 2.1., the reuse of code alone will not have a major impact on the software development process as a whole. Because more time is spent on requirements, design, and maintenance than on coding, these areas need to be addressed as well.

A final difficulty in achieving reusability at the code level is that a user may want to change or extend the function of the unit to be reused. This may require extensive knowledge about the implementation of the module, thereby negating much of the advantage. If these changes are to be made over several reusable components, the virtues are severely diminished.

Two active research projects that are pursuing this line of research are presented in [Cooprider and Flon, 1981] and [Gerhart, 1980].

2.3.2 Very High-Level Program-Producing Systems

A narrow view of reusability would culminate with the subject just described. But it appears to us that several other ways to view reusability hold greater promise for improving our ability to create software. A group of these approaches can be viewed as creating a complex system for program development. Such a system has several components, each of which comes in many different forms. In this section we try to present these forms in an organized manner.

The general idea is to create a processor that interacts with a programmer (or system analyst) and produces executable code for solving his problem. But this processor does not accept just some variant of the conventional high-level programming language. Rather, it accepts a language that is much closer to the problem domain and presumably requires the programmer to write much less than if he were using a conventional language. This language is a critical element. It may be a general-purpose language, in the sense that it is designed to describe a broad range of applications, or it may be a domain-specific language, constructed to be most useful for describing applications of a given domain. The language may be procedural or nonprocedural, the latter freeing the programmer from having to specify the precise order of computations. For describing data, the language may use a hierarchical, algebraic, or relational formalism. Because of the many characteristics distinguishing these languages from programming languages, we refer to them as specification languages, and to programs written in them as specifications. Some advice to the designers of such languages has been presented by [Balzer and Goldman, 1979] (Fig. 2.1).

The second major component of these systems is the processor itself. The processor is usually far more than just a translator from the specification language to some executable target language. It may consist of an environment into which a domain-specific language can be inserted. It may have a great

FIGURE 2.1
OUTLINE OF A VERY HIGH-LEVEL PROGRAMMING SYSTEM

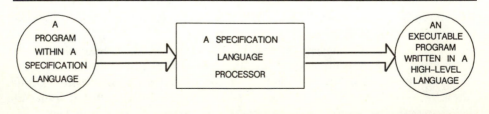

deal of information built into it, either about a given domain or about the process of creating a programming system in general. Nevertheless, despite this diversity, we can pose some specific questions about this generic processor:

☐ Does it produce the program directly from the supplied inputs or is it built to interact with an individual?

☐ Does it find incompleteness and/or inconsistencies in the specification? Is it guaranteed to find all of them?

☐ What capabilities of general use are provided, such as knowledge of arithmetic, transformations into efficient data structures, or theorem proving?

☐ How efficient is the processor as it translates a specification?

☐ How efficient is the resulting object code?

good Q's

In the next few sections we examine some approaches which have followed this model.

Reusable Design. The essential idea of reusable design is that a particular application domain should be studied in a formal way and that the artifacts of this study should be used to design software systems that automate that domain. The study leads both to an understanding of the domain and to various sets of outputs that describe concepts and processes occurring there. Subsequent efforts to automate specific instances of the domain make use of the artifacts already developed. The domain analysis can be reused for any system in the domain. A successful instance of this was already discussed in Section 2.2, namely, compiler writing. But now we wish to study the process of reusable design in its most general form. Two of the recent advocates of this approach are Neighbors and Freeman, who have developed a prototype system called Draco [Freeman and Neighbors, 1980; Neighbors, 1980].

There are two basic questions to be solved here. The first is, What is the output of a domain analysis? Several different kinds of objects will likely arise from study. These include data types from the domain, processes or important algorithms, and various constraints on the interactions between processes and types. How are these to be recorded for later use? Neighbors suggests that each domain will yield a different language. This unfortunately can lead to problems. The comprehension problem is multiplied and the implementation of the domain into others can be further complicated if the system designer must familiarize himself with several different languages.

The second major question is, What is done with the output of the domain analysis once it is written down? One approach would be to translate the types and processes into code modules written in some programming language. Another approach would be to extend an existing programming language with the new types and processes à la Simula for simulation.

Recently this approach has been effectively followed by Neighbors in his Ph.D. dissertation [Neighbors, 1980]. He has developed a computerized system called Draco to aid the translation of a domain specification into an executable program. Draco's essential functional steps are shown in Fig. 2.2.

From Fig. 2.2 we see that a software system is built in the following stages:

1. Determine the domain for analysis.
2. Do a domain analysis.
3. Create a domain language and library of concepts.
4. Create a parser and prettyprinter for concepts expressed in the domain language.
5. Define transformations that work from constructs of the output language.
6. Design a specific computerized system using the domain language. Then pass it to Draco, which will translate it into an executable form.

Neighbors reports in [Neighbors, 1980] that he has successfully built several systems, each being on the order of several thousand lines of code. He plans to scale up his examples in the near future. The practical use of this approach will ultimately depend upon several as-yet-untested points. One is that a good domain analysis is only as good as the domain analyst. Another concern is the potential growth in the domain languages that must be simultaneously mastered. Will the transformation system yield reasonably efficient programs? And most importantly, will debugging and maintenance be facilitated or hampered by this approach?

J. G. Rice advocates a similar approach in his book *Build Program Technique* [Rice, 1981]. Rice advocates the creation of what he calls an automatic software generation system (or ASGS). Such a system is composed of a

FIGURE 2.2
SCHEMATIC FOR DRACO

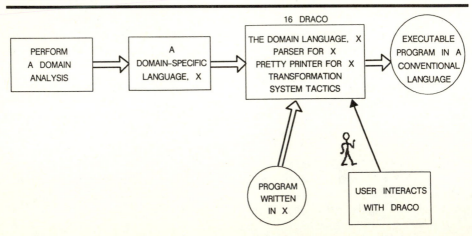

requirements statement language (RSL), an analyzer of the language, and translations of statements from the source to the target language (Fortran). Programs written in the RSL are translated by the ASGS into fully executable code. As in Neighbors' approach, this technique critically depends upon the quality of the domain analysis, the ease of use and appropriateness of the RSL, and the quality of the ASGS and of the resulting code. In Rice's book he tells of a major example that was worked out using the methodology he espouses.

Although there are still many questions to be studied and resolved in the area of reusable design, this subject appears to be a potentially effective avenue of research. Clearly, the compiler and simulation domains have been thoroughly and effectively analyzed with success. The prototypes built by Neighbors and Rice lead us to believe that gains are achievable in this direction (Fig. 2.3).

A Reusable Processor. An interesting contrast to the work of Neighbors and Freeman is the work of Prywes and his colleagues [Prywes, 1977; Prywes *et al.*, 1979]. Rather than reusing design, they have tried to provide a processor for a single, sophisticated specification language. The language is especially interesting in that it is nonprocedural. The programmer is not required to specify the order in which computation must be performed. This, according to Prywes, has a substantial effect on decreasing the amount of information that the programmer must provide. His language is called MODEL for "module description language." The language contains only two statement forms, one for describing data and one for describing relationships between variables (called an assertion statement). The MODEL processor is highly sophisticated. It works by first performing a syntactical analysis. Then

FIGURE 2.3
SCHEMATIC OF AN ASGS

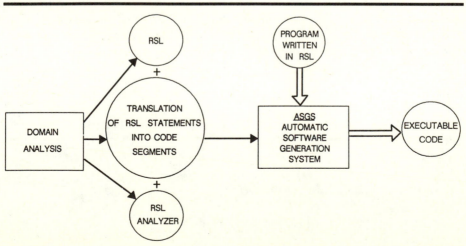

it creates a precedence matrix out of the statements, producing an order for the computations. Meanwhile, it checks for any incompleteness, ambiguity, or inconsistency that may exist. The eventual output consists of both a complete set of documentation (i.e., cross-reference listings of names and their use) and a program in a conventional programming language (PL/1).

A MODEL II program consists of a header, a data description, and a set of assertions. The header provides the usual sort of prologue information like the program's name, source, and target data, and the programmer's name. The data description part defines the data structures that will be used. MODEL II follows a hierarchical approach for describing data, similar in form to PL/1 structures. The assertions part consists of a set of declarative statements, which describe various relations between data items. The language offers no procedural mechanism such as iteration. In fact, the order in which statements are presented has no effect on the meaning of the program. Each individual statement is analyzed by the MODEL system, which establishes precedence relations between them (Fig. 2.4).

The MODEL language is unusual and is not for naive end users. However, a capable programmer should become comfortable using the language after a short period of time. One advantage of this overall scheme is that the systems analyst need only learn one new language. The fact that it is nonprocedural causes code compression in the original source. Good documentation is produced along with the code, which is a highly desirable feature. And finally, subsequent debugging can be done in the original source. Note that with the Draco system, the systems analyst would have to retransform at least part of the system. Prywes reports having built a major application for the U.S. Internal Revenue Service using his system.

Reusing Transformation Systems.   Several researchers have thoroughly investigated the approach of taking high-level operational specifications and transforming them into efficient programs. Researchers involved in this work include Arsac [1979], Burstall and Darlington [1977], Cheatham [Cheatham *et al.*, 1979], Manna and Waldinger [1977], and many others too numerous to mention here. Often the original programs are stated using a few mutually recursive procedures. The transformation system then successively

FIGURE 2.4
OVERALL PROCEDURE FOR USING MODEL II. FROM [PRYWES, 1979]

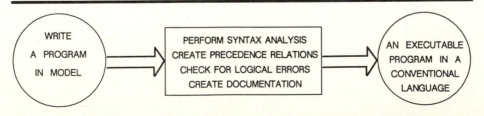

refines each function, perhaps introducing new variables, data structures, and iteration to produce the final efficient version. Complete catalogs of transformations have been developed by Standish *et al.* and by Arsac. This work has been very valuable in precisely formulating the types of transformations that can be done while preserving computational equivalence. It has also caused people to investigate the theoretical limits of the transformation technique. From our perspective of large-scale software design, the question seems to be whether these prototype systems will be capable of scaling up to a system of major size.

The researchers at USC's Information Sciences Institute are pursuing this line. Their SAFE project (specification acquisition from experts) has attempted to handle examples of a substantial size and to produce from each specification a reasonably efficient program. In [Balzer *et al.*, 1978] and [Balzer, 1981] two examples are shown. In both cases a specification is transformed into some executable form. It appears that the specification language has been changing over time, and [Balzer and Goldman, 1979] gives an exposition of the desirable properties of such languages.

As of the writing of this paper, their system has two components. The first component takes specifications that are written in English but are preparsed by hand. This preparsed natural language input is given to the front-end component, which tries to transform it into a high-level but operational specification. The specification language is called Gist, and it describes data using a relational formalism. The front-end component also attempts to discover any inconsistencies or ambiguities. The resulting output is handed to the second component. This is a processor that interacts with an analyst and permits him to apply various available transformations. The result is a fully efficient program. Future plans call for offering an alternative to natural language as the language for writing specifications by extending Gist to be more complete. (See Fig. 2.5.)

The research projects covered in this section are mostly in an early stage of development. Rather than draw any conclusions about their individual merits, we wish to make some general observations.

FIGURE 2.5
OVERVIEW OF THE SAFE SYSTEM

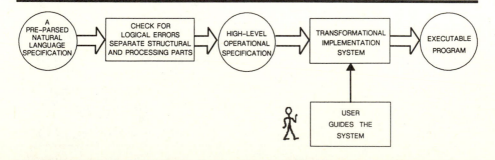

How to?

Good point ***

The specification language is a crucial element of all these systems. It must be sufficiently concise and yet descriptive. Too many of the specifications we have seen are more complex to read than the resulting programs.

The trend towards using relational statements for data description is a good one, and melds the best of database technology with more conventional programming language design theory.

If it is necessary to debug at the level of the output program, then these methods will not succeed. As there will be little or no recognizable relationship between the original specifications and the output program, it must be sufficient and economical to debug back at the specification level.

Application Generators.   Application generators are a form of software system that has found practical use in computing for many years. Their original purpose was very narrow; typically they were used to generate programs whose output is a series of reports (such as RPG). Later they were extended so that they could interface with an existing database, perform statistical operations, and display the results. The programmer writes statements provided by the application generator and the output is an executable program that accesses the database and prints some report. Several software product houses sell commercial application generators. An abbreviated list is seen in Table 2.3.

Suppose we consider the kind of capabilities these systems offer. Central to such a system is a nonprocedural language designed for a nontechnical person to use. In practice, this basically means that the user selects one of the items presented to him in a menu. The second basic element of

TABLE 2.3

SOME COMMERCIALLY AVAILABLE APPLICATION GENERATORS

Admins2	Admins Inc.
Ads	Cullinane Database Systems
Aims Plus	Aims Co.
Athena	Phoenix Systems Inc.
Cpg	Insac Software
Focus	Information Builders Inc.
Generation 5	American Management Systems
Info	Henco Inc.
Inform	Cortex Corp.
Mantis	Cincom Systems
Mark IV	Informatics Inc.
Nomad	National CSS
Oasis	Burroughs Corp.
Oracle	Relational Software
QBE	IBM
Ramis II	Mathematica
RIMS/MPG	Information and Systems Research

the application generator is built-in knowledge about an existing database management system or simply about the specification of files on the computer it is running on. The user of the application generator starts the program and goes through four phases, which are presented to him by the system. These are as follows:

1. File format design. The user must define all files, field names, and their attributes.
2. Print design. The user creates printing formats including column headers, sum totals, spacing, special characters, and so on.
3. System operations. This phase includes the main program, which prompts the end user as he creates his application program. The user selects to enter the file design phase or the print design phase, or he requests to use a special utility routine. The user can create special definitions or change the value of variables.
4. System utilities. Typical here are the operations of sorting on records or changing the values of certain fields as they are input.

After the programmer has completed these phases, the application generator will produce for him a fully executable program. For the systems mentioned in the above table, the output language is typically Cobol.

What are the advantages offered by this process? Clearly, one is the nonprocedural front end, which prompts the programmer as he creates arbitrary applications from data files. Another is the built-in knowledge concerning file creation, record input and output, report writing, and various logical operations on fields of records. Most importantly, the usual lengthy debugging periods associated with writing programs conventionally are avoided because the generated code has already been debugged, and because all modifications are made using the nonprocedural language. Therefore, we view application generators as an excellent example of reusability.

In Section 2.1 we emphasized that we were assuming a computer environment for developing large customized software systems. In this respect, the application generators mentioned above are severely restricted. Their use has primarily been confined to programs for report generation and/or small-scale database manipulation. However, one system developed by M. Zloof at IBM [Zloof, 1981] has progressed considerably beyond this level. Query-by-example/office-procedures-by-example is an attempt to extend the QBE application generator to a system that contains knowledge of word processing, electronic mail, graphics, security features, and general data processing. Objects in the language include letters, forms, charts, graphs, and audio documents. It appears that the less sophisticated end user can rapidly gain familiarity with the language and do useful programming in short order. Once again the nonprocedural nature of the interaction is the strongest feature.

Thus the critical research issue for the successful use of such systems is how to extend them so that they can express a wider range of computations while maintaining their already efficient operation. We hope to see this area studied in greater depth soon.

Prototyping. Prototyping can be a powerful tool in defining the requirements of a computerized system. However, prototypes have been dismissed as a practical approach because they are considered to be too expensive to build. Yet, [Gomaa and Scott, 1981] rejects the notion that prototypes are too expensive, arguing that the aid they give at the requirements stage is of the highest leverage. Although techniques such as PSL (problem statement language) [Teichrow and Hershey, 1977] or any of the methods that rely upon a specification do not show that the given specification agrees with the user's needs, they are in some measure consistent and complete. From a user's point of view, hands-on use of a prototype is an ideal way to determine if the projected system performs in the desired way.

Historically, two programming languages have proved themselves to be most useful in the task of creating complex systems fast (i.e., prototypes). These are LISP and APL. For example, Gomaa and Scott use APL. The criticism usually put forth is that these languages are inefficient for production systems. We do not intend to argue this point here. Future research must focus on mechanisms to make prototyping more economical and study how it can effectively be inserted into the software life cycle. This research can take several forms, as outlined by [Taylor and Standish, 1981]. They suggest that there be a study of (1) new prototyping languages, (2) the redevelopment of prototypes into efficient systems, and (3) incremental modification of a prototype into a production system.

Application generators can serve as a prototyping tool, as applications in rudimentary form can quickly be devised and running. End users can easily be involved in designing the reports aided by the use of the nonprocedural language. This would eliminate one commonly stated objection to prototypes, namely that only programmers familiar with esoteric languages can build them.

2.3.3 Programming Language Support

Most programmers think about computation using the concepts offered by their programming languages. Although it is impossible to quantitatively assess the extent to which a programming language influences our mental abilities to conceptualize a software system, there is wide agreement that it is substantial. Thus it comes as a delight to see a new programming language that supports, to a greater degree than before, the development of reusable software. The Ada programming language [United States Department of Defense, 1980] contains several mechanisms that aid in the specification and development of reusable code.

One of the features of Ada that support reusability is the package concept. This is a mechanism for defining an abstract data type. Methodologically, this is valuable because it supports information hiding, a basic concept of good system design. Although it is possible to create abstract data types in other languages, there it is necessary to create one's own conventions. In Ada, the definition of abstract data types is supported more effectively. It is likely that any future efforts to develop reusable code will make substantial use of the semantic rules of packages, even if they do not code the modules themselves into Ada.

A second feature provided by Ada that supports reusability is the generic procedure. As a simple example consider what one has to do to write a sorting procedure in Pascal. One is required to state both the type of the data that the sort will work on and the maximum number of elements it can handle. A consequence of this is that a routine for sorting at most 100 integers cannot be used to sort 100 real numbers. This adds to the complexity required of any software system. Generic procedures in Ada preserve the virtues of typing while eliminating the negative aspects.

2.3.4 Even Other Methods Exist

It is impossible to give appropriate coverage to all of the computer software development innovations on the horizon. In this section we want to mention one that is very different from those we have covered so far. We do this primarily to emphasize the diversity of invention in the software field and to reiterate our conviction that it is impossible to accurately predict the influence that any one technique may have in the future.

Programming productivity was recently raised in a major way by the invention of a new mode of programming. This mode was really entirely different from any previous method. Moreover, it captured a paradigm of computation that was so broad that many people have immediately gone on to use it. We are thinking of the spreadsheet concept and its generalization, spreadsheet programming.

By now our readers have all heard of VisiCalc. This is the product that introduced the notion of the spreadsheet. Briefly, one looks at an array of fields where each field can contain either textual, numerical, or formula data. Formulas for the computation of the value of a field can involve the values in other fields. With this sort of capability one can ask "what if" questions and run various scenarios.

We consider the spreadsheet program as an example of software reusability partially because of the growth of a secondary industry surrounding spreadsheets. Companies have been developing spreadsheet templates to cover a wide range of applications from checkbook balancing to cash flow projection to inventory control. These templates are just like reusable code modules, both in their positive and negative aspects. Moreover, many people who now use a computer do so by "programming" in VisiCalc, and not in

Basic or Pascal. By bringing a fairly simple and natural paradigm to the computing world, the spreadsheet has brought many new users to computers.

Although it is not clear that this innovation will have impact on the design of large, customized software, nevertheless its lessons are quite valuable. An interface to a computer-naive user is essential, and it is very powerful when developed properly. The impact of capturing a certain domain of application in a programming environment can be very great if it is done well. This should be a new direction of study in the computer research community.

2.4 RELATED ISSUES

Many nontechnical issues will still have to be considered even if we are able to develop effective means for reusability. Some of these are as follows:

- ☐ Contractual problems. These could involve deliverables or computer manufacturer support of special-purpose software such as application generators.
- ☐ Programmer training. The need to train people in a new technology is often overlooked as an essential item. This is something that must be done inhouse rather than through the current educational system.
- ☐ Facilitation within the government. Contracts for redesign and production rather than prototypes are needed to verify the applicability and limits of any new technology.
- ☐ Maintenance and modification. New thought must be given to this question, if the system is not written in a conventional language but is composed of reusable components or created for some high-level specification system.

1987 UPDATE

In the time since this paper was initially written significantly more industry attention has been given to practical application of reusability concepts to enhance productivity. Needless to say, this is a complex problem, and the basic issues as discussed earlier in this paper have not significantly changed. However, recently several major national thrusts toward a solution have been initiated. First, Ada is now here and real. The Department of Defense has taken a strong stand with a directive mandating Ada for all new DOD computer-based systems (not just embedded-computer weapon systems). Two conclusions about Ada are already clear from preliminary DOD efforts: (1) Ada is portable, and major reusability gains have been demonstrated at the systems level [Myers, 1987] from code programmed in Ada; and (2) the potential for "packages" (less than full systems) is very real for second-generation Ada systems.

Second, the DOD STARS [Office of Secretary of Defense, 1986] program has been recently reorganized and funded, and it has adopted as a major goal the support of reuse of existing, validated Ada components in future procurements. If favorable results can be achieved, there will be potential for major returns on investment. This will be important to DOD, and therefore, the STARS program will continue to flourish on this basis alone. Immediate STARS plans include development of special Ada-coded reusable packages.

Third, the issue of improved productivity has also achieved non-DOD prominence in the creation of the Software Productivity Consortium of Reston, Virginia [Software Productivity Consortium, 1987]. This association of large industrial corporations has established a research center to explore methods for reducing software development costs through advanced technology. At this writing, one of their key thrust areas is advertised to be reusability of software products. MCC in Austin, Texas, is likewise applying effort on several innovative approaches to reusability as part of the software engineering research activities under Lazlo Belady.

The net of all this activity is that the data processing industry has both recognized the huge potential for major cost savings through reusability and found ways to collect and focus significant national resources on this program, inspiring hope that real progress can be achieved in the near future.

References

Arsac, J. J. Syntactic source-to-source program manipulation. *Commun. Ass. Comput. Mach.*, vol. 22, pp. 43–54, 1979.

Balzer, R. M. A global view of automatic programming. In *Proc. 3rd Joint Conf. Artificial Intell.*, pp. 494–499, SRI Int., Aug. 1973.

Balzer, R. M. Transformational implementation. USC/ISI, Tech. Rep. ISI/RR-79-79, May 1981.

Balzer, R. M., and N. Goldman. Principles of good software specification and their implications for specification languages. In *Proc. Specifications of Reliable Software Conf.*, pp. 58–67, New York: IEEE, 1979.

Balzer, R. M.; N. M. Goldman; and D. Wile. On the transformational implementation approach to programming. *In Proc. 2nd Int. Conf. Software Eng.*, pp. 58–67, New York: IEEE, 1976.

———. Informality in program specifications. *IEEE Trans. Software Eng.*, vol. SE-4, pp. 94–103, Mar. 1978.

Belady, L. A., and M. M. Lehman. The characteristics of large software systems. In *Research Directions in Software Technology*, ed. P. Wegner. Cambridge, Mass.: MIT Press, 1979.

Biermann, A. W. Approaches to automatic programming. In *Advances in Computers*, ed. Rubinoff and Yovits, pp. 1–65. New York: Academic, 1976.

Burstall, R. M., and J. Darlington. A transformation system for developing recursive programs. *J. Ass. Comput. Mach.*, vol. 24, no. 1, pp. 44–67, 1977.

Cheatham, T. E.; J. A. Townly; and G. H. Holloway. A system for program refinement. In *Proc. 4th Conf. Software Eng.*, pp. 53–62. New York: IEEE, Sept. 1979.

Cooprider, L., and L. Flon. Meta-programming. Department of Computer Science, Univ. of Southern California, 1981.

Frank, W. L. What limits to software gains? *Computerworld*, pp. 65–70, May 4, 1981a.

———. Software productivity: Any breakthrough? *Computerworld*, July 13, 1981b.

Freeman, P., and J. M. Neighbors. Reuse project: Proposal for research on software construction using components. Department of Information and Computer Science, Univ. of California, Irvine, Oct. 1980.

Gerhart, S. Adaptable software components. Research proposal submitted to ARPA, Information Sciences Institute, Los Angeles, Calif., Nov. 1980.

Gomaa, H., and D. B. H. Scott. Prototyping as a tool in the specification of user requirements. In *Proc. 5th Conf. Software Eng.*, pp. 333–342. New York: IEEE, Mar. 1981.

Gordon, R. D. The modular application customizing system. *IBM Syst. J.*, vol. 19, no. 4, pp. 521–541, 1980.

Hammer, M., W. Howe, V. Kruskal, and I. Wladawsky. A very high-level programming language for data processing applications. *Commun. Ass. Comput. Mach.*, vol. 20, pp. 832–840, 1977.

Harrison, R. T. The IBM application customizer service. In *Approaches to System Design*, ed. R. Bout, New York: NCC.

Ivie, E. L. The programmer's workbench. *Commun. Ass. Comput. Mach.*, vol. 20, pp. 746–753, 1977.

Manna, A., and Z. Waldinger. Synthesis: Dreams → programs. tech. rep. STAN-CS-77-630, Stanford University, Nov. 1977.

McIlroy, M. D. Mass-produced software components. In *Software Eng. Concepts and Techniques, 1968 NATO Conf. Software Eng.*, ed. J. M. Buxton, P. Naur, and B. Randell, pp. 88–98, 1976.

Morrissey, J. H., and L. S. Wu. Software engineering—An economic perspective. In *Proc. 4th Conf. Software Eng.*, pp. 412–422. New York: IEEE, 1979.

Myers, Ware. ADA: First users pleased; prospective users still hesitant. *IEEE Computer Magazine*, vol. 20, no. 3, March 1987.

Neighbors, J. M. Software construction using components. Ph.D. dissertation, tech. rep. 160, Department of Information and Computer Science, Univ. of California, Irvine, 1980.

Office of Secretary of Defense. Software technology for adaptable reliable systems—STARS. Technical program plan. Washington, D.C., Aug. 6, 1986.

Personal Software, Inc. *VisiCalc Guide*. Boca Raton, Fla.: IBM Manual.

Prywes, N. Automatic generation of computer programs. In *Advances in Computers*, ed. M. Rubinoff and M. Yovits, vol. 16. New York: Academic, 1977.

Prywes, N. S.; A. Pnueli; and S. Shastry. Use of a nonprocedural specification language and associated program generator in software development. In *ACM Trans. Program. Lang. Syst.*, pp. 196–217, 1979.

Read, N. S., and D. L. Harmon. Assuring MIS success. *Datamation*, pp. 109–120, Feb. 1981.

Rice, J. G. *Build Program Technique: A Practical Approach for the Development of Automatic Software Generation Systems*. New York: Wiley, 1981.

Software Productivity Consortium. Technology development plan—Part I. Technical report 82001, March 1987.

Teichrow, D., and E. A. Hershey. PSL/PSA: A computer-aided technique for structured documentation and analysis of information processing systems. *IEEE Trans. Software Eng.*, vol. SE-3, pp. 41–48, Jan. 1977.

United States Department of Defense. *The Ada Language Reference Manual*. Dec. 1980.

Zloof, M. M. QBE/OBE: A language for office and business automation. *Computer*, vol. 14, pp. 13–23, May 5, 1981.

Zloof, M., and P. S. de Jong. The system for business automation (SBA) programming language. *Commun. Ass. Comput. Mach.*, vol. 20, pp. 385–395, 1977.

CHAPTER 3

Capital-Intensive Software Technology

PETER WEGNER
Brown University

3.1 CAPITAL-INTENSIVE TECHNOLOGY AND REUSABILITY

What is Capital?

Capital is a stock rather than a flow. In its broadest sense it includes the human population; non-material elements such as skills, abilities and education; land, buildings, equipment of all kinds; and all stocks of goods, finished or unfinished, in the hands of both firms and households.

—*Encyclopedia Britannica*, 1968

To flirt is capital.

—*The Mikado*, Gilbert and Sullivan

Striking similarities between industrial and software technology have led to considerable borrowing of the terminology of industry for corresponding software concepts. For example, the term *software engineering* emphasizes that the construction of software is an engineering task. Terms such as *software tools* and *software factory* suggest that paradigms of industrial production are being adopted for software production.

The terms *capital* and *capital-intensive*, first introduced in the context of industrial technology, can also be applied to software technology. Software technology, like the technology that fueled the industrial revolution, was labor-intensive in its youth and is becoming capital-intensive as it matures.

Economists such as Adam Smith used the term *capital* for one of three factors of production, along with *land* and *labor*. Because Karl Marx, in his book *Das Kapital*, emphasized the exploitation resulting from the ruthless use of capital to maximize profits, the term came to have bad connotations. The ensuing arguments between classical and Marxist economists about who should own capital resources have sometimes obscured the more central question of how capital resources should be harnessed for the benefit of mankind. We are here concerned with the public benefits of capital, irrespective of ownership. Our purpose is to understand how capital goods enhance our productivity in building bigger and better software systems and, more generally, in managing our growing stock of knowledge.

Technologies that rely heavily on capital goods are called capital-intensive. Intuition suggests that a production process is capital-intensive if it requires expensive tools or if it involves large startup expenditures. Software development is becoming increasingly capital-intensive; its tools are becoming more powerful and expensive, and it requires greater early investment to reduce later expenditures.

Machine tools of the industrial revolution and software tools such as compilers are both reusable resources. Any reusable resource may be thought of as a capital good whose development cost may be recovered over its set of uses. Thus it seems reasonable to identify capital goods with reusable resources and capital with reusability.

Capital goods such as a lathe or an assembly line are reusable resources for producing consumer goods. Capital goods such as compilers and operating systems are reusable resources for producing application programs. Programmers are reusable resources in the production of programs. Activities such as education that contribute to programmer productivity develop capital in that they enhance the reusability of people. The process of developing capital goods is called capital formation. Capital formation in software technology is dependent on the implementation of concepts and models rather than on the construction of physical machines. Both conceptual and physical capital involve the idea of reusability.

Reusability is a general engineering principle whose importance derives from the desire to avoid duplication and to capture commonality in undertaking classes of inherently similar tasks. It provides both an intellectual justification for research that simplifies and unifies classes of phenomena and an economic justification for developing reusable software products that make computers and programmers more productive. The assertion that we should stand on each other's shoulders rather than on each other's feet may be interpreted as a plea for both intellectual and economic reusability.

The initial economic motivation for the development of general-purpose computers was the reusability of computer hardware. General-purpose computers are a capital-intensive response to the information-processing needs of society. They allow critical computing resources such as the central processing unit to be reused one million times per second. Less critical resources such as the computer memory may be reused for programs and data with very different behavioral characteristics.

The changed economic balance between hardware and software has resulted in changed perceptions of what is capital-intensive. When hardware was the dominant cost in a computer system, attention focused on computer efficiency. Even Fortran was regarded with skepticism because its compiled code might be less efficient than machine language. Time-sharing operating systems were carefully crafted so that a single powerful processor could be shared (reused) by many users. With decreasing hardware costs, attention has shifted from the reusability of central processing units to the reusability of software and the productive use of people.

Technological changes that took several decades in the industrial revolution are being compressed in the computer revolution into a much shorter time. The greater speed of technical change means that capital investment must be recovered more quickly and that enhancement and evolution consume proportionately more resources than in a slowly changing technology. Maintenance and enhancement are the dominant costs in the software life cycle today.

Overview and Organization

The drive to create reusable rather than transitory artifacts has aesthetic and intellectual as well as economic motivations and is part of man's desire for immortality. It distinguishes man from other creatures and civilized from primitive societies.

We explore a variety of capital-intensive software activities, including (1) software components, (2) programming in the large, (3) knowledge engineering, and (4) accomplishments and deficiencies of Ada. Each topic is presented in a self-contained section that can be read independently. However, the article as a whole presents an integrated view of capital-intensive software technology that is greater than the sum of its parts.

Software components are the capital-intensive building blocks out of which large programs are constructed. In Section 3.2 we review the evolution of software components and examine the relation among subprograms, data and process abstraction, and object-oriented programming. We contrast the computation model of block-structured languages with that of distributed programming languages. The role of libraries as repositories of knowledge that organize the interaction of software components during both program development and program execution is examined. A taxonomy is developed that suggests that the study of software components is maturing into a sub-discipline of computer science with considerable structure and substance.

The evolution of life-cycle models from the waterfall model through the operational (rapid prototyping) model to the knowledge-based model is examined in Section 3.3. The tension between efficiency and modifiability in the design of large systems is discussed. We give examples of the reusability of concepts in both theoretical and experimental computer science, indicating that the value of research contributions and concepts can be measured by the same metric as software products. Application generators generate software components of high granularity in a specialized domain and take advantage of the reusability of both the generating mechanism and the environment in which generated software components are embedded.

Software technology is concerned not only with amplifying the productivity of the programmer but also with amplifying man's mental capacities in other areas. In Section 3.4 we suggest that knowledge engineering will play the same role in the management of knowledge that software engineering plays in the management of software. We introduce the concept of knowledge support environments to parallel that of program support environments. We examine the knowledge graph paradigm of navigation through graph-structured documents, the idea of dynamic documents, and aids to automatic authoring that have the potential of increasing the quality of writing by providing better tools for the creation and delivery of information. Note that automatic authoring also has the potential of decreasing the quality of writing by cheapening (in both senses of the word) the process of delivery.

Section 3.5 is about Ada, a prototypical example of capital-intensive software technology. We examine both the contributions and the weaknesses of Ada. We conclude that Ada has accelerated the evolution of software technology but that imposition of Ada as a standard for embedded computing could have a negative impact on software productivity. In particular, preoccupation with Ada diverts attention from other technologies with a far greater potential impact on productivity, such as interactive, graphics-based, workstation technology.

3.2 SOFTWARE COMPONENTS

Reusability of Software Components

I would like to see the study of software components become a dignified branch of software engineering. I would like to see standard catalogs of routines classified by precision, robustness, time-space requirements and binding time of parameters.

—M. D. McIlroy, 1969

The importance of subprogram libraries of reusable programs was recognized by Wilkes, Wheeler, and Gill as early as 1950. McIlroy reformulated this idea and proposed a reusable software components technology to parallel components technologies for products such as automobiles. Research on data abstraction, object-oriented programming, and modularity in the 1970s was motivated by the desire to develop a viable software components technology. Research on process abstraction and distributed computing in the 1980s has yielded interesting new perspectives on software components. In reviewing this research, we develop the beginnings of a taxonomy of software components. But first we briefly examine the different kinds of component reusability that contribute to software productivity:

1. Software components may be reused in a variety of applications.
2. They may be reused in successive versions of a given program.
3. They are reused whenever programs containing the component are executed.
4. They are reused by being repeatedly called during program execution.

The first two forms of reusability reduce the costs of program development and are of greater interest than the third and fourth forms, which illustrate the static and dynamic reusability of hardware.

At the present time, reuse of a component in successive versions of an evolving program appears to be a more important source of increased productivity than reuse of code in different applications. Components are rarely portable between applications, and even if they are, the incremental benefit of using a component in two applications is only a factor of two. But the number of versions of a system over its lifetime can number in the hundreds or the thousands.

Project libraries, which contain successive versions of all software components in a software project, have become a central tool in project management. They are a primary means for maintaining a managerial visibility and control over the status and progress of a project and are also invaluable in debugging and project maintenance. The use of libraries for tracking progress within a project, isolating errors during debugging, and localizing the effect of program changes contributes much more to reducing the cost of program development than the use of interproject libraries.

If we expand the notion of components to include software tools, then the contribution of reusable components to software productivity becomes much greater. Compilers, loaders, and debuggers are constantly reused during both program development and program execution. Reusability of application-independent tools contributes more to software productivity than reusability of application-dependent software components.

We may distinguish between two kinds of component reusability: reusability of components in building a variety of structures and reusability of resources in performing a variety of tasks. The relation of being a resource for a task is more general than that of being a component in a structure. Tools, concepts, and people that contribute to performing a task are not parts of the final structure, but they are reusable components of software technology.

There are many different kinds of reusability and many different potential meanings of the term *software component*. In the remainder of this section we review the properties and design alternatives of traditional software components.

Interfaces

An interface is what the user sees.

Software component interfaces specify invariant properties accessible to users of the component. Syntactic interfaces specify compile-time invariants that determine how components fit together. Semantic interfaces specify execution-time invariants that determine what the component computes.

The syntactic interface of a subprogram definition may be viewed as a socket, and subprogram calls may be viewed as plugs that are plugged in at the time of subprogram call. Subprogram parameters may be viewed as prongs whose size and shape depend on the parameter type. The number and type of prongs of a subprogram call must match the number and type of corresponding slots in the socket corresponding to the subprogram definition (see Fig. 3.1).

Syntactic interface specifications are a weak form of specification sufficient to determine that components fit together correctly, but insufficient to determine the correctness of computations of the resulting software structure. However, weak interface specifications are tractable and useful in the sense that they allow consistency between specifications and invocations of software components to be checked and enforced at compile time. Strong semantic interface specifications are intractable in the sense that they do not always exist and their correctness cannot always be verified. This distinction is intrinsic in the language design of Ada.

Ada separates the syntactic interface specification of a component from the body that implements the component. Ada's weak syntactic interface

FIGURE 3.1
PLUG-AND-SOCKET MODEL FOR SUBPROGRAMS

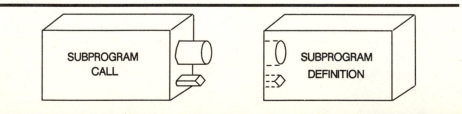

specifications have been criticized on the grounds that they are insufficient to determine program correctness. On the other hand, it can be argued that the design decision to use weak interface specifications as a basis for enforcing compile-time interface consistency is in fact one of Ada's strengths and represents an important contribution to language design.

One of the purposes of an interface specification is to capture invariant properties of the static program so that they can be checked and enforced by the compiler. Strongly typed languages such as Ada enforce compile-time type consistency by interface specifications. The programming language NIL,[*] developed by IBM at the T. J. Watson Research Center in Yorktown Heights, New York, is designed so that not only the type but also the state of initialization (type state) of variables is a compile-time invariant of the static program [Strom and Yemini, 1983]. It permits stronger compile-time consistency checks that guarantee proper initialization of variables before they are used and proper finalization of variables after they are used.

Programming systems may be characterized in terms of the internal interface specifications among their components. Interlisp and UNIX have weak interface specifications, while languages for application programming have strong interface specifications. The Ada environment requirements were a pioneering attempt to specify programming systems out of strongly typed components. NIL's notion of interfaces is even stronger than that of Ada, since not only the type but also the state of initialization of variables is known at compile time.

The tradeoffs between the flexibility and efficiency of very weak interface specifications and the guaranteed integrity of strong interface specifications need to be better understood. Strong interfaces serve to increase productivity during program development but may limit expressive power. Their cost-effectiveness is greater for application programs, where development and maintenance are the primary bottleneck, than for system programs, where efficiency is the primary consideration. In principle, a good compiler should be able to transform strongly typed modules specified by the user into efficient untyped internal modules, but we do not yet have sufficient experience to do this well.

Function and Data Abstraction

In the development of the understanding of complex phenomena, the most powerful tool available to the human intellect is abstraction. Abstraction arises from a recognition of similarities between certain objects, situations, or processes in the real world and the decision to concentrate on these similarities and to ignore, for the time being, their differences.

—C. A. R. Hoare, *Notes on Data Structuring*, 1972

---

[*]The acronym NIL stands for Network Implementation Language. It has nothing to do with the programming language Lisp.

FIGURE 3.2
FUNCTION ABSTRACTION

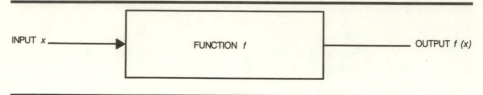

Many different abstraction mechanisms have been proposed as the basis for a software components industry, each representing different building blocks from which programs can be constructed and each resulting in different paradigms (methodologies) for programming. In this section we describe the features of function and data abstraction and illustrate design and interface issues with examples from programming languages such as Ada.

Function abstractions may be specified by input-output relations in which every input x determines a unique output $f(x)$ that depends only on x and on no other data (see Fig. 3.2). The user is aware only of the input-output specification and not of the way the function is implemented. The specification constitutes the interface to the user, and the implementation is hidden.

Function abstraction may be contrasted with data abstraction, in which the information hidden from the user includes data as well as function implementations. With data abstraction, an internal state "remembers" the effect of past operations and allows components to use past experience to modify future behavior. The effect of an operation f on an input x is no longer uniquely determined but may depend on the internal state s (see Fig. 3.3). An operation f on a state x may result in an output, $y = f(x,s)$, and a new state, $s' = g(x,s)$, just as in finite automata. A given data abstraction may in general support more than one operation sharing the same data structure.

FIGURE 3.3
DATA ABSTRACTION

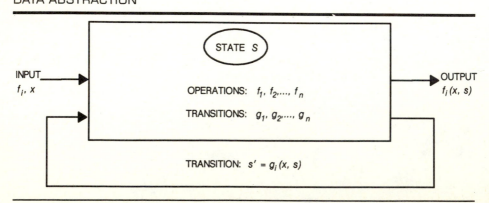

For example, a data abstraction for a stack generally supports push and pop operations and a test for the empty stack, all of which operate on the shared common state.

Whereas subprogram interfaces specify a single function f, data abstractions may specify a set of operations $f_1, f_2, \ldots, f_N$, each associated with a hidden state transition function $g_1, g_2, \ldots, g_N$. Each operation may be viewed as a socket that users who call the data abstraction are plugged into for the duration of a call.

In designing interfaces for data abstraction, the following issues must be addressed:

1. What kinds of resources should data abstractions provide to their users? Should they provide operations, types, variables, or some subset of these resources?

2. What rules should govern the granting of access rights to users of an abstraction?

Ada allows package interfaces to contain operations, types, variables, and other linguistic constructs. This wide interface (you can drive a truck through it) may be contrasted with the narrow interfaces of CLU, which permits just operations to be specified in the interface, and of NIL, which permits just types (of messages) to be specified in the interface.

Updatable interfaces may increase accessing efficiency but cause the component to lose control over information in the interface. Moreover, they violate the principle that interfaces be compile-time invariants. Interfaces become dependent on values of variables rather than on invariant interconnection properties of components. The tradeoffs between efficiency and integrity in choosing between wide and narrow interfaces are similar to those for global variables.

In Ada, access rights to abstractions declared in an enclosing block are inherited through the block structure mechanism. Access rights to library components are not restricted but must be redundantly mentioned in *with* clauses, thereby allowing the compiler to track dependencies among components and facilitating compile-time type checking for imported resources. Thus, "with Q" placed before a component P specifies that the resources of Q are imported into P.

Ada's compile-time binding of component interdependence may be contrasted to run-time interconnection facilities provided by operating systems. NIL embeds operating system facilities in a strongly typed programming language. It allows the programmer to establish dynamic interconnections by treating ports as updatable variables whose values are connections to ports in other processes. Here again, there are tradeoffs between the efficiency of compile-time binding and the flexibility of dynamic network interconnections.

Function and data abstraction determine different paradigms for programming associated with different partitionings of a computation into reusable and varying parts. Function abstraction emphasizes the reusability of functions of varying data, while data abstraction emphasizes the reusability of data objects for various operations that may be applied to them. With function abstraction programs are the primary capital goods and data are consumer goods, supplied as input by the consumer and returned as output to the consumer. With data abstraction, data objects are the primary reusable resource and functions are consumers with a shorter lifetime than the objects on which they operate.

Process Abstraction

Functions are abstract operations. Data abstractions are abstract variables. Processes are abstract computers.

Process abstractions are similar to data abstractions in having an internal state and a collection of operations that may transform the internal state. They differ from data abstractions in having an independently executing thread of control that determines the order in which operations become available for execution. They have ports through which users may obtain synchronized access to resources of the process. Access requests are placed in a queue from which they are removed only when the process is ready to handle them (see Fig. 3.4).

Two kinds of processes may be distinguished:

1. *concurrent processes*, which may communicate through shared data in a global memory, and
2. *distributed processes*, which have no shared data and communicate only by message passing.

Concurrent processes require a mechanism for protecting shared data from concurrent access. This may be accomplished by monitors [Hoare, 1974], which protect the set of operations of a data abstraction from con-

FIGURE 3.4
PROCESS ABSTRACTION

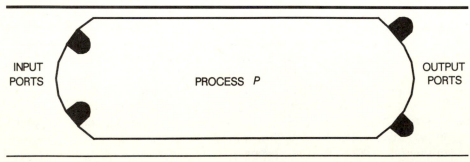

INPUT
PORTS

PROCESS *P*

OUTPUT
PORTS

current access by queuing all calls for sequential execution. An alternative mechanism is the atomic objects of Argus [Liskov and Scheifler, 1982], which permit concurrent read operations on a data abstraction but protect against concurrency during write operations.

Distributed processes do not need a mechanism for protecting data from concurrent access since there is no data outside a distributed process that needs to be protected. Ports can serve as the mechanism for data protection as well as the mechanism for process synchronization, thereby achieving linguistic economy.

In the design of interfaces for process abstraction the following issues must be addressed:

1. Are there essential differences between the interface needs of data and process abstraction?
2. What relation between interfaces and components is needed to support program evolution during both the development and the execution of long-lived distributed embedded systems?

The differences between the interface properties of Ada's data and process abstractions appear to be somewhat arbitrary. Ada's process (task) interfaces are narrower than its data abstraction interfaces, containing only entry points (operations). Process abstractions are first-class objects, which may be passed as parameters and appear as components of records and arrays, while subprogram and data abstractions are second-class objects [Wegner, 1983].

Ada allows interface specifications for both data and process abstraction to be compiled independently of their body (implementation). This represents an important step forward in language design, because it facilitates the reuse of software components in building large programs. Interfaces are specified and compiled early in program development since the resources they define may be needed by other components. Bodies that implement interface specifications are programmed much later by "body shops," since other components do not care how bodies are implemented, provided they deliver the resources promised in their specifications.

Interface specifications and bodies of a given Ada software component are weakly coupled during program development but strongly coupled during program execution, in the sense that the linkage between specifications and bodies cannot change during program execution. Ada is designed for program evolution during development, but it precludes evolution during program execution. This can be a severe limitation in long-lived, distributed embedded systems that must provide for evolution and modification while they are being used.

NIL has an approach to interface specification that is very different from that of Ada. Its interfaces specify properties of communication channels between components rather than of sockets at the receiving end of a communication channel. They are not tied to specific bodies but may be imported by any process that needs to use the interface for purposes of communication. Both calling and called processes must import the interface associated with the channel they will use to communicate. NIL permits output ports of a calling process to be dynamically connected to a new input port with a compatible interface specification during program execution. (Dynamic linking is discussed further later on.)

A given NIL process may import several different interface specifications and present different interfaces to each of the processes with which it communicates. This corresponds to the intuitive notion that any component (or person) is used in different ways by different components of its environment.

While Ada's separation of interface specifications and bodies represents an advance over previous software component technology, it places constraints on execution-time program evolution that can be avoided only by an even looser binding between interface and bodies, such as that found in NIL. This is just one of many examples illustrating that Ada's considerable contributions to language design represent the beginning rather than the end of our quest for a standard software components technology for evolutionary, embedded computing systems.

Software Components of Ada

Ada superimposes data and process abstraction on a Pascal-based language core.

Ada supports a variety of different kinds of software components. It has subprograms for function abstraction, packages for data abstraction, and tasks for process abstraction. It is a good language to illustrate the interaction among software components, both because it supports many kinds of components and because it goes wrong in interesting ways:

1. Ada's concern with efficiency resulted in software components that can communicate not only through interfaces, but also through shared global variables declared in textually enclosing environments, and through pointers to shared data in a "heap."
2. Ada does not properly integrate its data and process abstraction mechanisms. In particular, data abstractions (packages) are not protected against concurrent access by process abstractions (tasks).

Software components should normally communicate with their clients only through their interfaces. Communication through shared global data or pointers is not properly documented in the interface and results in imperfect, unverifiable abstractions. Components with shared global data are more like patients in a hospital connected to a life-support system by a variety of tubes than like truly autonomous entities (see Fig. 3.5). Patients can control ingestion of substances through the mouth but have no control over substances

FIGURE 3.5
GLOBAL AND POINTER VARIABLES

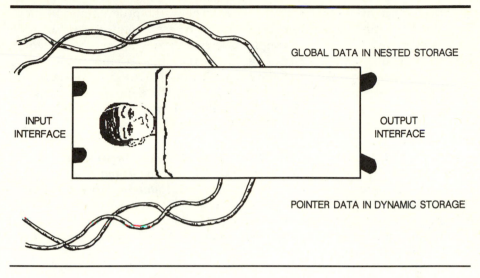

GLOBAL DATA IN NESTED STORAGE

INPUT
INTERFACE

OUTPUT
INTERFACE

POINTER DATA IN DYNAMIC STORAGE

entering the body through the life-support system. Software components
in Ada can similarly control ingestion and manipulation of data through
interfaces but have no control over global and pointer values.

The lack of protection of data abstraction against concurrent access by
process abstractions can result in erroneous programs, with errors that cannot
be caught at compile time or run time and with unpredictable effects that may
include the corruption of provably correct components. Erroneous programs
violate basic modularity prerequisites, since modules that have been proved
correct may be corrupted by unpredictable errors in erroneous modules.

The protection of shared data abstraction against concurrent access may
be realized by (1) replacing packages by protected data abstractions such
as monitors or (2) eliminating the possibility of sharing, both at the level
of variables and at the level of data abstraction. Linguistic constructs that
eliminate sharing are discussed in greater detail in the next section.

Distributed Processes

The strong modularity of distributed processes has its physical origins
in hardware requirements of distributed systems but derives its logical
importance as a paradigm for programming in the large.

Distributed processes model autonomous concurrently executing computers.
They are both logically and linguistically simpler than concurrent processes
with shared data. They provide a paradigm for a software components technology for large, long-lived, evolving programs that is more powerful than

that of data abstraction. We shall briefly examine some open design issues for distributed processes.

One important design issue is whether to allow the programmer to specify internal concurrency within distributed processes. Internal concurrency models large computers with multiple processes sharing a common memory. It greatly enhances the efficiency of certain kinds of computation, but it also increases the complexity of the programming language, requiring concurrency control within distributed processes to ensure disciplined access to shared data. Two kinds of processes are required, one to model distributed concurrency and the other to model internal concurrency within distributed processes.

Distributed processes with internal concurrency will be called *distributed concurrent processes* and may be contrasted with *distributed sequential processes*, which have no internal concurrency. Distributed sequential processes have a simpler model of computation because there is only one kind of concurrency rather than two. The problem of shared local data within distributed processes may be eliminated, and a single interprocess synchronization mechanism may be used for both process communication and synchronized data access.

Distributed sequential processes cannot express concurrent reading or writing of shared data structures. Access to a multiuser database such as that of an airline reservation system must be handled through a database server process that accepts queries sequentially through input ports. However, concurrency for such sequential queries may be reintroduced by an optimizing compiler [Strom and Yemini, 1983]. Figure 3.6 illustrates how queries arriving at an input port of a distributed sequential process may be compiled into concurrent queries of a distributed concurrent process. Such a compiler maps distributed sequential processes of a high-level user interface into distributed concurrent processes of an internal language that supports disciplined concurrent access to a shared database.

Distributed sequential processes allow the user to think concurrently at the logical level using distributed processes as the unit of concurrency. But they discourage the user from introducing explicit concurrency purely for

FIGURE 3.6

OPTIMIZATION OF DISTRIBUTED SEQUENTIAL PROCESSES

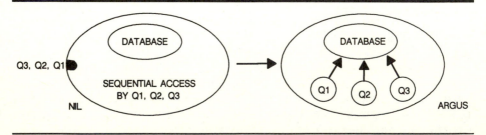

purposes of performance. In particular, they prevent the user from specifying optimizations requiring shared concurrent access to data structures, leaving such optimizations to smart compilers.

Distributed sequential processes determine a level of logical concurrency that may be either less than or greater than the level of physical concurrency during program execution. The optimization above introduces extra concurrency at execution time to improve efficiency. The reverse situation, where logical concurrency is greater than physical concurrency, arises when logically distributed processes are executed at a single physical location, either concurrently or sequentially. In this case, channels between distributed processes may be represented by shared variables so that remote procedure calls may be implemented as efficient transfers of control between components that share common storage. Sharing introduced by this kind of optimization is safe because it is introduced by the system rather than the user.

Distributed sequential processes permit neither local nor global sharing of data structures, but sharing plays a key role in both optimizations above. Increased concurrency is realized by sharing of data structures local to a process, while decreased concurrency allows channels to be replaced by shared data structures global to processes. The relation between sharing and optimizations that change the level of concurrency deserves to be further explored.

Another important design decision for distributed processes is the philosophy for recovery from failures. Programmable mechanisms provide control over recovery by the user, while transparent mechanisms free the user from this responsibility and place greater responsibility on the system. Argus provides programmable mechanisms while NIL hides the recovery mechanism from the user [Strom and Yemini, 1984].

Argus programs explicitly distinguish between volatile storage, which is destroyed by a crash, and permanent storage, which may be recovered with high probability. Argus allows the user to specify the granularity of recovery by atomic actions, which may abort or commit. The mechanism of atomic actions is used to recover from software failures and to define the granularity of transactions that need to be atomic in maintaining consistent states.

Recovery in NIL is transparent to the user. The system automatically takes periodic checkpoints and uses an optimistic recovery technique to recover from failures. Atomic actions are therefore not needed to recover from hardware failures. Software failures are handled by the NIL exception mechanism. All statements (including remote procedure calls) are atomic actions. A separate mechanism for defining atomic actions is therefore not needed.

Delegating responsibility for concurrency and recovery to the system makes the resulting language higher-level. But it requires a different model of the problem being solved and different language mechanisms to achieve the desired computational effect. For example, Argus handles hardware failures, software failures, and atomic transactions by the same language mechanism (atomic actions). NIL handles hardware failures transparently, software failures by the exception mechanism, and atomic transactions by serial processes, demonstrating a very different software design approach.

Recovery and internal concurrency are only two of many design issues for distributed processes. For example, distributed systems should have mechanisms for the dynamic creation and dynamic linking of processes so that they may evolve during execution. Mechanisms are needed for communicating with external devices, including external distributed processes with different hardware and software characteristics. A robust technology for distributed software components must transcend traditional programming language concepts and incorporate operating system and communication technology.

Objects, Classes, and Hierarchies

1. A thing that can be seen or touched, material that occupies space;
2. a person or thing to which action, thought, or feeling is directed;
3. what is aimed at: purpose, goal, end.

—Definition of *object*,
Webster's New World Dictionary, 2nd College Edition, 1984

The term *object* has become a ubiquitous buzzword that was independently adopted by the operating system, programming language, and database communities to denote software components having a hidden state and a set of operations or capabilities for transforming the state. Both data and process abstraction are object oriented, but the term has been most closely associated with Smalltalk [Byte, 1981], a programming language developed at Xerox PARC that superimposes hierarchical inheritance on data abstraction.

The set of classes of Smalltalk is organized as a tree structure with a root class called "object" containing properties possessed by all objects, such as the method "copy" for creating instances of any object. A subclass possesses all of the properties of the parent class as well as properties special to the subclass. Thus the class "vehicle," with methods "weight" and "owner" applicable to all vehicles, could have a subclass "car" with method "passengers" and a subclass "truck" with method "capacity." The subclass "car" could in turn have subclasses "Buick" and "Toyota."

By associating the superclass "car" with the subclass "Toyota," we permit callers of objects of the class "Toyota" to use methods and variables of the superclasses "car," "vehicle," and "object." A new class can simply specify incremental attributes and reuse attributes that it shares with already defined classes. Class hierarchies determine a capital-intensive paradigm for the flexible reuse of already defined data and program behavior in defining new system components.

There is a difference between inheriting attributes from a superclass and importing attributes from a global environment. Imported attributes may be invoked from within an object but cannot generally be called by users of the object. Inherited attributes can be directly invoked by callers. They can be exported to and inherited by callers. They become "owned" by the objects that inherit them and may be disposed of by their owners in any way deemed desirable. Inheritance is transitive: If *P* inherits from *Q* and *Q* inherits from *R*, then *P* inherits from *R*. Importing is not transitive.

In the terminology of ports, imported attributes determine additional output ports, while inherited attributes determine additional input ports callable by anyone that knows the name of the object. Introducing inheritance for distributed processes requires augmenting the set of input ports to include ports for inherited attributes.

Inheritance

The importance of multiple inheritance as a mechanism for system evolution is underlined by the fact that natural inheritance is based on the genes of two parents rather than one.

The Smalltalk paradigm of object-oriented programming is spreading to other language cultures. Class hierarchies of the Smalltalk variety have been used as a basis for extending a number of existing programming languages, and have resulted in Clascal (Pascal with classes) and C++ (C with classes). Lisp, which has a simple core that lends itself to extensions, has been extended to support classes, called flavors in the Lisp community [Weinred and Moon, 1981]. Lisp flavors may "mix in" methods and variables from more than one superclass, resulting in multiple inheritance of the attributes of several superclasses by a newly defined class. (The term *flavors* derives from Steve's ice cream parlor, where nuts and chocolate pieces can be mixed in to flavor a dish of vanilla.)

Inheritance may both enrich a class with extra features and specialize a class to perform a particular function. Consider for example a class "window," whose instances are windows on the screen of a personal computer. Windows have basic attributes such as a location on the screen. They may be enriched by inheriting attributes such as "border," "label," and "scroll." They may also inherit attributes such as "Lisp" or "Pascal" that specialize the window to a particular language. As shown in Fig. 3.7, enriching features may be mixed

FIGURE 3.7
INHERITED ENRICHMENT AND INHERITED SPECIALIZATION

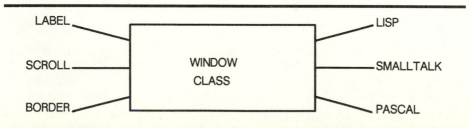

in to the class "window" without restriction, while features that specialize a window to a particular language are incompatible with each other. Thus inherited attributes may be subject to integrity constraints similar to those for databases. In its most general form an inheritance structure is a relation among templates that is automatically acquired by all instances as they are created.

An inheritance structure on software components mirrors the growth of knowledge in a database by building on what already exists rather than by starting from the beginning for every software component. Inheritance of attributes by software components is analogous to inheritance of acquired capital resources and inherited genes from one generation to the next in human societies. But inheritance of software components is more flexible because a component can be bound to different ancestors on different instances of execution. In some object-oriented systems, the binding may be changed even during execution. This corresponds to genetic engineers changing the ancestors of a person after he has been born.

Object-oriented languages of the Smalltalk variety have the following characteristics:

1. Objects with operations on an internal state are the primary software component. The internal state persists between successive operations and may, for long-lived objects, change the set of applicable operations while maintaining the identity of the object.
2. Operations and states may be inherited from previously defined classes by single or multiple inheritance so that new functionality may be incrementally defined in terms of previous functionality.

The first of these characteristics defines the essence of being object oriented. The second defines an attractive paradigm for organizing a library of classes so that new classes of objects can build on the properties of previously defined classes.

Class inheritance can be viewed as a structural relation of a library of components. Classes in Smalltalk can be thought of as library components, since they can be repeatedly reused either to create objects or as superclasses of lower-level classes. The class hierarchy of Smalltalk determines a tree-structured rather than a flat library. Class hierarchies provide a structured way of organizing components in a library so they can be systematically reused.

Library Structure and Design

Libraries promote the reuse of existing knowledge in the creation of new knowledge.

Program libraries are databases of reusable software components. Library design is concerned with organizing collections of software components so they can be easily created and used. Program libraries should contain not only software components but also tools for organizing knowledge, such as catalogs. In this respect they are like libraries of books or films. However, they differ from conventional libraries in that their customers are computers as well as people. Library tools for welding components together into programs must, therefore, be automatic. By the 1990s we are likely to have "intelligent libraries" that use knowledge about application domains in constructing composite programs from a library of software components.

In designing a program library the following issues must be considered:

1. What kinds of components can the library contain?
2. What is the granularity and domain of application of the library?
3. What kinds of clients (programs, people) will use the library?
4. How are components loaded, linked, and invoked?
5. How are components created, inserted, inspected, and retrieved?
6. What relations among components may be expressed?
7. What kind of knowledge is needed to aid programmers in building composite programs from libraries of software components?

In early programming languages like Fortran, subprograms are the only library components, although named common data blocks are effectively a second library. Fortran libraries are flat and require relations among programs to be implicit in the calling structure of subprograms.

In Ada, library components may be subprograms and packages but not tasks. Library structure is flat, but dependencies among components must be explicitly specified by *with* clauses. In Smalltalk, library components are organized into a hierarchy that allows new knowledge to be incrementally added to the library database. Programming environments such as UNIX may be viewed as libraries that support exceptionally diverse sets of clients and granularity within a single system. More generally, any database may be viewed as a library of persistent components whose lifetime is longer than that of the operation that accesses them.

Libraries may be characterized both by the kinds of components they contain and by the way that human and computer clients of the library use these components. Human clients include managers, analysts, and programmers with different needs and expectations. Computers also have multiple interfaces with software components, including compiler interfaces for program creation, tool interfaces for debugging, version control, and execution-time interfaces for module execution.

Libraries define a collection of resources external to a given component that complements the resources built up within a component while it computes. In block-structured languages the distinction between internal and external resources is coupled with the distinction between dynamic and static creation. Internal resources, represented by local variables, are created dynamically on entry to the block in which they are declared, while external resources, represented by components, are fixed prior to execution. Distributed-processing languages and operating systems generally allow execution-time creation and linking of components and thereby encourage the programmer to think of components as first-class objects whose properties are not dissimilar from properties of variables.

The extension of inheritance to concurrent and distributed processes is an interesting library design issue. Inheritance is essentially a block-structured compile-time mechanism for construction of types out of previously defined types. In the world of Lisp and of dynamically linked distributed processes, access rights to components are first-class objects and can be passed between processes dynamically. Dynamic passing of access rights is more flexible than the inheritance in Smalltalk but also requires more work on the part of the programmer. The flexibility of being able to inherit attributes dynamically can be important in long-lived systems that evolve during execution.

Taxonomy of Software Components

Classified information?

Software components may be classified as in Fig. 3.8. This taxonomy identifies state, inheritance, concurrency, and sharing as discriminating characteristics for the software components of different languages. It provides little guidance in classifying the large number of languages whose primary components are functions and subprograms (Fortran, Lisp, APL, Prolog), because they differ in their mechanisms for computation rather than intermodule communication. But it provides a rather satisfying, simply structured classification for languages with data and process abstraction and highlights key differences in the properties of their components.

The separation between data and process abstraction is based on the intuitive notion that data abstractions are passive while process abstractions are active. All operations in a data abstraction may be passively accessed at any time. Process abstractions control both *when* they accept an operation (by an input queue) and *where* they accept an operation (by an *accept* statement). Protected data abstractions, such as monitors, fall between data and process abstraction because they control when but not where they can be accessed. Monitors are generally implemented as specialized processes since the monitor queue is subject to precisely the same scheduling rules as queues associated with input ports of processes.

Our taxonomy of software components is tentative and shows that software components technology is in a state of transition. Programming languages like Ada were designed as sequential languages and have concurrency as a special feature, not properly integrated into the language. As concurrency becomes the norm, process abstraction will become the central abstraction mechanism, and both data and function abstraction will be defined as

FIGURE 3.8
TAXONOMY OF SOFTWARE COMPONENTS (WITH EXAMPLES)

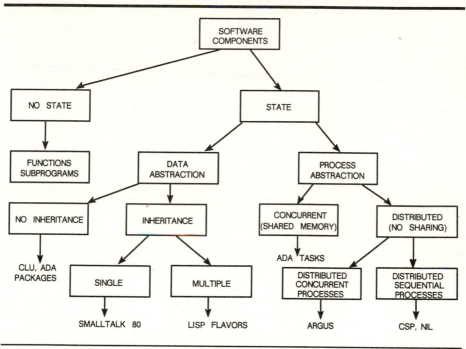

specialized forms of process abstraction. When this happens, data abstraction may well disappear as a distinct concept.

Our analysis suggests that the user model of computation for process abstraction will be that of distributed sequential processes. This requires the user to be aware of concurrency between distributed processes, while concurrency within distributed processes (if any) is hidden from the user and introduced for purposes of optimization by the system. Sharing of data by concurrent processes is likewise hidden from the user and managed by the system.

3.3 PROGRAMMING IN THE LARGE

Changing Paradigms of Software Technology

The change from a program-centered to a data-centered view of programming is comparable to the shift from the earth-centered to the sun-centered view of the solar system brought about by the Copernican revolution.

—Charles Bachman, Turing Lecture, 1973

As a first approximation, the evolution of software technology can be characterized by the following phases:

1950s	stand-alone programs (transient data, subprograms)
1960s	operating systems, databases (managing banks, airplanes)
1970s	software engineering (life cycle, abstraction, methodology)
1980s	interface technology (personal computers, modular languages)
1990s	knowledge engineering (intelligent components, for computers, for people).

In the early days of computing the paradigm for programming was writing subprograms that realized algorithms rather than modeling complex evolving real-world systems. Emphasis was on computations with transient data structures that could be discarded once the computation was completed. Programs were the primary capital goods and data was a consumer good in the sense that it was supplied as input and returned as output to the consumer. Subprogram libraries for common algorithms were regarded as the principal capital-intensive mechanism for reducing the programming effort.

As applications became larger and more ambitious, their nature changed to data management and embedded computing applications with non-transient data structures representing the state of an evolving system or organization. Data became a primary capital resource since programs often had a shorter lifetime than the data structures on which they operated.

Embedded computer applications, such as those that control banking operations, airline reservations, or aircraft flight, require two databases—one for the application and the other for program development. The application database contains both permanent and transient facts about the domain of discourse, while the program development database includes current and old versions of software components as well as specialized tools for testing or otherwise manipulating the components.

By 1970, perceived similarities between constructing large software systems and large physical structures, such as bridges and buildings, led to the birth of the discipline of software engineering. The life-cycle model caused attention to shift from software products, such as individual subprograms, to the process of software development.

The personal computer revolution of the 1980s has ushered in a new technology of man-computer interfaces. It involves the use of high-resolution multiple-window screens that simulate multiple piles of papers on a desktop. Multiple views of programs and data can be handled well by the emerging interface technology. The improved man-computer interface technology is being supplemented by an improved intermodule interface technology based on a distributed rather than a block-structured model of computation. Its aim is to provide a sounder framework for software components technology than that provided by current block-structured languages.

By the 1990s, interface technology will have become sufficiently capital-intensive to increase our system-building capability by several orders of magnitude. Ambitious software systems that failed in the past will become technologically feasible. For example, computer-aided instruction, which got a bad name in the 1960s and the 1970s, is likely to become cost-effective in the 1990s; it could materially change the style and pace of learning in schools and universities. Flat-screen technology could cause paper books to be replaced by much more versatile computer books. Knowledge databases could play an active role in amplifying our mental abilities, both in everyday activities and in research that extends the frontiers of knowledge.

Life-Cycle Paradigms

Life-cycle models provide a uniform framework for problem solving within which reusable methodologies and tools can be developed.

Attempts to understand the process of program development have led to a progression of life-cycle models, including the static waterfall model, the more dynamic operational model, and the futuristic knowledge-based model. These can be briefly described as follows:

The Waterfall Model: Requirements → Design → Implementation → Maintenance. In the waterfall model the development of software proceeds through a number of stages. Each stage has documentary output that serves as the input to the next stage. Early stages specify an informal behavioral abstraction of *what* is computed. This abstraction is progressively refined into a formal implementation of *how* the behavior can be realized. Maintenance and enhancement are performed on the implemented program.

The Operational Model: Executable Specification → Transformations → Efficient Implementation. In the operational model software development proceeds from an executable problem-oriented specification (rapid prototype) through a sequence of transformations to a more efficient implementation-oriented realization [Zave, 1984]. Early stages are independent of computational resources. Transformations from the problem-oriented specification to an efficient implementation are automatic wherever possible. Maintenance and enhancement changes are performed on the problem-oriented specification, which is then optimized.

The Knowledge-Based Model: Project Database, Knowledge-based Assistant. In the knowledge-based model software development is under the control of a knowledge-based activity coordinator, which coordinates access by multiple developers and users and logs the states and history of all information in the project database. The computer is an active partner in program development.

The model provides a framework for automating a variety of life-cycle models, including the waterfall and operational models.

Waterfall Model.   The waterfall model was developed in the late 1960s—before knowledge-based automation—and is viable with a noncomputerized project database. We now have considerable experience and data for projects using this model. For example, Boehm [1981] draws on a database of 63 projects in developing a constructive cost model—"Cocomo"—for estimating levels of effort and time schedules for software projects. His results show that the uniformities hypothesized by the model do in fact exist. In spite of such successes, however, the waterfall model has the following drawbacks:

1. It is geared to program development by humans rather than computers.
2. It does not provide feedback concerning requirements and design behavior till late in the implementation phase.
3. Documentation is manual, voluminous, static, and incomplete.
4. Maintenance and enhancement are performed on low-level, already-optimized implementations rather than on problem-oriented specifications.
5. The behavioral abstraction paradigm with its inflexible separation between behavior and implementation may be inappropriate for automatic life-cycle management.

The waterfall model embodies development procedures prevalent in the 1960s, before the potential of the computer as an active partner in program development was fully understood. The manual nature of requirements, design, and implementation activities requires the system designer to make the major system development decisions and cast them in concrete without any feedback from the computer. Voluminous documentation of static system structure at successive points in system evolution is required, leaving little energy for documenting the process of program development. Moreover, program development is regarded as complete once an implementation is delivered. Maintenance is performed by patching the implementation without any redesign or redevelopment.

Life-cycle automation requires an underlying abstraction paradigm that is amenable to automation. The traditional behavioral abstraction paradigm of the waterfall model identifies abstraction with external behavior and implementation with internal code structure. Program development by refinement of behavioral abstraction is not easily automated. Formal specifications and verification that specifications realize intended behavior are motivated by analogies with mathematics and reflect a manual rather than an automated view of the meaning of program modules. The complexity of specification and verification systems provides a warning that this form of abstraction may be unnecessarily complex and suggests that alternative abstraction paradigms should be sought.

Operation Model.   The operational life-cycle model is based on operational rather than behavioral abstraction. An operational abstraction of a system or module captures its behavior by an executable specification in terms of a problem-oriented model of computation. Instead of hiding the implementation mechanism, an operational abstraction explicitly uses the implementation as a basis for specifying behavior. An executable specification is as formal as a behavioral specification, but its behavior is specified implicitly (and automatically) by its set of executable computations rather than by an implementation-independent formal specification.

Operational abstraction determines a process-oriented paradigm for problem solving. Instead of verbal requirements and a design that determines the modular structure of the implementation, an executable model for an idealized computing environment is developed directly and tested by a high-level interpreter. This provides early feedback to both the end user and system designer on the functionality of the intended system, and it serves as a basis for developing an optimized, acceptable efficient realization of the prototype.

Transformation of an executable specification into an acceptably efficient realization is a complex task that requires human decisions as well as automated implementation. But this task is more amenable to automation than the classical program development paradigm because we start from a formal executable system that captures program behavior by a process-oriented abstraction.

The operational life-cycle model is competitive with the waterfall model even in a manual environment because of the feedback provided by executable specifications. The payoff of the operational model lies in its greater compatibility with automated program development.

Knowledge-Based Model.   Knowledge-based program development systems based on the operational life-cycle paradigm have the potential to increase software productivity by several orders of magnitude.

The knowledge-based model is effectively a specialization of the artificial intelligence paradigm of expert systems applied to the domain of program development. It needs three kinds of databases:

- [ ] A general-purpose, domain-independent environment.
- [ ] A special-purpose, project-oriented set of tools.
- [ ] A project database with multiple versions of application programs.

Knowledge of the program development process is encoded into a collection of expert systems that make use of knowledge in each of the three databases. The expert systems are called upon either explicitly by the programmer or implicitly during the performance of a program development task.

The development of a knowledge-based software assistant is a very ambitious task whose realization has been estimated to require 15 years of cooperative effort by several institutions [Balzer *et al.*, 1983]. However, it provides a framework for a quantum leap forward in capital-intensive software technology. Moreover, expert system technology has reached a level of maturity that should be capable of sustaining systems of this magnitude.

Maintenance, Enhancement, and Evolution

> Plus ça change, plus c'est la même chose. (The more it changes, the more it stays the same.)

Complex structures, both natural and social, are generally the result of evolutionary development rather than a single creative act. This is also true of large software systems. A new programming language such as Ada evolves from experience in the design and implementation of previous languages such as Pascal, and in turn forms a basis for the design of future languages. Successful programming systems such as UNIX evolved from small beginnings. They achieved their success by having a simple core to which facilities could easily be added.

Maintenance and Enhancement.   Large software systems must be constructed so that modification and evolution can be accomplished in a time proportional to the magnitude of the changes rather than to the size of the system.

Large systems that are easily maintained and enhanced have the property of local modularity and are constructible in an evolutionary manner from primitive components. They can be constructed by incremental "builds" of subsystems that can be independently tested and verified. Therefore, an adequate solution of the maintenance and enhancement problem depends on an evolutionary system structure not only for a large system as a whole but also for its component subsystems. Maintainable systems require not only static modularity but also dynamic modularity that facilitates incremental development, testing, and rapid prototyping. Solving the maintenance problem requires an evolutionary life-cycle methodology that allows complex systems to evolve from a simple core by multiple independent extensions. Failing to find a simple expandable core may result in system rigidity even if the system has a high degree of modularity. The additional requirements on modularity needed to support evolutionary development are an important area of study.

Iterative enhancement [Basili and Turner, 1975] is an example of an evolutionary life-cycle approach. It involves using a skeletal implementation (rapid prototype) as a starting point for iterative redesign of what has already been produced and evolutionary addition of new features until the system is completed. When the set of tasks needed to complete a project can be predicted, they can be listed in a project control list and systematically scheduled. The approach is useful even when the set of subtasks and the end result are incompletely defined. For example, the present chapter was developed by iterative enhancement of an incomplete specification, starting from a brief discussion of the capital-intensive nature of Ada and growing by iterative revision and expansion to its present scope and size. The technique of iterative enhancement was first developed in the context of software engineering but is just as pertinent to the writing of articles and books, where evolution is part of the process of creation. Text-editing systems and other computerized knowledge engineering aids greatly facilitate evolutionary development of manuscripts and are having a profound impact on the writing habits of both technical and nontechnical authors.

Evolutionary Flexibility.   Lack of evolutionary flexibility contributed to the failure of technologically advanced countries like Great Britain in coping with competition from countries whose industrial development occurred later in time. It could similarly lead to the passing of the current U.S. lead in the software field to countries like Japan whose software technology is less dependent on old software systems and management structures. Inability to adjust to changing technology was a cause of great pain and social dislocation in the industrial revolution. Evolutionary flexibility, both for individuals and for the technology as a whole, should be a primary goal of information technology.

There may be a distinction between evolution in the large, for very large organizations with time horizons measured in decades or centuries, and evolution in the small, for smaller (but still large) organizations with time horizons measured in months or years. Adaptation to changing technology is a matter of evolution in the large, while development, maintenance, and enhancement of a particular system are a part of evolution in the small. Tuning of a system for a particular set of tasks and time horizons may increase its cost and reduce its efficiency for narrower classes of applications and constrain its adaptability for broader classes of applications.

Maintainable systems should be modular both in the small, to allow modification of functional components in specific applications, and in the large, to allow changes in major components of the technology, such as the change from sequential to concurrent programming or from central processing units to distributed processing hardware. Systems should be designed not only for evolution in the small for short time horizons, but also for evolution in the large for long time horizons, so that they are robust with regard to extension in both space and time.

The problem of evolutionary flexibility arises in its most acute form in the context of adaptation to a changing technology. Maintenance and enhancement typically account for 80 percent of total life-cycle costs. Adaptive systems that can acquire and subsequently use knowledge, such as expert systems or theorem provers, must have databases designed for evolution.

Evolution involves reusability in response to change. Thus evolutionary systems are capital-intensive, according to our definition. Evolution, adaptation, and maintainability are synonyms for reusability.

Reusable Concepts and Models

Research in any discipline is judged largely by the degree to which its products are reusable.

Reducibility and Equivalence.   Reducibility of a problem B to a problem A means that the techniques used in solving problem A may be reused in solving problem B. Reducibility is thus another way to express reusability. A compiler reduces programs in a problem-oriented language to equivalent programs in an executable machine language (a language for which the program execution problem is already solved). The reducibility of the context-free grammar-parsing problem to the matrix multiplication problem permits the algorithm for matrix multiplication to be reused in parsing a context-free grammar. All reducibility results are effectively equivalence-preserving mappings of a problem from a less familiar form to a previously encountered form.

Equivalence is effectively two-way reducibility. Having proved B equivalent to A, we can reuse all of A's known properties in talking about (or executing) B and vice versa. In defining any equivalence class, we are effectively factoring attributes of the domain of discourse into primary attributes that are reusable for all elements of the class and secondary attributes that may, for the time being, be ignored. Different choices of equivalence class determine different abstractions with different choices of what is regarded as fixed or variable. For example, program-centered and data-centered programming can be distinguished by differences in the choice of equivalence relations.

By defining equivalence-preserving transformations we can navigate within an equivalence class and examine secondary attributes for invariant primary attributes. For example, transformations on functionally equivalent program specifications allow us to navigate from a program representation suited to human understanding to a representation suited to computer efficiency. Life-cycle models of program development provide a framework for navigation within an equivalence class from a requirements specification through a design specification to an implementation that permits flexible enhancement. One of the objectives of expert systems is to codify knowledge about such equivalence classes to facilitate the automation of such goal-directed navigation.

Models. Model building is closely connected with reusability. Mathematical logic is concerned with the development of models of valid reasoning that may be reused for all interpretations of nonlogical symbols in specific domains about which we wish to reason. The first-order predicate calculus is a framework for reasoning about mathematical objects such as sets, functions, and predicates. Systems of computational logic such as dynamic and temporal logic specialize the predicate calculus to permit reasoning about domains of computational objects such as programs. Systems of modal logic allow reasoning in situations where the modality of an assertion may be other than conventionally true or false (for example, there may be quantitative or qualitative probabilities of being true).

Semantic models provide a framework for expressing the meaning of programs and programming languages in terms of operational semantics, which models the process by which results are computed, or denotational semantics, which attempts to model meaning by abstract mathematical denotations. Denotational models are less dependent on a particular model of computation than operational models. But operational models provide insight into the model of computation and may be useful to designers and implementors in understanding what actually happens during execution. The greater abstraction of denotational models provides greater potential reusability, but they may require greater overhead of interpretation and provide less intuitive understanding than operational models. If reusability is to be enhanced, the choice of an abstraction to model computation should be governed by the purposes for which the abstraction is to be used.

Invariance and Regularity. Discovery of invariants is a basic paradigm for both mathematical and computational abstraction. The input-output relation of a function is an invariant for all programs that realize the function. Invariants of the program state during execution are used as a basis for program verification. A program $P(x)$ is an invariant that determines a uniform rule of computation for all arguments x in the domain of P. The programming process involves the creative discovery of invariants during the specification, verification, and realization of programs. Many of the practical tasks in software engineering can be formulated in terms of the discovery of reusable invariants in a class of computations or class of concepts. The notion of invariance is, therefore, another way to view reusability.

Pattern recognition and regularity are further aspects of reusability that are closely related to invariance. Pattern recognition is concerned with the discovery of reusable patterns in classes of phenomena. Regularity may be defined as the opposite of randomness, and has given rise to some interesting theories relating to the capturing of regularity (nonrandomness) of long digit sequences by short descriptions [Chaitin, 1975]. The abstract theory of regularity could yield practical insights that facilitate the automation of regularity in industrial processes and programming activities.

Application Generators

Application generators strive for reusability in a domain that is narrower than a general-purpose programming language but broader than a specific application.

Application generators such as RPG or Nomad synthesize high-granularity software components over a specialized domain and provide an environment for efficient use of the generated software component. The environment generally contains utilities such as a text editor, a database, and file-handling facilities. Since these utilities are used only with generated software components, they can be custom designed for this purpose. Application generators can thus take advantage of two kinds of reusability: (1) reusability of the mechanism for generating software components, and (2) reusability of utilities in providing a service for generated components.

The specialized nature of generated software components is an advantage not only in developing the generating mechanisms but also in developing the environment that supports generated components. The class of generable software components may be specified by a generic program family with richer parameterization facilities than traditional generic programs. Specification of parameter values for a generated software component can be guided by the computer, requiring the user to answer a sequence of questions. The choice of a domain of discourse for an application generator and the design of the generic program generator and parameter interface require a deep understanding of the problem domain.

Application generators for office automation generally have simple user interfaces, such as a questionnaire with questions about office procedures that translate into parameter values of generic software components. Simple interfaces allow users unfamiliar with computers to generate application systems directly but are not a necessary requirement for all application generators. Some domains, such as the domain of compilers, may require technical knowledge of programming to generate applications. If the application being generated is important, there is no reason to insist on simple user interfaces. Production-quality systems in any domain should probably be generated by highly skilled persons expert in both computing and the application domain. Flexibility and evolutionary modifiability of components of an application generator may well be more important than simple user interfaces.

Application generators will make increasing use of expert systems that allow computers to use the knowledge of "experts" in the automatic performance of intelligent tasks in their domain of specialization [Stefik *et al.*, 1982]. For example, office automation systems will make increasing use of expert knowledge in automating office procedures. This requires the integration of software engineering techniques for creating application environments with knowledge engineering techniques for creating expert systems. A number of recently formed companies are developing application generators that will facilitate development of expert systems in specific areas from reusable, prepackaged software components.

3.4 KNOWLEDGE ENGINEERING

People-oriented Knowledge Engineering

> The computer revolution will fundamentally amplify man's ability to manage knowledge, just as the industrial revolution fundamentally amplified man's ability to manage physical phenomena.

Knowledge engineering is a body of techniques for managing the complexity of knowledge—just as software engineering is a body of techniques for managing the complexity of software. It is as old as knowledge itself. Euclid's *Elements*, a magnificent piece of knowledge engineering, provided a basis for managing geometrical knowledge, and the classification techniques of Linnaeus are an important example of knowledge engineering in biology. These and other milestones in the development of science are as important for their contributions to the management of knowledge as for their contributions to knowledge itself. Knowledge engineering is capital-intensive in the sense that reusability is a primary consideration in the development of books, expert systems, and other structures for the management and use of knowledge.

The computer's potential as a tool for knowledge engineering was realized as early as 1945, when Vannevar Bush examined techniques for fundamentally reorganizing knowledge and proposed a device called a memex for the storage, retrieval, and management of knowledge [Bush, 1945]. In the 1960s, Douglas Engelbart proposed a systematic research program on the use of computer technology to augment man's intellectual capabilities [Howerton and Weeks, 1963]. Now personal computer technology may allow us to realize their pioneering ideas at an affordable cost.

Feigenbaum, who introduced the term in the context of artificial intelligence, defined knowledge engineering as "the art of bringing the tools and principles of artificial intelligence to bear on application problems requiring the knowledge of experts for their solution" [Feigenbaum, 1977]. This definition views knowledge engineering as the art of representing knowledge so that it can be used by computers to perform intelligent tasks.

The present view is broader. Building knowledge structures to aid human understanding is now seen as the primary objective of knowledge engineering, and intelligent computer problem solving is considered a derivative objective, legitimized by the first objective. The current goal—and motivation—for knowledge engineering is to amplify human intelligence, not to substitute computer intelligence for it. Knowledge engineering involves educational technology, cognitive science, and human-factors research. The technology of managing the modular presentation of complex knowledge structures has some of the flavor of software engineering, but it must also consider the human factors associated with animation, user interaction, multiple windows, and other techniques for improving man-computer communication.

Personal computers have caused fundamental changes in the way we absorb, manage, and use knowledge. New ways of representing and organizing knowledge to exploit interaction, animation, and multiple windows must be developed. More effective techniques for the management of knowledge by humans will complement artificial intelligence techniques for its management by computers, and will result in an environment that integrates human and computational management of knowledge. By the 1990s, knowledge engineering will be as important a subdiscipline of computer sciences as software engineering is today.

Electronic Books

> University teachers should initially be appointed to full professorships and suffer a reduction in rank or salary whenever they publish a book or a paper. Then results will be published only if they are sufficiently important to warrant a personal sacrifice.

Restructuring existing knowledge to make it more accessible to humans involves more than putting existing repositories, such as the Library of Congress, on computers and accessing them through information retrieval systems. It involves restructuring existing knowledge so that it can be flexibly presented in different formats for use in different contexts. The technology for such restructuring is not well understood, but its nature is illustrated by recent developments in computerized printing and computer-based learning.

Computers are revolutionizing printing technology to allow rapid, inexpensive reproduction of high-quality text. Word processing systems increase an author's control over the production, layout, and modification of text. Soon computers will be used not only for writing and printing books but also for reading them. Book-size computers with flat panel displays will make electronic books a reality. The greater bandwidth of man-computer interfaces will qualitatively change the nature of man-computer communication; it will make communication of knowledge more effective than today's conventional reading of hard-copy books.

While hard-copy books consist of a linear sequence of pages, materials on a computer may have a graph structure with different entry points for readers with different backgrounds. With multiple windows, the reader can pursue several lines of thought simultaneously or view a given object at several levels of detail. The computer can use interactive responses to tailor the graph traversal mode to the individual user's interests and skill level. Each node of the graph structure can include dynamically animated pictures, texts, and programs; for example, the mathematician may animate proof development, while the computer scientist may animate program development and execution.

A family of different hard-copy books could be obtained by printing out nodes of the graph structure in a particular linear order for particular kinds of students. It is conjectured that flexibility in the pace and order of presentation, combined with the power of animation (possibly augmented by voice input and output), can, if properly used, increase enormously the student's capacity to absorb and understand both elementary and advanced knowledge.

Knowledge Support Environments

> One of the principal objects of research in any department of knowledge is to find the point of view from which the subject appears in its greatest simplicity.
>
> —J. Willard Gibbs

By analogy with the program support environment of software engineering, a computer support system for authors, students, and researchers involved in creating, learning, and using a body of knowledge will be called a *knowledge support environment*. Its desirable features would include systematic support for thinking about problems at multiple levels of abstraction and for solving problems by divide-and-conquer strategies. Support for both top-down and bottom-up problem-solving strategies would be included. Methods for exploring the design space (solution space) to determine what is possible and methods for testing the consequences of design decisions by executing partial designs (rapid prototypes) would be supported.

Knowledge support environments would include both facilities for management of knowledge by the human user and facilities for expert systems and interactive man-computer problem solving. Such environments are being developed at Xerox PARC, by manufacturers of personal computers such as the Apollo, Perq, and Sun, and at universities such as Carnegie-Mellon, MIT, and Brown.

Graph Structures of Frames

> Support environments for authors will receive the same kind of attention in the 1990s that support environments for programmers have received in the 1970s and 1980s.

The knowledge-graph paradigm suggests the organization of knowledge as a graph structure of frames with different entry points and modes of traversal. Knowledge graphs can be used to represent advanced as well as elementary knowledge. For example, a computer-based learning environment for a programming language such as Ada would include not only introductory material but also a literature of well-documented, prototypical "real" programs that examined issues in software methodology. They would be part of a production program support environment. Authors could make use of its tools for production programs, and students could easily switch from the education mode to the production mode.

In working with knowledge graphs, it is useful to define individual frames as objects of an abstract data type, which will, in the case of programming examples, have a text component, a program component, a question component, and an answer component, plus operations for manipulating each. A programming language (authoring language) is needed that allows frames in different domains to be declared as different abstract data types. Editors, graph-walking algorithms, answer interpreters, and other tools for creating and using knowledge graphs also need to be defined. Knowledge graphs will require both domain-independent tools that operate on graphs and frames independently of the knowledge domain being considered and domain-dependent tools that know about objects of particular knowledge domains such as programs, forms, and circuits.

If computer documents consisting of graph structures of frames become a standard mechanism for representing books and computer-based learning materials, then the number of frames produced in the next 30 years will be very large. Thus capital-intensive aids for reducing the labor and increasing the quality of frame-based documents will be important. Tools can free authors from low-level tasks and guide them in the higher-level tasks of developing insight, understanding, and examples. Work on graphical authoring tools for computer documents has been under way at Brown for several years [Feiner *et al.*, 1982].

Dynamic Documents

One of the strengths of computer-based knowledge engineering is the ability to switch easily between different levels of abstraction and different views of conceptual objects to gain a more complete understanding of the domain of discourse.

Dynamic documents are intended to be "read" from computers and may combine traditional text with dynamically changing figures and user-interaction facilities. Such documents are particularly effective in presenting information about inherently dynamic objects or processes such as algorithms. The idea of viewing algorithms as processes whose intermediate states are intrinsically interesting rather than as static input-output relations has been explored in depth by Brown and Sedgewick in the context of sorting algorithms [Brown and Sedgewick, 1984].

The key to engineering dynamic documents for algorithms is to find a representation of intermediate states that gives the reader insight into the execution process. In the case of sorting algorithms, the representation of intermediate states of a partially sorted vector as a graph, with the magnitude of each element plotted against its current position in the vector, provides remarkable insights into the variety of mechanisms by which sorting algorithms massage elements of a random vector into a sorted vector.

The contrast between the representation of algorithms as input-output relations and as processes with intermediate states is analogous to the contrast between denotational and operational semantics for programming languages. To understand conceptual products such as algorithms or programming languages, it is necessary to understand both their static characterization as input-output relations or denotations and their dynamic characterization as processes with interesting intermediate states.

Both graph-structured frames and dynamic documents are novel forms of knowledge presentation that are not possible with traditional textbooks. Both are suited for presenting elementary educational material or more advanced material to users of the knowledge or to researchers attempting to extend the frontiers of knowledge. In each case there is an immediate payoff in small documents, constructible with ad hoc techniques, but there is also the promise of much larger payoffs in large documents that extend the user's intellectual reach in significant ways. Clearly, the two styles should be combined, since it is useful for frames to have dynamic components and for dynamic documents to be organized as graph-structured frames.

Computer Authoring Technology

Books are large knowledge structures whose problems of management— by both authors and readers—resemble those of large software systems. They are quintessential capital goods, requiring an intense effort to produce and being reusable by many readers.

Methods for authoring computer textbooks are likely to differ from those for traditional textbooks. Organizing large knowledge domains into graph-structured text modules will require new approaches. The rich visual structure of frames will require authors to think not only about the meaning of words but also about the meaning and communication power of pictures. A disadvantage of the modular approach is that it may violate the subject matter's natural continuity, but the advantage is that it requires authors to decompose knowledge systematically into manageable pieces.

Authors of the future may have computerized writing assistants that function like prettyprinters for programming languages in creating user-friendly representations of knowledge. Writers of textbooks would no longer have to worry about the surface structure of books at the user interface but could concentrate on creating a knowledge database of facts, relations, and pictures from which books could be created by intelligent authoring assistants. The intelligence level of automatic authoring assistants would increase as the task of converting knowledge databases into user-friendly learning materials became better understood.

Creators and readers of a computer textbook will form a social community whose members can communicate directly via a computer message system.

Authors could make text available incrementally, receive instantaneous feed-back from readers, and rapidly respond to such feedback. Man-computer communication may be used not only for machine display of knowledge but also for communication among its community of creators and users. Such social interaction will permeate all work in knowledge engineering. Computers will affect the sociology of knowledge production by providing a new mode of communication among scholars.

With conventional printing technology, books can be enhanced only by means of costly new editions. Computer technology, on the other hand, permits continuous incremental enhancement once development of the book has been completed, thereby allowing previously impossible improvements in quality and adaptation to changing requirements. To illustrate the advantages of incremental enhancement, let's compare the life cycle of a program and that of a book. Studies have shown that 80 percent of the effort of supporting a program over its life cycle is in maintenance and enhancement. With conventional printing technology, the only form of "maintenance and enhancement" is printing a second edition, which is time-consuming and expensive. Computer printing technology, by allowing cheap incremental maintenance and enhancement, could allow the author a much more active role in both the production and enhancement processes.

Knowledge support environments are capital-intensive because they facilitate building and using capital goods. They also encourage capital-intensive practices—initial investments to increase subsequent productivity—by both authors and readers.

3.5 ACCOMPLISHMENTS AND DEFICIENCIES OF ADA

Ada—A Case Study in Capital-Intensive Software Technology

Ada is the second woman mentioned in the Bible—the first after Eve:

> Ada and Zillah hear my voice
> Ye wives of Lamech hearken to my speech
>
> —Genesis 4:23

Ada was developed to reduce the cost and improve the reliability of software. It is a careful, comprehensive attempt by the world's largest user of software—the U.S. Department of Defense (DOD)—to develop a capital-intensive framework for software technology [United States Department of Defense, 1983]. Moreover, the Ada effort is extraordinarily well documented, both in terms of the process by which decisions were made and in terms of its requirements and products.

Ada's development began in 1975 with a sequence of programming language requirements, finalized as STEELMAN in 1978 [Wasserman, 1980]. A language for meeting these requirements was developed in 1980. However, DOD realized that a language was only a small, if central, component in capital-intensive software technology and thus developed a set of environmental requirements, called STONEMAN, during 1978–81. In 1983, STONEMAN was supplemented by METHODMAN, a set of methodology requirements, and by STARS (Software Technology for Adaptable, Reliable Systems) [*Computer*, 1983], an intensive study of technology transfer requirements. Thus the Ada effort has involved four successively broader layers of activity:

☐ language (reusable by people, computers),

☐ environment (reusable tools),

☐ methodology (reusable concepts), and

☐ technology (education, measurement, integration).

Each of these layers is capital-intensive in the sense of requiring large up-front expenditures to improve later productivity. The improved productivity is achieved by several forms of reusability. Languages are reused by people in writing programs and by computers in compiling and executing them. Environments provide both run-time support and reusable software tools for enhancing programmer productivity. Methodologies determine reusable concepts and techniques for effective problem solving. Technology requirements integrate language, environment, and methodology and address the process of technology transfer.

Ada was designed to support the development of large programs composed of reusable software components. Some of Ada's language features that support such reusability are the following:

1. A rich variety of program units including subprograms, packages, and tasks. Program units have syntactic interface specifications, which determine the way they may be interconnected in building composite program structures.

2. Systematic separation between visible syntactic interface specifications and hidden bodies, which allows the programmer to separate concerns about module interconnection from concerns about how the module performs its task.

3. Strong typing, which imposes constraints on module interconnections and allows consistency between formal parameters of module definitions and actual parameters of module invocations to be enforced at compile time.

4. Generic program units, which are parameterized templates for generating software components. They allow reusable uniformities of a family of software components to be captured by a single generic definition.

5. Program libraries with separately compiled reusable program units.

Ada supports a greater variety of software components (abstraction mechanisms) than previous programming languages. This richness is a strength because it increases Ada's expressive power, but it is also a weakness because the different abstraction mechanisms are not well integrated.

The economic benefits of a language like Ada will be determined in part by the technical quality of its language features but in even greater measure by the size of its user community. The real economic payoff comes from standardization that amortizes the cost of development over a large programming community and increases the potential reusability of program modules and tools developed in the language. The objectives of the Ada effort were to achieve a quantum leap forward in capitalization and productivity by combining technical excellence at the level of language features and tools with political and educational mechanisms for rapidly diffusing technical advances over a wide base of users.

The potential benefits of reusability of tools may be illustrated by a recent study of the U.S. Army's software systems. Its 91 major software systems were developed in 43 different languages on 58 computer systems from 29 manufacturers. Each system had its own custom-built support software. In an ideal world of standardized software, the 43 languages could have been replaced by a single language—with great savings in software cost and considerable increases in quality of support. For example, a medium-size system with 10,000 lines of application code that makes use of 100,000 lines of system code would require only 10,000 lines rather than 110,000 lines of new code, and the system would be more reliable because the code could be debugged in a secure environment.

Achieving these savings would require standardization of the environment as well as the language. The Ada approach is to standardize on a Kernel Ada Program Support Environment (KAPSE) of nonportable operating system facilities whose interface to the outside world is specified in Ada. The facilities of the KAPSE interface may be used by a much larger set of portable tools than are specified in Ada. Standardization of the environment requires standardization of both the KAPSE interface and the set of tools provided to the user. A standardized environment would allow the 58 systems in the Army example above to be replaced by a single system.

Ada—A Process or a Product?

There is no doubt that we have learned a great deal from the process of developing Ada. But the adoption of Ada as a standard may unduly constrain the evolution of software technology.

The strong economic arguments for adopting Ada as a standard language can be balanced by equally strong arguments for viewing standardization as premature. Ada was developed in a period of rapidly changing software technology. Its requirements for language and environment design represent a static snapshot of an exploding technology at an arbitrary point in its evolution rather than a stable and mature point of equilibrium appropriate for standardization. Moreover, its initial narrow goals of language standardization have become submerged in much more ambitious and elusive goals of environment standardization. Whereas Ada's language standardization was systematically addressed by the world's top experts in language design, environment standardization is being addressed in an ad hoc way by a volunteer committee [Fisher, 1984]. Ada's goals have become so diluted and diffuse that they embrace the whole of software technology. Standardization on Ada could have a negative impact on software productivity by channeling resources into Ada that could be more productively used for developing mainstream Ada-independent software technology.

The arguments against standardization on Ada can be summarized as follows:

1. Ada has involved far more innovation than originally intended because it was developed in a period of transition—from sequential to distributed programming languages and from time-sharing to interactive modes of computer usage. It was innovative in its attempt to integrate the technology of data abstraction and concurrency. It was also innovative in its comprehensive attempt to integrate language, environment, and methodology for large evolutionary software systems. Because Ada breaks new ground in so many areas, there are many loose ends in both its language and environment design. This is compounded by the fact that computer technology has evolved so rapidly that the hardware and software assumptions on which Ada was based are almost obsolete.

2. Ada is a child of 1970s programming language technology. Its block structure paradigm for language design was dominant in the 1970s but may be replaced by a message-oriented distributed model of computation in the 1980s and 1990s. Its mechanisms for modularity (subprograms, packages, tasks, generics, types) are not well integrated with each other and are based on a transient technology [Strom *et al.*, 1984].

3. Ada is a child of 1970s life-cycle technology. It was developed in accordance with the waterfall life-cycle model, with a requirements and design phase, and is currently in the middle of its implementation phase. However, this life-cycle model does not accommodate prototyping, so that products cannot be tested before being cast in concrete. The prototyping approach advocates throwing away the prototype and starting over to achieve results that are less dependent on early preconceptions. Application of this philosophy to Ada suggests that we throw Ada away and use what we have learned from Ada to develop a new well-integrated language, environment, and methodology.

4. Ada is a child of 1970s environment technology. Its environmental requirements were developed to be compatible with the time-sharing technology of the 1950s and 1960s, before the advent of interactive workstations with high-resolution graphics interfaces. Environment technology has changed even more rapidly than language technology. Although the editing, debugging, and project management tools of proposed Ada environments of the late 1980s would be a definite advance over current

embedded computing technology, they would be out of date even if they became available in 1990. There is a danger that their widespread introduction in the 1990s could constrain the adoption of the more productive and cheaper interactive environment technology of personal workstations.

5. Requirements for Ada Program Support Environments are language-dependent. The APSE requirement that tools be developed in Ada—and largely for Ada—constrains the scope of Ada environments and makes tool development more expensive. The adverse effects of making the environment Ada-dependent may dominate the consequences of design decisions at the language level. This is a flaw in the overall Ada concept at the system integration level. It would not be surprising if Ada, just as other very large systems, had its primary problems at this level. The tendency to lavish great care on the internal design of macrocomponents (such as the language) but to exercise weaker control over relations among macrocomponents is a feature that Ada shares with other very large systems.

One of the strongest arguments for Ada is that the mere existence of a standard is more important than the product on which we standardize. According to this argument, the economic benefits of a common language with common subroutine libraries and a common environment will far outweigh any possible differences in quality or approach among candidate programming languages. But these advantages are balanced by potential disadvantages.

1. Inadequacies of the standard propagate to all its users, causing products that use the standard to be inferior to those that do not.
2. Once a standard is adopted it may be inflexible, preventing progress. This disadvantage is especially acute in a rapidly changing technology.
3. The inadequacies of a standard may be propagated to other standards that use it as a basis. For example, using a language as a basis for an environment propagates language inadequacies to the environment and constrains the environment design to be dependent on the language.

Ada's standardization may cause problems in each of these areas. Its imperfect software components may give rise to unreliable software systems with components that might be erroneous, particularly for concurrent systems. It standardizes a transitional 1970s language and environment technology that is being rendered obsolete by technological advances, and it may stand in the way of a transition to more productive languages and environments. The use of the language as a basis for the environment is running into trouble in part because it is the wrong kind of language and in part because of our inadequate understanding of environment standardization.

Ada is pioneering new ground in attempting to develop an environment for components with strongly typed interfaces. In addition, it must overcome the linguistic imperfections of its software components. Language-based environments were successful in the case of UNIX (based on C) and Interlisp, but their strength derives not from behavioral standardization on tool sets but from operational standardization on a uniform set of internal system interfaces. In the context of Ada this corresponds to standardization on the KAPSE Interface. This has been attempted by a KAPSE Interface Team, which designed a Common Apse Interface Set [Ada Joint Program Office, 1983]. But issues in the standardization of internal system interfaces are not well understood, particularly in the presence of strong typing, and standardization may well be premature. Developing Ada-based interface standards may not be as productive an approach as starting from a demonstrably proven base, such as Unix, and extrapolating from this base—just as Ada extrapolated from Pascal.

Reusable software technology requires standardization not only of languages and environments, but also of major software subsystems like communication, database, and workstation subsystems. Little is being done to coordinate language standardization with subsystem standardization. There is an opportunity in the development of large DOD software systems, such as WIS with its budget in excess of $30 billion over 15 years, to develop communication, database, and workstation subsystems that could become de facto standards for other very large applications. Subsystem standardization could provide dividends in productivity that dominate those of language standardization.

The problem of standards in software technology is complex because of the strong interaction among its diverse elements. Standards are needed not only for languages and environments, but also for software acquisition, life cycle methodology, documentation, and a whole range of other technological elements. Standardization on one element, such as language, means that it must remain fixed while other elements evolve. This can be an advantage if we are confident that the standard is appropriate and stable, but can seriously constrain and distort overall evolution of the technology if the standard is inappropriate.

Conclusion

Just as the Eskimo has many different words for snow, we have many words for reusability. A plausible conclusion is that reusability of the resources we create is as important in our lives as snow is in the life of the Eskimo.

Reusability has provided us with a single metric for examining a variety of software activities—software components, programming in the large, knowledge engineering, and Ada.

In the area of software components, the shift from sequential to concurrent models of computation has opened up new dimensions in language and environment design. Sequential programming languages such as Pascal and Ada were based on the block structure paradigm. Concurrent programming languages are still in the preparadigm stage of development, but the plug-and-socket distributed sequential processes paradigm appears attractive on the grounds of both simplicity and logical expressiveness. The programming language NIL embodies this new paradigm. Its components are free from the textual bonds of block structure, can perform autonomous concurrent computations, can be linked and reconfigured dynamically while they are executing, and are designed for systems that may evolve during program execution as well as during program development. NIL's greater autonomy, on the other hand, carries with it responsibilities to efficiently implement data protection, communication, and recovery.

In the area of programming in the large, there is intense debate about a paradigm shift from the waterfall life-cycle model to an interactive model that uses the computer as an integral part of the problem-solving process. The new paradigm includes a shift from behavioral to operational specification, with emphasis on rapid (early) prototyping. It aims to provide automatic transformations from high-level operational specifications to efficient implementations. This paradigm has yet to prove itself. But there is no doubt that the availability of cheap computing power as an almost free resource in interactive problem solving will have a profound impact on the problem-solving process.

Knowledge engineering has been redefined to emphasize augmenting rather than replacing human intelligence. Knowledge management is less ambitious than artificial intelligence but can provide a framework within which both computers and humans function more intelligently. Knowledge engineering (in the new sense) subsumes software engineering, since software engineering is simply knowledge engineering applied to the specialized domain of software. But software engineering needs domain-independent knowledge-management tools for tasks like documentation, authoring, and library management. Program support environments for software development are therefore dependent on good knowledge support environments. Capital-intensive software technology requires a knowledge support environment for programmers to be productive, and in turn provides the technology that allows good knowledge support environments to evolve.

Our discussion of Ada took a broad view, examining the capital-intensive nature of the language, environment, methodology, and technology. We indicated that Ada involved far more innovation than originally intended, in part because it had the misfortune of being developed during a period of technological transition from sequential to concurrent software components and from batch to interactive environments. Its careful attempt at standardization might have succeeded had the technology been more stable, but instead the effort has resulted in a transitional product that mirrors the transitional language and environment technology that spawned its development.

The U.S. Department of Defense should hitch its wagon to STARS of the future rather than the past. It should build on the ideas of Ada but bypass

Ada as a product. Perhaps it could support a new competition to specify language and environment designs for the technology of the late 1980s and the 1990s. New requirements would probably start with environment and interface requirements at the KAPSE and UNIX levels, continue with communication requirements for software components and libraries, and add language requirements once the others had been agreed upon. Greater emphasis would be placed on the standardization of communication interfaces and less on the standardization of computation primitives.

Reopening the language and environment standardization issue will delay adoption of a standard. But this delay may well occur anyway because of the inadequacies of Ada implementations and the pressures of new technology. A reexamination of language and environment standards could be sponsored by the DOD Software Engineering Institute proposed as a central feature of the STARS program.

Many of us who work in the field of software technology feel that the 1980s are more exciting than the 1970s and that the 1990s may prove to be even more so. Living in a period of rapid technological change provides both an opportunity and a responsibility for shaping the future. It requires us to be more innovative and to take greater risks than in a period of greater stability. But worthwhile progress can be achieved only by taking some risks, making some hard decisions, and investing in the future.

The French maxim "Reculer pour mieux sauter" (draw back to better jump) echoes the capital-intensive sentiment of giving up present profit for future productivity and suggests that drawing back from a commitment strengthens our ability to face the future.

APPENDIX: NOTES ON RELATED ISSUES

Note: In the original article, these notes were boxes in the main text.

Electronic Steam Engines

Large central processors are the steam engines of the computer revolution. The shift from large central processors to personal computers is comparable to the shift from steam engines to combustion engines and electric motors. The 19th-century transition from cumbersome energy supplies to cheaper, more accessible sources of energy is being paralleled in the 1980s by a shift from inaccessible large computing engines to accessible small computing engines in every home and appliance.

Watt's engine marked the real beginning of the age of steam. In 1765, while repairing a Newcomen pump, James Watt recognized one of the machine's main disadvantages. Condensation of the steam inside the cylinder lowered the pressure to provide suction. Newcomen's machine introduced cold water to condense the vapor, but every time the steam condensed, the cylinder cooled off. Thus, much of the new steam was wasted in reheating the cylinder.

Watt's first innovation was the condenser, a separate compartment in which the steam was made to condense. He kept the cylinder insulated by surrounding it with a steam jacket. His most important contribution, however, was in obtaining rotary motion. In 1782, he constructed a double-acting engine that, through a series of cogged wheels, transformed the rocker arm's alternating movement into a rotary movement. Later, Watt equipped his engine with a governor and a pressure gauge.

The first Watt engine was installed in a coal mine in 1784, the same year that Arkwright and Crompton achieved the complete mechanization of spinning. The industrial revolution was entering its most active phase, and within a few decades, the technological picture changed radically. By 1800, 52 of Watt's engines were operating in various types of mines, one had been applied to a drop hammer, and 84 had been installed in cotton mills.

Why UNIX is Successful

UNIX may well be the most successful example to date of a system of reusable software components. Its features and philosophy therefore deserve careful study. The UNIX shell is both a command language and a programming language [Bourne, 1978]. Commands may be executed either under user control from a terminal or under program control from a file. Commands are like subprograms in having a name and parameters, but the number and type of parameters may be variable, allowing a given command to handle a wider range of options than a typical subprogram. UNIX supports composition of commands by filters that transform an input stream to an output stream and pipes that allow the output stream of one command to be the input stream of a successor. Filters and pipes provide a data flow model of communication between components that complements the traditional control flow model. Uniform character stream data flow gives filters and pipes the operational flexibility of single-type languages like Lisp.

The UNIX file system provides a single tree-structured name space for both user and system software components. The system makes no assumptions about file structure, allowing it to be determined entirely by the programs that use files. Late and flexible binding of file names to files occurs at the time that a command is executed. Components in files are first-class objects that may be massaged as data or executed as programs.

The UNIX environment breaks down traditional distinctions such as that between command languages and programming languages, between execution under terminal control and programmer control, between user models of computation. It enhances reusability of components by allowing a given component to be reused by application programmers and system programmers, from terminals or within command language programs, for program development or for execution. The flexible command language and versatile file system combine to provide powerful operations for creating, managing, and executing reusable software components that are much richer than those for program libraries in traditional programming languages.

Abstraction and Reusability

The relation between function and data abstraction is captured in lambda notation by the expressions $[\lambda x \cdot f(x)]$ and $[\lambda f \cdot f(x)]$. The function abstraction $[\lambda x \cdot f(x)]$ can be applied to an argument a in the domain of f to yield $f(a)$. It captures the reusability of the function f for a range of values of the variable x. In contrast, the expression $[\lambda f \cdot f(x)]$ allows the set of functions applicable to x to vary. It may be thought of as data abstraction because it captures the reusability of a data object x for a range of applicable functions f. This example illustrates that different abstractions of the expression $f(x)$ correspond to different choices of what is to remain fixed (reusable) and what is to be allowed to vary.

Argus and NIL

Argus [Liskov and Scheifler, 1982] supports distributed concurrent processes called *guardians*. Guardians communicate with each other by message passing. Concurrent processes within a guardian communicate through shared variables. Synchronization of access to shared local data is realized by atomic objects that have their own locks for read and write access control. Argus has two synchronization mechanisms: remote procedure calls for interprocess synchronization between guardians, and atomic objects for shared data synchronization within guardians.

NIL [Strom and Yemini, 1983] supports distributed sequential processes. Its primitives are simpler than those of Argus because there is just one kind of concurrency and no shared variables. It does not allow concurrent access to shared data to be specified at the user level. Providing concurrency for logically sequential queries of a database is regarded in NIL as an optimization that is the responsibility of the system rather than the user. If efficient and reliable mechanisms for realizing such concurrency can be developed, possibly with the aid of pragmas that allow the user to indicate input ports for which concurrency optimizations are appropriate, then the NIL approach will become state of the art.

Smalltalk

Objects in Smalltalk represent their internal state by *instance variables*, and have operations called *methods*, which are invoked by messages from other objects. Messages specify the name of the object being called, the name of the method to be invoked, and actual parameters of the invoked method. They are like procedure calls of conventional languages, but binding of the method name in the message to the method actually invoked occurs at execution time rather than at load time.

Objects are created from *class definitions*, which specify methods and instance variables common to objects of a class. Classes correspond to types in traditional languages. The complete set of variables and methods available in a class includes not only those directly defined in the class but also those defined in superclasses of the class.

Dynamic Linking

One aspect of the execution-time environment is the loading and linking of library components. Languages like Fortran and Ada have a loading and linking phase prior to execution and require the set of components and their bindings to each other to be invariant during execution. Loading and linking are relegated to an operating system whose operation is not under the control of the programmer.

This limitation is unduly static and makes an artificial distinction between program evolution during program development and during program execution. An alternative is to allow loading and linking to be performed by programming language commands during program execution. This approach is taken in NIL, which allows processes to be loaded dynamically by executing a create instruction, and which also allows ports of a created process to be dynamically connected to ports of other processes both at process creation time and during subsequent execution of the process. The processes of a NIL computation may include compilers that compile new processes and add them to the library concurrently with the execution of other processes, so that they become available dynamically to processes already executing. Moreover, any given process of the library can have multiple instantiations, each with a different set of port connections to other processes.

This dynamic flexibility in resting and linking processes contrasts sharply with the static relations among components in Pascal and Ada. Ada was carefully designed to support evolution of programs during program development, but contains no provision for evolution of programs during execution. Languages like NIL, on the other hand, are designed to support program evolution during both program development and execution. They attempt to combine the dynamic advantages of languages like Lisp with the static advantages of strong typing. They provide an extra dimension of reusability technology for the development of long-lived multimodule programs.

Fifth-Generation Computers

The Japanese fifth-generation computer project is an attempt to create a capital-intensive technology for knowledge engineering [Feigenbaum and McCorduck, 1983]. Its central theme is to add intelligence to the high-bandwidth interface technology of fourth-generation personal computing systems. Its proposed architecture includes a database machine and a problem-solving and inference machine. Its proposed system programming language is the logic programming language Prolog. Its software includes support for natural language and speech understanding and problem solving over a wide set of problem domains. The project includes not only technical goals such as increasing productivity and saving energy, but also social goals such as coping with an aging society. Some researchers regard the project as overambitious, but it has a worthwhile set of goals, which, even if not achieved in their entirety, could catalyze an integrated research effort that could give Japan a technological lead in developing computing systems for the 1990s.

The basic premise of the Japanese fifth-generation computer project is that our prime concern in the 1990s will be the processing and management of knowledge. A logic-based language was chosen as the system programming language because logic was perceived to be the basic tool for managing and manipulating knowledge. The hardware emphasizes the management of knowledge databases, the software emphasizes problem solving and inference, and the user interface emphasizes knowledge acquisition by understanding natural language inputs.

The Japanese have done the computing profession a service by presenting their vision of an integrated knowledge engineering environment in such a clear and public manner. This has placed the goal of achieving such an environment squarely in the public domain. But the Japanese have a clearer vision and are pursuing the goal with greater single-mindedness than other nations and may therefore be the first to achieve the goal, with all the commercial and other advantages that this entails.

Operational and Behavioral Thinking

The distinction between operational and behavioral thinking is not restricted to life-cycle models. It arises in many areas of computer science and also in mathematics and physics. Operational semantics differs from denotational and axiomatic semantics. Mathematics has a behavioral view of model building and abstraction. The difference between mathematical and computational views of the world is essentially a difference between behavioral and operational approaches to model building. In physics, relativity theory and quantum theory are operational models because they take operations performed by an observer into account in formulating the model. Operational models of physics may be contrasted with the Platonic notion of absolute space and time that underlies Newtonian mechanics. Note, however, that operational semantics in computer science is defined in terms of the internal structure of states, while operationalism in physics explains natural phenomena in terms of the way they are observed and has a distinctly operational flavor.

Evolution of Organizations

The evolution of software systems may be viewed as a special case of the evolution of organizations with both human and computer components. There is a considerable literature on the structure, social dynamics, and adaptability of organizations. At a very general level, Toynbee's pessimistic study of the genesis, growth, breakdown, and disintegration of civilizations is about the failure of organizations to adapt to changing environments and suggests that radical renewal must supplement gradual change as a mechanism for system evolution [Toynbee, 1947]. The text *Organizations*, which is a source book for Simon's Nobel prizewinning work on formal models of organizational behavior, is a good starting point for readers interested in this area [March and Simon, 1958]. *Organization Development* presents an analytical framework for the development of organizations in terms of flows of information among their components [Schein *et al.*, 1973]. Holland explores the problem of adaptation for both natural and artificial systems, emphasizing the response of such systems to changing environments [Holland, 1975]. The similarity of models of large industrial organizations and large computer systems is reflected in the computer literature in anthropomorphic terminology such as *actors* and *societies* of interacting computer programs [Hewitt, 1977]. Milner's *A Calculus of Communicating Systems* is a formal (algebraic) model of communicating systems whose components may be people or computers [Milner, 1980]. The study of evolutionary behavior of mixed man-computer systems and of interfaces that allow creativity and growth of people in a computer environment is central to the development of a reusable software technology that combines current efficiency with adaptability to change.

Specialization—the Converse of Abstraction

An abstraction characterizes a class of phenomena by their common (invariant) attributes and hides (ignores) distinguishing attributes of instances that are not common to the complete class. Greater abstraction results in greater reusability and reduces the costs of problem solving by distributing the cost of developing the abstraction over its uses, but the converse process of making distinctions between instances of an abstract class is also an essential ingredient in problem solving. The lawyer thrives on distinguishing new cases from precedent-setting abstractions established by previous cases. Good information engineering requires shedding excessive generality by making distinctions that provide new insights or allow efficient solution of the problem at hand.

The converse of the process of abstraction may be referred to as specialization. Specialization may be technically defined in terms of contexts which constrain the generality of the abstraction and may be used as a basis for optimization [Scherlis, 1981]. The formal notion of specialization has been applied to toy problems, such as specializing the "reverse list" function to finding the last element of the reversed list, and to more substantive problems such as the derivation of algorithms for context-free grammars and graph problems. Examples of the practical use of specialization include supplying parameters to procedures, constraining a type to a subtype in order to realize greater space or time efficiency, selecting an alternative in a menu-driven graphics application, zooming in to obtain more detail in a graphics display, and specializing a requirements specification to a particular program design.

Since specialization is as ubiquitous and important a concept as abstraction, mechanisms for specialization deserve to be classified and formalized as rigorously as those for abstraction. Schemes for navigation within an equivalence class should make equal use of controlled specialization and abstraction as central tools in problem solving.

Compiler Generators

PQCC, the production-quality compiler-compiler developed by Wulf, is an interesting example of an application generator in an area where a lot of expert knowledge is available [Wulf, 1980]. Compiler-compilers generate programs for a spectrum of programming languages and target machines whose range of variation must be carefully defined. They can make use of the very considerable knowledge of compiler writing accumulated over the last 20 years. Wulf adopts the strategy of breaking down the compiler development process into a large number of subtasks such as parsing, syntactic analysis, and flow analysis. Each is handled by a specialized software component with knowledge about that particular task. The program being compiled is transformed from its source language form through a sequence of intermediate representations to its compiled form by a sequence of applications of expert subsystems. The problems of identifying subtasks, encoding expert knowledge about each subtask, providing a mechanism for subtasks to work cooperatively on a large task, and defining the complete spectrum of applications must initially be handled manually. These tasks could eventually be automated so that not just a single component but a collection of cooperating components could be generated.

The Knowledge Industry

The production of knowledge is an economic activity governed in part by market forces of the economy, in the view developed by Machlup in a comprehensive study of the economics and the substance of the knowledge explosion [Machlup 1980]. The importance of knowledge as a product of our economy is shown by the size of the education industry, the growth of the computer industry, and the average age at which people start contributing to the economy. The latter has increased from the early teens during the industrial revolution to over 20 for college graduates and over 25 for doctors and lawyers.

Knowledge is a stock of capital goods, and its production is a capital-intensive activity. The growing importance of the knowledge industry demonstrates that man is becoming an increasingly capital-intensive animal.

Knowledge Graphs

Knowledge graphs that can be entered at different points and traversed in different ways impose a modular, interactive discipline on both creators and users of knowledge. They are a basic representation not only for electronic books but also for computer games, such as Adventure, that fascinate by allowing players to explore new graph-structured worlds. Since the hardware technology to support their effective use is only now being developed, we have little experience with building large knowledge graphs, but we can describe their general features.

Knowledge graphs will probably have a domain-independent interconnection structure that facilitates several modes of graph traversal, such as browsing, retrieval, learning, referencing, and authoring. Each node will have a domain-dependent internal structure containing, for example, programs (when representing programming knowledge) or proofs (when representing mathematical knowledge). Graph creators and users will have a domain-independent set of operations for navigating the graph and domain-dependent operations for manipulating objects in each domain. Zog [Robertson *et al.*, 1981] is an early example of this kind of general-purpose system.

Personal Authoring Tools

Knuth has developed a system for writing books about programs that integrates document formatting, program editing, and compiling into a single system, called Web [Knuth, 1982]. In this system, a program Weave assembles text and programs into a single readable document that reflects the process by which the program was created. A program Tangle allows programs in the document to be extracted, compiled, and executed.

Knuth's system is recursively illustrated by a 200-page description of Weave and Tangle produced by his system. It presents a remarkably clear, well-structured account of these nontrivial programs and illustrates their value for document formatting and word processing. Such systems are evolving into tools that can materially assist authors in the mechanics of authoring, thereby freeing more of their time for the substantive organization and development of ideas.

The Web system is currently restricted to Pascal programs and, to be effective, requires knowledge of TEX, Web, and Pascal and the use of a systematic programming methodology. It is a personal knowledge engineering tool tuned for use by specific individuals rather than by a large user community. Knowledge support environments for specific authors will in general start from a general-purpose environment of editing and knowledge management tools and then include special-purpose tools for supporting the requirements and habits of specific authors. Authors are likely to benefit by investing some of their time in the development of special authoring tools to support their own special needs.

Reusability in Ada

The Ada effort has spawned a remarkably large number of terms that are near-synonyms of reusability, including the following:

commonality—reusability of a language by many people;

portability—reusability of a program or software tool on many computers;

modularity—reusability of software components in larger applications;

maintainability—reusability of the unchanged part of a program when a small change is made; and

evolution—reusability of a system as it evolves in response to changing needs.

Strategic Decisions of Ada

The major strategic decisions in the development of Ada included

1. language requirements that extrapolate from block-structure languages to encompass data abstraction and concurrency,
2. choice of Pascal as a base for the language,
3. language-dependent environment requirements that require tools to be written in the language and largely for the language, and
4. methodology and technology requirements (STARS) strongly coupled to the language.

The first two decisions were reasonable given the language technology of the 1970s but deserve to be reexamined in the new circumstances of the 1980s. The third and fourth decisions have unduly constrained environment development and have channeled resources away from the development of productive software by forcing simple environment ideas to be implemented by means of a complex language not intended for that purpose.

Acknowledgments

This article owes a great deal to Rob Strom and Shaula Yemini, who introduced me to the world of NIL and distributed processing. Dennis Allison, Brian Dalio, Rob Rubin, Bruce Shriver, and the students of my software engineering course contributed to its debugging.

Partial support for this work was provided by ONR and DARPA under Contract N00014-83-K-0146 and ARPA Order No. 4786, and by IBM Yorktown Heights.

References

Ada Joint Program Office. *Common Apse Interface Set*. Version 1.0, Aug. 1983.

Bachman, C. W. The programmer as navigator. *Comm. ACM*, Nov. 1973.

Balzer, R.; T. Cheatham; and C. Green. Software technology in the 1990's: Using a new program. *Computer*, vol. 16, no. 11, pp. 39–45, Nov. 1983.

Basili, V. R., and A. J. Turner. Iterative enhancement, a practical technique for software development. *IEEE Trans. Software Engineering*, Dec. 1975.

Boehm, B. *Software Engineering Economics*. Englewood Cliffs, N.J.: Prentice-Hall, 1981.

Bourne, S. R. The UNIX shell. *Bell System Technical J.*, July–Aug. 1978.

Brown, M., and R. Sedgewick. Techniques for algorithm animation. Technical report CS-84-02, Brown University, Providence, R.I., Jan. 1984.

Bush, V. As we may think. *Atlantic Monthly*, July 1945.

Byte. Special issue on Smalltalk. Aug. 1981.

Chaitin, G. J. Randomness and mathematical proof. *Scientific American*, 1975.

Computer. Special issue on the DOD STARS program. Vol. 16, no. 11, Nov. 1983.

Feigenbaum, E. A. Case studies in knowledge engineering. *Proc. Fifth Int'l Conf. Artificial Intelligence*, Aug. 1977.

Feigenbaum, E., and P. McCorduck. *Fifth Generation Computers*. Reading, Mass.: Addison-Wesley, 1983.

Feiner, S.; S. Nagy; and A. van Dam. An experimental system for creating and presenting interactive graphical documents. *ACM Trans. Graphics*, Jan. 1982.

Fisher, G. Chairman's letter. *Ada Letters*, Mar.–Apr. 1984.

Hewitt, C. Viewing control structures as patterns of passing messages. *Artificial Intelligence*, June 1977.

Hoare, C. A. R. Monitors: An operating system structuring concept. *Comm. ACM*, Oct. 1974.

Holland, J. *Adaptation in Natural and Artificial Systems: An Introductory Analysis with Applications to Biology, Control, and Artificial Intelligence*. Ann Arbor, Mich.: University of Michigan Press, 1975.

Howerton and Weeks, eds. A conceptual framework for the augmentation of man's intellect. In *Vistas in Information Handling*, vol. 1. Spartan, 1963.

Knuth, D. E. The WEB system for program documentation. Stanford University report, Stanford, Calif., 1982.

Liskov, B., and R. Scheifler. Guardians and actions: Robust support for distributed programs. *Proc. POPL Conf.*, Jan. 1982.

Machlup, F. *Knowledge: Its Creation, Distribution, and Economic Significance*. Princeton, N.J.: Princeton University Press, 1980.

March, J. G., and H. A. Simon. *Organizations*. New York: Wiley, 1958.

Milner, R. A calculus of communicating systems. *Lecture Notes in Computer Science*, no. 92. New York: Springer-Verlag, 1980.

Robertson, G.; D. McCracken; and A. Newell. The Zog approach to man-machine communication. *Int'l J. Man-Machine Studies*, 1981.

Schein, E. H., *et al. Organizational Development*. Reading, Mass.: Addison-Wesley, 1973.

Scherlis, W. Specialization. *Proc. POPL Conf.*, Jan. 1981.

Stefik, M., *et al*. The Organization of Expert Systems—A tutorial. *Artificial Intelligence*, Mar. 1982.

Strom, R., and S. Yemini. NIL, an integrated language and system for distributed programming. *Proc. Sigplan 83 Symp. Programming Language Issues in Software Systems*, June 1983.

———. Optimistic recovery: An asynchronous approach to fault tolerance in distributed systems. *Proc. FTCS-14*, June 1984.

Strom, R.; P. Wegner; and S. Yemini. Ada is too big. Draft report, IBM, Yorktown Heights, Apr. 1984.

Toynbee, A. J. *The Study of History*. Oxford University Press, 1947.

United States Department of Defense. *Ada Reference Manual*. ANSI/MIS-STD 1815, Jan. 1983.

Wasserman, A. I., ed. Requirements for higher order computer programming languages—STEELMAN. In *Tutorial on Programming Language Design*, pp. 298–315. Los Alamitos, Calif.: Computer Society Press, 1980.

Wegner, P. On the unification of data and program abstraction in Ada. *Proc. Principles of Programming Conf.*, Jan. 1983.

Weinreb, D., and D. Moon. *Lisp Machine Manual*. MIT, 1981.

Wulf, W. A. PQCC: A machine-relative compiler technology. Report no. CMU-CS-80-144, Carnegie-Mellon Univ., Pittsburgh, Pa., 1980.

Zave, P. The operational versus the conventional approach to life cycle development. *Comm. ACM*, Feb. 1984.

COMPOSITION-BASED SYSTEMS

CHAPTER 4

CLASSIFICATION OF REUSABLE MODULES

RUBÉN PRIETO-DÍAZ*
GTE Laboratories Inc.

4.1 INTRODUCTION

In 1967, McIlroy proposed the idea of a software components catalog from which software parts could be assembled, much as is done with mechanical or electronic components [McIlroy, 1969]. In the late 70s, this idea was applied in a limited domain by Lanergan and Poynton with excellent results [Lanergan and Poynton, 1979]. They identified and classified a lot of code and standard structures that could be used in many of their applications.

More recently, Japanese software factories have reported great improvements in programmer productivity through reusability by integrating known techniques from different disciplines like resource management, production engineering, quality control, software engineering, and industrial psychology [Matsumoto, 1980; Kim, 1983; Tajima and Matsubara, 1984]. Furthermore,

©1987 IEEE. Based on a paper published in *IEEE Software* 4(1):6–16, 1987. This research was supported in part by National Science Foundation grant MCS-83-04439 and by the Consejo Nacional de Ciencia y Tecnología, México.

*The author is currently at CONTEL Technology Center.

old software inventories, which are recognized as very valuable assets, are being "retrofitted" for reusability by improving their structure, documentation, maintainability, and modifiability [Gomez, 1979; Morrissey and Wu, 1979; Miller, 1980; Lyon, 1981].

Important

For code reuse to be attractive, it must require less effort than the creation of new code. Code reuse involves three steps: (1) accessing the existing code, (2) understanding it, and (3) adapting it. A classification scheme is central to code accessibility. Code understanding depends on both reuser experience and program characteristics such as size, complexity, documentation, and programming language. Code adaptation depends on the differences between requirements and the features offered by existing components and on the skills of the reuser. Research has focused on understanding and adaptation, as supported by numerous studies relating cognitive psychology, programming, and reusability [Love, 1977; Brooks, 1978; Gordon, 1979; Jeffries *et al.*, 1981; Soloway and Ehrlich, 1983; Curtis, 1983; Selby, 1984], but the role of classification has received little attention.

Classification of a collection is central to making code reusability an attractive approach to software development. If the collection is organized by attributes related to software requirements, then the probability of retrieving nonrelevant components is reduced. This in turn enhances understanding and adaptation. A classified collection is of no use without a search-and-retrieval mechanism, and an effective retrieval system requires a well-defined classification structure. Furthermore, the classification and retrieval system must help its users discriminate among very similar items in the collection. A retrieved sample may contain several very similar components differing only in minor implementation details. The user must select the components that require the least adaptation effort.

Typically, the user inspects each element in the sample to select the best. This process alone may discourage a potential user from using the collection, especially if the collection is large. A system to evaluate very similar components is needed to help users select the components that require the least conversion effort. A proper classification scheme must be based on an integrated solution—*a classification scheme embedded in a retrieval system and supported by an evaluation mechanism.*

The main features to be sought in a classification scheme are expandability, adaptability, and consistency. Expandability means that new classes can be added with minimal disturbance to the present collection, that is, with a minimum of reclassification problems. Adaptability means that the scheme can be customized to a particular environment. Consistency means that components from different collections in the same class share the same attributes. This feature allows different organizations to share their collections.

In this chapter we present a model of the code reuse process as the basis of our work followed by a brief introduction to faceted classification as used in library science. Faceted schemes, in contrast with hierarchical classification schemes such as Dewey decimal, are very flexible and well suited for dynamic collections subject to continuous expansion and change. Next, we describe our software classification scheme and the use of a conceptual graph to measure conceptual closeness among terms of the same facet. We use conceptual closeness to improve retrieval by selecting closely related terms for new queries when a retrieval operation fails. Ordering of terms by their conceptual distance is facilitated by faceted classification. Following this discussion, we describe the library system and the evaluation mechanism. The evaluation mechanism ranks functionally equivalent components by the effort required to reuse them. The final sections include a sample session with the prototype library system, a discussion on using the prototype to validate our approach, and directions for further research.

4.2 A REUSE MODEL

Reuse is the use of previously acquired concepts or objects in a new situation. Reusability is a measure of the ease with which one can use those previous concepts or objects in the new situation. Ideally, reuse is a matching process between new and old situations and, when matching succeeds, duplication of the old object's actions. This very general view assumes that knowledge has been coded at different levels of abstraction and stored for future reuse [Freeman, 1983].

In well-established disciplines like civil or electrical engineering, reuse is based on the existence of previously coded knowledge. There are two different levels of reuse to consider: (1) the reuse of ideas or knowledge and (2) the reuse of particular artifacts and components. In civil engineering, for example, the reuse of ideas consists of applying general engineering concepts, such as standard design equations for determining the dimensions and materials of a beam. In contrast, the reuse of components might consist of selecting the beam that best meets design criteria from a set of standard beam shapes, cross sections, and materials.

A design is typically based on standard components. Electrical engineers, for example, consult component catalogs, check which available part best fits the design constraint, and, in some cases, relax the original design requirements to take advantage of existing components. In real design problems, the number of alternatives is usually large and several combinations of components may give feasible solutions, thus creating a selection problem. Components are usually acquired rather than created, and they are described by standard attributes that capture their functional characteristics. The same observations are valid for software reuse as practiced in software factories (Japanese factories in particular).

We propose a model for reusability based on these observations and on the assumption that available components usually do not match the requirements perfectly, making adaptation the rule rather than the exception. Our approach is to provide an environment that helps locate components and that estimates the adaptation and conversion effort necessary for their reuse. The reuse process is as follows:

☐ A set of functional specifications is given. The user then searches a library of available components to find the candidates that satisfy the specifications.

☐ If a component that satisfies all the specifications is available, reusing it becomes trivial.

☐ More typically, several candidates exist, each satisfying some specifications. We call them similar components. In this case, the problem becomes one of selecting and ranking the available candidates based on how well they match the requirements and on the effort required to adapt the nonmatching specifications.

☐ Once an ordered list of similar candidates is available, the reuser selects the easiest to reuse and adapts it.

The following algorithm illustrates this process:

```
given a set of specs
begin
  search library
  if identical match then terminate
  else
    collect similar components
    for each component
      compute degree of match
    end
    rank and select best
    modify component
  fi
end
```

Selecting similar components is a classification problem. The degree of similarity depends on how the collection is organized. We group closely related components by carefully selecting relevant attributes and meaningfully organizing them. The classification scheme is a central component in the reuse process. Before presenting our classification scheme, we introduce some basic classification principles from library science.

4.3 CLASSIFICATION PRINCIPLES

Classification is grouping like things together. All members of a group, or class, produced by classification share at least one characteristic that members of other classes do not. Classification displays the relationships among things and among classes of things. The result is a network or structure of relationships. In defining an object, for example, reference is made to the class that contains the object being defined, and reference is then made to characteristics that differentiate the object from other members of the same class.

A *classification scheme* is a tool for the production of systematic order based on a controlled and structured index vocabulary. This index vocabulary is called the *classification schedule*. It consists of the set of names or symbols representing concepts or classes, listed in a systematic order to display the relationships between classes [Buchanan, 1979].

There are two kinds of relationships a classification scheme must be able to express: *hierarchical* and *syntactical*. Hierarchical relationships are based upon the principle of subordination or inclusion, while syntactical relationships are created to relate two or more concepts belonging to different hierarchies. Typical classification schemes are strictly hierarchical, with syntactical relationships presented as *compounded classes*. For example, the compounded class "respiration of birds" relates the term *respiration* from the class "processes" with the term *birds* from the class "taxonomy."

Classification schemes can be either enumerative or faceted. The enumerative (or traditional) method postulates a universe of knowledge divided into successively narrower classes that will include all the possible compounded classes. These are then arranged to display their hierarchical relationships. Dewey decimal classification is a typical example of an enumerative hierarchy, where all possible classes are predefined.

The faceted method, as used in library science, relies not on the breakdown of a universe, but on building up or *synthesizing* from the subject statements of particular documents [Ranganathan, 1967]. By this method, subject statements are analyzed into their component elemental classes, and these classes are listed in the schedule. Their generic relationships are the only relationships displayed. When the classifier using such a scheme has to express a compound class, she does so by assembling its elemental classes. This process is called *synthesis*, and the arranged groups of elemental classes that make up the scheme are the *facets*. The elements or classes that make up a facet are called *terms*.

Facets are sometimes considered as perspectives, viewpoints, or dimensions of a particular domain. An example faceted scheme is as follows:

Process facet
    Physiology
        Respiration
        Reproduction

Animals' habitat facet
    Water animals
    Land animals

Zoologists' taxonomy facet
  Invertebrates
    Insects
  Vertebrates
    Reptiles

A partial enumerative version is as follows:

Physiology
  Respiration
  Reproduction

Water animals
  Physiology of water animals
    Respiration of water animals
    Reproduction of water animals
Land animals
  Physiology of land animals
    Respiration of land animals
    Reproduction of land animals

Invertebrates
  Physiology of invertebrates
  (etc.)

Both schemes can be used to express the same number of classes. The difference is that in the enumerative scheme classes with more than one elemental
component are listed ready-made, while with the faceted scheme the classifier
will have to make multielement classes by synthesis.

The difference between enumerative and faceted classification is better
illustrated by going through the classification process as conducted in library
science [Maltby, 1975]. A class that best describes or represents the title to
be entered into the library is selected from the classification schedule. In the
Dewey decimal system [Dewey, 1979], for example, if we want to classify the
title *Structured Systems Programming*, we look at the hierarchical structure and
try to find the predefined class that best describes the title. Figure 4.1 shows
a partial expansion of the Dewey hierarchy showing the classes relevant to
our title.

A problem typical of enumerative schemes is traversing the hierarchical
tree to find the appropriate class. In this case the librarian could end the
traversal in any of the following classes: 001.61 (systems analysis), 001.642 5
(software), 003 (systems), 620.72 (systems analysis), or 620.73 (systems
construction). Implicit in the use of this kind of classification scheme is the
expertise of the librarian in both the classification scheme and the subject
matter or domain of the title: this expertise enables him to decide which is the
most appropriate class. This is usually a difficult task because more than one

FIGURE 4.1
A PARTIAL EXPANSION OF DEWEY DECIMAL HIERARCHY

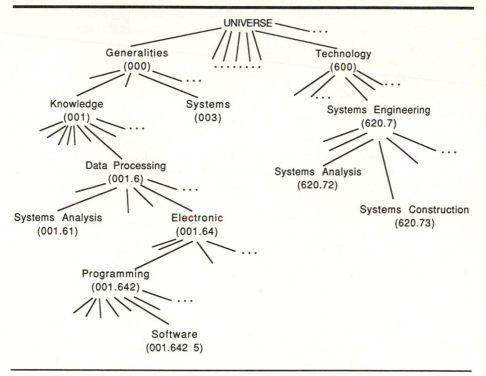

class may be applicable. To compensate for ambiguity cross-references are established. The title of our example is classified as 001.642 5 (software) but cross-references are made to the other classes. Cross-referencing is a cumbersome and error-prone process.

Faceted classification, on the other hand, is straightforward. A faceted scheme may have several facets, and each facet may have several terms, but facets and terms are derived from analysis of a representative sample of the collection to be classified. A partial listing of a hypothetical faceted scheme is shown below.

Entities facet	*Activity facet*
programs	programming
designs	design
systems	evaluation
structures	analysis
.	.
.	.
.	.

To classify the example title we select from each facet the term that best describes each of the concepts in the title. For this example, we select *systems* from the entities facet and *programming* from the activity facet. The resulting synthesized class is "systems/programming." This classification approach basically tailors the class to a perfect fit; in enumerative schemes the librarian must shop from a collection of standard sizes for the best fit.

Faceted scheme features are very attractive for classifying reusable software. Besides the perfect-fit characteristic, we can order facets by their relevance to the users of the collection. We could order our faceted scheme above with activity as the first facet and entities as the second. The resulting classification of our title would be "programming/systems," which emphasizes the activity. This *citation ordering* enhances search-and-retrieval performance (recall and precision) when used to organize a database.

Another important feature of faceted schemes is the ordering of terms within each facet. Terms can be ordered according to how closely related they are to each other (conceptual closeness). For example the terms in the facet "planets of the solar system" can be ordered by their size, by their distance from the sun, or even alphabetically, depending upon which order is more meaningful to the user. This feature provides a means to find similar items in a collection—an essential feature for reusability, as we explain later.

Other benefits of faceted schemes include expandability and flexibility. Adding a new class to an enumerative scheme would generate several cross-references from related classes in other hierarchies, while new classes in a faceted scheme can be easily added as new terms in their respective facets. Dealing with a predefined hierarchy is difficult when some of its nodes experience rapid growth, as is the case in classes representing new technologies such as computers, genetics, and so on. Faceted schemes are more flexible, more precise, and better suited for large, continuously expanding collections such as collections of reusable software components.

In library science, faceted schemes are constructed by selecting a representative sample from the collection to be classified—a process called *literary warrant* [Vickery, 1960]. Related terms from the selected titles are grouped together and facets defined from such groups. Facets are then given a citation order, and terms within each facet are ordered arbitrarily to satisfy user needs. Literary warrant generates collection-specific customized schemes. However, as new titles are added to the collection, new terms are easily added to the classification scheme.

4.4 SOFTWARE CLASSIFICATION

Existing software classification schemes are enumerative and usually very general. They are designed for the end user (the user not interested in adaptation). Moreover, current schemes are not organized by reusability-related attributes but by area of application, type of problem solved, or hardware make. Examples include the ACM Computing Reviews Scheme, AFIPS's Taxonomy of Computer Science and Engineering, schemes for functional collections (GAMS, SHARE, SSP, SPSS, IMLS, etc.), and schemes for commercial software catalogs (ICP, IDS, IBM Software Catalog, Apple Book, etc.). Furthermore, with the current proliferation of commercially available software, many catalogs display long listings in a few general classes and display some classes with no listings—proving the need for more specific and flexible schemes.

The faceted scheme we proposed [Prieto-Díaz, 1985] is based on the assumptions that collections of reusable components are very large and growing continuously and that there are large groups of similar components—even in very specific classes. The scheme has a component description format based on a standard vocabulary of terms, imposes a citation order for the facets, and provides a metric for conceptual distances between terms in each facet. This metric helps select closely related components. A mechanism has been added to evaluate the similarity of items, helping the user to select the best.

Software components can be described by (1) the function they perform, (2) the way they perform it, and (3) their implementation details. These descriptors fall naturally into facets that can be ordered by their relevance to reusability. A component descriptor thus is a tuple of terms where each term is an attribute value of a selected facet.

We have derived a preliminary schedule for classifying functionally identifiable code fragments of medium size (50 to 200 source lines of code). More than 400 program descriptions and source listings from several commercial software catalogs and programming textbooks were used to determine which attributes are relevant to describing programs. We observed that program descriptions consist of two parts: one describing the functionality (what it does) and the other describing the environment (where it does it). Implementation details or realization (how it does it) were not usually included in a description.

If a description is to be used as both a classification code and a retrieval key, it must be brief, succinct, and semantically rich—it must consolidate in a single descriptor the "what," "where," and "how" of a program.

Functionality

Programs performing the same function for the same application have more similarity in their implementation details than programs performing the same function in different applications. Intuitively, a search program used in a compiler, for example, may be functionally similar to a search program used in a database system. Both may even be implementations of the same algorithm. However, it is more likely that the compiler search deals with a particular data structure often found in compilers like symbol tables while the data base search deals with data structures common to database systems, like

B-trees. Although functionally equivalent, the implementations of these programs may be very different.

In all of the program descriptions in our collection, we observed imperative statements. Although imperative statements are typically characterized by the triple <*action, object, agent*>, the agent (the conductor of the action) in our sample is always implied as being the program itself. To represent program functionality, we chose a slightly modified version, <*function, object, medium*>, because this version describes better what a program does. *Function*, which is a synonym for *action*, is the name of the specific primitive function performed by the program (for example, move, start, or compare). *Object* refers to the objects manipulated by the program (such as characters, lines, variables). *Medium*, which replaced *agent*, refers to entities that serve as the locale of the action, such as the data structures that in many cases are the supporting structures for the functions (like table, file, tree, and line). To classify for reusability, the medium, a very relevant attribute, must be made explicit. In the sample analyzed, only 45 percent of the descriptions mentioned the medium used. In most cases medium was identified by direct code inspection. Some examples of triples of the form <*function, object, medium*> are as follows:

<input, character, buffer>
<substitute, tabs, file>
<search, root, B-tree>
<compress, lines, file>

Sugarman reported a successful case of describing entities with modified imperative statements for classification [Sugarman, 1981]. In that study, a model describes dissertation abstracts with triples of the form <*operation, objects, properties*>. Sixty-five percent of all sentences found in a sample of 167 dissertation abstracts were written in this triplet format. A classification and retrieval test showed better performance than techniques based on keywords.

Environment

There are two environments for any program: the internal environment (where the program is executed) and the external environment (where the program is applied). Internal environmental differences relate to software portability; program functionality usually remains unchanged when a program is adapted to a new environment. External environmental differences, on the other hand, require modifications of the program's design or specifications; such differences arise when a new set of requirements is proposed for an existing system. This type of adaptation is more typical of reusability, and it is the type we address.

Knowing a program's intended application and its external environment provides *indirect* knowledge of its general characteristics. Some implementation details can be inferred from the external environment. These details include certain programming practices, style, data structures used, information manipulated, and particular computational methods and algorithms.

From our experimental sample, we selected environment-related words and grouped them into three major groups: (1) terms describing the type of system, (2) terms describing the functional area, and (3) terms describing the location or setting of the application. Three corresponding facets were defined: system type, functional area, and setting. System-type terms refer to functionally identifiable, application-independent modules, usually including more than one component. Examples of system type include report-formatter, lexical-analyzer, scheduler, retriever, expression-evaluator, and interpreter. In our term-grouping experiment, some system-type terms were found in catalog descriptions of software systems, but most were obtained from source code listings and design documents. Functional-area terms describe application-dependent activities, usually defined by an established set of procedures in an area of application. Examples are general-ledger, cost-control, and purchasing. Setting describes where the application is exercised. This captures details of how to conduct certain operations. For example, a manufacturing control program in a print shop may have a slightly different implementation than a manufacturing control program in a chemical plant. The differences here are mainly in the form of control and in the objects handled. Functionally, they may be the same programs. Examples of settings are print shop, chemical plant, and department store.

Citation order is based on relevance to users. Assuming that the typical users of the collection are software engineers designing and building new systems from components, we selected the following citation order: function, objects, medium, system type, functional area, and setting. Table 4.1 shows a partial listing of the scheme.

Classifying a component consists of selecting the sextuple that best describes the component. Some examples are these:

<add, integers, array, matrix-inverter, modeling, aircraft-manufacture>
<compress, files, disk, file-handler, DB-management, catalog-sales>
<compare, descriptors, stack, assembler, programming, software-shop>

Vocabulary Control

Describing code with a tuple of specially selected terms is not problem free. Synonyms can produce different descriptors for the same component. In the case of functionality, for example, the descriptor <move, words, file> and the descriptor <transfer, names, file> may be two different descriptions of the same program. To avoid duplicate and ambiguous descriptors a *controlled vocabulary* is required.

A terms thesaurus is needed to group all synonyms under a single concept. The term that best describes the concept is selected as the *representative* term. The thesaurus is used for vocabulary control and for broadening

TABLE 4.1
PARTIAL LISTING OF THE FACETED CLASSIFICATION SCHEDULE

| | | FACETS | | |
{function}	{objects}	{medium}	{system-type}	{functional-area}	{setting}
add	arguments	array	assembler	accounts-payable	advertising
append	arrays	buffer	code-generation	accounts-receivable	aircraft-manufacture
close	backspaces	cards	code-optimization	analysis-structural	appliance-store
compare	blanks	disk	compiler	auditing	association
complement	buffers	file	DB-management	batch-job-control	auto-repair
compress	characters	keyboard	expression-evaluator	billing	barbershop
create	descriptors	line	file-handler	bookkeeping	broadcast-station
decode	digits	list	hierarchical-DB	budgeting	cable-station
delete	directories	mouse	hybrid-DB	capacity-planning	car-dealer
divide	expressions	printer	interpreter	CAD	catalog-sales
evaluate	files	screen	lexical-analyzer	cost-accounting	cemetery
exchange	functions	sensor	line-editor	cost-control	circulation
expand	instructions	stack	matrix-inverter	customer-information	classified-ads
format	integers	table	pattern-matcher	DB-analysis	cleaning
input	lines	tape	predictive-parsing	DB-design	clothing-store
insert	lists	tree	relational-DB	DB-management	composition
join	macros	.	retreiver	modeling	computer-store
measure	pages	.	scheduler	programming	.
modify	.	.	.	.	.
move	.	.	.	.	.

the index vocabulary. These uses enhance recall performance. A thesaurus can also control the size of the schedules, either by increasing the number of terms assigned to a particular group or by breaking up groups of terms. The ambiguity of the term *list*, for example, is resolved by selecting one of the two contexts: measure or output. Examples of thesaurus entries from the actions facet are as follows:

Term	*Synonyms*
add	increment/total/sum
close	release/detach/disconnect
compare	test/relate/match/check/verify
complement	negate/invert
measure	count/advance/size/enumerate/list
move	transfer/copy
open	connect/attach
output	print/echo/show/write/display/list/put
substitute	replace/convert/change/update/map

Conceptual Closeness

A very important feature of this scheme is the introduction of a conceptual graph to measure closeness among terms in a facet. The conceptual graph is an acyclic directed graph in which the leaves are terms and the nodes are supertypes that denote general concepts relating two or more terms. Weights in the edges are user assigned: The closer the user perceives a relationship of a term to a supertype, the smaller the weight.

Figure 4.2 shows a partial weighted conceptual graph for some function names. In this example the supertypes are all related to the notion of *function* (symbolized by *), which is the facet name. Closeness is then measured by the closest path between any two terms. For example, *measure* is closer to *add* (6) than to *move* (16). We used a software engineering perspective for weight assignment in this particular graph.

One practical application of a closeness measurement happens during retrieval. If a particular term in a query does not match any available descriptions in the collection, the system tries the nearby terms to retrieve descriptions of closely related items.

Constructing conceptual graphs for more than a few terms is time-consuming. However, we observed that in most cases conceptual distances between new terms and terms of an initial graph could be estimated outside the graph, thus simplifying the process. We also observed that the graph's basic structure remains very stable as the collection expands. Constructing it is a one-time investment (although a substantial one). Minor tuning is required as users provide feedback on retrieval performance.

FIGURE 4.2
A PARTIAL WEIGHTED CONCEPTUAL GRAPH FOR THE FUNCTION FACET

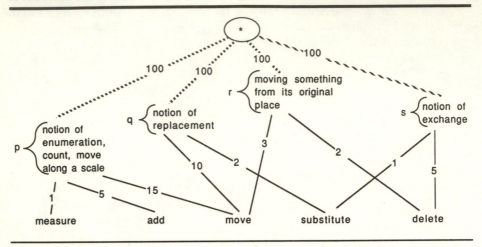

Figure 4.3 presents an abstract view of the scheme. Each component σ has a descriptor d_σ that is an ordered set of terms from each facet F_i. Every term in a facet is related to one or more supertypes by means of a weighted conceptual graph. During retrieval, a query is a valid descriptor $d_{\sigma 1}$ of terms selected from each facet. If there is no match in the collection for $d_{\sigma 1}$, closely

FIGURE 4.3
ABSTRACT VIEW OF THE PROPOSED CLASSIFICATION SCHEME

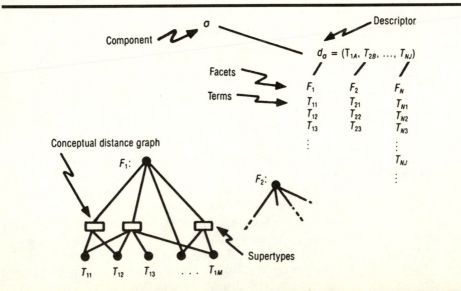

related terms are selected according to distances in the conceptual graphs to make new descriptors d_σ. Matches on the new descriptors will retrieve components closely related to components described by $d_{\sigma 1}$.

4.5 LIBRARY SYSTEM

We integrated the faceted classification scheme, the conceptual distance model, and a mechanism to evaluate and rank functionally equivalent components into a prototype library system. Figure 4.4 shows a SofTech Structured Analysis and Design Technique (SADT) level 0 diagram of the library system for reusable code fragments.

The library system consists of a group of procedures that help in query construction and evaluation of the retrieved sample for potential reusability. The catalog is the database of component descriptors. The query system (boxes 1, 2, and 3 in Fig. 4.4) uses the classification scheme to interactively generate component descriptors.

The user inputs descriptive terms and is guided by the system in selecting valid terms from the classification schedules. The thesaurus resolves

FIGURE 4.4
SADT LEVEL 0 ACTIGRAM FOR A LIBRARY SYSTEM

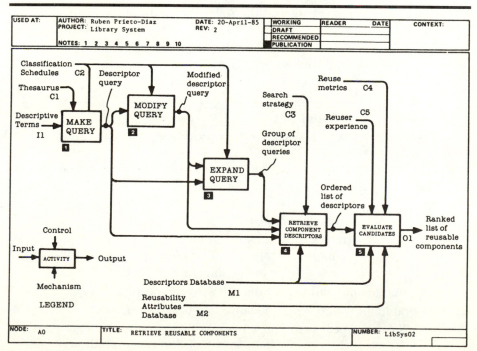

ambiguities. A query is a sextuple descriptor of a component and may be modified by replacing terms with wild cards, in a prescribed relevance order. This mechanism generalizes a query. We can also replace wild cards with specific terms to specialize a query. A more detailed illustration of this mechanism is shown in the sample session in Section 4.7.

A query can also be expanded. Closely related terms are selected from the conceptual graphs to construct new queries ordered by their relevance to the original query, from most to least related. Query expansion, a central feature of the library system, is an interactive process controlled by the user. It can be initiated by the system, when the original query returns the empty set, or by the user. Query expansion is illustrated in Section 4.7. Retrieval (box 4 in Fig. 4.4) is implemented by a relational database system where each program descriptor is a tuple in the database with pointers to source code, documentation, and other relevant information.

Evaluation (box 5 in Fig. 4.4) is a system for normalization and ranking. Reusability-related metrics for each retrieved component are normalized first. The sample is then ranked according to the estimated reusability effort required to reuse the components. A detailed description of the evaluation system follows.

4.6 EVALUATION MECHANISM

The evaluation system is based on the following assumptions:

☐ The collection of components is very large.
☐ There are several functionally equivalent components in any particular class.
☐ Reusers have different abilities.
☐ Programs have different attributes.
☐ The reuser needs help selecting the easiest component to reuse.

We selected five program attributes as the most relevant indicators of reuse effort. We then chose a metric for each indicator [Prieto-Díaz, 1985].

Attribute	Metric
Program size	Lines of code
Program structure	Number of modules, number of linkages, and cyclomatic complexity
Program documentation	Subjective overall rating (1 to 10)
Programming language	Relative language closeness
Reuser experience	Six levels in two areas: programming language and domain of application.

For these five metrics to be effective we had to define a criterion that would minimize reuse effort. The best component for reusability (the one that would require the least amount of effort to be reused) would have attributes as follows:

$$
\begin{aligned}
\text{Size} &= \text{small} \\
\text{Structure} &= \text{simple} \\
\text{Documentation} &= \text{excellent} \\
\text{Programming language} &= \text{same}
\end{aligned}
$$

Reuser experience (explained below) is a modifier for the first three attributes. Reusers have their own criteria, based mainly on experience, for determining what "small," "simple," and "excellent" mean.

We can define a reuser experience profile and determine how size, structure, and documentation criteria change with level of experience. Since these criteria do not have precise values, we used fuzzy set theory as a basis to evaluate them. Most humans reason in categories with fuzzy boundaries: "John is tall," "Today's temperature is pleasant," "This is a short program." Fuzzy logic is "a kind of logic using graded or qualified statements rather than ones that are strictly true or false" [Zadeh, 1984].

A fuzzy set is a class with fuzzy boundaries, which may be characterized by associating a membership grade in the class with every object that could be in the class. A fuzzy function maps a set of values in a fuzzy set to the interval [0, 1]. Thus, if the domain is the concept of "small program" measured in lines of source code, then this function can be represented as

$$\text{smallprogram: lines} \rightarrow [0, 1].$$

For example, this mapping might assign a 20-line component a degree of membership in the small program class of .7, while assigning a 40-line component only a .4 degree of belonging in the same class. Fuzzy distinctions like "small" or "large" are represented by an S-shaped curve. In our system fuzzy functions determine the degree of membership a component has in the favorable categories for each of the first three attributes listed earlier.

Fuzzy modifiers are "operations that change the membership function of a fuzzy set by spreading out the transition between full membership and nonmembership, by sharpening that transition, or by moving the position of the transition region" [Zadeh, 1984]. We use reuser experience as a fuzzy modifier by sharpening and moving the transition region of a program attribute's fuzzy function. A change in the transition region of the fuzzy function for the "small" component concept as a function of program size in lines of source code is illustrated in Fig. 4.5.

Program structure and documentation quality functions are modified in the same way as the program size function is. In the case of documentation

FIGURE 4.5
REUSER EXPERIENCE AS MODIFIER FOR SMALL COMPONENT

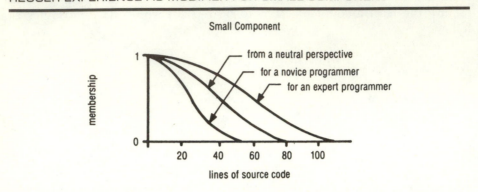

quality, what is modified is its overall relevance to program understanding. For an experienced programmer, a high documentation quality value may contribute less to reuse effort than the same high rating would contribute for a novice programmer.

Programming language is another function modifier for size and structure. What is considered a small component may depend on the programming language used. For example, a large component in APL may have fewer lines of code than a small component in assembly language. This idea is illustrated in Fig. 4.6.

We implemented reuser experience as a modifier for size, structure, and documentation functions by shifting the transition regions by amounts proportional to reuser experience. For the evaluation subsystem, we assumed

FIGURE 4.6
PROGRAMMING LANGUAGE AS MODIFIER OF COMPONENT SMALLNESS

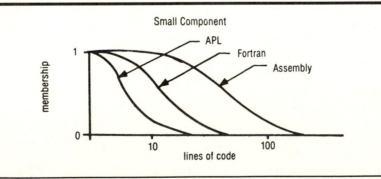

FIGURE 4.7
USER EXPERIENCE AS MODIFIER FOR ATTRIBUTE FUNCTIONS

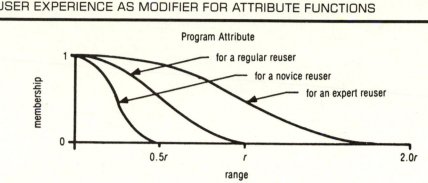

that the spread of the membership functions varied with experience from one half to twice the normal range for a regular user, as shown in Fig. 4.7.

We implemented this evaluation technique based on fuzzy functions and modifiers in the library system; the evaluation subsystem is box 5 in Fig. 4.4. Specific S-shaped fuzzy functions were defined for program attributes, programming languages, and reusers and tested in a limited environment [Prieto-Díaz, 1985].

4.7 SAMPLE SESSION

We present a sample session with the library system to illustrate its basic functions. The system has been implemented in C under UNIX Berkeley 4.2 and with the University of California Troll/USE prototyping tool as the underlying database system. The database used in this example consists of about 200 program descriptors and their corresponding data (such as reuse metrics, short English descriptions, and author).

Forming the Query

A user request starts the interactive session to form the query. The library system asks the user to select a representative term from the thesaurus of each facet until all six terms that form the query have been selected. For example, if the reuser is looking for a component to change backspaces to multiple lines (to expand compressed text in a text formatting system), he will select the query:

substitute/backspaces/file/text-formatter/program-development/software-shop

The objective of the dialog is to create as specific a query as possible and to try it in the collection first. If there is no match, then the user may go into query modification mode to modify or expand the query.

Query Modification

In query modification mode, the query can be generalized or specialized. The generalization process consists of an orderly replacement of terms by the "any" metasymbol (*) to obtain the *most relevant generalizations* of the completely defined query. Most relevant generalizations are created by removing less relevant facets in the established citation order. For the complete query of this example the most relevant generalizations are as follows:

substitute/backspaces/file/text-formatter/program-development/*

substitute/backspaces/file/text-formatter/*/*

substitute/backspaces/file/*/*/*

substitute/backspaces/*/*/*/*

substitute/*/*/*/*/*

Specialization consists of placing terms back into the query. The reuser conducts query generalization and specialization interactively in any order or combination to generate the desired query. This lets the reuser test different sample retrievals. In this example we tried the last of the most relevant generalizations and retrieved 19 components (in alphabetical order).

```
Modified Query:
      substitute/*/*/*/*/*/
   (g)eneralize (s)pecialize (k) OK as is    k
Modified Query:
      substitute/*/*/*/*/*/ Sample Size = 19   view? y/n    y
NUMBER     FUNCTIONALITY                    DESCRIPTION
10033   substitute/backspaces/file    convert backspaces into multiple lines
10025   substitute/characters/file    transliterate characters by command line
 9105   substitute/descriptors/file   update file descriptor
10050   substitute/files/file         update existing files-append new ones
10059   substitute/files/file         replace or delete files from archive
 9107   substitute/instructions/file  replace two word inst by one word
10037   substitute/integers/file      convert integer to char string
10018   substitute/patterns/file      substitute string for occurrences of patterns
 9110   substitute/pointer/file       resolve label relative address
 9100   substitute/pointers/table     replace reference in look-up table
 9101   substitute/pointers/table     update location in look up table
 9102   substitute/pointers/table     change pointer in look up table
 9104   substitute/pointers/list      link next line
10101   substitute/reals/buffer       convert float to string
10038   substitute/string/file        convert string to integer
```

```
10031   substitute/tabs/file        convert tabs to equivalent number of blanks
10032   substitute/tabs/file        convert runs of tabs into blanks
 9108   substitute/variables/file   resolve variable relative address
 9109   substitute/variables/file   fill up macro arguments
            view? y/n       n
         Are you satisfied with this sample? y/n      n
```

Only five components show some relevance to our original request (10033, 10025, 10038, 10031, and 10032). If this sample were large, as should be expected in a well-populated collection, it would have taken a long time to visually extract the components relevant to the query. Such extraction is done with query expansion mode.

Query Expansion

In query expansion mode, the selected (original or modified) query is used as a reference for creating new queries of closely related terms. The criterion for term selection is conceptual distance from the reference term, and conceptual distances are calculated from a conceptual graph. Terms are ordered from conceptually closest to conceptually farthest; each ranking step is called a conceptual level. Expansion can be requested for any facet where a term is present in the query, and the range of the expansion can be increased as desired. Each expansion creates a new query. A five-level expansion using "substitute/backspaces" as the reference query produces (in order of conceptual closeness):

substitute/quotes

substitute/blanks

substitute/digits

substitute/tabs

substitute/characters

These expanded keywords retrieve the following sample.

```
Retrieving expanded query .....
   Sample Size = 4
NUMBER        FUNCTIONALITY                 DESCRIPTION
10033  substitute/backspaces/file  convert backspaces into multiple lines
10031  substitute/tabs/file        convert tabs to equivalent number of blanks
10032  substitute/tabs/file        convert runs of tabs into blanks
10025  substitute/characters/file  transliterate characters by command line
       view? y/n       n
     Are you satisfied with this sample? y/n       y
   >>>  sample saved in: -----> expanded.txt
      (q)uitting (c)ontinue      c
```

The result is a sample of the components conceptually closest to our original request. Next we rank the sample by expected reusability effort. Here we enter user profile and target language:

```
Continuing for component selection......
    Enter user profile name:  prieto
    Enter target language:  F77
Numbr  Wght  Sz  Cpx  Doc  Lang     Functionality
10033  5.39  26  4    9    pascal   substitute/backspaces/file
10031  4.86  38  7    9    pascal   substitute/tabs/file
10032  4.73  43  8    9    pascal   substitute/tabs/file
10025  4.65  41  13   9    pascal   substitute/characters/file
    view?  y/n     n
      >>> Weighted sample in:  ----> 'dbprottyp/selection.txt'
        (q)uitting (r)epeat    q
```

The components are ranked by an overall weight factor. In this particular example, it turned out that all components were coded in the same language, so the language conversion factor was a constant.

4.8 VALIDATION

Given the amount of work required to create a practical library of components, classify them, and then try to build software with them, we limited our validation to tests that predict, to a certain degree, the behavior of a scaled-up library system. We conducted three evaluations: retrieval, classification, and reuse effort estimation.

Retrieval

We tested retrieval effectiveness by comparing recall and precision values of our system to those of a database retrieval system with data not organized by a classification scheme. Recall is the proportion of relevant material retrieved from the collection. Precision is the proportion of retrieved material that is relevant. We first evaluated the effect of citation order by comparing performance of most relevant generalizations to that of partial generalizations. (If $d_c = <v_1, v_2, v_3>$ is a complete query, then $d_m = <v_1, v_2, *>$ is a most relevant generalization and $d_{p1} = <v_1, *, v_3>$ and $d_{p2} = <*, v_2, v_3>$ are partial generalizations.) Next, we evaluated conceptual ordering by comparing the performance of expanded queries to that of regular queries. In both evaluations, while recall was reduced by about 50 percent precision improved over 100 percent [Prieto-Díaz, 1985].

Classification

We tested the classification scheme for ease of use, accuracy, and consistency. A set of five programs, the faceted schedules, some classification rules, and an example of how to classify a program were given to 13 graduate computer science students. The participants were asked to classify each program and to comment about any difficulties experienced during the process. For accuracy and consistency, we compared the classifications returned. Consistency was 100 percent for terms selected from the function and object facets and 60 percent for terms from the medium facet. That is, all students classified the function and object facets with the same term and 8 out of 13 students classified the medium facet using the same term. Environment facets were not used in the experiment because the programs in the sample were generic. Comments from the participants confirmed the simplicity of the classification process—a necessary feature for the librarian.

Reuse Effort Estimation

We asked reusers to rank functionally equivalent components. We then compared their ranking to the system ranking. With a target application and some implementation constraints, we gave five candidate programs and their respective detailed documentation to six participants. For three of the five programs, ranking correlation was 100 percent—the participants and the system ranked the components in the same order.

Because of the relatively small size of the collection and the limited number of participants, the results, although very encouraging, are only indicative, not conclusive. We are now scaling up the collection and making it available through a refined version of our prototype in a production environment at GTE Laboratories.

4.9 RESEARCH FOLLOW-UP

Some research questions remain open, such as standardization of the classification schedules, the incorporation and classification of logic structures, and the validation of reuse effort estimation metrics.

This work, although in a preliminary state of development, is a promising approach to reusability, especially in the short term. It can be incorporated into current state-of-the-art software development environments with minimum effort and offers a high payoff potential.

REFERENCES

Brooks, R. Using a behavioral theory of program comprehension in software engineering. In Wilkes, M. V. (ed.), *3rd International Conference on Software Engineering*, pp. 196–201. Atlanta, Ga.: IEEE, May, 1978.

Buchanan, B. *Theory of Library Classification*. London: Clive Bingley, 1979.

Curtis, B. Cognitive issues in reusability. In Perlis, A. (ed.), *Workshop on Reusability in Programming*, pp. 192–197. Newport, R.I.: ITT Programming, September 1983.

Dewey, M. *Decimal Classification and Relative Index.* 19th ed. Albany, N.Y.: Forest Press, Inc., 1979.

Freeman, P. Reusable software engineering: Concepts and research directions. In Perlis, A. (ed.), *Workshop on Reusability in Programming*, pp. 2–16. Newport, R.I.: ITT Programming, September 1983.

Gomez, J. E. An interactive Fortran structuring aid. In Bauer, F. L. (ed.), *Proceedings of the Fourth International Conference on Software Engineering*, pp. 241–244. Munich, West Germany: IEEE, September 1979.

Gordon, R. D. Measuring improvements in program clarity. *IEEE Transactions on Software Engineering* SE-5(2):79–90, March 1979.

Jeffries, Robin; Althea A. Turner; Peter G. Polson; and Michael E. Atwood. The process involved in designing software. In Anderson, J. R. (ed.), *Cognitive Skills and Their Acquisition*, pp. 255–284. Hillsdale, N.J.: Lawrence Erlbaum, 1981.

Kim, K. H. A look at Japan's development of software engineering technology. *Computer* 16(5):26–37, May 1983.

Lanergan, R. G., and Poynton, B. A. Reusable code: The application development technique of the future. In *Proceedings of the IBM SHARE/GUIDE Software Symposium*. Monterey, Calif.: IBM, October 1979.

Love, T. An experimental investigation of the effects of program structure on program understanding. *ACM SIGPLAN Notices* 12:105–113, March 1977.

Lyon, M. J. Salvaging your software asset (tools based maintenance). In Orden, A. (ed.), *AFIPS Proceedings of the National Computer Conference*, pp. 337–341. Chicago, Ill.: May 1981.

Maltby, A. *Sayers' Manual of Classification for Librarians*. London WCI: André Deutch Ltd., 1975.

Matsumoto, Y. SWB system: A software factory. In Hunke, H. (ed.), *Software Engineering Environments*, pp. 305–318. New York: North-Holland, 1980.

McIlroy, M. D. Mass produced software components. In *Software Engineering Concepts and Techniques*, pp. 88–98. Brussels 39, Belgium: Petrocelli/Charter, 1969. Paper presented at the 1969 NATO Conference on Software Engineering.

Miller, J. C. Structured retrofit. In *Techniques of Program and System Maintenance*, pp. 85–86. Lincoln, Nebr.: Etnotech, 1980.

Morrissey, J. H., and Wu, L. S. Y. Software engineering: An economic perspective. In Bauer, F. L. (ed.), *Proceedings of the Fourth International Conference on Software Engineering*, pp. 412–422. Munich, West Germany: IEEE, September 1979.

Prieto-Díaz, R. A software classification scheme. Ph.D. thesis, Department of Information and Computer Science, University of California, Irvine, 1985.

Ranganathan, S. R. *Prolegomena to Library Classification*. Bombay, India: Asia Publishing House, 1967.

Selby, R. W. A quantitative approach for evolving software technologies. Ph.D. thesis, Department of Computer Science, University of Maryland, December 1984.

Soloway, E., and Ehrlich, K. What do programmers reuse? Theory and experiment. In Perlis, A. (ed.), *Workshop on Reusability in Programming*, pp. 184–191. Newport, R.I.: ITT Programming, September 1983.

Sugarman, J. H. The development of a classification system for information storage and retrieval purposes based upon a model of scientific knowledge generation. Ph.D. thesis, School of Education, Boston University, 1981.

Tajima, D., and Matsubara, T. Inside the Japanese software industry. *Computer* 17(3):34–43, March 1984.

Vickery, B. C. *Faceted Classification: A Guide to Construction and Use of Special Schemes.* London: Aslib, 1960.

Zadeh, L. A. Making computers think like people. *IEEE Spectrum* 21(8):26–32, August 1984.

CHAPTER 5

INTERFACE ISSUES IN A SOFTWARE PARTS TECHNOLOGY

JOHN RICE

Department of Computer Science, Purdue University

HERB SCHWETMAN

Microelectronics and Computer Technology Corporation (MCC)

A mature software parts technology will include tens of thousands of software parts available in a common environment. In principle, a programmer can attempt to combine any two available parts, so the technology must provide robust mechanisms to insure reliable and meaningful parts composition. In this chapter existing approaches are briefly surveyed, and we note that the principal mechanism in current use is syntactic (or type) checking, which may occur at compile time (Pascal), load time (Ada), or run time (Intel 432). There must also be a subsequent semantic checking either at load time or at run time.

We describe an interface specification structure for all checking required for the highly reliable use of software parts. We identify three levels of interfaces and associated syntactic and semantic checking: global, part specific, and problem specific. At the global level, most of the checking is syntactic. For part-specific checking, not only must the data be of the correct type, but it must be valid for the part; for example, a parameter might have to be not only an integer, but a valid index into a particular array. Problem-specific checking checks whether data is appropriate to the problem; for example, not only a matrix, but a matrix with certain properties. The essential role of standards and conventions is discussed, and an assessment of the tradeoffs is made.

5.1 INTRODUCTION

The discussion of Wasserman and Gutz [1982] on the future of programming includes for the medium term "the development of certified software components—a body of rigorously tested and thoroughly documented software modules will be created and made available for easy incorporation in new systems." More recently, the Department of Defense STARS program has focused on reusable software parts as a major approach to improving software productivity [Batz *et al.*, 1983]. One of the major technical issues in software parts is how to define the interfaces between parts; this is sometimes called the *semantic interface problem*. We address this problem here.

We first introduce some background about software parts and the programming environment that will be required to support a software parts technology. We then define the semantic interface problem and present our solution of it. This paper is an outgrowth of a previous study of the development of a software parts technology [Comer, 1980]. The comments of Doug Comer, Larry Snyder, and Peter Denning influenced our views considerably.

5.1.1 Background

The need for sharing and reusing code has been recognized for many years; the subroutine library concept was conceived in the late 1940s. A current example is the SHARE program library, a repository of subroutines donated by users of large IBM systems. Prospective users can obtain copies of selected routines and incorporate them into their own software. It is our opinion that, while many of these routines are quite useful, the number of routines that fail to work as desired make this library an unreliable source of software. We believe that much volunteered software is unreliable and hence a collection of such software is almost useless. See [Rice, 1971] and [Cowell, 1984] for more discussion.

Much more successful are commercial subroutine libraries from IMSL, Inc., and NAG, Ltd., which provide a library of subroutines for common mathematical and statistical procedures. Each routine is listed and described in a reference manual [IMSL, 1987; NAG, 1986], and its quality is assured by the seller. Because they are in the business of providing software, sellers have become proficient in the construction, distribution, and maintenance of these software components. Today, a programmer operating in a computing center that makes these libraries available is wasting time and money if he does not use them. We refer to these two libraries by the term MATH in later discussion.

The UNIX operating system [Bell System, 1978] (UNIX is copyrighted by Bell Telephone Laboratories) supports parts-based computing in another manner. In UNIX, the user has access to a large number of programs, each of which performs a simple function. By using the *pipe* mechanism these programs can be assembled into larger commands that perform more complex functions. Each program is written to take input from the *standard input file*. Two programs can be connected by a pipe; this means that the standard output of the first program is the standard input of the second. Thus sequences of programs can be connected by linear streams of characters. The large number of programs available on UNIX and the pipe mechanism give UNIX programmers an environment in which software parts are used as building blocks. The UNIX programmer's manual describes each part in terms of its functions, inputs, outputs, and error conditions. Since the source form for every program in UNIX is on-line, existing parts can be tailored to meet a specific need. This is usually much less costly than starting from scratch.

There are other examples. APL programmers have access to sets of *idioms*; these are predefined functions that perform certain desired tasks. A user can invoke an idiom to perform a needed function instead of writing a new function.

Many people are trying to distribute sets of software parts for microprocessors. One example is Scientific Enterprises, Inc., with a product called XM-80 Software Components. This is a set of macros for use with the Macro-80 relocatable assembler for the Z80 microprocessor (Macro-80 is a product of Microsoft, Inc.). The XM-80 routines perform many commonly needed functions. Each macro is described with a data sheet [Scientific Enterprises, 1981].

The goal of the STARS effort [U.S. Dept. of Defense, 1983] is to develop large sets of software parts in the form of Ada packages. Packages are to be developed for a variety of application areas, and the hope is not only to reuse software, but also to provide a *lingua franca* for practitioners in various disciplines and subdisciplines (outside of computer science).

5.1.2 Goals

The goal of a software parts technology is the development of a programming environment in which reusing code is the norm, not the exception. We feel strongly that a programmer, when faced with a programming task, should start looking for existing software parts instead of starting to write.

Consider the steps routinely taken in the design and fabrication of digital electronic components:

☐ Obtain specifications: These could include the function of the components in terms of inputs and outputs, the required speed, size, power consumption, and logic type.

☐ Search catalogs: Catalogs of components, usually integrated circuits or chips, are searched until the right set of parts can be located.

☐ Order parts.

☐ Design interconnections.

☐ Build a bench model; test and refine.

☐ Obtain printed circuit boards or wire wrap boards.

☐ Fabricate in pilot quantities.

☐ Redesign to reduce costs and improve performance, possibly using customized components; produce new design for high-volume or critical items.

This is a good model of how programming should proceed in the future with a software parts technology. Only in the case of a high-volume item (or when extreme performance is needed) would the designer consider fabricating new components. The designer is not building chips and is not operating at the level of discrete components. The parts are at a higher functional level. This comparison is explored in more detail in [Comer *et al.*, 1980] and [Wasserman and Gutz, 1982].

5.1.3 Requirements

In order for a software parts technology to become useful, at least three features have to be present:

1. a large supply of useful, reliable parts;
2. a catalog of parts, making them easy to locate and evaluate; and
3. a mechanism for putting parts together to form more complex objects.

There must also be economic justification; if programming based on software parts catches on, it will be because it makes sense economically.

We can evaluate MATH and UNIX with respect to these requirements. For MATH:

1. The libraries provide a large supply of reliable parts within the area of mathematical and statistical applications.
2. The MATH documentation lists and describes each routine well.
3. The interconnection scheme is not part of the library; interconnection is accomplished by writing a main (or driver) program.

For UNIX:

1. The UNIX library of commands and programs constitutes a fairly exten-sive set of parts; these meet a large variety of needs in several areas, including text handling, data handling, and interactive inquiry.
2. The UNIX programmer's manual is a comprehensive list of all programs; it is usually on-line and augmented with a KWIC index.
3. The pipe mechanism described above serves as the interconnection scheme; the major limitation of the pipe is that it is limited to transmitting a single stream of characters.

5.2 INTERFACES: EXISTING AND POTENTIAL

5.2.1 Framework

We have mentioned a number of nascent software parts environments and their related interfaces. These interfaces can be classified by when the inter-face is checked and what type of checking is done; existing examples are shown in Table 5.1.

Semantic checking at compile time is difficult because it requires all code and data objects to be present. Furthermore, certain semantic checks cannot be made in advance of executing or pseudoexecuting the program. We believe that very little semantic checking will be done at compile time, and we know of no current example of this being done.

Semantic checking is more feasible at load time, when all the code is present and one can check that the arguments to all procedures form well-posed computations. That is, one not only verifies that procedure arguments are individually of the correct type, but also that the combination of types and attributes satisfies certain constraints. Still, this checking is necessarily incomplete and requires additional facilities in the loader. Indeed, it is not clear that such checking is more than sophisticated syntax checking.

Note that, with detailed checking and many data attributes, it is infeasible to have strong type checking in the sense that a single procedure accepts

TABLE 5.1
THE TIMES AND TYPES OF INTERFACE CHECKS WITH EXAMPLES

	Type of Checking	
	Syntax	Semantic
When done		
Compile-time	Pascal	—
Load-time	Ada	—
Run-time	Intel 432	Protran

only a single combination of types and attributes. Consider a matrix multiply procedure and the possible choices for type of elements (real, integer, etc.), precision of elements, precision of product, row size, and column size. If each procedure could handle just one combination, 400,000 distinct procedures would be required just to handle real matrices of size 20 by 20 or less and 10 or less digits of precision. However, for example, it is feasible to check at load time whether the product precision is less than or equal to each of the two input precisions.

We will not discuss the details of all the mechanisms of checking shown in Table 5.1. The facilities of Pascal and Ada are very widely known; those of the Intel 432 are discussed in [Intel, 1982]. We discuss the Protran example [Aird and Rice, 1983], as it is a newer and less widely known system.

5.2.2 Semantic Checking at Run Time

The Protran system [Aird and Rice, 1983] is an extension of Fortran that adds numerous problem-solving capabilities to Fortran. It uses as software parts about 100 of the programs from the IMSL library. These parts are invoked internally so that many syntactic-matching problems are avoided; the system uses the syntax to select the appropriate software parts so that the matching is automatically correct. If the syntax is incorrectly specified, then the language processor catches the error and there is no attempt to use a software part. A simple example of Protran code follows:

```
$DECLARATIONS
    VECTOR Y(4), YSTART(4), F(4)
    MATRIX TABLEY(50,4)
$ASSIGN YSTART = (0,-1.0,1.0,3.1415926)
$DIFEQU Y' = F(T,Y); ON(1.0,10.0); INITIAL = YSTART
    ERRTARGET = .0001; NOUTPUT = 91; SOLUTION = TABLEY
    DEFINE
    ====
    F(1) = Y(1) - T*Y(2) + SIN(T*Y(3))
    F(2) = Y(2)*Y(3) - COS(T*Y(1) - Y(4))
    F(3) = EXP(-Y(3)*T)*T*Y(4)
    F(4) = COS(Y(1)*Y(4)*T) - SIN(Y(2)*Y(3)*5)
    ====
$PRINT TABLEY
$END
```

Protran does further checking at run time and formally identifies two types of run-time errors: problem formulation and numerical. A *problem formulation error* occurs where the problem setup is incorrect. For example, one might have specified a solution of three differential equations but given a vector of initial conditions only of length 2. Or one might have SUM F(X); FOR(X = A,B,STEP) when STEP has the value 0 (or STEP = −0.1 and A is larger than *B*). A *numerical error* occurs where the algorithm in the software part fails. For example, if one asks for a solution of the linear system $AX = B$ for a matrix A and vectors X and B and if the matrix A is singular, then Protran sets an error condition and marks X as undefined.

The Protran system provides three options for action when a problem formulation or numerical error occurs: ignore, warn, or abort. The first two are primarily for use in experimental codes; the default action is to abort the computation.

5.3 AN INTERFACE SPECIFICATION STRUCTURE

In this section we present a detailed proposal for a general structure for interface specification. This structure allows for all the checking discussed above and provides a balance between flexibility, efficiency, and completeness. Several examples are given. Realistic testing of this structure has not been made.

The encoding of the interface information has two conflicting objectives: It should be efficient and it should be extendible to arbitrarily complex data structures. One danger is that one might need something like 27 bytes to indicate that the following byte is a character. We propose a treelike interface structure that

- [ ] allows simple data items to be specified simply,
- [ ] explicitly exhibits the information that can be used for type checking at compile or load time,
- [ ] allows one to specify many complex data structures in terms of existing simpler ones, and
- [ ] provides complete generality for data structures.

5.3.1 Definition of the Structure

The specification structure has three conceptual levels:

Level 1: $<$type$>$ + $<$L1$>$ + $<$size$>$
Level 2: $<$length$>$ + $<$L2$>$ + $<$data structure$>$ + $<$qualifier$>$
Level 3: $<$data$>$

We assume that the computing environment uses bytes; other hardware can be accommodated by packing or by replacing bytes by words. The elements on each level are defined as follows: First of all,

$<$type$>$ = one of a small set of basic data types encoded
into one byte.

This is usually the type of the lowest-level element in the data structure. We suggest that the types should be

> CHARACTER
> BIT
> BLANK
> LIST
> INTEGER
> REAL
> MIXED

The MIXED type is for more complex data structures whose specifications are given at the second level. The BLANK type is to specify that the second-level data have been checked already and found to be correct, even though the second-level specification is not detailed. This type is intended for situations where efficiency requires that data not be moved or reformatted unnecessarily. The LIST type is for a list of items, each of which is specified at a lower level.

Other elements are defined as follows:

$< L1 > =$ 0 or 1. Zero means that the size of the data (in bytes) is given by $<$size$>$. One means that the size of the data is given by the integer in the next $<$size$>$ bytes of the level 1 specifications.

$< size > =$ an integer whose function was just described.

$< length > =$ an integer, the number of bytes in the remainder of the second-level specification.

$< L2 > =$ 0 if the data structure is encoded in $<$ data structure $>$ as a standard data structure.

$< data structure > =$ an integer. If $< L2 > = 0$, this integer encodes one of the 128 standard data structures; otherwise this integer specifies the number of following bytes that give the name of the nonstandard data structure as a character string.

It seems that 128 is more than enough standard data structures, but the list is perhaps longer than one might initially guess. For example, the standard data structures should include the following:

1-D-ARRAY	BINARY-TREE	PROCEDURE-TEXT	LIST
2-D-ARRAY	NAME-LIST	PROCEDURE-OBJECT-CODE	CODE-SEGMENT
3-D-ARRAY	MATRIX	EXPRESSION-TEXT	DIRECTORY
UNASSIGNED	VECTOR	FILE	ARGUMENT-LIST
QUEUE	STACK	HEAP	BIT-MAP

This illustrates the need for many data structures beyond the usual ones.

<qualifiers> = a set of information that is appropriate
for the given data structure.

The length of the qualifiers is not fixed. For example, the qualifiers for
1-D-ARRAY could be name, lower index bound, lower index range, upper
index range, and upper index bound; the qualifiers for MATRIX could be
name, storage format, property, number of rows, number of columns, row
range, and column range; and the qualifiers for NAME_LIST could be name,
number of pairs, name lengths, and value lengths.

In addition to the normal qualifying information, every data type also
has two final special qualifiers for more complex data structures. The next-
to-last qualifier allows one to replace the normal element specification by a
new specification using the two levels of the structure defined here. The last
qualifier is an integer that specifies the number of qualifiers added to the data
structure.

<data> = The actual data. As illustrated below, this structure
is recursive, so that the data may contain
combinations of data structures specified by the two
levels of the interface structure.

5.3.2 Six Examples

It is tedious to illustrate all the possible combinations of these definitions,
but we give six example specifications of data: (1) two real numbers, (2) a
complex composite data structure, (3) a tree of real, positive-definite band
matrices, (4) a matrix with elements of a binary tree of character strings, (5)
the argument list for a procedure, and (6) the list of arguments for the same
procedure, plus a list of names associated with the tree. We use a verbose
form of the specification to make the examples more readable.

EXAMPLE 1

Two real numbers, 1.321 and 48.695.

Level 1: REAL + 0 + 2
Level 2: 0
Level 3: .1321E + 1, .48695E + 2

EXAMPLE 2

A general region in a rectangular domain with a set of grid lines. This example
originates from a system for solving partial differential equations. The interface
specifications consist of two real procedures with two real arguments, one two-

dimensional integer array, three one-dimensional real arrays, two one-dimensional integer arrays, and one one-dimensional character array. This is an example of a special data structure created within our interface definition structure.

Level 1: OTHER + 0 + 1

Level 2: 33 + 1 + 11 + "REGION-GRID", "DOMAIN 6B",
        <I1>, <I2>, . . . , <I9>, 1, 0

Level 3: <D1>, <D2>, . . . , <D9>

The 33 on level 2 specifies there are 31 bytes after the 11 which, in turn, specifies that "REGION-GRID" has 11 characters. Here <I1>, <I2>, and so on are single-byte codes for the nine elements of the data structure. If <I1>, <I2> =   X, C for the X procedure and the character array, then <D1>is the data specification

REAL + 0 + 1
12 + 0 + PROCEDURE + "X6B", 2, REAL, REAL, OBJECT, 812, 0, 0
(812 bytes of machine code)

and <D2> is the specification

CHARACTER + 0 + 1
13 + 0 + 1-D-ARRAY + "TYPES", 0, 0, 98, 250, 0, 0
(98 character strings)

EXAMPLE 3

A binary tree BMAT of depth 5 of real, positive definite, band matrices of order 40, range 20, and bandwidth 5.

REAL + 1 + 1
7 + 0 + BINARY-TREE + "BMAT", 5, 1, 0
REAL + 0 + 63
10 + 0 + MATRIX + " ", 40, 20, 5, 5, POSITIVE DEFINITE, 0, 0
(63 matrices = 27,720 real numbers)

EXAMPLE 4

A band matrix BMB of order 40, range 20, and bandwidth 5 of each consisting of a 63 character string and a six character string.

LIST + 0 + 1
13 + 0 + MATRIX + BAND, "BMB", 0, 5, 5, 40, 20, 2, 0
CHARACTER + 0 +. 440
6 + 0 + LIST + " ", 2, 0, 0
(440 entries, each consisting of a 63 character string and a six character string = 30,360 character strings)

EXAMPLE 5

The argument list for the linear equation solver M_SOLVE is of the form
MATRIX = <name>, SOLUTION = <name>, RIGHT_SIDE = <name>,
ORDER = <integer expression>, ACCURACY = <keyword>. The specification
of this argument list is

LIST + 0 + 0
15 + 0 + ARGUMENT-LIST + "M_SOLVE", 5, MATRIX, MATRIX,
MATRIX, INTEGER, CHARACTER, 0, 0

EXAMPLE 6

The set of arguments for M_SOLVE could be specified alternatively by separating
the five arguments and providing more detail about each of them. The specification could then be

MIXED + 0 + 5
6 + 0 + LIST + " ", 5, 1, 0
REAL + 0 + 400
11 + 0 + MATRIX + "A", FULL, SYMMETRIC, 100, 100, 20, 20, 0, 0
(400 real numbers of the matrix A)
REAL + 0 + 1
10 + 0 + MATRIX + "A", FULL, 100, 10, 6, 0, 1, 0
REAL + 0 + 0
2 + 0 + UNASSIGNED
(No data for X, it is an output argument)
REAL + 0 + 40
15 + 0 + MATRIX + "B", FULL, 0, 100, 10, 20, 2, "FULL", 0, 0
(40 real numbers of the matrix B)
INTEGER + 0 + 1
0
20 (= the order of the linear system to be solved)
CHARACTER + 0 + 1
0
HIGHACC (= the keyword to request a high-accuracy solution)

5.4 PROBLEM FORMULATION CHECKING

The underlying concern of interface checking is that the user may make
mistakes in using the software. This concern is particularly high when large
numbers of software parts are invoked indirectly. Syntactic checking is the
simplest kind of checking and has the largest payoff. However, experience
shows that further checking is needed in order to provide really high reliability, and thus we have been led to the elaborate specification structure
presented in this paper and the related checking. We now carry this theme
forward to problem formulation checking. That is, we examine the entire set

of inputs to a software part to see if they define a well-posed computation. We illustrate the situation with the linear equation procedure M_SOLVE introduced in Example 5 of the previous section; similar situations occur in other computational areas.

Many software parts are somewhat generic in nature; for example, a part for sorting might sort integers, reals, or character strings. A more complex example is a part that solves linear systems of equations. Consider M_SOLVE, whose argument list was specified in Example 5. It is generic in the sense that it solves linear systems of different types (real, complex, or double precision). However, for the computation to make sense, the matrices involved must be compatible in size (the row ranges of A and B must agree and the row and column bounds of X must be as large as the row and column ranges of B). The checking of types might or might not be possible at compile time, but the compatibility in size can only be checked at run time when M_SOLVE is invoked with actual arguments.

The size compatibility checking is easily done by the prologue of M_SOLVE using the information given in the specification of Example 6. More subtle is the problem of checking the validity of the SYMMETRIC specification. Given this specification, the procedure M_SOLVE should use an algorithm that takes advantage of the symmetry to reduce the computational work by half. If the standard algorithms are used directly, there is no need for checking, since there is no failure if the matrix A is mismarked as symmetric. A robust software part would perform this checking anyway, at a reasonable computational cost. The work of solving a linear system is of the order of $N^3/6$ operations for an N-by-N matrix, while the checking requires work of the order $N^2/2$. Recall that the BLANK data type allows one to specify that a property like SYMMETRIC has already been checked and found to be present.

If the matrix A is specified to be positive definite, then an even more difficult checking problem arises. To check that A is actually positive definite is a computation equal to that of solving the linear system, and it is unreasonable for the part's prologue to check this property. If the Cholesky algorithm is used to solve the system, it will fail in a specific easily detectable way and no special check is needed. However, one might also use SOR iteration on the linear system, as this method always converges if A is positive definite. If A is not positive definite, then the iteration may continue indefinitely. This would, at least, eventually be identified as a failure and thus signal that the matrix A was not positive definite.

Of course, some matrix property specifications could (1) allow for very efficient solution of the system, (2) be very expensive to check, and (3) cause no obvious or easily computable failure condition to occur when the specification is not met. An example of such a property is TENSOR PRODUCT, for which ADI iteration is an extremely efficient solution method. Note that the naive test of substituting the computer solution into the linear system to see if the equations are satisfied is not a reliable checking procedure. However, more sophisticated versions of this approach (e.g., using sensitivity analysis) can provide high (but not complete) reliability.

It requires progressively more effort to provide higher and higher levels of reliability in the composition of software parts. Absolute reliability requires infinite effort in general, although it might be achievable in some small areas of computation. Those who strive for absolute reliability should be amused by the article [Davis, 1972] on the nature of mathematical proofs. Davis shows that even proving that the integer C is the sum of two given integers A and B is fraught with pitfalls.

5.5 TRADEOFFS IN INTERFACE CHECKS

5.5.1 Gains: Higher Reliability and Faster Software Production

The primary goal of a software parts technology is faster and cheaper software production. The goal of an elaborate interface specification structure is to achieve high reliability also. These goals are justified, and we believe that the interface structure proposed here allows one to achieve high reliability. We make two additional points: (1) There is an important situation when interface checking and its attendant costs are not required for high reliability, and (2) the economy in software production is for the users of software parts, not the creators.

Interface checking is needed when a part must be designed for use everywhere and thus cannot trust that its input is correct. However, the input might be trusted when several software parts are composed to form a larger part. The principle of modular software construction leads to the component parts retaining their identity within the larger part, so we could have the epilogue of one part putting the output data into a particular form. Thus we visualize an optimization phase in software production where a new part is constructed and then redundant processing and checking at the interfaces is removed to improve efficiency. The structure of parts as *prologue + nucleus + epilogue* facilitates this optimization.

One should expect a reusable software part to cost 5 or 10 times as much to create as an instance of it in a particular application. A software part must be designed, created, and validated for general use; a specific instance needs only be correct in a narrow scope of one application. A software part must be documented so that users from widely different backgrounds can understand what it does and how to use it; a specific instance needs only be documented within one context. A software part must have its performance measured systematically and this information (along with much more) put into a catalog entry; a specific instance often does not have its performance measured at all. We believe that a common source of inadequate software parts has been code lifted from a particular application and stamped as general-purpose with only superficial changes.

5.5.2 Costs: Bulkier Data, Interface Overhead, and Slower Execution

There is no doubt that reliability will cost more; the question is how much more. Interface overhead manifests itself as slower execution, so the costs are in the use of more memory and more CPU time. We believe the extra memory costs are modest but that the extra CPU time costs are not. We discuss tactics to minimize the costs of reliability but note that these costs are inherently high. However, they are no higher in a software parts technology than elsewhere.

In programs built from reusable parts, data becomes bulkier because it is tagged with information to be used in checking. For a single number, this might double or triple the memory required. However, most bulky data is of some very systematic nature (e.g., a vector of 10,000 real numbers or a file of 10,000 identically structured records). The interface specification structure presented here allows one to tag these data all at once and with a small penalty in memory. It is true that one could be very inefficient here, but we do not expect this tagging to increase memory requirements significantly.

The overhead of interface checking can be significant. All one has to do is to put two or three small parts in the inner loop of some major computation, and one can easily arrange to spend 50 to 90 percent of the CPU time in interfacing checking. This cost might be perfectly acceptable in prototype code development but totally unacceptable in a production code; in between, the interface overhead could perhaps be removed as discussed earlier. Interface overhead that cannot be removed by optimization is probably essential to the reliability of the software, and other approaches are liable to be just as costly. For example, in the inner loop example just mentioned, if previously unseen external data enters that must be checked, then one cannot optimize away the checking and retain reliability.

The following statement is supported by much observed evidence:

Expect to pay as much to check the correctness of an answer as to obtain the answer in the first place.

There are gross exceptions to this statement in both directions, but it underscores that run-time checking of problem formulation and solution correctness should be expected to be costly. Such costs are very high, for example, in the solution of differential equations. These problems permeate programs for control (e.g., in robots, refineries, airplanes, and nuclear power plants) and the best efforts so far have not been able to check correctness in as little time as it takes to solve the problem.

5.5.3 Timing: Compile Time, Load Time, or Run Time?

As a general principle, one should do checking as early as possible. Thus the compiler should check as much as it can, but since it usually does not process either the whole program or its data, there is only so much it can do. The loader has access to all the subprograms of a program, so it can complete some syntactic checking left undone by the compiler. Still, much checking should be done at run time, and this checking is potentially the most expensive. One cannot check the validity of the input to a linear equation solver unless one has the input and attempts to solve the system.

In more and more computing environments, what appears to the user as run time includes pieces of compile time and load time. An interpretative language often translates the input into an internal code before executing the program; some checking could be done during the language translation instead of during execution. Other systems have multiple levels of language processing; one can realistically visualize systems with four languages (e.g., ELLPACK to PROTRAN to Fortran 77 to C) where various semantic and syntactic checking is appropriate for each one.

R EFERENCES

Aird, T. J., and Rice, J. R. PROTRAN: Problem solving software. *Advances in Engineering Software* 5:202–206, 1983.

Batz, J.; Cohen, P.; Redwine, S.; and Rice, J. The application specific task area. *IEEE Computer* 16:78–85, 1983.

Bell System Technical Journal. UNIX time-sharing system. Special issue. Vol. 57, no. 2, July–August, 1978.

Comer, D.; Rice, J.; Schwetman, H.; and Snyder, L. Project quanta. CSD-TR 366, Computer Science Department, Purdue University, 1980.

Cowell, W. R. *Sources and Development of Mathematical Software*. Englewood Cliffs, N.J.: Prentice-Hall, 1984.

Davis, P. J. Fidelity in mathematical discourse: Is one and one really two? *American Mathematical Monthly* 79:252–263, 1972.

IMSL, Inc. *Library Reference Manual*. Houston, 1987.

Intel Corp. *Intel 432 Reference Manual*. 1982.

NAG, Ltd. *Library Reference Manual*. Oxford, England, 1986.

Rice, J. R. *Mathematical Software*. New York: Academic Press, 1971.

Scientific Enterprises, Inc. *XM-80 vl. 2 Language Reference Manual*. Wilsonville, Ore., 1981.

United States Department of Defense. *Software Technology for Adaptive, Reliable Systems (STARS): Program Strategy*. 1 April, 1983.

Wasserman, A. I., and Gutz, S. The future of programming. *Communications of the ACM* 25:196–206, 1982.

CHAPTER 6

ENHANCING REUSABILITY WITH INFORMATION HIDING

D. L. PARNAS
Queen's University

P. C. CLEMENTS[*]
Naval Research Laboratory

D. M. WEISS
Software Productivity Consortium

6.1 INTRODUCTION

A number of reasons are commonly cited for not reusing software. Among them are these:

1. The specifications of the software are either nonexistent or sufficiently ambiguous so that it is not possible to determine exactly what the software does without examining all of the source code. However, if the software is complex enough to make reusability attractive, then it is complex enough to thwart any effort to specify its behavior in this fashion.

2. The software performs a specialized task that resembles the required task, but the cost of changing the software to perform the required task is greater than the cost of writing new software.

From *ITT Proceedings of the Workshop on Reusability in Programming*, Newport, R.I., 1983. Reprinted with permission of the authors.

[*] On leave, at the Computer Science Department, University of Texas at Austin.

3. Although the software to perform the required task may exist, nobody on the new project knows about it or those who know of its existence don't know how to find it.

4. Software that can perform the required task is available, but it is so general that it is too inefficient for the task.

In this paper we show how a well-known software design principle ameliorates this situation. The next section discusses the principles that guide our design. We then present a complete picture of software that is being built according to these principles. In a concluding section, we discuss the above problems in reusing software and show how our design supports reusability.

6.2 BACKGROUND AND GUIDING PRINCIPLES

The unit of software that we would like to be able to reuse is the *module*. In our terminology a module is a work assignment for a programmer or programmer team. Each module consists of a group of closely related programs. The module structure of a system is the decomposition of the program into modules and, for each, the assumptions that the teams responsible for other modules are allowed to make about it. We call the set of assumptions for each module the *interface* to the module.

The overall goal of the decomposition into modules is reduction of software development and maintenance cost by allowing modules to be designed, implemented, and revised independently. These properties are synonymous with reusability. Specific goals of the module decomposition are the following:

1. Each module's structure should be simple enough that it can be understood fully.

2. It should be possible to change the implementation of one module without knowledge of the implementation of other modules and without affecting the behavior of other modules.

3. The ease of making a change in the design should bear a reasonable relationship to the likelihood of the change being needed. It should be possible to make likely changes without changing any module interfaces; less likely changes may involve interface changes, but only for modules that are small and not widely used. Only very unlikely changes should require changes in the interfaces of widely used modules. There should be few widely used interfaces.

4. It should be possible to make a major software change as a set of independent changes to individual modules; that is, except for interface changes, programmers changing the individual modules should not need to communicate. If the interfaces of the modules are not revised, it should be possible to run and test any combination of old and new module versions.

In keeping with the goals above, the software design we present in Section 6.3 is composed of many small modules. They have been organized into a tree-structured hierarchy; each nonterminal node in the tree represents a module that is composed of smaller modules, which are represented by the node's descendants. The hierarchy is intended to achieve the following additional goals:

5. A software engineer should be able to understand the responsibility of a module without understanding the module's internal design.
6. A reader with a well-defined concern should easily be able to identify the relevant modules without studying irrelevant modules. This requires that the reader be able to distinguish relevant modules from irrelevant modules without looking at their internal structure.

Design Principle

Our module structure is based on the decomposition criterion known as information hiding [Parnas, 1972]. According to this principle, system details that are likely to change independently should be the secrets of separate modules; the only assumptions that should appear in the interfaces between modules are those that are considered unlikely to change. For example, every data structure is private to one module; it may be directly accessed by one or more programs within the module but not by programs outside the module. Any other program that requires information stored in a module's data structures must obtain it by calling programs on the module's interface.

Applying this principle is not always easy. It attempts to minimize the expected cost of software over its period of use and requires that the designer estimate the likelihood of changes. Such estimates are based on past experience and usually require knowledge of the application area[1] as well as an understanding of hardware and software technology.

In large systems, it is important to classify potential changes. One can always classify them as changes to accommodate new hardware, changes in required behavior, or changes in implementation details independent of the first two. Some actions may require changes of two or three types. The structure we illustrate in this paper is appropriate for many other applications. Later projects have found it useful to start with this structure and modify the lower levels to fit their own detailed requirements.

Module Description

Three ways to describe a module structure based on information hiding are (1) by the *roles* played by the individual modules in the overall system operation, (2) by the *secrets* associated with each module, and (3) by the *facilities*

---

[1]This is sometimes called *domain analysis*.

provided by each module. Our module guide describes the module structure by characterizing each module's secrets. Where useful, we also include a brief description of the role of the module. The description of facilities is relegated to the module specifications (e.g., [Parker *et al.*, 1980]). Each module has a precise abstract specification that tells exactly what the module does. The module guide tells which module(s) will require a change. The module specification tells how to use that module.

For some modules we find it useful to distinguish between a *primary secret*, which is hidden information that was specified to the software designer, and a *secondary secret*, which arises from implementation decisions made by the designer.

Although we have attempted to make the decomposition rules as precise as possible, the possibility of future changes in technology makes some of the boundaries fuzzy. Some sections of the module guide point out fuzzy areas and discuss additional information that must be used to resolve ambiguities.

Illustrating Solutions to Complex Problems

Most of the problems of software design are problems of scale. Problems that are insignificant for small programs can be overwhelming for large ones. Reusability is just such an issue. With a library of 20 programs, there is no real problem reusing something if it is there. With 20,000 programs, the problem is obvious.

To show how our techniques work, we give a fairly large extract from our module guide [Britton and Parnas, 1981] in Section 6.3. The design we present is the module structure of the A-7E flight software produced by the Naval Research Laboratory. NRL is completely rebuilding this software to demonstrate and evaluate modern software engineering techniques. The A-7E flight software is a hard-real-time program that processes flight data and controls complicated displays for the pilot. It computes the aircraft position using an inertial navigation system and must be highly accurate. The current operational system is one big module. It is very difficult to identify the sections of the program that must be changed when certain requirements change. Our software is structured to meet the goals mentioned earlier but must still meet all accuracy and real-time constraints.

6.3 A-7E MODULE STRUCTURE

Top-Level Decomposition

The software system consists of the three modules described below.

1. Hardware-Hiding Module. The Hardware-Hiding Module includes the programs that need to be changed if any part of the hardware is replaced by a new unit with a different hardware/software interface but with the same

general capabilities. This module implements *virtual hardware*, abstract devices that are used by the rest of the software. The primary secrets of this module are the hardware/software interfaces described in chapters 1 and 2 of the requirements document.[2]

The secondary secrets of this module are the data structures and algorithms used to implement the virtual hardware.

2. Behavior-Hiding Module.

The Behavior-Hiding Module includes programs that need to be changed if there are changes in the sections of the requirements document that describe the required behavior. The content of those sections is the primary secret of this module. These programs determine the values to be sent to the virtual output devices provided by the Hardware-Hiding Module.

3. Software Decision Module.

The Software Decision Module hides software design decisions that are based upon mathematical theorems, physical facts, and programming considerations such as algorithmic efficiency and accuracy. The secrets of this module are not described in the requirements document. This module differs from the other modules in that both the secrets and the interfaces are determined by software designers. Changes in this module are more likely to be motivated by a desire to improve performance than by externally imposed changes.

Notes on the Top-Level Decomposition

Fuzziness in the above classifcations is unavoidable for the following reasons:

1. The line between requirements definition and software design has been determined in part by decisions made when the requirements documents are written; for example, weapon trajectory models may be chosen by system analysts and specified in the requirements document, or they may be left to the discretion of the software designers.
2. The line between hardware characteristics and software design may vary. Hardware can be built to perform some of the services currently performed by the software; consequently, certain modules can be viewed either as modules that hide hardware characteristics or as modules that hide software design decisions.
3. Changes in the hardware or in the behavior of the system or its users may make a software design decision less appropriate.
4. All software modules include software design decisions; changes in any module may be motivated by efficiency or accuracy considerations.

[2]See [Heninger *et al.*, 1978]. These chapters define the host computer for the program and the software interfaces of all the input and output devices with which the program must interact.

To reduce the fuzziness, we have based our decomposition on the current requirements document. In particular:

1. The line between requirements and software design is defined by our requirements document. When the requirements document specifies an algorithm, we do not consider the design of the algorithm to be a software design decision. If the requirements document only states requirements that the algorithm must meet, we consider the program that implements that algorithm to be part of the Software Decision Module.

2. The line between hardware characteristics and software design is based on estimates of the likelihood of future changes. For example, if it is reasonably likely that future hardware will implement a particular facility, the software module that implements that facility is classified as a hardware-hiding module; otherwise, the module is considered a software design module. In most cases we have taken a conservative stance; the design is based on the assumption that drastic changes are less likely than evolutionary changes.

3. A module is included in the Software Decision Module only if it would remain correct, albeit less efficient, when there are changes in the requirements document.

4. A module will be included in the Software Decision Module only if its secrets do not include information documented in the software requirements document.

Second-Level Decomposition

1. Hardware-Hiding Module

The Hardware-Hiding Module comprises two modules.

1.1. Extended Computer Module. The Extended Computer Module hides those characteristics of the hardware/software interface of the avionics computer that we consider likely to change if the computer is modified or replaced.

Avionics computers differ greatly in their hardware/software interfaces and in the capabilities that are implemented directly in the hardware. Some avionics computers include a hardware approximation of real numbers, while others perform approximate real number operations by a programmed sequence of fixed-point operations. Some avionics systems include a single processor; some systems provide several processors. The Extended Computer provides an instruction set that can be implemented efficiently on most avionics computers. This instruction set includes the operations on application-independent data types, sequence control operations, and general I/O operations. The Extended Computer is a multiprocessor but may also serve as a single processor.

The primary secrets of the Extended Computer are the number of processors, the instruction set of the computer, the processor state transitions, the processor-addressing restrictions, and the processor's self-test capabilities.

The structure of the Extended Computer Module is given under "Third-Level Decomposition."

1.2 Device Interface Module.   The Device Interface Module hides the peripheral device characteristics that are considered likely to change. Each device might be replaced by an improved device capable of accomplishing the same tasks. Replacement devices differ widely in their hardware/software interfaces. For example, all angle-of-attack sensors measure angle-of-attack, but they differ in input format, timing, and the amount of noise in the data.

The Device Interface Module provides virtual devices to be used by the rest of the software. The virtual devices do not necessarily correspond one-to-one to physical devices because all of the hardware providing a capability is not necessarily in one physical unit. Further, there are some capabilities of a physical unit that are likely to change independently of others; it is advantageous to hide characteristics that may change independently in different modules.

The primary secrets of the Device Interface Module are those characteristics of the present devices documented in the requirements document and not likely to be shared by replacement devices.

The structure of the Device Interface Module is given under "Third-Level Decomposition."

Notes on the Hardware-Hiding Module Decomposition

Our distinction between computer and device is based on the current hardware and is the one made in the requirements document. Information that applies to more than one device is considered a secret of the Extended Computer; information that is only relevant to one device is a secret of a Device Interface Module. For example, an analog-to-digital converter is used for communicating with several devices; it is hidden by the Extended Computer although it could be viewed as an external device. As another example, there are special outputs for testing the I/O channels; they are not associated with a single device. These too are hidden by the Extended Computer.

If all the hardware were replaced simultaneously, there might be a significant shift in responsibilities between computer and devices. In systems like the A-7E such changes are unusual; the replacement of individual devices or the replacement of the computer alone is more likely. Our design is based on the expectation that this pattern of replacement will continue to hold.

2. Behavior-Hiding Module

The Behavior-Hiding Module consists of two modules: a Function Driver Module supported by a Shared Services Module.

2.1 Function Driver Module.   The Function Driver Module consists of a set of modules called function drivers; each function driver is the sole controller of a set of closely related outputs. The outputs are either part of a virtual device or provided by the Extended Computer for test purposes. The primary secrets of the Function Driver Module are the rules determining the values of these outputs.

The structure of the Function Driver Module is given under "Third-Level Decomposition."

2.2 Shared Services Module.   Because all the function drivers control systems in the same aircraft, some aspects of the behavior are common to several function drivers. We expect that if there is a change in that aspect of the behavior, it will affect all of the functions that share it. Consequently we have identified a set of modules, each of which hides an aspect of the behavior that applies to two or more of the outputs.

The structure of the Shared Services Module is found under "Third-Level Decomposition."

Notes on the Behavior-Hiding Module Decomposition

Because users of the documentation cannot be expected to know which aspects of a function's behavior are shared, the documentation for each function driver will include a reference to the Shared Services Module that it uses. A maintenance programmer should always begin his inquiry with the appropriate function driver. He will be directed to the Shared Services Module when appropriate.

3. Software Decision Module

The Software Decision Module has been divided into (1) the Application Data Type Module, which hides the implementation of certain variables, (2) the Data Banker Module, which hides the data-updating policies, (3) the Filter Behavior Module, which hides models of physical filters, (4) the Physical Models Module, which hides algorithms that simulate physical phenomena, (5) the Software Utility Module, which hides algorithms that are used in several other modules, and (6) the System Generation Module, which hides decisions that are postponed until system generation time.

3.1 Application Data Type Module.   The Application Data Type Module supplements the data types provided by the Extended Computer Module with data types that are useful for avionics applications and do not require a computer-dependent implementation. These data types are implemented using the data types provided by the Extended Computer; variables of these types are used just as if the types were built into the Extended Computer.

The secrets of the Application Data Type Module are the data representation used in the variables and the programs used to implement operations on those variables. Units of measurement are part of the representation and are hidden. Where necessary, the modules provide conversion operators, which deliver or accept real values in specified units.

The structure of the Application Data Type Module is given in the section on third-level decomposition.

3.2 Data Banker Module.   Most data are produced by one module and consumed by another. In most cases, the consumers should receive a value as up-to-date as practical. The time at which a datum should be recalculated is determined both by properties of its consumer (e. g. , accuracy requirements) and by properties of its producer (e. g. , cost of calculation, rate of change of value). The Data Banker Module acts as a middleman and determines when new values for these data are computed. The Data Banker obtains values from producer programs; consumer programs obtain data from Data Banker access programs. The producer and consumers of a particular datum can be written without knowing whether or not the Data Banker stores the value or when a stored value is updated. In most cases, neither the producer nor the consumer need be modified if the updating policy changes.

The Data Banker provides values for all data that report on the internal state of a module or on the state of the aircraft. It also reports events involving changes in the values that it supplies. The Data Banker is used as long as consumer and producer are separate modules, even when they are both submodules of a larger module. The Data Banker is not used if consumers require specific members of the sequence of values computed by the producer, or if a produced value is solely a function of the values of input parameters given to the producing program.

The choice among updating policies should be based on the consumers' accuracy requirements, how often consumers require the value, the maximum wait that consumers can accept, how rapidly the value changes, and the cost of producing a new value. This information is part of the specification given to the implementor of the Data Banker.

The structure of the Data Banker Module is given under "Third-Level Decomposition."

3.3 Filter Behavior Module.   The Filter Behavior Module contains digital models of physical filters. They can be used by other programs to filter potentially noisy data. The primary secrets of this module are the models used for the estimation of values based on sample values and error estimates. The secondary secrets are the computer algorithms and data structures used to implement those models.

3.4 Physical Models Module.   The software requires estimates of quantities that cannot be measured directly but can be computed from observables using mathematical models. The primary secrets of the Physical Models Module are the models; the secondary secrets are the computer implementations of those models.

The structure of the Physical Models Module is given under "Third-Level Decomposition."

3.5 Software Utility Module.

The Software Utility Module contains those utility routines that would otherwise have to be written by more than one other module. The routines include mathematical functions, resource monitors, and programs that signal when all modules have completed their power-up initializations.

Because users of the documentation cannot be expected to know which routines are used by more than one module, the documentation of the using modules will always contain references to the Software Utility Module.

The secrets of the module are the data structures and algorithms used to implement the programs.

3.6 System Generation Module.

The primary secrets of the System Generation Module are decisions that are postponed until system generation time. These include the values of system generation parameters and the choice among alternative implementations of a module. The secondary secrets of the System Generation Module are the method used to generate a machine-executable form of the code and the representation of the postponed decisions. The programs in this module do not run on the on-board computer; they run on the computer used to generate the code for the on-board system.

The structure of the System Generation Module is given in the next section.

Third-Level Decomposition

Descriptions of lower-level modules are included in this section only when particularly illustrative. Missing module numbers indicate omissions. Figure 6.1 shows the complete module hierachy, down through the fourth level.

1. Hardware-Hiding Module

1.1 Extended Computer Module

1.1.1 Data Module.

The Data Module implements variables and operators for real numbers, time intervals, and bit strings. The primary secrets of this module are the data representations and the data-addressing and manipulation instructions built into the computer hardware. Specifically, the primary secrets are the representation of numeric objects in terms of hardware data types, the representation of bit strings, and the way bits are accessed within

FIGURE 6.1
THE A-7E SOFTWARE MODULE STRUCTURE

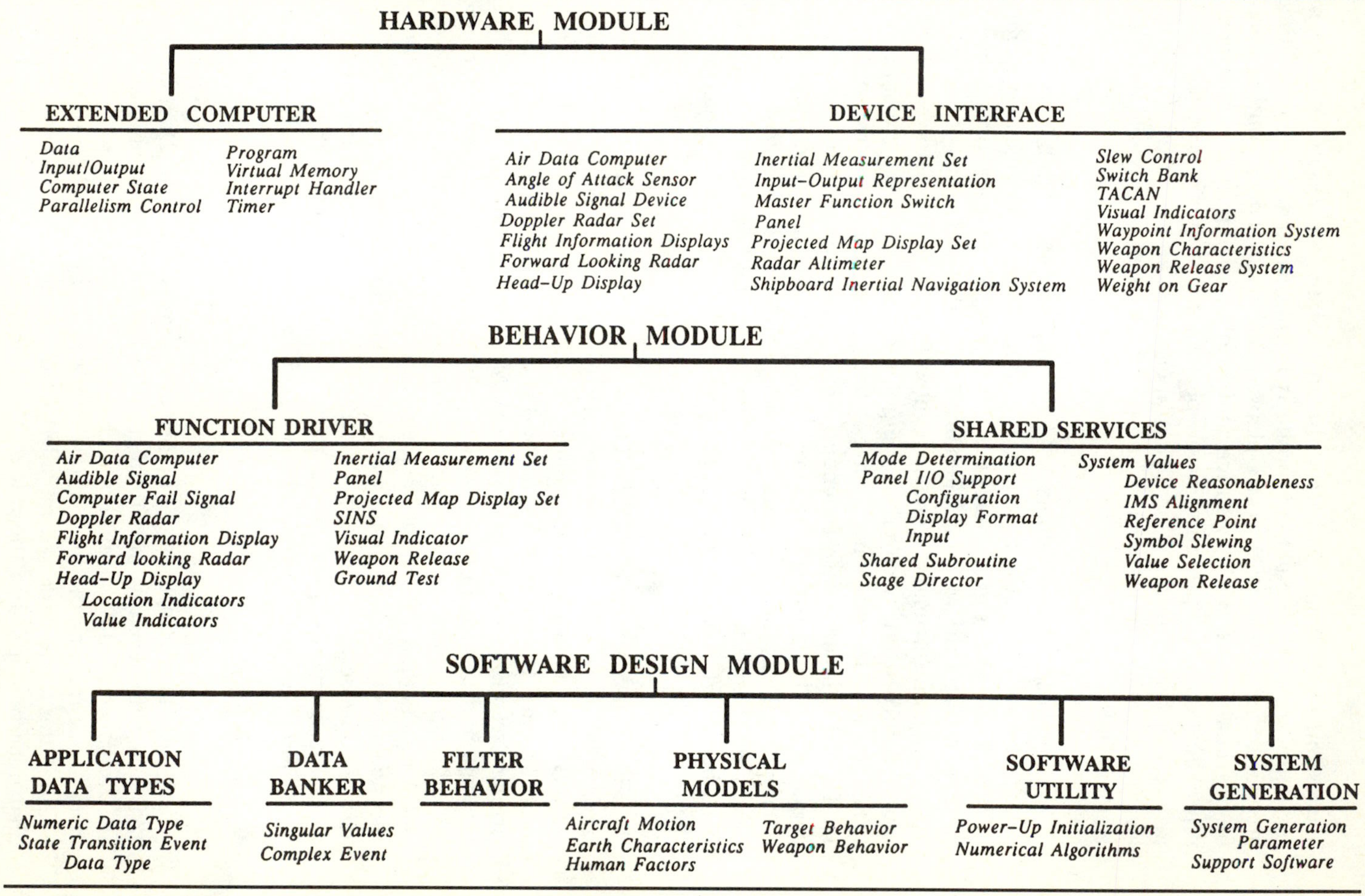

HARDWARE MODULE

EXTENDED COMPUTER

Data
Input/Output
Computer State
Parallelism Control
Program
Virtual Memory
Interrupt Handler
Timer

DEVICE INTERFACE

Air Data Computer
Angle of Attack Sensor
Audible Signal Device
Doppler Radar Set
Flight Information Displays
Forward Looking Radar
Head–Up Display
Inertial Measurement Set
Input–Output Representation
Master Function Switch
Panel
Projected Map Display Set
Radar Altimeter
Shipboard Inertial Navigation System
Slew Control
Switch Bank
TACAN
Visual Indicators
Waypoint Information System
Weapon Characteristics
Weapon Release System
Weight on Gear

BEHAVIOR MODULE

FUNCTION DRIVER

Air Data Computer
Audible Signal
Computer Fail Signal
Doppler Radar
Flight Information Display
Forward looking Radar
Head–Up Display
Location Indicators
Value Indicators
Inertial Measurement Set
Panel
Projected Map Display Set
SINS
Visual Indicator
Weapon Release
Ground Test

SHARED SERVICES

Mode Determination
Panel I/O Support
Configuration
Display Format
Input
Shared Subroutine
Stage Director
System Values
Device Reasonableness
IMS Alignment
Reference Point
Symbol Slewing
Value Selection
Weapon Release

SOFTWARE DESIGN MODULE

APPLICATION DATA TYPES

Numeric Data Type
State Transition Event
Data Type

DATA BANKER

Singular Values
Complex Event

FILTER BEHAVIOR

PHYSICAL MODELS

Aircraft Motion
Earth Characteristics
Human Factors
Target Behavior
Weapon Behavior

SOFTWARE UTILITY

Power–Up Initialization
Numerical Algorithms

SYSTEM GENERATION

System Generation
Parameter
Support Software

a bit string. The primary secrets also include the representation of times for hardware timers, but the module is unconcerned with how the timers are started or how they measure elapsed real time. The secondary secrets of this module are the way range and resolution requirements determine representation, the procedures for performing numeric operations, the procedures for performing bit string operations, and the way the memory location of an array element is computed given the array name and the element index.

1.1.4 Computer State Module. The Computer State Module keeps track of the current state of the Extended Computer, which can be either *operating, off,* or *failed,* and signals relevant state changes to user programs. The primary secret is the way that the hardware detects and signals state changes. Specifically, the primary secrets are how the hardware behaves when the power is turned on; what effect the go/no-go timer has on the state of the machine; how the hardware behaves when it enters malfunction states; how malfunctions in hardware functions are detected and reported; how many actual states the hardware has, and what hardware transitions are possible, what internal malfunctions cause transitions from *operating* to *failed;* and what causes transitions to *off* and to *operating.* After the Extended Computer has been initialized, this module signals the event that starts the initialization for the rest of the software.

1.1.8 Virtual Memory Module. The Virtual Memory Module presents a uniformly addressable virtual memory to the other Extended Computer submodules, allowing them to use virtual addresses for both data and subprograms. It provides diagnostic facilities for testing the memory. The primary secrets of the Virtual Memory Module are the hardware addresses for data and instructions, the various ways that different areas of memory are addressed, the way the memory tests are performed, the criteria used to judge results, and the timing characteristics that affect test evaluation. The secondary secrets of the module are the policy for allocating real memory to virtual addresses, the programs that translate from virtual address references to real instruction sequences, the parts of memory that are checked when a diagnostics program is run, and the algorithm used to check that memory.

1.2 Device Interface Module

1.2.1 Air Data Computer. The primary secrets of the Air Data Computer (ADC) are the way raw measurements are obtained for barometric altitude, true airspeed, and Mach number; the scale, offset, and format of the input data items; the way the built-in test operates and the method used to determine if the test was passed or failed; and the device-dependent operations that must be applied to the raw measurements from the device in order to produce correct barometric altitude, true airspeed, and Mach number.

1.2.2 Angle-of-Attack Sensor. The primary secrets of the Angle-of-Attack (AOA) Sensor are the method used to read angle of attack, the value encoding of the data words from the devices, the corrections applied by this module, and the circumstances under which the AOA is unreliable.

1.2.8 Head-Up Display. The primary secrets of the Head-Up Display (HUD) Module are the particular sequence of operations necessary to enable and positon the various HUD symbols; the scale and offset of the data words for numeric displays; the method used to generate the symbols, that is, which symbols are hardware produced and which are produced by software actions such as superimposing basic symbols; the reasons for restrictions on certain symbols, such as why the in-range cue and the lower-solution cue are exclusive, why the pull-up cue must flash when it is on, and why the flight path marker cannot be turned on unless the vertical velocity and acceleration displays are enabled; and the symbols that have hardware-controlled blinking.

The secondary secrets of this module are the method used to cause certain symbols to be removed from the display and the way the HUD test pattern is generated.

1.2.12 Master Function Switch. The Master Function Switch hides a suite of five switches and reports which is currently depressed. Its primary secret is the encoding of the data and the hardware interconnections and exclusions among the switches.

1.2.20 Weapon Release System. The primary secrets of the Weapon Release System are the method for causing weapons to be prepared and released; details of the armament release panel (ARP), armament station control unit, and pilot's grip stick hardware, such as operations necessary to perform certain functions and the encoding of values; the way that the ready and active weapon stations are identified; and the station priority scheme. The maximum settings of the ARP interval and quantity switch, and the number of stations and weapon types are secrets at program design and write time; the actual values are inserted during program assembly.

2. Behavior-Hiding Module

2.1 Function Driver Module

2.1.7 Head-Up Display. The primary secrets include where the movable HUD symbols should be placed; when a HUD symbol should be on, off, or blinking; and what information should be displayed on the fixed-position displays.

2.1.8 Inertial Measurement Set. The primary secrets include rules for what scale to use for the IMS velocity measurements, when to initialize the velocity measurements, and how much and when to rotate the IMS platform for alignment with real-world north, east, and vertical.

2.1.13 Weapon Release.   The primary secret of this module is the set of rules that determine when to prepare and release a weapon.

2.2 Shared Services Module

2.2.1 Mode Determination Module.   The Mode Determination Module determines the system modes, as defined in the requirements document, and the local modes (aliases for system modes), as defined in the individual function driver documents. It signals the occurrence of mode transitions and identifies the current modes. The primary secrets of the Mode Determination Module are the mode transition tables in the requirements document and the local mode definitions: what causes transitions among the requirements-defined modes. The secondary secrets of this module are the representation of the correspondence between defined mode names and the defining modes, the algorithm for signaling mode changes, and the representation of the mode transition criteria.

2.2.4 System Value Module.   The System Value Module computes a set of values. Although some values are used by more than one function driver, the module may include a value that is only used in one function driver if the rule used to calculate that value is the same as that used to calculate other shared values. The secrets of the System Value Module are the rules in the requirements for computing the values. The shared rules in the requirements specify such things as (1) selection among several alternative sources, (2) applying filters to values produced by other modules, or (3) imposing limits on a value calculated elsewhere. The Sytem Value Module is also responsible for signaling events that are defined in terms of the values it computes.

3. Software Decision Module

3.4 Physical Models Module

3.4.1 Aircraft Motion Module.   The Aircraft Motion Module hides models of the aircraft's motion, which are used to calculate aircraft position, velocity, and attitude from observable inputs. Secrets of the module include the methods of converting the aircraft's potential energy to kinetic energy; the ratio(s) of thrust to drag when the aircraft is accelerating with maximum indicated normal acceleration; and basic physics logic, such as the equations of motion and acceleration and the geometry of torques and lever arms.

3.4.2 Earth Characteristics Module.   The Earth Characteristics Module hides models of the earth and its atmosphere. This set of models includes models of local gravity, curvature of the earth, air pressure, magnetic variation, local terrain, rotation of the earth, Coriolis force, and atmospheric density. Secrets of the module also include how the angles and slant range to impact point are determined for air-to-ground launch weapons; how trajectories are determined for air-to-air launch weapons; which, if any, of these calculations must be performed periodically instead of on demand; which weapons characteristics and which values are used in calculation of trajectories and how they are used; and in which reference frame the calculations are implemented.

3.4.5 Weapon Behavior Module.   The Weapon Behavior Module contains models used to predict weapon behavior after release.

6.4 CONCLUSIONS

Software that is structured in a well-defined and well-documented fashion lends itself to reuse. In particular, we show how the four problems mentioned in the introduction can be overcome.

1. Information hiding demands precise specification. It is impossible to use the principle of information hiding unless you provide a substitute for the information that you are hiding. The specifications for our modules remove the first obstacle to software reuse.
2. The fact that all of our software is designed to be easy to change in itself increases the likelihood that it will be reused. Further, information hiding leads to separation of concerns. Device-dependent code will be in one module, physical models somewhere else. This makes it easier to reuse the device-dependent code with a different physical model, or to reuse the physical models with different devices.
3. A module guide of the kind shown serves as a software catalog. Users can characterize the software they seek by the same secrets that characterize the software described in the catalog. The hierarchical nature of the catalog lends itself to rapid convergence to that part of the existing system that will most likely provide the needed software.
4. Our software is designed to be flexible, not general. The distinction is discussed in [Parnas, 1978]. We do not make software that is designed to be used without change in many situations; that would be too inefficient. Instead, we have designed the software so that it is easy to adapt to a new situation. We are able to tune the software to our particular situation, but confine that tuning to specific modules so that the software can be readjusted when the situation changes.

Information hiding and abstraction are two sides of the same coin. The value of abstraction has always been that results developed in terms of an abstraction may be reused for any valid model of that abstraction. We have shown in this paper that by developing and cataloging abstractions, we can greatly increase the likelihood that some of the software we write will be reused.

REFERENCES

Britton, K., and Parnas, D. A-7E software module guide. Naval Research Laboratory memorandum report 4702, 1981.

Heninger, K.; Kallander, J.; Parnas, D., and Shore, J. Software requirements for the A-7E aircraft. Naval Research Laboratory memorandum report 3876, 27 November 1978.

Parker, A.; Heninger, K.; Parnas, D.; and Shore, J. Abstract interface specifications for the A-7E device interface module. Naval Research Laboratory memorandum report 4385, 20 November 1980.

Parnas, D. On the criteria to be used in decomposing systems into modules. *Communications of the ACM* 15(12): 1053–1058, 1972.

Parnas, D. Designing software for ease of extension and contraction. Presented at Third International Conference on Software Engineering, Atlanta, 10–12 May 1978.

ACKNOWLEDGMENT

Ms. Kathryn Britton, now with IBM in Research Triangle Park, North Carolina, is a coauthor of our software module guide, parts of which have been included in this paper.

ABOUT THE AUTHORS

Dr. David Lorge Parnas, born 10 February 1941 in Plattsburgh, New York, is Professor of Computing and Information Science at Queen's University in Kingston, Ontario. Previously he was Lansdowne Professor of Computer Science at the University of Victoria in Victoria, British Columbia. Professor Parnas was also Principal Investigator of the Software Cost Reduction Project at the Naval Research Laboratory in Washington, D.C. He has also taught at Carnegie-Mellon University, The University of Maryland, the Technische Hochschule Darmstadt, and the University of North Carolina at Chapel Hill. Dr. Parnas is interested in all aspects of software engineering. His special interests include program semantics, language design, program organization, process structure, process synchronization, and precise abstract specifications. He initiated and led an experimental redesign of a hard real-time system, the on-board flight program for the U.S. Navy's A-7 aircraft, in order to evaluate a number of software engineering principles. He is also involved in the design of a language involving new control structures and abstract data types. An avid cyclist, Dave is best remembered by many students for lecturing with his pants tucked into his socks.

Paul Clements is on leave from the Naval Research Laboratory where he was the Principal Investigator of the Software Cost Reduction project. He is currently pursuing his doctoral degree in Computer Science at the University of Texas at Austin, specializing in real-time and distributed systems software engineering. He has a Master of Science degree in Computer Science from the University of North Carolina at Chapel Hill. He has performed research in software engineering for the past eight years, specializing in modularization and abstract interface specification problems.

Dr. David Weiss is a principal member of the technical staff at the Software Productivity Consortium, where he is responsible for methodology and measurement, especially in support of reuse and prototyping. Previously, he spent a year as a senior analyst with the Office of Technology Assessment working on an assessment of computing technology needed for the Strategic Defense Initiative. Before OTA, he was with the Naval Research Laboratory, where he directed research in software engineering and software measurement, and participated in the transfer of modern software engineering practices into the Navy. At NRL he was also a member of the Software Cost Reduction project, whose purpose was to provide a well-engineered model of a complex real-time system. During the 1985–1986 academic year he was a visiting scholar at The Wang Institute, where he lectured on and conducted a project class in the application of the NRL software cost reduction methodology. He is also a retired marathoner.

CHAPTER 7

PRINCIPLES OF PARAMETERIZED PROGRAMMING

JOSEPH A. GOGUEN
University of Oxford, and SRI International

7.1 INTRODUCTION

Both the costs and the demands for software are enormous and growing rapidly. One way to diminish these effects is to maximize the reuse of software. This paper argues that *parameterized programming* can greatly extend opportunities for software reuse and illustrates the technique with some examples in the OBJ language.

This paper is a very substantial revision and expansion of [Goguen, 1984]; new material includes OBJ3-based examples, more powerful default views, improved motivation from software engineering, discussions of order-sorted algebra and logical programming, several new language features, and many new examples. This paper does not attempt to develop the semantic basis of parameterized programming, but rather to motivate it from a programming

Supported in part by Office of Naval Research contracts N00014-85-C-0417 and N00014-86-C-0450, NSF Grant CCR-8707155, and a gift from the System Development Foundation to the Center for the Study of Language and Information at Stanford University.

language point of view. In addition, it argues that parameterized programming is powerful enough so that higher-order functions are not needed in the underlying programming language; specifically, we show that typical higher-order functional programming techniques can be implemented, often with greater flexibility and clarity, by using parameterized modules, and that a typical application, namely hardware verification, is readily captured in the simpler formalism. One appendix develops default views, another sketches the OBJ3 implementation, while a third enumerates language features that support parameterized programming.

7.1.1 Parameterized Programming

Successful software reuse depends upon the following tasks being sufficiently easy:

1. finding old parts that are close enough to what you need,
2. understanding those parts,
3. getting them to do what you need now, and
4. putting them all together correctly.

Under these conditions, total programming time, and especially debugging and maintenance time, can be greatly reduced. Objects, theories, views, and module expressions provide formal support for these tasks. The basic idea of parameterized programming is a strong form of abstraction: to break code into highly parameterized mind-sized pieces. Then one can construct new programs from old modules by instantiating parameters and transforming modules. Actual parameters are modules in this approach, and interface specifications include semantic as well as syntactic information.

The Ada [U.S. Dept. of Defense 1983] notion of a generic package provides only part of what is needed. In particular, Ada generic packages provide no way to document the *semantics* of interfaces, although this feature can greatly improve the reliability of software reuse and can also help retrieve the right module from a library (as discussed in [Goguen, 1986a]). Also, Ada provides only very weak facilities for combining modules; for example, only one level of module instantiation is possible at a time.

It may happen that there is a software part we want to reuse, but it is not in exactly the right form, or perhaps we have combined some modules and now we want to improve the efficiency of the combination. Then a promising approach is to apply some program transformations [Burstall and Darlington, 1977; Balzer, 1981; Scherlis, 1986]. Parameterized programming allows us to achieve such goals by modifying parameterized modules, either before or after combination or instantiation, so that they can fit a wider variety of applications. Among possible modifications are the following:

1. extend a module, by adding to its functionality;
2. rename some of its external interface;

3. restrict a module, by eliminating some of its functionality;
4. encapsulate some existing code;
5. combine (add) two or more modules; and
6. modify the code inside a module.

All of these can be accomplished with module expressions, in a way that still guarantees the preservation of (selected) program properties, given in the form of theories. In addition to having parameters, modules can also import other modules, that is, rely upon their being just as they are (although this could be viewed as a special case of parameter instantiation, it is more convenient to treat it separately; see Section 7.3).

As an example of parameterized programming, consider a parameterized module LEXL[X] that provides lists of Xs with a lexicographic ordering, where the parameter X can be instantiated to any preordered set. Thus, if ID is a module that provides identifiers (and in particular, words) with their usual (lexicographic) ordering, then LEXL[ID] provides a lexicographic ordering on sequences of words (i.e., on "phrases," such as book titles). And LEXL[LEXL[ID]] provides a lexicographic ordering on sequences of phrases (such as lists of book titles) by instantiating the ordering that LEXL[X] requires with the one that LEXL[ID] provides, namely lexicographic ordering. Similarly, given a module SORTING[Y] for sorting lists of Ys (again for Y any preorder, and assuming that SORTING[Y] imports LEXL[Y]), we can let Y be LEXL[ID] to get a program SORTING[LEXL[ID]] that sorts lists of book titles.

Let us look at this example a little more closely. In general, a module can define one or more data structures, with various operations among them, possibly importing some data structures and operations from other modules.[1] For example, LEXL[X] should define or import lists of X's and provide a binary relation L1 << L2 meaning that list L1 is the same as or comes earlier in the ordering than L2. The requirement theory for LEXL is PREORD, the theory of preordered sets, and hereafter we will use the notation LEXL[X :: PREORD] for this. To instantiate a formal parameter with an actual parameter, it is necessary to provide a *view*, which binds the formal entities in the requirement theory to actual ones. If there is a default view of a module M as a preorder, we can just write LEXL[M]; for example, if M = ID, there is an obvious view that selects the built-in lexicographic ordering relation on identifiers. LEXL[ID] in turn provides another lexicographic ordering, and a default view from PREORD using this ordering makes it legal to write SORTING[LEXL[ID]].

A useful insight (perhaps best expressed in [Burstall 1985] is that programming in the large is a kind of *functional programming*, in which evaluating (what we call) a module expression is a kind of functional expression

---

[1]It is worth mentioning that modules may also have internal states; although this feature is neither discussed in this paper nor implemented in OBJ, the reader may consult [Goguen and Meseguer, 1987a] and [Goguen and Meseguer, 1982a] for further information about our approach to this important issue.

evaluation; in particular, there are no variables, assignments, or effects (side or otherwise), and functions are applied to arguments; this can provide a formal basis for software reuse. However, there are also some significant differences between ordinary functional programming and module expression evaluation in parameterized programming, including semantic interfaces, limited (but sufficient) higher-order syntax, and evaluation in context, producing not just a single module, but also embedding it in its context, that is, placing it in a graph of modules. Appendix B lists linguistic features that support parameterized programming.

7.1.2 OBJ

To make our discussion of parameterized programming concrete, it is necessary to have a fixed programming language in which to give examples, and we will use OBJ for this purpose. However, the reader should understand that this requires explaining many features of OBJ not directly related to parameterized programming.

OBJ has four kinds of entity at its top level: objects, theories, views, and reductions. Objects and theories are both modules and can import other previously defined modules. Because of such importation dependencies, an OBJ program is conceptually a graph of modules, rather than a sequence (see Section 7.3). Modules have *signatures* that introduce new types and new operations among both new and old types. Note that we will generally use the word *sort* instead of *type* because of the many very different meanings that have been assigned to *type*. Also, note that the word *operation* generally means *function* in this paper, because we are dealing with a functional language.

An OBJ *object* gives executable code for the sorts and operations in its signature; these operations may create, select, interrogate, or modify data. Thus the object concept includes both "types" in the traditional programming language sense (that is, a domain of values for variables together with operations that access those values) and algorithms. All this is in general conformity with methodology espoused, for example, by Jackson [1975]. An OBJ *theory* defines properties that may (or may not) be satisfied by an object; this concept is found in no other programming language. Both kinds of module can be parameterized, and a parameterized module comes with one or more theories to define its interfaces.

A *view* is a binding of the entities in a theory signature to entities in a module, and it is also an assertion that the module satisfies the properties stated in the theory. Thus a view both indicates how to apply a parameterized module to an actual parameter and asserts its semantic appropriateness.

An OBJ *reduction* evaluates a given expression relative to a given object (including its imported objects) by interpreting equations as rewrite rules. In particular, OBJ supports pattern matching and rewriting modulo attributes (including associativity and commutativity; see Section 7.2.5). OBJ is interactive, and when an OBJ program gets to the stage where it can be executed, it has survived a great deal more checking than most compilers provide, including both syntactic and semantic consistency checks.

OBJ embodies basic design choices that are quite different from those of other programming languages, even current functional programming languages. Indeed, OBJ is the only language we know with the following properties:

1. It supports parameterized programming, including
   - both objects (executable code) and theories (nonexecutable properties),
   - parameterized modules with interface theories,
   - views for instantiation (binding) and for property assertion, and
   - module expressions for constructing complex (sub)systems.

2. It is a *logical* programming language, that is, a language whose statements are sentences in some rigorous logical system (see Section 7.2.5 for more detail); in fact, OBJ is based on *order-sorted logic*, which is the logic of subsorts, providing a precise basis for the following:
   - exception handling;
   - multiple inheritance;
   - retracts, which allow the benefits of both strong typing and untyped programming; and
   - multiple representations for data abstractions.

3. It has user-definable *evaluation strategies*, defined on an operation-by-operation basis, rather than globally, to control the order of evaluating subterms, providing eager and lazy evaluation as well as more complex options. Also, efficient default evaluation strategies are computed by strictness analysis if the user fails to provide an explicit strategy.

4. It has rewriting *modulo attributes*, including associative, commutative, identity, and idempotent.

It has been well argued by advocates of Prolog that a logical programming language has certain important advantages: program simplicity and clarity (which can greatly ease program understanding, debugging, and maintenance), separation of logic and control, and identity of program logic with proof logic. In such a language, a high-level description of what a program does actually is a program, that is, one can execute it; such languages can also be considered as efficiently executable specification languages. Besides OBJ, which is based upon order-sorted equational logic, other logical programming languages include pure Prolog [Colmerauer *et al.*, 1979], pure Lisp [McCarthy *et al.*, 1966], and CDS [Berry and Currien, 1985]. Some other languages based on algebraic semantics include Larch [Guttag *et al.*, 1985], Asspegique [Bidoit *et al.*, 1985], Obscure [Lerman and Loecky, 1985], and Act One [Ehrig and Mahr, 1985]; it seems fair to say that all these have been significantly influenced by OBJ.

Hope [Burstall and Goguen, 1980] and Miranda [Turner, 1985] are higher-order functional programming languages based on rewrite rules. ML [Harper *et al.*, 1986] is an elegant higher-order imperative language with a well-defined functional sublanguage; moreover, it is in the process of acquiring a module facility inspired in part by Clear's. Guttag, Horowitz, and Musser [1978] describe a system for the symbolic execution of algebraic abstract data types, and Levy and Sirovich [1977] describe the TEL system for specifying semantics with equations. Other related systems are due to Hoffmann and O'Donnell [Hoffmann and O'Donnell, 1982; O'Donnell, 1985], Lucas and Risch [1982], and Prywes and Pnueli [1983], all of which are first-order, and there is also the elegant work of Backus [1978], which is higher-order functional programming for a fixed set of rewrite rules and data types.

The experimental OBJ systems implemented so far have been used for many applications, including: debugging algebraic specifications [Goguen *et al.*, 1983]; rapid prototyping [Goguen and Meseguer, 1982b]; defining programming languages in a way that immediately yields an interpreter (see [Goguen and Parsaye-Ghomi, 1981] and the elegant work of Mosses [1983, 1985]); specifying software systems (e.g, the GKS graphics kernel system) [Duce and Fielding, 1987]; an Ada configuration manager [Gerrard, 1989]; the MacIntosh QuickDraw program [Nakagawa and Futatsugi, 1987]; OBJ in itself [Coleman *et al.*, 1987]; and specifying, simulating, and verifying hardware (see [Stavridou, 1987] and Section 7.4.7). Many of these applications were produced under an experiment sponsored by the British Alvey Project, and will be collected, with more recent work, in a book on the practical use of OBJ [Coleman *et al.*, 1989]. OBJ is also being combined with Petri nets, thus allowing structured data in tokens [Battiston *et al.*, 1987], and is the basis for programming a massively parallel machine to execute rewrite rules directly [Leinwand and Goguen, 1987,1988]; we believe that OBJ on such a machine should greatly outperform a conventional language on a conventional machine, by direct concurrent execution of rewrite rules.

7.1.3 Acknowledgments

I wish to thank Professor Rod Burstall for his extended and ongoing collaboration on Clear and its foundations, which inspired the parameterization mechanism of OBJ; Dr. José Meseguer for his invaluable contributions to every aspect of OBJ, including its theoretical foundations, implementation, and applications; Timothy Winkler for his heroic efforts in implementing OBJ3, his many suggestions concerning its design and theory, and his very valuable comments on this paper; Professor Jean-Pierre Jouannaud for his efforts to educate me on the theory and practice of rewrite rules, and for his work on the theory and implementation of OBJ2's rewrite rule engine; Dr. Kokichi Futatsugi for his enormous efforts in implementing the rest of OBJ2, including his design of the distinctive OBJ2 syntax; Aristide Megrelis for his work on the OBJ3 parser; Drs. Claude and Hélène Kirchner for their work on the theory and practice of order-sorted rewriting, embodied in the OBJ3 rewrite engine; Professor David Plaisted for his many suggestions about the design of OBJ, and for his implementation of OBJ1; Dr. Joseph Tardo for his pioneering and courageous implementation of OBJT; Drs. James Thatcher, Eric Wagner, and Jesse Wright for their initial collaboration on abstract data types; Dr. Peter Mosses for his many valuable suggestions and for his valiant attempts to use a very early version of OBJ3; and Dr. Victoria Stavridou for her inspiring early efforts to use OBJ3 for hardware specification and verification.

7.2 OBJECTS

The most important OBJ unit is the *object*, which encapsulates executable code. Syntactically, an object begins with the keyword `obj` and ends with `endo` or `jbo`.[2] The name of the object occurs immediately after the `obj` keyword; following this is the word `is`, and then the body of the object. For unparameterized objects, the name is a simple identifier, such as STACK-OF-INT, PHRASE, or OBJ14. Parameterized objects have more complex names, as discussed in Section 7.4. Optionally, the name of the object can be repeated after the object ending keyword to enhance readability. For example,

```
obj PHRASE is
    . . . . .
endo PHRASE
```

By convention, all OBJ keywords are lower case, while object names are all upper case plus possibly special characters.

7.2.1 Strong Sorting

We believe that a programming language should have a strong but flexible type system; however, to avoid the confusion associated with the many uses of the word *type*, we shall instead use the word *sort*. Among the advantages of strong sorting are that it can catch meaningless expressions before they are executed, separate logically and intuitively distinct concepts, enhance readability by documenting these distinctions, and, when the notion of subsort is added, support overloading, coercions, multiple representations, and error handling without the confusion found in many programming languages [Goguen and Meseguer, 1987b]. Of course, this may involve additional declarations, but with a modern (e.g., structural) editor, it is little trouble to insert declarations, and many could even be inserted automatically.

---

[2]OBJ has the uniform convention that ending keywords can be of the form `end` <x> where x is the first letter of the corresponding initial keyword, or possibly the first plus some additional letters. The initial keyword spelled backwards, as in `jbo`, is an archaic form preserved from earlier versions of OBJ.

Ordinary unsorted logic offers the dubious advantage that anything can be applied to anything; for example,

$$\texttt{first-name(not(age(3 * false))) iff } 2^{\text{birth-place(temperature(329))}}$$

is a well-formed expression. Although beloved by Lisp and Prolog hackers, unsorted logic is too permissive. Unfortunately, the obvious alternative, many-sorted logic, is too restrictive, since it does not support overloaded function symbols, such as `_+_` for integer, rational, and complex numbers. Moreover, strictly speaking, an expression like `(-4 / -2)!` does not even parse (assuming that factorial only applies to natural numbers), since `(-4 / -2)` looks to the parser like a rational rather than a natural. This problem can be solved by extending order-sorted algebra with *retracts*, which provide sufficient expressiveness, while still banishing truly meaningless expressions, as discussed in Section 7.2.3.

7.2.2 Operation and Expression Syntax

We believe it is worth some extra implementation effort and processing time to support syntax that is as flexible, informative, and close to users' intuitions and standard usage as possible. In particular, OBJ users can define any syntax they like for operations, including prefix, postfix, infix, or more generally, *mixfix*, to make it maximally appropriate for any given problem domain; this is similar to ECL [Cheatham, 1966]. Obviously, there are many opportunities for ambiguity in parsing such a syntax. OBJ's convention is that an expression is well formed if and only if it has exactly one parse (or more precisely, a unique parse of least sort; see Section 7.2.3). In keeping with the interactive nature of the language, the OBJ parser gives information about the difficulties it encounters, helping the user to correct these difficulties before reattempting to parse. (This is not yet fully implemented.)

We now discuss operation syntax. The argument and value sorts of an operation should be declared at the same time as its syntactic form. We distinguish two cases. The first is the usual parenthesized-prefix-with-commas functional form. For example,

```
op f : S1 S2 -> S3 .
```

declares the function `f(X,Y)` of sort `S3` for `X` of sort `S1` and `Y` of sort `S2`. (Commas are required as separators in well-formed expressions using this syntactic form.) The general syntax for such declarations is

```
op <op-identifier> : <sort-list> -> <sort> .
```

where *<op-identifier>* is a string of characters, possibly including spaces, but

definitely excluding the underbar character "_" and not consisting entirely of
spaces. Such declarations must be terminated with a period.

The general mixfix case uses place-holders indicated by an underbar
character, as in the prefix declaration

```
op top_ : Stack -> Int .
```

for top as used in expressions like top push(A,B). Similarly, the outfix form
of the singleton set formation operation, as in {4}, is declared by

```
op { _ } : Int -> Set .
```

and the infix form for addition, as in 2 + 3, is declared by

```
op _+_ : Int Int -> Int .
```

while a mixfix declaration for conditional is

```
op if_then_else_fi : Bool Int Int -> Int .
```

Incidentally, OBJ provides such a built-in conditional operation for each
available sort, so that users do not have to define it themselves.

Between the : and the -> in an operation declaration comes the *arity* of
the operation, and after the -> comes its *value sort* (also called co-arity); the
<arity, value sort> pair is called the *rank* of the operation, and all these sorts
must have been previously declared. The general syntax for mixfix operation
declarations is

```
op <form> : <sort-list> -> <sort> .
```

where *<form>* is a nonempty string of characters containing exactly as many
underbars as there are sorts in *<sort-list>*; a terminating period is required,
and the *<form>* may contain spaces between other characters, but may not
consist of just spaces. Forms consisting of just one underbar are also prohib-
ited, since this corresponds to a subsort declaration, for which the notation
of order-sorted algebra is preferred (although some earlier versions of OBJ
took the opposite point of view). Constant declarations have no underbars
and empty arity.

Operations with the same rank but different forms can be declared
together, using the keyword ops; for example,

```
ops zero one : -> S .

ops (_+_)(_*_) : S S -> S .
```

The parentheses are required in the second case to indicate the boundary between the two forms. Here is a simple example illustrating the syntax given so far; it defines strings of bits.

```
obj BITS is
  sorts Bit Bits .
  ops 0 1 :  -> Bit .
  op nil :  -> Bits .
  op _._ : Bit Bits -> Bits .
endo BITS
```

A typical expression using the syntax of BITS is 0 . 1 . 0 . nil.

When strong sorting is not sufficient to prevent ambiguity in an expression that uses overloaded operations and subsorts, then a qualification notation can be useful. In particular, if the same operation symbol has been introduced in more than one module, then to avoid ambiguity and thus parse failure, the operation symbol can be qualified by its module name. For example, to distinguish the bit 0 above from the natural number zero, one can write (0).BITS. Module qualifiers can also be applied to mixfix operations, as in (X is-in file1).M47; the parentheses are not optional here. Sometimes module qualification doesn't work, but sort qualification does. For example, one might write (X is-in Set1 union Set2).Nat to indicate that the expression is natural-number valued (as might be used for bags) rather than truth valued (as might be used for sets). Qualification by sort can be distinguished from qualification by module as long as distinct names are involved, which is provided for by the convention used in this paper that module names are all upper case, while sort names only have an upper-case letter at the beginning.

7.2.3 Subsorts

To handle cases where things of one sort are also of another sort—for example, all natural numbers are also rational numbers—and cases where expressions may have several different sorts, we use order-sorted algebra, sometimes abbreviated *OSA*. The essence of order-sorted algebra is to provide a subsort partial ordering among sorts, and to interpret it semantically as subset inclusion, as in Nat < Rat, which means Nat ≤ Rat (we use < instead of ≤ simply for typographical convenience). OSA also supports multiple inheritance, in the sense that a given sort can have more than one distinct supersort.

Although many-sorted algebra has been quite successful for the theory of abstract data types, it can produce some very awkward code in practice, primarily due to difficulties in handling erroneous expressions, such as dividing by zero in the rationals, or taking the top of an empty stack. In fact there is no really satisfying way to define either rationals or stacks with many-sorted algebra (see [Ehrig and Mahr, 1985] for some examples of just how awkward things can get). However, order-sorted algebra overcomes these obstacles through its richer type system, which supports subsorts and overloaded operations and allows functions to be total that would otherwise have to be partial, by restricting them to a subsort. OSA is only slightly more difficult than many-sorted algebra, and essentially all results generalize from the many-sorted to the order-sorted case without complication. Although this paper omits the technical details, OSA is a rigorous mathematical theory. Moreover, OSA solves the *constructor-selector problem* [Goguen and Meseguer, 1987b], which, roughly speaking, is to define inverses, called *selectors*, for all constructors; the solution is to restrict each selector to the largest subsort where it makes sense. For example, considering pop and top as selectors for the constructor push, they are only defined on nonempty stacks. [Goguen and Meseguer, 1987b] shows not only that OSA solves this problem, but also that many-sorted algebra cannot solve it. OSA originated in [Goguen, 1978] and is best developed in [Goguen and Meseguer, 1989] and [Goguen and Meseguer, 1987b]; some nice alternative approaches have been given by Gogolla [1984, 1985], Wadge [1982], Reynolds [1980], and others.

OBJ directly supports *subsort polymorphism*, which is operator-overloading consistent under subsort restriction. By contrast, languages like ML [Harper *et al.*, 1986] and Hope [Burstall, MacQueen, and Sanella, 1980] support *parametric polymorphism*, following ideas of Strachey [1963] and of Milner [1978]. OBJ's parameterized modules provide a similar capability, but with instantiations declared explicitly, rather than automatically determined by unification; Section 7.4.6 further contrasts these approaches.

A term over an order-sorted signature is considered well formed iff it has a *unique* parse of lowest sort; [Goguen and Meseguer, 1989] and [Goguen and Meseguer, 1987b] show that under certain mild and natural assumptions, order-sorted terms do in fact always have well-defined least sorts. Sometimes subexpressions are not of the expected sort, and must be "coerced" to it. This is trivial from a subsort to a supersort; for example, if the operation + is only defined for rationals, then (2 + 2) is fine when 2 is a natural number, because Nat < Rat. It is less trivial the other way; for example, consider (-4 / -2)! where ! is only defined for natural numbers. At parse time, we cannot know whether the subexpression (-4 / -2) will turn out to be a natural number, so the parser must consider it a rational; in fact, the expression (-4 / -2)! *does not parse* in the conventional sense. However, we can give it the benefit of the doubt by having the parser insert a *retract*, a special operation symbol (r:Rat>Nat in the example below) that just lowers the sort, to be removed at run time if the subexpression really is a natural, but otherwise remaining behind as an informative error message. Thus the parser turns the expression (-4 / 2)! into the expression (r:Rat>Nat(-4 / 2))! which at run time becomes first (r:Rat>Nat(2))! and then (2)!, using the (automatically provided) key equation

```
r:Rat>Nat(X) = X
```

where X is a variable of sort Nat. [Goguen, Jouannaud, and Meseguer, 1985] describes the mathematical and operational semantics of retracts, based on order-sorted algebra and order-sorted rewriting.

Exceptions have both inadequate semantic foundations and insufficient flexibility in most programming and specification languages. Algebraic specification languages sometimes use partial functions, which are simply undefined under exceptional conditions. Although this can be developed rigorously, as in [Kaphengst and Reichel, 1977], it is unsatisfactory in practice because it does not allow error messages or error recovery. For some time, we have been exploring rigorous approaches that allow users to define their own exception conditions, error messages, and exception handling. Unfortunately, the error algebra approach [Goguen, 1977] used in OBJT and OBJ1 sometimes lacks initial models [Plaisted, 1982], but the current OSA approach seems entirely satisfactory.

The basic form of a subsort declaration in OBJ is

```
subsort  <sort1> <  <sort2> .
```

meaning that the set of things of *<sort1>* is a subset (not necessarily proper) of the things of *<sort2>*. The form

```
subsorts  <sort-list1> <  <sort-list2> < . . . .
```

can also be used, meaning that each sort in *<sort-list1>* is a subsort of each sort in *<sort-list2>*, and so on; the elements of the various lists must be separated by blanks. OBJ checks for cycles of subsorts, and complains if it finds any. (But OBJ does not complain about syntactic ambiguities purely due to the subsort relation, since it regards each expression as having the smallest possible sort.) The *signature* of an object consists of the sorts, subsort relation, and operations defined in it, where each operation has a form, arity, and value sort.

Using subsorts, we can give a somewhat better representation for bit strings than that in the previous subsection:

```
obj BITS1 is
   sorts Bit Bits .
   subsorts Bit < Bits .
   ops 0 1 : -> Bit .
   op _ _ : Bit Bits -> Bits .
endo
```

A typical expression using this syntax is 0 1 0 .

Many programs represent data in more than one way, and then convert between representations, using whichever representation is most convenient or efficient. This is *multiple representation*; for an example, consider Cartesian and polar coordinates for points in plane geometry. Other programs may convert from one sort of data to another in an irreversible way; for example to apply integer addition to two floating point numbers, the floating point numbers might be truncated; this is an example of coercion. Multiple representation can be considered a special case of coercion, since the selectors for one representation, when applied to a data item of another, can be thought of as mediated by functions that change the representation. The difference is that the conversions between multiple representations are necessarily reversible [Wadler, 1987]. OSA provides a rigorous semantics for all this (see [Goguen and Meseguer, 1987b] for details; these features are not yet implemented in OBJ3).

7.2.4 Attributes

It is natural and convenient to consider certain properties of an operation as *attributes* that are declared at the same time as its syntax. These properties include axioms like associativity, commutativity, idempotence, and identity that have both syntactic and semantic consequences, as well as others that affect order of evaluation, parsing, and so on. In OBJ, such attributes are given in square brackets after the syntax declaration. For example,

```
op _or_ : Bool Bool -> Bool [assoc] .
```

indicates that or is an associative binary infix operation on truth values. This means that the parser does not require full parenthesization; for example, the term (true or (false or true)) can be written (true or false or true), and the deparser will omit all unnecessary parentheses; the attribute declaration also gives the semantic effect of an associativity axiom. The assoc attribute is only meaningful for a binary operation with arity A B and sort C when C < A and C < B; however, retracts can be inserted in other cases.

Similarly, binary infix operations can be declared commutative with the attribute comm, which is semantically a commutativity axiom, but also has operational consequences for matching (see Section 7.2.5). An identity attribute can be declared for a binary operation in which each sort in its arity is a subsort of the value sort. For example, in

```
op _or_ : Bool Bool -> Bool [assoc id: false] .
```

the attribute id: false gives the effects of the identity equations (B or false = B) and (false or B = B). An identity attribute can be a term as well as just a constant. If the identity for an operation o is a constant operation symbol i, and if all three sorts in the rank of o are the same, then i need not have been already declared, and its introduction as an attribute is considered its declaration. OBJ3 currently implements the identity attribute by generating new equations; if it only makes sense to have a left or a right identity, then that is all that is generated. For example,

```
op nil :  -> List .
op _ _ :  Int List -> NeList [id: nil] .
```

In addition, operations can be declared idempotent with attribute idem.
    Each sort S has a built-in equality operation with syntactic form

```
op _==_ : S S -> Bool .
```

Any operation with rank of the form S S -> Bool can be given the equality
attribute, which makes it equal to the built-in equality. For example, one
could write

```
op _iff_ : Bool Bool -> Bool [equality] .
```

Similarly, any Bool-valued binary operation can be given the attribute lex,
which declares it equal to the built-in lexicographic ordering operation on
its arity sort. All OBJ built-in objects have built-in lexicographic orderings,
and the default lexicographic ordering for user-defined objects is determined
by the order in which operations are declared; operations that are declared
earlier are placed earlier in the ordering. (The features in this paragraph
were in OBJ1 but are not yet in OBJ3.)
    An integer precedence attribute can be given for parsing; the lower the
integer, the more binding the operation. For example, the built-in object INT
might have declarations

```
_+_ : Int Int -> Int [assoc prec 8] .
_*_ : Int Int -> Int [assoc prec 5] .
```

so that the expression A + B * C is parsed as expected, A + (B * C).
    Giving an operation the memo attribute causes the results of evaluating
any term headed by this operation to be saved; thus the work of reduction
is not repeated if that term appears again [Michie, 1968]. The user can give
the memo attribute to any operations that she wishes. OBJ uses hashing to
implement this efficiently; in this respect term-rewriting systems have an
advantage over unification-based systems like Prolog. Memo also causes
OBJ to use structure sharing for common subexpressions, which can greatly
reduce term storage requirements in some problems.
    Finally, operations can be given "E-strategy" attributes to control the
order of evaluation, as discussed in Section 7.2.5.

7.2.5 Semantics

So far we have only considered syntax. But every programming language
must also have semantics. OBJ has both an abstract denotational semantics
based on order-sorted algebra and a more concrete operational semantics
based on order-sorted rewriting. The semantics of an object is determined

by its equations. Equations are written declaratively and interpreted operationally as rewrite rules, which replace instances of left-hand sides by the corresponding instances of right-hand sides. The operational and denotational semantics are discussed in the following subsections.

The basic syntax for an equation in OBJ is

    eq <*exp1*> = <*exp2*> .

where both <*exp1*> and <*exp2*> are well-formed OBJ expressions. There are also conditional rewrite rules, with syntax

    ceq <*exp1*> = <*exp2*> if <*bexp*>

where <*bexp*> is an expression of sort Bool (the built-in object BOOL is implicitly imported into every module, to help parse <*bexp*> conditions). Such a conditional rule can be thought of as a pattern-driven demon that fires only when its <*bexp*> is true. All these expressions can use variables that have been previously declared with the syntax

    vars <*var-name-list*> : <*sort*> .

where the variable names are separated by commas or by blanks. For example,

    vars I J K : Nat .

(The keyword var can be used if just one variable is declared.) Variables can also be introduced on the fly with notation like X : Nat, where the sort is given after the colon. Because of overloading, it is sometimes necessary to declare a sort for an equation to get it to parse as desired. This can be done with the syntax

    eq-as <*sort*> <*exp1*> = <*exp2*> .

    ceq-as <*sort*> <*exp1*> = <*exp2*> if <*exp2*> .

It would also be possible to let the parser determine the sorts of undeclared variables according to the convention that they have the highest sort that makes sense. If necessary to circumvent this convention, undeclared variables could be qualified with their sorts, as in X:Sort. However, our belief in the value of declarations for enhancing readability has made us reluctant to implement this feature.

Operational Semantics. We can illustrate computation by term rewriting with a simple LIST-OF-INT object. (The protecting INT line below indicates that the INT module, for integers, is imported; module importation will be discussed in Section 7.3.)

```
obj LIST-OF-INT is
  sorts List .
  protecting INT .
  subsorts Int < List .
  op _ _ : Int List -> List .
  op length_ : List -> Int .
  var I : Int .
  var L : List .
  eq length I = 1 .
  eq length I L = 1 + length L .
endo
```

Let us now evaluate some expressions over this object. An expression *<exp>* to be evaluated is presented to OBJ with the syntax

```
reduce <exp> endr
```

which is evaluated in the context of the last module entered into the system. One can also give a different module *<mod>* to be used as context, with syntax

```
reduce-in <mod> <exp> endr
```

and one can give a sort to be used for parsing *<exp>* with syntax

```
reduce-as <sort> <exp> endr
```

One can even give both, with the syntax

```
reduce-in-as <mod> <sort> <exp> endr
```

A reduce command is executed by matching the expression with the left-hand sides of equations, and then replacing the matched subexpression with the corresponding substitution instance of the right-hand side; that is, evaluation proceeds by applying rewrite rules.

For example,

```
reduce length 17 -4 329 endr
```

is evaluated in LIST-OF-INT, and gives

```
result Int: 3
```

by the following sequence of rewrite rule applications:

```
length 17 -4 329 =>
1 + length -4 329 =>
1 + (1 + length 329) =>
1 + (1 + 1) =>
1 + 2 =>
3
```

where the first step uses the second rule, with left-hand side length I L, matching I to 17 and L to −4 329. The second step also uses this rule, but now matching I to −4 and L to 329; this match works by regarding the integer 329 as a List, since Int is a subsort of List. The third step simply uses the first rule, and the last steps use the built-in arithmetic of INT. Execution proceeds until it reaches a term to which no further rules can be applied; such a term is called a *normal* (or *reduced*) *form*.[3]

Let us now consider a more sophisticated integer list object with associative and identity attributes:

```
obj LIST-OF-INT1 is
  sorts List NeList .
  protecting INT .
  subsorts Int < NeList < List .
  op _ _ : List List -> List [assoc id: nil] .
  op _ _ : NeList List -> NeList [assoc] .
  op head_ : NeList -> Int .
  op tail_ : NeList -> List .
  var I : Int .
  var L : List .
  eq head I L = I .
  eq tail I L = L .
endo
```

We now give some test cases using this object. For example,

```
reduce 0 nil 1 nil 3 endr
result NeList: 0 1 3
```

is carried out in LIST-OF-INT1 by applications of the identity axiom modulo associativity, as follows

```
0 nil 1 nil 3 =>
0 1 nil 3 =>
0 1 3
```

---

[3]Most functional programming languages require users to declare constructors such that a term is reduced if and only if it consists entirely of constructors. OBJ does not make any use of such constructors, thus achieving greater generality; however, the technique is available as a compiler optimization.

Similarly, we have

```
reduce head(0 1 3) endr
result Int: 0

reduce tail(0 1 3) endr
result NeList: 1 3

reduce tail(nil 0 1 nil 3) endr
result NeList: 1 3
```

The identity attribute is implemented by adding rules, rather than by pattern matching modulo identity. A subtle point is that sometimes further rules must be generated to get the correct effect of matching modulo identity. For example, the first equation of the LIST-OF-INT1 object has as a special case, with L = nil, the equation head I = I, which is added to the rulebase by the OBJ compiler. Sometimes it is also necessary to generate new "extension" rules for associative operations, but this topic is beyond the scope of the present paper; see [Kirchner *et al.*, 1987].

OBJ has a built-in polymorphic binary infix Bool-valued operation _==_ on every sort, to tell whether or not two ground expressions are equal. This is computed by reducing the two expressions to normal form and then comparing the normal forms for syntactic identity. For example, _==_ on Bool itself is just _iff_. The operation == really is equality on a sort, provided that the rules for expressions of that sort are Church-Rosser and terminating with respect to the given evaluation strategy (these notions are discussed in the next subsection), since these conditions guarantee that normal forms will be reached. The negation =/= of == is also available. Finally, recall that the conditional

```
if_then_else_fi : Bool S S -> S
```

is built in for every available sort S.

Order of Evaluation.   In general, a large tree will have many different sites where rewrite rules might apply, and the choice of which rules to try at which sites can strongly affect efficiency and even termination. Most modern functional programming languages have a uniform lazy (i.e., top-down, or outermost, or call-by-name) semantics. But since raw lazy evaluation is unacceptably slow, lazy evaluation enthusiasts have built clever compilers that figure out when an "eager" (i.e., bottom-up or call-by-value) evaluation can be used with exactly the same result; this subject is called *strictness analysis* [Mycroft, 1981]. OBJ is more flexible, since each operation can have its own evaluation strategy. Moreover, the OBJ programmer gets this flexibility with minimum effort, since the OBJ compiler determines a default strategy if none is explicitly given. This can be done at interactive speed because strictness analysis is much easier for first-order programs than for higher-order programs.

More precisely, an *E-strategy* (*E* for "evaluation") is a sequence of integers given as an operation attribute to help determine where and in what order to apply rules. For example, `if_then_else_fi` has strategy (1 0), which says evaluate the first argument until it is reduced, then apply rules at the top (indicated by 0); whereas `_+_` (say, on `Int`) might have strategy (1 2 0), which says evaluate both arguments before attempting to add them. The keyword `strat` is used in the attribute list for user-defined E-strategies, as in

```
op _+_ : Int Int -> Int [strat (1 2 0)] .
```

A negative number −j indicates that the jth argument is to be evaluated lazily. For example, "lazy cons" is

```
op cons : Sexp Sexp -> Sexp [strat (-1 -2)] .
```

A `reduce` command at the top level of OBJ is interpreted as a demand, and it is this that gets lazy evaluation to move. Many interesting and subtle evaluation strategies can be expressed in this notation. Strictness analysis determines default E-strategies by examining the rules for a given operation to see which of its arguments have nonvariable terms; those are the arguments that must be evaluated before rules are applied at the top.

Sometimes the order of applying rules does not matter, in the sense that if one starts with a term t_0 and rewrites it in two different ways, using any number of rules in any order and obtaining terms t_1 and t_2, then there is another term t_3 such that both t_1 and t_2 can be rewritten to t_3. A rule set with this desirable property is called *Church-Rosser*. Another desirable property for a rule set is *termination*, in the technical sense that there are no infinite sequences of rewrite rule applications. A rule set that is terminating (in this sense) can be checked for the Church-Rosser property by the Knuth-Bendix algorithm [Knuth and Bendix, 1970]; a rule set that is both terminating and Church-Rosser is called *canonical*. Although we cannot assume that all rewrite rule sets are terminating, the rules defining the operations of an abstract data type can always be chosen to be both Church-Rosser and terminating [Bergstra and Tucker, 1980]. However, further functions defined over these structures may well fail to have terminating rule sets, for example, if they implement procedures for problems that are only semidecidable. The Knuth-Bendix algorithm extends to a completion procedure that can often produce a canonical rule set from one that is terminating. Huet and Oppen [1980] give a good survey of term rewriting systems. Foundations for all this in OSA may be found in the references [Meseguer, Goguen, and Smolka, 1987; Goguen, Jouannaud, and Meseguer, 1985; Kirchner, 1987; Smolka *et al.*, 1989].

Denotational Semantics. Whereas the operational semantics of a programming language shows how computations are done, its denotational semantics should give precise meanings to programs in a conceptually clear and simple way. The denotational semantics of OBJ is algebraic, as in the algebraic approach to abstract data types [Goguen, Thatcher, Wagner, and Wright, 1975; Goguen, Thatcher, and Wagner, 1978; Zilles, 1974; Guttag, 1975]; that is, the denotation of an object is an *algebra*, a collection of sets with functions among them. In a logical programming language (in the sense of the next subsection) like OBJ, the already established proof theory of the underlying logical system applies directly to programs, and complex formalisms like Scott-Strachey denotational semantics and Hoare axiomatic semantics are not needed. The *initial algebra* approach [Goguen, Thatcher, and Wagner, 1978; Meseguer, and Goguen, 1985] takes the unique (up to isomorphism) initial algebra as the most representative model of the equations (there may of course be many other models), that is, as the representation-independent standard of comparison for correctness. [Burstall and Goguen, 1981, 1982] show that an algebra is *initial* if and only if it satisfies the following properties:

1. No junk: Every element can be named using the given constant and operation symbols.
2. No confusion: All equations true of the algebra can be proved from the given equations.

Under certain mild conditions, the rewrite rule operational semantics agrees with initial algebra semantics. Since OBJ is based on order-sorted algebra, it is important to note that the above result of Burstall and Goguen easily extends to this case: the conditions are just that the rule set is Church-Rosser and terminating (this result is shown in [Goguen, 1980]; see also [Wand, 1980]). OSA, and thus OBJ, provides a completely general programming formalism, in the sense that any partial computable function can be defined, according to an as-yet-unpublished theorem of Dr. José Meseguer; see [Bergstra and Tucker, 1980; Meseguer and Goguen, 1985] for similar results about total computable functions. The formalism seems especially convenient and natural for nonnumerical processing, but in fact, it also handles numerical applications quite well.

Logical Programming.   The original vision of *logic programming* called for using pure first-order predicate calculus directly as a programming language [Kowalski, 1974]. As has been well argued by advocates of Prolog, this confers some important benefits: program simplicity and clarity, separation of logic and control, and identity of program logic with proof logic. In such a language, a high-level description of what a program *does* actually *is* a program; that is, one can execute it. Unfortunately, Prolog [Colmerauer *et al.*, 1979; Sterling and Shapiro, 1986] only partially realizes this vision, since it has many features with no corresponding feature in logic (e.g., cut, `is`, and `assert`), and also lacks some important features of logic (e.g., semantic equality and true negation).

We believe that the many advantages claimed for logic programming are compromised to the extent that it fails to realize a pure logic. Consequently, a major research goal has been to create powerful programming languages that are based upon pure logic and support truly practical programming. An important advantage of such languages is that they are more convenient for parallel machines, since the compiler and operating system can exploit whatever concurrency is actually available in the program and the particular target machine, because programs are not tied down to particular control strategies (sequential control in traditional imperative languages, and tasking, rendezvous, etc., in imperative languages with explicit concurrency). To this end, we have taken the broad view [Goguen, 1986] that a logical programming language L consists of a well-understood[4] logical system[5] I together with two subclasses of sentence called *statements* and *queries*, such that

☐ an L program P is a finite set of statements,

☐ every program P has an *initial model* (where initial models are standard or most prototypical as described in the previous subsection), which gives its denotational semantics,

☐ operational semantics is given by a (reasonably efficient) form of deduction in I, and

☐ a query is satisfied in an initial model of P if and only if it can be proven from P (this is a form of completeness).

To complete this picture, we may define an *answer* to a query to be some property of a proof of the query; for example, we might extract a value for each variable that occurs in the query (this definition has evolved over some period of time in collaboration with Dr. José Meseguer). This notion of logical programming refines the perhaps more familiar notion of *declarative programming*, in which programs tell what properties the result should have, rather than how to calculate that result. We claim that programs in logical programming languages are easier to read, understand, write, debug, reuse, modify, maintain, and verify. We also claim that it is easier to build environments to support such languages; in particular, it is easier to build debuggers. (See [O'Keefe, 1985] for a discussion of serious difficulties that arise in trying to implement a debugger that can handle Prolog's cut.) Logical programming can be given a precise grounding in the notion of *institution* [Goguen and Burstall, 1985], and this is in part responsible for the cleanliness and simplicity of the various languages that we have designed.

---

[4]In particular, there should be reasonably simple notions of sentence, deduction, model, and satisfaction, preferably with a completeness theorem, saying that the notion of deduction is fully adequate for the notion of model, that is, that given any set P of sentences, another sentence s can be deduced from P if and only if every model of P satisfies s.

[5]More precisely, what Burstall and Goguen call an institution [Goguen and Burstall, 1985].

Logical programming in this general sense includes

- ☐ functional programming, where the logic is some kind of equational logic, that is, a logic of substitution of equals for equals;
- ☐ relational (i.e., predicate, or Horn clause) programming, where the logic is first-order Horn clause logic (without equality); and
- ☐ multiparadigm programming, where the underlying logical systems are unified. In particular, unified relational and functional programming results from using Horn clause logic with equality, as in Eqlog [Goguen and Meseguer, 1986]; unified functional and object-oriented programming results from using reflective equational logic, as in FOOPS [Goguen and Meseguer, 1987a]; and triparadigm programming results from using reflective Horn clause logic with equality, as in FOOPlog. (As shown in [Goguen and Meseguer, 1982a], there is another somewhat simpler semantics for FOOPS and FOOPlog based on hidden sorts, rather than on reflexivity.)

Some other logical programming languages include pure Prolog [Colmerauer *et al.*, 1979], pure Lisp [McCarthy *et al.*, 1966], and CDS [Berry and Currien, 1985]. Some other systems using equational logic are Larch [Guttag, Horning, and Wing, 1985], Asspegique [Bidoit *et al.*, 1985], and Act One [Ehrig and Mahr, 1985]. A logical programming language wears its semantics on its sleeve and does not need the complex machinery of Scott-Strachey-style "denotational" semantics [Scott and Strachey, 1971; Stoy, 1977] or Hoare-style "axiomatic" semantics [Hoare, 1969]. In fact, I claim that if a language can only be given a semantics in one of these styles, but not as a logical programming language, then it is too complex. Most functional programming languages are not logical programming languages, since they have neither a supporting notion of deduction nor a model-theoretic semantics for their programs.

OBJ provides the capabilities of functional programming in a simple, elegant, and logically precise way, based on order-sorted algebra and parameterized modules. However, really practical programming should also handle input/output, files, windows, dynamic databases, and, most generally, objects having their own local states, as in FOOPS [Goguen and Meseguer, 1987a].

Propositional Calculus Example.   This subsection presents a decision procedure for a theory of practical interest, the propositional calculus. This decision procedure is due to Hsiang [1981]); the OBJ3 code given in this subsection evolved from OBJ1 code originally written by David Plaisted [Goguen, Meseguer, and Plaisted, 1983]. This example is a good illustration of the associative, commutative, and precedence attributes. It also involves some details about importing other modules that will only become clear in the next section. The rules in the object PROPC below reduce valid propositional formulas, in the standard connectives and, or, implies, not, xor (exclusive or), and iff, to the constant true, and reduce all other formulas to a canonical form in the connectives xor, and, true, and false. Here QID is the protecting imported module of identifiers that begin with an apostrophe, for example 'a, and BOOL is extending imported, to permit associative extensions to be generated (see the next section for discussion of these issues). These rules are Church-Rosser and terminating modulo the axioms corresponding to the attributes [Hsiang, 1981].

```
obj PROPC is
   sort Prop .
   extending BOOL .
   protecting QID .
   subsorts Id Bool < Prop .

   op _and_ : Prop Prop -> Prop [assoc comm idem id: true prec 2] .
   op _xor_ : Prop Prop -> Prop [assoc comm id: false prec 3] .
   vars p q r : Prop .
   eq : p and false = false .
   eq : p xor p = false .
   eq : p and (q xor r) = (p and q) xor (p and r) .

   op _or_ : Prop Prop -> Prop [assoc prec 7] .
   op not_ : Prop -> Prop [prec 1] .
   op _implies_ : Prop Prop -> Prop [prec 9] .
   op _iff_ : Prop Prop -> Prop [assoc prec 11] .
   eq : p or q = (p and q) xor p xor q .
   eq : not p = p xor true .
   eq : p implies q = (p and q) xor p xor true .
   eq : p iff q = p xor q xor true .
endo
```

Here are some sample executions in the context of this object:

```
   reduce 'a implies 'b iff not 'b implies not 'a endr
   result Prop : true

   reduce not('a or 'b) iff not 'a and not 'b endr
   result Prop: true

   reduce 'c or 'c and 'd iff 'c endr
   result Prop: true

   reduce 'a iff not 'b endr
   result Prop: 'a xor 'b

   reduce 'a and 'b xor 'c xor 'b and 'a endr
   result Prop: 'c
```

The first three expressions reduced above are tautologies, while the fourth is true iff exactly one of `'a` and `'b` is true, and the fifth is true iff `'c` is true. Note that `'a`, `'b`, `'c` are propositional variables in the sense that anything of sort `Prop` can be substituted for them while still preserving truth; in particular, `true` and `false` can always be substituted. This example illustrates a particular advantage of programming in a logical language: Even if the given equations did not define a decision procedure, as long as they are all true, then the results of reduction are always correct; in particular, anything that reduces to `true` is definitely a tautology. Section 7.4.7 uses the `PROPC` object in a hardware verification example.

7.3 HIERARCHICAL STRUCTURE

It is easier to understand a program if it is broken into modules, each of which is mind-sized and has a natural purpose. This in turn facilitates both debugging and reusability. When there are many modules, it is helpful to make the hierarchical structure of module dependency explicit, so that whenever one module uses data or operations declared in a second, the second must be explicitly imported to the first and must also be defined earlier in the program text. A program developed in this way has the abstract structure of an acyclic graph of abstract modules. Note that such a hierarchy differs from a Dijkstra-Parnas hierarchy of abstract machines because higher-level modules are not implemented by lower-level (less abstract) machines; rather, higher-level modules include lower-level modules.

More exactly now, a directed edge in an acyclic graph of modules indicates that the higher (target) module imports the lower (source) module. The context of a given module is the subgraph of other modules upon which it depends, that is, the subgraph of which it is the top. Parameterized modules can also occur in such a hierarchy, and are treated in essentially the same way as unparameterized modules. (This discussion is a bit oversimplified, since OBJ contexts must reflect not only submodule relations, but also the more general view relations that may hold among modules; we return to this after views are defined in Section 7.4.)

In addition to representing program structure in a clear and convenient way, the module hierarchy has some more specific applications. It can be used to maintain multiple mutually inconsistent structures as subhierarchies; this is useful for keeping available more than one way to do the same or related things, such as in a family of partially overlapping system designs; that is, the module hierarchy can be used for configuration management. It can also be used to keep information from different sources in different places, and to maintain multiple inconsistent worlds. This could be useful in artificial intelligence applications to explore the consequences of various mutually inconsistent assumptions, in the context of some shared assumptions. Hierarchical structure could also be used to reflect access properties of a physically distributed database.

7.3.1 Importing Modules

OBJ has three modes for importing modules, with syntax

      <importing-kw> <mexp-list> .

where *<importing-kw>* is one of the modes using, extending, or protecting, and *<mexp-list>* is a list of module expressions (in particular, *<mexp-list>* could be just one module, such as INT). By convention, if a module M imports a module M′ that imports a module M″, then M″ is also imported into M; that is, importing is a transitive relation. (This convention can be modified by information hiding, as discussed in Section 7.3.4 below.) A given module M′ can only be imported once into M, in a single mode.

    The meaning of the three import modes is related to the initial algebra semantics of objects. An importation of module M′ by M is

1. protecting iff M′ adds no new data items of sorts from M, and identifies no old data items of sorts from M (no junk and no confusion),
2. extending iff M′ identifies no old data items of sorts from M (no confusion), and
3. using if there are no guarantees at all.

The using mode is implemented by copying the imported module's text, without copying the modules that it imports. But if desired, these can also be copied, just by listing them in the using *<mexp-list>* as well. In this case, the module names must be written in an order that respects their hierarchy; that is, if B is a submodule of A that we also want copied, then B should follow A in *<mexp-list>*.

    Sometimes one may want to modify the attributes of an imported operation. The syntax is the same as for originally declaring it; that is, write

      op *<op-decl>* [*<attr-list>*] .

to indicate that the attributes in *<attr-list>* are to overwrite those previously given for this operation; this allows deleting attributes just by not mentioning them. However, it is not meaningful to delete rewrite modulo attributes for a redeclared operation under a using importation.

    For an extending importation, the E-strategies associated with imported operations may have to be recomputed, according to the following rules:

1. If an imported operation has an explicit strategy, then use it (if the attributes of the operation are redeclared, then use the new strategy, if there is one; if there isn't, then nullify the old strategy);
2. if not, and if there are no new rules, then use the inherited computed strategy; but
3. if there are new rules, then recompute the strategy and use the new one.

A `protecting` importation has the advantage that it guarantees that the E-strategies of imported operations do not need to be recomputed, and thus the code from imported modules can just be shared. Note that OBJ does not check whether the user's import declarations are correct, since this could require arbitrarily difficult theorem proving and would therefore render the language impractical. However, the consequences of an incorrect import mode declaration can be serious: incomplete reductions in some cases and inefficient reductions in others. Recall that BOOL is implicitly `protecting` imported into every module, to ensure that conditional equations can be used. This convention can be overridden by giving an explicit `extending BOOL` declaration; `using BOOL` is not meaningful, since a `using` importation that is not an extending importation will identify true with false, which is not only not useful, but also will interfere with the built-in `==` and `if_then_else_fi` operations.

7.3.2 Built-ins

Programming systems usually provide a number of built-in data types—for example, numbers and identifiers. A sufficiently powerful language need not provide such built-ins, since they can be defined; but building in the most frequently used data types can make a great difference in efficiency and convenience. OBJ has built-in objects BOOL, NAT, INT, RAT, FLOAT, TUPLE, ID, and QID. BOOL provides the expected syntax and semantics for Booleans, such as infix associative `and`, `or`, and `iff`, infix `implies`, prefix `not`, and the truth values `true` and `false`. NAT, INT, and RAT provide natural numbers, integers, and rationals, respectively, while FLOAT provides floating point numbers, each with the usual operations. TUPLE provides n-tuples for all $n > 1$, with ith-selectors for $0 < i < n + 1$. ID and QID provide identifiers, with only the operations of equality and lexicographic order built in. QID identifiers begin with the apostrophe symbol, for example, `'a`, `'b`, `'1040`, and `'aratherlongidentifier`. Data elements from ID lack the initial apostrophe, and therefore must be used very carefully to avoid massive parsing ambiguities.

OBJ objects can also encapsulate Lisp code, but since this paper is primarily concerned with parameterized programming, the details are omitted. However, it is worth noting that all of OBJ's built-ins were actually implemented this way, and the possibility of implementing other efficient built-in data structures and algorithms is always available to sophisticated users.

7.3.3 Libraries

For code to be reusable, it and anything that it relies upon (its context) must be known. This requires understanding of what the code does, and where to find it and its context. Libraries provide a convenient way to store and retrieve modules and their contexts. The basic OBJ library unit is a file, which may contain modules, views, and other top-level OBJ commands, including reduction commands and the `in` (or `input`) command, which reads in and executes one or more files. For example,

```
in library62 mysys test4
```

reads the files `library62`, `mysys`, and `test4` in that order, adding to the current context whatever modules and views they contain, executing whatever commands they contain, including nested `in` commands, and checking that a consistent context is formed as they are added to the database. The context of a given file of modules and views can be preserved by prefacing the file with an `in` command pointing to whatever they depend upon. A related command, `get`, extracts modules from a named file and adds them to the current context. For example,

```
get STACK ARRAY from alibrary
```

will get the objects `STACK` and `ARRAY` from `alibrary`. Of course, this command is more dangerous than `in`, since it may not preserve contexts.

Allowing files to include top-level OBJ commands is very convenient and flexible. For example, after constructing a particular multimodule context, OBJ1 could expand storage, execute some illustrative examples, and then store the results away with its `photo` command. Unix directories provide a convenient way to organize files into libraries, since a given directory can have subdirectories named by keywords, with further named subdirectories, and so on. For example, I have put the propositional calculus decision procedure in my file `obj/prop/propc.obj`, its test cases in `obj/prop/propc-test.obj`, and the results of running them in `obj/prop/propc-test.log`; the subdirectory `obj/prop` also contains code for some other approaches to the propositional calculus. Note that files and subdirectories can be cross-referenced; for example, a given file can be shared among several subdirectories. However, files are a relatively crude way to implement libraries, and we hope to do better in some future design.

7.3.4 Information Hiding

A very basic problem in programming is to control the complexity of large programs. Complexity does not just grow linearly with the size of programs, but seems to be more nearly exponential. *Information hiding*, also called abstraction or encapsulation, addresses This problem [Parnas, 1972a, 1972b]. For example, the representation of an abstract data type in an Ada package can be hidden. Information hiding involves modularization but goes further by declaring that some information inside a module *cannot* be accessed from outside. This tactic can insure that a data representation can be changed just by reimplementing its operations. There is no need to search through an entire program for subtle uses of the old representation; there can't be any, because the only operations that can be used outside are the operations that the module actually exports.

There are various approaches to describing what to hide in a strongly typed modular language. In OBJ, sorts and operations are visible unless declared hidden. Sorts can be declared hidden with the keyword `hsorts`, and operations with the attribute `hidden`.

7.3.5 Interaction

Programming can be greatly eased by running simple syntactic and semantic checks at program entry time, rather than later at compile or execution time. Such checks should be incremental and interactive, and are one reason for the popularity of structural editors and similar facilities. For example, OBJ1 immediately reported expressions that failed to parse or had more than one parse, and it also provided diagnostic information generated by a spelling checker. When reading from a file, OBJ1 inserted such information as comments; then the user could see those comments when later editing that file. When the editor (EMACS) was exited, OBJ1 retried only the edited objects. OBJ1 also had commands to show the sorts, subsorts, operations, and equations currently in use in any part of its database, commands to trace execution; commands to undo and edit any desired module, or even a whole file; a command to resume executing a previously interrupted session; and `help` and `photo` commands. The `photo` command recorded the results of a given session in a designated file. Experience shows that a good interactive user interface can tremendously improve programmer productivity by reducing the time required to find spelling and other syntax errors, and by eliminating the need to reprocess modules upon which a corrected module depended. (These facilities are not yet implemented in OBJ3.)

7.4 PARAMETERIZATION

Parameterized modules are the basic building blocks of parameterized programming, and theories, views, and module expressions go well beyond the capabilities of Ada generics. A theory defines the interface of a parameterized module, that is, the structure and properties required of an actual parameter for meaningful instantiation. A view expresses that a certain module satisfies a certain theory in a certain way (note that some modules can satisfy some theories in more than one way); that is, a view describes a binding of an actual parameter to a requirement theory. Instantiation of a parameterized module with an actual parameter, using a particular view, yields a new module. Module expressions describe complex interconnections of modules, possibly adding, deleting, renaming, or modifying functionality.

Module composition in parameterized programming is more powerful than the purely functional composition of traditional functional programming, in that a single module instantiation can compose many different functions all at once. For example, a generic complex arithmetic module CPXA can be easily instantiated with any of several real arithmetic modules as actual parameter:

☐ single-precision reals, CPXA[SP-REAL],
☐ double-precision reals, CPXA[DP-REAL], or
☐ multiple-precision reals, CPXA[MP-REAL].

Each instantiation involves substituting dozens of functions into dozens of other functions. While something similar is also possible in higher-order functional programming by coding up modules as records, it is much less natural. Furthermore, with parameterized programming, the logic can be first-order, so that understanding and verifying the code can be simpler. Moreover, semantic declarations are allowed at module interfaces (given by requirement theories), and module expressions allow many interesting transformations and combinations other than application.

Our approach to parameterization was inspired by the Clear specification language [Burstall and Goguen, 1977; Burstall and Goguen, 1980]; in fact, OBJ can be regarded as an implementation of Clear. In particular, the notion of view was developed in collaboration with Rod Burstall for use in Clear. Clear's approach was in turn inspired by some ideas in general system theory [Goguen, 1971]. A key idea is the use of colimits of diagrams of theories to determine the result of module expression evaluation. Although colimits are beyond the scope of this paper, they give a precise foundation for parameterized programming, and moreover, a foundation that is independent of the particular choice of an underlying logical system.

Any logical programming language (in our sense) can be given the features for parameterized programming described in this paper. This includes Eqlog, FOOPS, and FOOPlog, as well as OBJ, so that the various combinations of functional, relational, and object-oriented programming are all covered. These languages also seem to have great potential as efficiently executable knowledge representation languages, and many of their features can be redescribed in the idiom of that field; this is entirely consistent with the original conception of Clear. Parameterized programming is also applicable to languages like Ada and (impure) Prolog; however, some additional ideas are needed to handle states, for which see LIL, as described in [Goguen, 1986a].

7.4.1 Theories

Theories express properties of modules and module interfaces. In general, OBJ theories have the same structure as objects; in particular, theories have

sorts, subsorts, operations, variables, and equations; can import other theories
and objects; can be parameterized; and can have views. The difference is that
objects are executable, while theories just define properties. Semantically, a
theory has a *variety* of models, all the (order-sorted) algebras that satisfy it,
whereas an object has just one model (up to isomorphism), its initial algebra.

We now give some example theories, declaring structure and properties
that we might want satisfied for a given module to perform correctly. The
first is the trivial theory TRIV, which requires nothing except a sort, here
designated Elt.

```
th TRIV is
   sort Elt .
endth
```

The next theory is an extension of TRIV, requiring that models also have a
given element of the given sort, here designated *.

```
th TRIV* is
   extending TRIV .
   op * : -> Elt .
endth
```

Of course, this enrichment is equivalent to

```
th TRIV* is
   sort Elt .
   op * : -> Elt .
endth
```

which may seem clearer.

Next, we give the theory of preordered sets (which are like partially
ordered sets but without the antisymmetric law). Its models have a binary
infix Bool-valued operation <= that is reflexive and transitive.

```
th PREORD is
   sort Elt .
   op _<=_ : Elt Elt -> Bool .
   vars E1 E2 E3 : Elt .
   eq E1 <= E1 = true .
   ceq E1 <= E3 = true if E1 <= E2 and E2 <= E3 .
endth
```

The theory of an equivalence relation also has a binary infix Bool-valued
operation; it is denoted _eq_ and is reflexive, symmetric, and transitive.

```
th EQV is
  sort Elt .
  op _eq_ : Elt Elt -> Bool .
  vars E1 E2 E3 : Elt .
  eq (E1 eq E1) = true .
  eq (E1 eq E2) = (E2 eq E1) .
  ceq (E1 eq E3) = true if (E1 eq E2) and (E2 eq E3) .
endth
```

Finally, we give the theory of monoids, which will later serve as a parameter requirement theory for a general iterator that in particular gives sums and products over lists.

```
th MONOID is
  sort M .
  op _*_ : M M -> M [assoc id: e] .
endth
```

The possibility of expressing semantic properties, such as the associativity of an operation, as part of the interface of a module is another aspect in which parameterized programming has an advantage over traditional functional programming. For example, one can certainly write a (second-order) function to iterate any given binary function (such as integer addition) over lists, but traditional functional programming cannot express the requirement that the binary function must be associative, although this semantic requirement is needed for many applications.

7.4.2 Parameterized Modules

Let us now consider some parameterized modules. First, here is a parameterized LIST object:

```
obj LIST[X :: TRIV] is
  sorts List NeList .
  subsorts Elt < NeList < List .
  op _ _ : List List -> List [assoc id: nil] .
  op _ _ : NeList List -> NeList [assoc] .
  op head_ : NeList -> Elt .
  op tail_ : NeList -> List .
  op empty?_ : List -> Bool .
  var X : Elt .
  var L : List .
  eq head X L = X .
  eq tail X L = L .
  eq empty? L = L == nil .
endo
```

Modules can have more than one parameter. The two-parameter case has the form [X :: TH1, Y :: TH2], and if the two theories are the same, we can just write [X Y :: TH]. Next we give a parameterized theory, for vector spaces over a field F.

```
th VECTOR-SP[F :: FIELD] is
  sort V .
  op _+_ : V V -> V [assoc comm id: 0] .
  op _*_ : F V -> V .
  vars F F1 F2 : F .
  vars V V1 V2 : V .
  eq (F1 + F2)* V = (F1 * V)+(F2 * V) .
  eq (F1 * F2)* V = F1 *(F2 * V) .
  eq F * (V1 + V2) = (F * V1) + (F * V2) .
endth
```

The requirement theories of parameterized modules must have been defined earlier in the program; in this case, FIELD must be defined earlier in the program text.

Even though the code is very similar to that for LIST, it seems worth doing STACK; this example is a well-known benchmark because it has been done in so many different formalisms, and in fact, it seems quite a good illustration of the power of order-sorted algebra.

```
obj STACK[X :: TRIV] is
  sorts Stack NeStack .
  subsorts Elt < NeStack < Stack .
  op empty : -> Stack .
  op push : Elt Stack -> NeStack .
  op top_ : NeStack -> Elt .
  op pop_ : NeStack -> Stack .
  var X : Elt .
  var S : Stack .
  eq top push(X,S) = X .
  eq pop push(X,S) = S .
endo
```

This seems about as simple a program as one could desire. Many other parameterized modules are given later in this paper.

7.4.3 Views

A module can satisfy a theory in more than one way, and even if there is a unique way, it can be arbitrarily difficult to find. We therefore need a notation for describing the particular ways that modules satisfy theories. For example, NAT can satisfy PREORD with the usual "less-than-or-equal" ordering, but "divides" and "greater-than-or-equal" are also possible; each of these cor-

responds to a different view. Thus, an expression like LEXL[NAT] (where
LEXL has requirement theory PREORD, as in Section 7.1.1) would be ambiguous if there were not a definite convention for default views.

More precisely now, a view v from a theory T to a module M, indicated
$v: T \rightarrow M$, consists of a mapping from the sorts of T to the sorts of M
preserving the subsort relation, and a mapping from the operations of T to
the operations of M preserving arity, value sort, and the attributes assoc,
comm, id:, and idem (to the extent that they are present), such that every
equation in T is true of every model of M (a view from one theory to another
is what logicians call a theory interpretation [Burstall and Goguen, 1980]).
The mapping of sorts is expressed in the form

```
sort S1 to S1' .
sort S2 to S2' .
    . . .
```

and the mapping of operations is expressed in the form

```
op o1 to o1' .
op o2 to o2' .
    . . .
```

where o1, o1', o2, and so on may be operation forms, or forms plus
value sort, or forms plus value sort and arity, as needed for disambiguation;
moreover, o1', o2', and so on can be derived operations (i.e., terms with
variables). Thus each mapping can be considered a set of pairs. These two
sets of pairs together are called a *view body*. The syntax for defining a view at
the top level of OBJ also includes names for the source and target modules,
and possibly a name for the view. For example,

```
view NATD from PREORD to NAT is
  sort Elt to Nat .
  op _<=_ to divides .
endv
```

defines a view called NATD from PREORD to NAT using the divisibility relation.

When the user feels that there is an obvious view to use, it is annoying to
have to write out that view in full detail. Default views often allow omitting
views within module expressions, by capturing the intuitive notion of the
"obvious view." This subsection is limited to general discussion and examples;
Appendix A gives details.

A view can be internal, null, or explicit. Internal views have first priority
when they exist. An internal view from a given theory is explicitly included
inside a module with the syntax

```
view <th-name> is <sort-map> <op-map> endv
```

The target is the including module, and need not be explicitly mentioned. It is an error to have more than one included view with the same source theory in a given module.

Null views are next in priority. A null view can be considered as the extreme case of an abbreviated view in which the view is abbreviated to nothing. Views can be abbreviated according to a definite set of rules; these rules have corresponding inverses for reconstructing the intended view from the abbreviation. Given a view $v: M \rightarrow M'$, there are two rules for abbreviating sorts. The first is that any pair of the form S to S can be omitted. The second is that a pair S to S' can be omitted if S is not shared between M and M' and if S' is the sort in M' having the same order as S has in M, where the order of a sort in a module is given by the order in which sorts are introduced in the body, imported modules, and parameters of the module; see Appendix A for details.

As a special case, every module has a default view from TRIV with its primary sort as the target for Elt. For another example, the default view from PREORD to NAT is

```
view NATV from PREORD to NAT is
  sort Elt to Nat .
  op _<=_ to _<=_ .
endv
```

In the following abbreviated view:

```
view NATD from PREORD to NAT is
  op _<=_ to divides .
endv
```

the pair Elt to Nat has been omitted.

There are also conventions for omitting operation pairs from a view $v: M \rightarrow M'$. First, any pair of the form o to o can be omitted. For example, the default view from PREORD to NAT has Elt to Nat and _⇐_ to _⇐_. Second, a pair o to o' can be omitted if o is not shared, if the sorts in the arity and value sort of o are contained in their counterparts in o', and if o and o' have the same order in their respective modules, as detailed in Appendix A. Finally, if o to o' is a pair, and if o and o' have attributes id: e and id: e' respectively, then e to e' can be omitted. For example, the default view from MONOID to NAT is

```
view NAT* from MONOID to NAT is
  sort M to Nat .
  op _*_ to _*_ .
  op e to 1 .
endv
```

where e maps to 1 because the id: attribute of * is preserved. The following is a nondefault view of NAT as a MONOID.

```
view NAT+ from MONOID to NAT is
  op _*_ to _+_ .
  op e to 0 .
endv
```

where `e to 0` could also be omitted, again by preservation of the `id:` attribute.

Explicit views have last priority among default views. If there is no internal or null view $T \rightarrow M$, but there is exactly one view $v: T \rightarrow M$ explicitly declared at the top level, then v is the default view from T to M. (If there is more than one explicit view, we might take the most recently declared as default, but issue a warning that there is more than one explicit view.)

Next, we give a view that involves a parameter in the target module

```
view LISTM from MONOID to LIST[X :: TRIV] is
    op _*_ to _ _ .
    op e to nil .
  endv
```

(This view can actually be abbreviated to a null view.) Parameterized views are also possible, but we do not give an example here. Of course, it is necessary to instantiate parameterized views; the syntax for this is just the same as for instantiating parameterized modules.

The following view involves a derived operation.

```
view NATG from PREORD to NAT is
  vars L1 L2 : Nat .
  op L1 <= L2 to L2 <= L1 .
endv
```

This maps `<=` in PREORD to `=>` in NAT, using variables to mark the argument places in the operation forms.

When it is otherwise impossible to distinguish among operations or sorts having the same name, but coming from different modules, qualifiers can disambiguate an expression by explicitly indicating the module where an operation is declared.

If a non-null view is only used once, say to instantiate a parameterized module, it can be defined on the fly where it is used, with the syntax

```
view <mexp> is <sort-map> <op-map> endv
```

For example, if the view NATD had not already been defined, we could get the same result as SORTING[NATD] from

```
SORTING[view NAT is op _<=_ to divides .    endv]
```

(This very useful feature is due to Timothy Winkler.)

Composition of views can also be useful, because sometimes the view that you want is a composition of views that you already have. Given views $v1: M1 \rightarrow M2$ and $v2: M2 \rightarrow M3$, their composition is denoted $v1 * v2$, which has source $M1$ and target $M3$.

So far in discussing views, we have largely ignored the hierarchical structure of modules. Although the source components of the operation mapping of v involve only operations from M itself, the target components can be terms involving anything that M' imports; indeed, they do not have to involve operations from M' itself at all. Hence, a view $v: M \rightarrow M'$ may be meaningless unless the modules imported by M are also imported by M'; otherwise there can be equations in M whose translations make no sense in M'.

A given module can in general be seen in many different ways from the outside; that is, in general there are many different views into it, and thus many different interfaces into which it can fit. It may be convenient to document these with internal and explicit views. An internal view $T \rightarrow M$ is appropriate for documenting the most important view of M as T, since it will always be used as the default. Other views of M as T can then be given explicitly outside of M.

The documentation aspect of views is unique to parameterized programming and seems very practical. In principle, theorem-proving technology can be used to verify that a given mapping is a view, that is, that the semantic properties specified in the source theory really are satisfied by the target module. But in practice, this is not usually worth the trouble, and views should be seen as documenting the programmer's intentions and beliefs about the semantic properties of modules; an intermediate stage that often may be practical is to give paper and pencil proofs with the usual informal rigor of mathematics. These proofs could be given as comments, or stored in auxiliary files. Furthermore, programmers can put axioms from any logical system they like in source theories, and can even use natural language assertions (i.e., comments) as if they were axioms.

7.4.4 Instantiation

This subsection discusses instantiating the formal parameters of a parameterized module with actual modules. This construction requires a view from each formal parameter requirement theory to the corresponding actual module (actually, it suffices for each view to include the formal requirement theory in its source theory). The result of such an instantiation replaces each requirement theory by its corresponding actual module, using the views to bind actual names to formal names and avoiding multiple copies of shared submodules.

Let us consider the `make` command, which applies a parameterized module to an actual module via a view, and then adds the result to the OBJ database (if a module name is used instead of a view, then the default view of that module from the requirement of the parameterized module is used, if there is one). For example, if `P[X :: PREORD]` is a parameterized object, then we can form

```
make P-NATD is P[NATD] endm
```

using the explicit view NATD, while

```
make NATLIST is LIST[NAT] endm
```

uses the default view from TRIV to NAT to instantiate the parameterized module LIST with the actual parameter NAT. Similarly, we might have

```
make REAL-LIST is LIST[REAL] endm
```

where REAL is the field of real numbers, using a default view from TRIV to REAL, or

```
make REAL-VSP is VECTOR-SP[REAL] endm
```

using the default view from FIELD to REAL. More interestingly,

```
make STACK-OF-LIST-OF-REAL is STACK[LIST[REAL]] endm
```

uses two default views. In general,

```
make M is P[A] endm
```

is equivalent to

```
obj M is protecting P[A] . endo
```

where A may be either a module or a view. Thus make is redundant, and in fact it was not implemented in OBJ2. Expressions like LIST[NAT], STACK[LIST[REAL]], and P[NATP] are called module expressions, as discussed further in Section 7.4.5.

Sometimes it is convenient to import a module expression with its formal parameters instantiated by those of a parameterized module into which it is imported. For example:

```
obj LEXL[X :: PREORD] is
  protecting LIST[X] .
  view MONOID is op _*_ to _ _ . endv .
  op _<<_ : List List -> Bool .
  vars L L' : List .
  vars E E' : Elt .
  eq L << nil = false .
  eq nil << L = not L == nil .
  eq E L << E' L' = if E == E' then L << L' else E <= E' fi .
endo
```

Here LIST[X] uses the default view of X as TRIV. Then

```
make NATLEX is LEXL[NAT] endm
```

uses the default view of NAT as PREORD to give a lexicographic ordering on lists of natural numbers, and

```
make NATLEXLD is LEXL[NATD] endm
```

orders lists of NATs by the divisability ordering on NATs.

```
make PHRASE is LEXL[QID] endm
```

uses the lexicographic ordering on QID to give a lexicographic ordering on lists of identifiers (and thus for example on titles of books), and

```
make PHRASE-LIST is LEXL[PHRASE] endm
```

uses the lexicographic ordering on PHRASE to give a lexicographic ordering (for example, on lists of book titles). We could of course do this in one fell swoop as

```
make PHRASE-LIST is LEXL[LEXL[ID]] endm
```

Ada does not allow such a complex module expression and would force use of the two-step approach.

Environments for ordinary programming languages are functions from names to values (perhaps with an extra level of indirection); but environments for parameterized programming languages (which are called *contexts* in this paper) must also store relationships between modules. Section 7.3 discussed the submodule inclusion relation that arises from module importation, giving rise to an acyclic graph structure. If we also store views in contexts, with their source and target modules, we get a general graph structure. If submodule inclusions are seen as views, then the submodule hierarchy appears as a subgraph of this graph of views. Since internal views in parameterized modules must be instantiated when the including module is instantiated, parameterized programming actually involves defining and instantiating parameterized contexts.

There is an interesting further generalization of instantiation. First, notice that any parameterized module can be seen as a view $p: R \to B$ from the requirement theory R (or the sum of all requirement theories, if there are more than one) into the body B, which necessarily already includes R. For example, STACK[X :: TRIV] is just the inclusion view STACK: TRIV $\to$ STACKBODY, where the STACKBODY code is the same as was given in Section 7.4.2 above for STACK, except for replacing the name STACK[X :: TRIV] by just STACKBODY. Then, given any binding view $b: R \to A$ to an actual module A, we can form the instantiation $p[b]$, which substitutes A into B after translation by p of R; more precisely, the result of the application is given by what is called a pushout in category theory, as developed in the semantics of Clear [Burstall and Goguen, 1977, 1981]. With this technique, a single body can be parameterized in many different ways. Thus, Ada's idea to separate the "body" and "specification" (really, interface) parts of modules was good, but it is much more flexible if views are added.

7.4.5 Module Expressions

Module expressions not only permit defining, constructing, and instantiating complex combinations of modules, they also permit modifying modules in various ways, thus making it possible to use a given module in a wider variety of contexts. The major combination modes are instantiation (as discussed above) and sum. Among possible modifications are enriching a module, by adding to its functionality; restricting a module, by eliminating some of its functionality; renaming parts of a module; and modifying a module (or module combination), for example, to improve its efficiency. Such transformations can easily take account of data structures. All this makes possible a broad range of program transformations right inside of programs. No other programming language that we know has such a feature in the language itself.

The simplest module expressions are the constants, which are the built-in data types BOOL, NAT, INT, QID, ID, and FLOAT, plus any user-defined unparameterized modules available in the current context. The theory TRIV is also built in. Another built-in module is n-ary parameterized TUPLE, which forms n-tuples of sorts for any $n > 1$; all n of its requirement theories are TRIV. For example, TUPLE[INT,BOOL] is a module expression whose principal sort consists of pairs of an integer and a truth value. Another example is TUPLE[LIST[INT],INT,BOOL]. One can also write sort names instead of module names, for example, TUPLE[LIST[Int],Int,Bool], with the same result.

Renaming uses a view body, that is, a sort mapping and an operation mapping, to create a new module from an old one, with syntax

(*<sort-map>* *<op-map>*)

where either map can be deleted if empty, and where each map consists of pairs of the form sort S to S' or op o to o', which pairs must be separated by commas. A renaming is postfixed to a *<mexp>* after a *, and it modifies the syntax of the *<mexp>* by applying the pairs that are given. For example, we can use renaming to modify the PREORD theory to get the theory of an equivalence relation, as follows:

```
th EQV is using PREORD * (op _<=_ to _eq_) .
  vars E1 E2 : Elt .
  eq (E1 eq E2) = (E2 eq E1) .
endth
```

Similarly, functionality can be hidden in a module with the `hide` command, having syntax

    (hide sorts <*sort-list*> ops <*op-list*>)

which is also applied postfix following a *. Sometimes it may be more convenient to indicate which sorts and/or operations are to be visible, using the syntax

    (hide except sorts <*sort-list*> ops <*op-list*>)

Another important module-building operation is the sum, written

   <*mexp*> + ... + <*mexp*>

which denotes a new module that adds (sums, or combines) all the information in its summands. Submodules can be imported by more than one summand; for example, in A + B, both A and B may protect or extend NAT, INT, or other modules; such multiply imported modules should be shared.

There are actually three modes for summand modules in a sum, just as there are for imported modules, and the foregoing is syntactic sugar for the case where all modules are added in the extending mode. The most general syntax is

    +<*mode*> <*mexp*> +<*mode*> <*mexp* > ... +<*mode*> <*mexp*>

where <*mode*> can be ex, pr, or us, where ex can always be omitted, and where an initial +ex can be omitted, and any other +ex can be replaced by just +. For example,

    P +pr INT +us Q .

The sum construction can also be applied to views, with the syntax

    +<*mode*> <*view*> +<*mode*> <*view*>...+<*mode*> <*view*>

and the same conventions for abbreviation as for modules. The source of the sum view is the sum of its sources, and the target of the sum view is the sum of its targets.

To enrich a module expression, we need only import it into a module and then add the desired sorts, operations, and equations; thus we really do not need explicit enrichment transformations for module expressions. Earlier versions of OBJ had an image transformation with capabilities of renaming and instantiation; but since it did not use theories to describe interfaces, it now seems rather undisciplined and has been abandoned, even though it can be given a respectable semantics using colimits [Goguen, Meseguer, and Plaisted, 1983].

Nested Modules. Nesting modules within other modules allows scoping conventions that are much more convenient for some cases than those otherwise in force. If the enclosing module is parameterized, then all its enclosed modules implicitly inherit that parameterization, and all are automatically instantiated when the enclosing module is instantiated. Other nested modules at the same level as a given one and lexically above it are inherited by it, while nested modules below it or inside other modules at the same level are not. In particular, the content of a module M' that is inside a module M is not exported by M; indeed, M' is available only to code inside M and textually below M'. This provides a convenient way to hide implementation details, and allows local names, local data types, and local operations. However, some notational apparatus for circumventing this convention should also be available. Combined with parameterization and information hiding, nesting gives a potent generalization of the traditional block structure concept. (We hope to implement this in some future version of OBJ.)

Top-Down Development. It might seem at first that parameterized programming is limited to a bottom-up development style. But in fact, there are many ways to realize a top-down style in parameterized programming:

1. Write a theory T that describes some desired behavior, and then write a module M with a view $T \rightarrow M$. Here M may be either an object or another theory.
2. Write a parameterized module that realizes the desired behavior if its parameters are instantiated according to their requirement theories.
3. Write a module that realizes the desired behavior if the right modules are imported; write "stubs" (i.e., skeletal code) for the modules to be imported, and then elaborate them later. Often, one wants to use the requirement theories themselves as stubs, and OBJ2 provided this as a convenient default [Futatsugi, Goguen, Meseguer, and Okada , 1987].

Of course, a given step of downward development could involve any two, or even all three of these strategies, and any number of steps could be taken.

Optimizing Transformations. The transformations on module expressions that we have described so far seem reasonably comprehensive and convenient for programming in the large, but they do not address the problems of programming in the small (i.e., of module construction) or of enhancing program efficiency. These issues seem to require transformations that can modify the internal structure of modules. A graphics-based system that constructs rewrite rules from their dynamic effects on generic elements is described in [Goguen, 1987]. Although this provides a convenient way to build modules for a language like OBJ, it does not address interactions among the components of complex module combinations. Such issues are addressed by recent developments in the program transformation literature that emphasize the *process* of programming and in particular involve recording major design decisions for later manipulation. For example, the inferential programming of Scherlis and Scott [Scherlis and Scott, 1983; Scherlis, 1986] is concerned with these matters and with being able to reason about program derivations, including commitment and specialization steps that make programs less abstract. Parameterized programming, with its machinery for handling structure and semantics, seems to complement the concerns of inferential programming very nicely, and it should be quite worthwhile to combine the two approaches.

For purely functional programming (as in OBJ), the following transformations seem especially useful:

1. Memoize, that is, add the `memo` attribute to certain operations.
2. Transform a set of equations that define an operation by case analysis on constructors into a single equation that uses `if_then_else_fi`.
3. Represent lists as trees.

The first transformation changes an object in a very simple way, just adding the attribute `memo`. This has no effect on the denotational semantics,[6] but it can make the operational semantics much more efficient. The second transformation changes the equations in an object into a more efficient form, while preserving the denotational semantics.[7] For example, this transformation would change

```
eq f(0) = 1 .
eq f(s N) = (s N) * f(N) .
```

for f : Nat->Nat and where s_ : Nat->NzNat is the successor function, into

```
eq f(N) = if N == 0 then 1 else N * f(p N) fi .
```

where p_: NzNat->Nat is the predecessor function. This transformation requires knowing the selectors for the given constructors [Goguen and Meseguer, 1987]; in this case, p_ is the selector for the constructor s_.

The third transformation is more complex but still preserves denotational semantics in a more general sense[8] and can transform a linear-time algorithm to logarithmic time.

In general, transformations should be parameterized modules with interface theories to express their semantic requirements; however, if there are no

---

[6] The initial algebra is the same since the operations and equations are the same.

[7] Here the set of all equations that follow from the given equations remains the same, so the initial algebra is also the same.

[8] The two initial algebras are not equal, but are isomorphic on a subsignature.

semantic requirements, then such transformations could be postfixed to module expressions with *. Sometimes an internal view has to be deleted when its including module is transformed, since it may be unclear how to transform its source theory without using expensive theorem proving. Moreover, an included view can even become invalid; for example, if some of the operations used in an internal view get hidden, then the view is no longer valid.

Major issues for optimizing transformations include their correctness and whether or not they really improve performance: Before applying one, you should be sure that its preconditions are met, and that it really will help. In the imperative case, major difficulties arise from side effects and global interactions, which can be quite unconstrained in this programming style. This suggests investigating optimizing transformations for an object-oriented language like FOOPS, which has a declarative style, while preserving the essential power of imperative programming, which (in my opinion) is access to persistent storage. FOOPS is actually a logical language, with semantics based on order-sorted equational logic with hidden sorts (see [Goguen and Meseguer, 1987a]), which is a generalization of abstract data types to abstract machines [Goguen and Meseguer, 1982a]. The FOOPS design also embodies parameterized programming as described in this paper, including parameterized modules with requirement theories instantiated by views. FOOPS has OBJ as its functional sublanguage for defining data structures; simple and rigorous data structure definitions can make many transformations simpler, clearer, and more general. Moreover, the use of requirement theories and views makes it easier to document and verify semantic requirements for the correctness of transformations, thus making transformation a safer process.

The closely related subject of *implementations* has developed in the abstract data type literature as an abstraction of Hoare's early work on the correctness of data representations [Hoare, 1972] and by now is rather extensively studied. A key idea is to relax the notion of having the same denotational semantics, so that nonisomorphic algebras may nevertheless have the same behavior. A first version of this concept was introduced in [Goguen, Thatcher, and Wagner, 1976], as a subquotient relation; see [Goguen and Meseguer, 1982a; Beierle and Voss, 1985; Orejas, 1985] for more recent developments.

In [Goguen and Burstall, 1980], the structuring mechanisms discussed in this paper are considered horizontal structure, while implementations are considered vertical, in the sense that they relate structures at different (higher and lower) levels of abstraction. Also, some very general laws relating the composition of implementations with horizontal structure are proposed in [Goguen and Burstall, 1980], while some mathematics of vertical structure is developed in [Goguen and Meseguer, 1982a]. This seems a promising direction for the further development of parameterized programming.

7.4.6 Higher-Order Functions Considered Unnecessary for Higher-Order Programming

Higher-order logic is useful in many areas, such as the foundations of mathematics (e.g., type theory), extracting programs from correctness proofs of algorithms, describing proof strategies (as in LCF tactics [Gordon *et al.*, 1979]), modeling traditional programming languages (as in Scott-Strachey semantics), and studying the foundations of the programming process. Perhaps the main advantage of higher-order programming over traditional imperative programming is its capability for structuring programs (see [Hughes, 1984] for some cogent arguments and examples). However, a language with sufficiently powerful parameterized modules does not need higher-order functions. We do not *oppose* higher-order functions as such; however, we *do* claim that they can lead to horribly complex programs and that they can and should be avoided in programming languages. Parameterized programming provides an alternative basis for higher-order programming that has certain advantages. In particular, as shown in the following, typical higher-order functional programming examples are easily coded as OBJ programs that are quite structured, flexible, and rigorous. Moreover, we can use theories to document any semantic properties that may be required of functions.

One classic functional programming example is motivated by the following two instances: (1) `sigma` adds a list of numbers; and (2) `pi` multiplies them. To encompass these and similar examples, we want a function that applies a binary function recursively over suitable lists. Let's see how this example looks in vanilla higher-order functional programming notation. First, a polymorphic list type is defined by something like

```
type list(T) = nil + cons(T,list(T))
```

and then the function we want is defined by[9]

```
function iter : (T -> (T -> T)) -> (T -> (list(T) -> T))
axiom iter(f)(a)(nil) => a
axiom iter(f)(a)(cons(c,list)) => f(c)(iter(f)(a)(list))
```

so that we can write

```
sigma(list) => iter(plus)(0)(list)
pi(list) => iter(times)(1)(list)
```

---

[9]Most people find the rank of `iter` rather difficult to understand. It can be simplified by uncurrying with products, and convention also permits omitting some parentheses; but these devices do not help much. Actually, we feel that products are more fundamental than higher-order functions, and that eliminating products by currying can be misleading and confusing.

For some applications of iter to work correctly, f must have certain semantic properties. For example, if we want to evaluate pi(list) with as many multiplications as possible in parallel, then f must be associative. (The algorithm first converts list into a binary tree, and then does all the multiplications at each tree level in parallel.) Associativity of f implies the following *homomorphic* property, which is needed in the correctness proof:

```
iter(f)(a)(append(list)(list')) =
f(iter(f)(a)(list))(iter(f)(a)(list')
```

for list and list' of the same type. Now, for the empty list nil to behave correctly, a must be an identity for f.

Now let's do this example in OBJ. First, using mixfix syntax _*_ for f improves readability somewhat; but much more significantly, we can use the requirement theory MONOID to assert associativity and identity axioms for actual arguments of a generic iteration module:

```
obj ITER[M :: MONOID] is
  protecting LIST[M] .
  op iter : List -> M .
  var X : M .
  var L : List .
  eq iter(nil) = e .
  eq iter(X L) = X * iter(L) .
endo
```

where e is the monoid identity. Note that LIST[M] uses the default view from TRIV to MONOID. (This code uses an associative list concatenation, but it is also easy to write code using a cons constructor in OBJ.)

We can now instantiate ITER to get our two examples. First,

```
make SIGMA is ITER[NAT+] endm
```

sums lists of numbers, while

```
make PI is ITER[NAT*] endm
```

multiplies lists of numbers (the views used here were defined in Section 7.4.3 above; note that a default view could be used for PI).

Any valid instance of ITER has the homomorphic property, which in the present notation is written

```
iter(L L') = iter(L) * iter(L')
```

and it is natural to state this fact with a theory and view, as follows:

```
th HOM[M :: MONOID] is
  protecting LIST[M] .
  op h : List -> M .
  var L L' : List .
  eq h(L L') = h(L) * h(L') .
endth

view ITER-IS-HOM[M :: MONOID] from HOM[M] to ITER[M] endv
```

This view is parameterized, because the homomorphic property holds for *all* instances; to obtain the appropriate assertion for a given instance ITER[A], just instantiate the view with the same actual parameter module A. Since semantic requirements on argument functions cannot be stated in a conventional functional programming language, all of this would have to be done outside of such a language. But OBJ can not only assert the monoid property, it can even prove that this property implies the homomorphic property using methods described in [Goguen, 1988].

Some have argued that it is actually much easier to use higher-order functions and type inference to get such declarations and instantiations automatically. However, the notational overhead of encapsulating a function in a module is really only a few keywords, and these could even be generated automatically by a structural editor from a single keystroke; moreover, this overhead can often be shared among many function declarations. There is also some overhead due to variable declarations. As discussed in Section 7.2.5, this can be reduced to almost nothing by two techniques: (1) let type inference give a variable the highest possible sort; and (2) declare sorts on the fly with a qualification notation. (We have not implemented this for OBJ3, because explicit declarations can save human program readers much effort in doing type inference.) Sort and operation declarations are needed in any approach, but our notation for them could be slightly simplified, if someone thought it worth the trouble. However, our view has been that the crucial issue is to make the structure of large programs as clear as possible; thus tricks that slightly simplify notation for small examples are of little importance, and they are of negative value if they make it harder to read programs.

On the other hand, our notation for instantiation can often be significantly simplified, for example, if nondefault views are needed, or if renaming is needed to avoid ambiguity when there is more than one instance of some module in a given context. For example,

```
make ITER-NAT is ITER[view NAT is op _*_to _+_ . endv] endm
```

is certainly more complex than iter(plus)(0). However, we could just let ITER[(+).NAT] denote the above module, and we could even let iter[(+).NAT] denote the iter function itself, with the effect of creating the module instantiation that defines it, unless it is already present. Indeed, this is essentially the same notation used in functional programming, and it avoids the need to give distinct names for distinct instances of iter. Let us call this *abbreviated operation notation*. It can also be used when there is more than one argument, as well as for sorts; note that the expression iter[[+].NAT] uses default view conventions so that Elt maps to Nat (rather than Bool), and e maps to 0. This notation also allows writing just + for _+_; the rule is that underbars can be omitted in single-keyword operation forms. (This feature is not yet implemented in OBJ3.)

An alternative is to model polymorphism within order-sorted algebra; here one could declare certain parameterized objects to be polymorphic within some syntactic scope and obtain the usual kind of polymorphism with a first-order logic. However, I am not sure that this is worth the trouble, because it is rare to need many different instantiations of the same function symbol that cannot be handled by very simple module expressions.

For a second example, let us define the traditional function map, which applies a unary function to a list of arguments. Its interface theory requires a sort and a unary function on it (more generally, we could have distinct source and target sorts, if desired).

```
th FN is
  sort S .
  op f : S -> S .
endth

obj MAP[F :: FN] is
  protecting LIST[F] .
  op map : List -> List .
  var X : S .
  var L : List .
  eq map(nil) = nil .
  eq map(X L) = f(X) map(L) .

endo
```

Now we can instantiate MAP in various ways. The following object defines some functions to be used in later examples.

```
obj FNS is
  protecting INT .
  op sq_ : Int -> Int .
  op dbl_ : Int -> Int .
  op _*3 : Int -> Int .
  var N : Int .
  eq dbl N = N + N .
  eq N *3 = N * 3 .
  eq sq N = N * N .
endo
```

Our first instantiation of this uses the default view from FN to FNS, which maps f to sq_, since sq_ is the first operation introduced in FNS.

```
obj TEST1 is protecting MAP[FNS] .    endo
```

Here is a sample reduction:

```
reduce map(0 1 -2 3) endr
result NeList: 0 1 4 9
```

Next, we give some reductions in objects using in-line nondefault views with operation abbreviation:

```
reduce-in MAP[(dbl).FNS] map(0 1 -2 3) endr
result NeList: 0 2 -4 6

reduce-in MAP[(3).FNS] map(0 1 -2 3) endr
result NeList: 0 3 -6 9
```

The following module does another classical functional programming example, applying a given function twice; some instantiations are also given.

```
obj 2[F :: FN] is
   op 2x : S -> S .
   var X : S .
   eq 2x(X) = f(f(X)) .
endo

reduce-in 2[FNS] 2x(3) endr
result Int: 81

reduce-in 2[(dbl).FNS] 2x(3) endr
result Int: 12

reduce-in (2[2[FNS]]*(op (2x).2[2[FNS]] to g)) g(3) endr
result Int: 43046721
```

Let us consider this last example more carefully. Since 2 applies f twice, the result function 2x of the first instantiation applies sq_ twice, that is, raises to the fourth power; then the second instantiation applies that twice, that is, raises to the 16th power. The renaming is given to prevent syntactic ambiguity of 2x, but could be avoided by using qualification.

To summarize, the difference between parameterized programming and higher-order functional programming is essentially the difference between programming in the large and programming in the small. Parameterized programming does not just combine functions, it combines modules. This parallels one of the great insights of modern abstract algebra, that in many important examples, functions should not be considered in isolation, but rather in association with other functions and constants, along with the axioms that they satisfy, and with their explicit sources and targets. Thus the invention of abstract algebras (for vector spaces, groups, etc.) parallels the invention of program modules (for vectors, permutations, etc.); parameterized programming makes this parallel more explicit, and also carries it further, by introducing theories and views, to document semantic requirements on function arguments and on module interfaces, as well as to assert provable properties of modules (as in the above homomorphic property). As we have already noted, it can be more convenient to compose modules then to compose functions, because a single module instantiation can compose many conceptually related functions at once, as in the complex arithmetic (CPXA) example mentioned in Section 7.4. On the other hand, the notational overhead of theories and views is excessive for applying just one function. However, this is exactly the case where our abbreviated operation notation can be used to advantage. And we should not forget that it can be much more difficult to reason with higher-order functions than with first-order functions; in fact, the undecidability of higher-order unification means that it will be very difficult to mechanize many aspects of such reasoning. Also, it is much easier to compile and interpret first-order programs. Poigné [1983] has found some significant difficulties in combining subsorts and higher-order functions, and we hope to have been convincing that subsorts are very useful. It is the experience of many programmers, and not just naive ones, that higher-order notation can be very difficult to understand and to use.

7.4.7 Hardware Specification, Simulation, and Verification

This subsection develops a computer hardware verification example. The crucial advantage of using a logical programming language here is that the reductions really are proofs, because the programs really are logical theories. The file shown after this paragraph begins by reading in the propositional calculus object (from Section 7.2.5) with the in command; this is an excellent example of software reuse, since PROPC was written years before we thought of using it for hardware verification [Goguen, Meseguer and Plaisted, 1983]. Next, Time is defined for use in input and output streams, which are functions from Time to Prop. A requirement theory LINE is defined, and then a NOT gate using it. The object F introduces two symbolic variables, t and f0, which are a generic time and input stream, respectively. Finally, two NOT gates are composed and applied to F1. Evaluating expressions in this context corresponds to proving certain theorems, in this case that the double NOT gate acts as an identity on input streams, while either single NOT gate reverses the polarity of its input stream. See [Goguen, 1988] for a precise statement of the first theorem proved here, and for a detailed justification that the reductions given below really give proofs.

```
in propc

obj TIME is sort Time .
  op 0 : -> Time .
  op s_ : Time -> Time .
endo

th LINE is protecting TIME + PROPC .
  op f : Time -> Prop .
endth

obj NOT[L :: LINE] is
  op g : Time -> Prop .
  var T : Time .
  eq g(0) = false .
  eq g(T) = not f(T) .
endo

obj F is protecting TIME + PROPC .
  op t : -> Time .
  op f0 : Time -> Prop .
endo

obj 2NOT is protecting NOT[NOT[F]*(op g to f1)]*(op g to f2) .
endo

reduce f2(s s t) iff f0(t) endr
result Bool: true

reduce f2(s t) iff not f1(t) endr
result Bool: true

reduce f1(s t) iff not f0(t) endr
result Bool: true
```

This code actually ran in our current OBJ3. Parameterized modules make this code much more readable than it would be otherwise. The same techniques seem effective for much more complex examples of hardware specification, simulation, and verification, as shown in Goguen [1988].

7.4.8 View Calculus

What can we conclude from all this? I would like to conclude that it is better to factorize code with parameterized modules than with higher-order functions, and that in fact higher-order functions should be avoided whenever possible. From this, one could conclude that the essence of functional programming cannot be the use of higher-order functions and therefore must be the lack of side effects. However, I feel that the true essence may well be having a solid basis in equational logic, because this not only avoids side effects, but more importantly, it supports simple equational reasoning about programs and transformations, as needed for powerful programming environments.

Instead of seeing parameterized programming as a way to supplant higher-order programming, one can view it as an interesting direction for generalizing higher-order logic, since the calculus of views must confront issues beyond those formalized in the lambda-calculus, including the following:

1. The basic types (which are the unparameterized modules, including BOOL, NAT, MONOID, and PREORD, as well as whatever a user chooses to define) denote not just classes of functions, but categories of models (order-sorted algebras in the case of OBJ).

2. Similarly, parameters range not just over classes of functions, but over classes of modules, and these classes are subject to semantic constraints (e.g., equations).

3. Modules are of two kinds, theories and objects, with loose and initial semantics, respectively.

4. Parameterized modules represent functors between classes of models.

5. Views are not just a minor addition here, but a major new dimension that may come to dominate modules.

These points perhaps deserve some elaboration, since they suggest it might be awkward to code up parameterized programming into some form of denotational semantics (e.g., in the style of [MacQueen *et al.*, 1984]) or into some form of type theory (e.g., in the style of Pebble [Burstall and Lampson, 1984], PX [Hayashi and Nakano, 1987], or Martin-Löf's type theory [Martin-Löf, 1982]). Although such an encoding could be valuable in theoretical studies, it is not the sort of notation that programmers should have to deal with in practice[10]; it would be rather like trying to program with Gödel numbers. Moreover, it does not emphasize what seem to be the really fundamental entities. For, just as types play a secondary role as indices for functions in the typed lambda-calculus, and objects play a secondary role as indices for morphisms in category theory, so it may be that modules play a secondary role as indices to views in parameterized programming.

Since its first-order proof theory is a major advantage claimed for our approach, it is interesting to see how far parameterization can be pushed without endangering this asset. It is possible to achieve the equivalent of parameters that are themselves parameterized by using nested parameterized modules. This corresponds to what type theory calls *dependent types*. However, it remains unclear whether there are significant applications for the more exotic possibilities suggested by type theory. It also seems interesting to inquire whether a suitable categorical semantics can be developed, either in terms of colimits of theories, as in Clear [Burstall and Goguen, 1980], or in

---

[10]One can of course code up lambda-calculus or type theory in OBJ, but that is quite another issue.

terms similar to the Cartesian closed category characterization of the lambda-calculus. Seeley's locally Cartesian closed categories [Seeley, 1964] seem relevant, as do Cartmell's S-categories [Cartmell, 1986], since the extending hierarchy of parameterized module inclusions is preserved under instantiation; also his hierarchical categories seem interesting. There is also some interesting recent work by John Gray on dependent abstract data types. Altogether, this appears to be an area that would reward further exploration.

7.5 CONCLUSIONS AND FUTURE RESEARCH

Parameterized programming is a powerful technique for the general and reliable reuse of software. Reusability is enhanced by the flexibility of the parameterization mechanism, which admits other modules as actual parameters and supports the easy construction of complex combinations of modules. Reliability is enhanced since semantic properties of modules can be verified once and for all (to any desired degree of formality), and module interfaces can also include semantic requirements. This paper has described several features of parameterized programming, including: (1) theories, which declare properties of modules and interfaces; (2) views, which connect theories to modules; (3) module contexts, which describe the context of a module as an acyclic graph of imported modules; (4) module expressions, which produce new modules by combining and modifying old modules; and (5) default views, which can greatly ease the effort of writing views, often reducing them to null views. Module expressions can be considered a generalization of program transformations, thus extending the power and expressiveness of both paradigms. These ideas have been illustrated with simple examples in the OBJ language, but should also be considered proposals for other language design efforts, including advanced Ada environments and modules for Prolog. OBJ is a logical programming language, based on order-sorted equational logic, that incorporates these ideas and others from modern programming methodology. Future research will aim at further extending parameterized programming, at implementing parameterized programming for multiparadigm languages (in particular, combined functional, logic, and object-oriented programming), at building a massively parallel machine for executing such languages very efficiently, and at further developing the relevant mathematics, including view calculus.

APPENDIX A: DEFAULT VIEWS

Most technical details of default views have been deferred from the main text to this appendix. In parameterized programming, views have a source and a target module. However, here we make simplifying assumptions so that we can ignore module structure and just consider signature morphisms. To start with, we ignore equations and the fact that views must preserve them.

Given a set S of sorts, an S-sorted *signature* Σ is an $S^* \times S$-indexed family of sets $\{\Sigma_{w,s} \mid w \text{ in } S^*, s \text{ in } S\}$; let $|\Sigma| = \cup_{w,s} \Sigma_{w,s}$. For o in $\Sigma_{w,s}$ let us call $<w, s>$ the *rank* of o, w the *arity* of o, and s the sort of o. Although OBJ is actually based on order-sorted algebra, every order-sorted signature is in particular a many-sorted signature, satisfying some extra restrictions that arise from the partial order on S. We assume that every operation o in a signature Σ is assigned a set attr(o) of attributes, chosen from `assoc`, `comm`, `idem` and `id`: $<gnd\text{-}term>$, without explicitly indicating how this set arises (here $<gnd\text{-}term>$ denotes any ground term in the currently available operations of an appropriate sort).

Definition 1. Let Σ and Σ' be signatures with sort sets S and S'. Then a *view* $\phi: \Sigma \rightarrow \Sigma'$ is a pair $<f, g>$ where $f : S \rightarrow S'$ is monotone and $g = \{g_{w,s} : \Sigma_{w,s} \rightarrow \Sigma'_{fw,fs} \mid w \text{ in } S^*, s \text{ in } S\}$.

OBJ actually supports a more general notion of view that maps operations in Σ to terms over Σ'. However, since this appendix is concerned with default views, we may take the above definition as basic.

Fact 1. If $\phi = <f, g>: \Sigma \rightarrow \Sigma'$ and $\psi = <f', g'>: \Sigma' \rightarrow \Sigma''$ are views, then so is their composition, $\phi;\psi : \Sigma \rightarrow \Sigma''$, defined to be $<f ; f', g; g'_f>$, where $(g; g'_f)_{w,s} = g_{w,s}; g'_{fw,fs}$.

We distinguish among the following kinds of view:

1. Explicit: declared and named at the top level of OBJ, using the syntax `view_from_to_is_endv`.
2. Abbreviated: computed from a partial description, using the abbreviation rules given below.
3. Null: abbreviated to nothing.
4. Internal: defined inside the target object; there can be at most one internal view in a given module having a given source theory.

Definition 2: Given modules M and M', the *default view* from M to M' (if any) is given by the following (ordered) rules:

1. If there is an internal view $M \rightarrow M'$, then it is the default view;
2. otherwise, if there is a null view $M \rightarrow M'$, then it is the default view;
3. otherwise, if there is only one explicit view $M \rightarrow M'$, then it is the default view.

Of course, it is possible that there is no default view $M \rightarrow M'$.

To keep this discussion independent of module structure, we assume that certain priority orderings are somehow given, both on the sorts and on certain sets of operations in a signature. Orderings for the OBJ module hierarchy are given as follows.

Definition 3.   The *primary sort* of a module M is given by the following (ordered) rules:

1. The primary sort of M is the first sort introduced in M (if any), either through a sort declaration (if any) or as the primary sort of the first explicitly imported module in M (if any), whichever occurs first in the text of M;

2. otherwise, it is the primary sort of the first parameter requirement theory of M;

3. otherwise, it is `Bool`, the primary sort of the implicitly imported module `BOOL`.

Fact 2.   Every module has a unique primary sort.

The secondary, tertiary, . . . , sorts of a module are defined as follows: The secondary sort is the primary sort of the module structure that remains after deleting the primary sort; the tertiary sort is the primary sort of the structure that remains after deleting both the primary and secondary sorts; and so on. It follows that the secondary, tertiary, . . . , sorts of a module are also uniquely determined, if they exist. From now on, we assume that every signature comes with an injective order function $n: S \to \mathrm{Nat}$, with $n(s) = 1$ when s is primary, $n(s) = 2$ when s is secondary, and so on. This will again enable us to ignore module structure.

Definition 4.   Let O be a subset of the operations $|\Sigma|$ available in M. Then the *primary operation in O relative to M* is

1. the operation in O that is first introduced (according to textual order) in M in an explicit `op` or `ops` declaration, if there is one;

2. otherwise, the primary operation in O relative to the first module expression explicitly imported into M, or if there is none in the first, then in the second, and so on;

3. otherwise, the primary operation in O relative to the first parameter requirement theory of M, or if there is none, then relative to the second requirement theory of M, and so on;

4. otherwise, the primary operation in O relative to `BOOL`;

5. otherwise, there is no primary operation in O relative to M.

Let $o1$ be the primary operation in O relative to M. Then $o2$, the secondary operation in O relative to M, is the primary operation in $O - \{o1\}$ relative to M. Similarly, the tertiary operation in O relative to M is the primary operation in $O - \{o1, o2\}$ and so on recursively. (Note that the preceding clauses are ordered differently from those defining primary sort.)

Given a view $M \to M'$ with signature mapping $<f, g>: \Sigma \to \Sigma'$ and given an operation o in Σ, we say that o' in Σ' *subsumes* o iff $f(\mathrm{arity}(o)) \leq \mathrm{arity}(o')$ and $\mathrm{sort}(o') \leq f(\mathrm{sort}(o))$ and $\mathrm{attr}(o) \subseteq \mathrm{attr}(o')$.

Fact 3. Given a module M, rename every sort and operation of M so that the new names are disjoint from the old names, call the resulting module M' and let $v: M \rightarrow M'$ be the renaming as a view. Then the default view $u: M' \rightarrow M$ satisfies $v * u = \mathrm{id}_M$ and $u * v = \mathrm{id}_{M'}$ provided that the textual ordering of operations in M is compatible with the subsumption ordering (with respect to the identity view on M), in the sense that if o is subsumed by o' (for o and o' distinct in M) then o is introduced earlier than o' in M.

We may consider a view $\langle f, g \rangle$ to be given by two sets of ordered pairs, the first for sorts and the second for operations:

```
(s1 to s1'), (s2 to s2'), ...
(o1 to o1'), (o2 to o2'), ...
```

Definition 5. Given a view ϕ from Σ to Σ' with sort sets S and S' respectively, call a sort s in S *shared* iff it is also in S'. Similarly, an operation o in $|\Sigma|$ is *shared* iff o is also in $|\Sigma_{f(rank(o))}|$. Given o in $|\Sigma|$, let us call those operations o' in $|\Sigma|$ that have the same rank and attributes as o the *cohorts* of o. Then an *abbreviation* of ϕ is a subset of the pairs defining ϕ, obtained according to the following rules:

1. A pair of the form (s to s) can be omitted.
2. A pair (s to s') can be omitted if s is not shared and $n(s) = n(s')$.
3. A pair of the form (o to o) can be omitted.
4. A pair (o to o') can be omitted if o is not shared and if o' has the same order among the operations that subsume o as o has among its cohorts.
5. A pair (i to i') can be omitted if there is a pair (o to o') where o has identity i and o' has identity i'.

Proposition 1. If ψ is an abbreviation of two views ϕ and ϕ', then $\phi = \phi'$. In fact, ϕ can be reconstructed from ψ by the following (ordered) rules:

1. If there is no sort pair for a shared sort s in S, then add (s to s).
2. If there is no sort pair for a nonshared sort s in S of order n, and if s' in S' also has order n, then add (s to s').
3. If there is no operation pair for a shared operation o in Σ, then add (o to o).
4. If there is no operation pair for a nonshared o in Σ and if o' has the same order among the operations in $\Sigma_{w,s}$ that subsume o as o has among its cohorts, then add (o to o'). (If there is more than one such operation, it would be appropriate for OBJ to inform the user which operation it has chosen.)
5. If o has identity i in Σ and o' has identity i' in Σ', if there is no operation pair for i, and if (o to o') is an operation pair, then add (i to i').

It now follows that there is at most one null view from any given module to another. Although our null view conventions work well for simple examples, it cannot be expected that they will always produce exactly the view that the user really wants at the moment. One way to get a bit more from these conventions is to permit explicitly defined sort and operation orderings that differ from the default orderings. Different default views can then be defined based on these new orderings. (This idea is due to Timothy Winkler.) Our abbreviated operation notation is also very helpful in simplifying views.

The composition of two null views is not necessarily a null view, as the following example shows:

```
th MONOID is sort Elt .
   op _*_ : Elt Elt -> Elt [assoc id: 1] .
endth

th CMONOID is sort Elt .
   op _+_ : Elt Elt -> Elt [assoc comm id: 0] .
endth

th R is sort Elt .
   op _+_ : Elt Elt -> Elt [assoc comm id: 0] .
   op _*_ : Elt Elt -> Elt [assoc id: 1] .
endth
```

The first two theories describe monoids and commutative monoids respectively; think of the third as rings, though we have not written all the equations. Now the null view D0 from MONOID to CMONOID necessarily maps * to + and 1 to 0, while the null view D1 from CMONOID to R maps + to + and 0 to 0. Now the null view D01 from MONOID to R maps * and 1 to themselves, whereas the composition D0 * D1 maps * to + and 1 to 0. (This is a counterexample to a claim in [Goguen, 1984].)

Although this appendix has only discussed views that are signature morphisms, the conclusions apply to the more general views that OBJ actually supports (which may map operation symbols to terms) because the only pairs that can be omitted are those that map to a single operation symbol. In particular, a null view is necessarily a signature morphism.

Appendix B: Linguistic Support for Parameterized Programming

This appendix lists some features that support parameterized programming. It is preferable that these features actually be in the language, but it suffices for them to be part of an environment for the language; such an approach has been suggested [Goguen, 1986a] to provide parameterized programming for Ada.

Modularity.   Breaking a program into parts, each of which is "mind-sized" and has a natural function, maximizes conceptual clarity, modifiability, understandability, and reusability.

Parameterization.   To maximize reusability, software modules should be parameterized, so that by substituting different parameters, a given module can be reused in many different ways. Actual parameters should not merely select among predefined behaviors, but rather should themselves be modules, possibly hierarchical.

Theories.   Theories declare structural and semantic properties that may (or may not) be satisfied by other modules. Theories are first-class citizens: They are named, can import other theories and objects, and can even be parameterized.

Requirement Theories.   Reliability could be a problem for parameterized modules that behave correctly only if certain properties are satisfied by the context in which they are used. Parameterized programming permits the explicit declaration of interface structure and properties in requirement theories. For critical applications, theorem proving could be used to verify that the properties are satisfied, while testing or even inspection might suffice for others. Just being able to state properties explicitly is a significant improvement in documentation capability.

Views.   A view is an assignment from required entities declared in a source theory to actual entities in a target module; for parameter instantiation, a view may be used to bind the formal entities in a parameterized module's interface to actual entities. A view is also an assertion that its target module satisfies the properties declared in its source theory. Views are first-class citizens that can be named, can import modules, and can even be parameterized. The integration of objects, theories, and views provides a very flexible wide-spectrum language capability.

Hierarchical Structure.   Particularly when modules are being instantiated and then reused in other modules, it is helpful to keep explicit track of the hierarchical structure of program development, showing exactly where and how modules use other modules.

Information Hiding.   To insure that a program does not depend on the way that some abstraction is actually implemented, it is desirable to hide implementation details; this means insuring that only operations in the declared interface can be used by other modules. This principle of information hiding, also called abstraction or encapsulation, includes the notion of abstract data type.

Module Expressions.   A software design is explicitly represented as a sequence of modules and views. Such a sequence can be considered a script that actually constructs a software system from its components when executed. These scripts may include module expressions that tell how to combine, instantiate, and transform previously constructed modules. Modifiability is enhanced by the ability to edit and then re-execute such scripts.

Module Transformation.   Sometimes it is necessary to transform a module (or combination of modules) before it can be reused, for example, to change the syntax or semantics of some operations, to add some new functionality, to delete some old functionality, or to improve efficiency. Language features for these tasks significantly augment the power and utility of parameterized programming; conversely, one could say that parameterized programming significantly augments the power of transformational programming (also called derivational or inferential programming).

Simplicity.   An economical and conceptually coherent syntax and semantics will maximize one's intuitive grasp of program text; then programs are easier to reuse, as well as to modify. One way to achieve this simplicity is to base the semantics of a language on some simple logical system, in such a way that statements of the language are sentences in the logic, and the operational semantics of the language is given by deduction in the logical system. We call this approach *logical programming*; it means that the specification and execution levels of programming are identified. (See Section 7.2.5).

Formal Semantics.   A simple underlying semantics for a language not only greatly enhances the understandability of programs, but is also essential for program verification; moreover, it is useful for retrieving modules from a library using semantic keys. Subsorts, as in OBJ, also support exception definition and handling, for overloaded mixfix syntax, for coercions, and for multiple representations.

Libraries.   In order to make the most effective use of parameterized programming, it is necessary to actually get hold of modules that do what one wants. This requires a library, preferably with cataloging, retrieval, version control, and so on.

Interactive Program Development.   An interactive programming environment can ease the actual process of parameterized programming; for example, through an interactive cycle of running simple test cases, finding bugs, and structural editing. A good environment will perform many syntactic and even semantic checks on programs before permitting them to be executed.

The advantages of modularity and abstraction (including data abstraction) lie primarily in control of detail; this is particularly important in view of the numerous changes that inevitably accompany large program development efforts. The semantic requirements associated with parameterized modules provide a kind of high-level documentation that can reduce the possibilities for misunderstanding and thus facilitate program debugging, maintenance, and reuse, as well as library access. Module expressions provide another kind of high-level documentation, showing design decisions, including commitments at various levels of detail. Theories and views provide documentation for semantic properties of modules.

Appendix C: History and Implementations of OBJ

OBJ was originally designed in 1976 by Goguen [Goguen, 1977] as a language for error algebras, an attempt to extend algebraic abstract data types to handle errors and partial functions in a simple, uniform way. This first design also used ideas from Clear [Burstall and Goguen, 1977, 1981] for parameterized modules. First implementations of OBJ were done from 1977 to 1979 at UCLA by Joseph Tardo as OBJ0 and OBJT [Tardo, 1981; Goguen and Tardo, 1979], using error algebras plus an "image" construct for parameterization. David Plaisted implemented OBJ1 by enhancing OBJT during 1982–83 at SRI; improvements included matching modulo associativity and/or commutativity, hash-coded memo functions, and a highly interactive environment [Goguen, Meseguer, and Plaisted, 1983]. OBJ2 [Futatsugi, Goguen, Jouannaud, and Meseguer, 1985; Futatsugi, Goguen, Meseguer, and Okado, 1987] was implemented during 1984–85 at SRI by Kokichi Futatsugi and Jean-Pierre Jouannaud, following a design in which José Meseguer and Joseph Goguen also participated, based on order-sorted algebra [Goguen, 1978; Goguen and Meseguer, 1989, 1987b; Goguen, Jouannaud, and Meseguer, 1985] rather than on error algebra; also, OBJ2 provided Clear-like parameterized modules, theories, and views, although not in full generality. The OBJ3 implementation currently being developed at SRI by Timothy Winkler, José Meseguer, Claude and Hélène Kirchner, and Aristide Megrelis has syntax quite close to OBJ2. However, it has a different implementation based on a simpler and more efficient operational semantics for order-sorted algebra [Kirchner *et al.*, 1987], and it provides more sophisticated module expressions, including default views, for which Timothy Winkler deserves special credit. OBJ2 and OBJ3 can also be seen as implementing Clear. OBJ as used in this paper extends OBJ3 in fairly modest ways that we hope to see implemented soon.

Other implementations of OBJ1 include UMIST-OBJ from the University of Manchester Institute of Science and Technology [Coleman *et al.*, 1987], Abstract Pascal at the University of Manchester [Latham, 1987], and MC-OBJ at the University of Milan [Cavenathi *et al.*, 1987]; the first two are written in Pascal and the third in C. In addition, a Franz Lisp version of OBJ2 has been done at Washington State University [Sridhar, 1986]. At SRI, we are currently extending OBJ in the directions of relational and object-oriented programming, to Eqlog [Goguen and Meseguer, 1986] and FOOPS [Goguen and Meseguer, 1987a], respectively.

OBJ3 was implemented at SRI on Sun3s in (Kyoto) Common Lisp, and therefore should be easy to port to any machine with a C compiler. To get started, the only commands you really need are `obj`, `in`, and `q`, which get you into OBJ from the operating system level, read a file within OBJ, and quit OBJ, respectively. The recommended way to work is to first edit a file; then go to OBJ and read in the file, making a log file of the execution so you have a record of any problems that arise; then go back and re-edit the source file. It is convenient to do this in a shell within an editor like Emacs.

OBJ's top-level statements for declaring objects, modules, and views can all be seen as commands whose effect is to add something to the OBJ database, which is therefore constructed incrementally. A general engine for term rewriting actually does the reductions, consulting the database to get the rules for a given context. Reductions do not change the database in any way (although they may change memo tables). OBJ3 comes with a small library of modules that seem especially reusable, and some examples.

OBJ3 lacks a convenient declarative way to handle persistent objects; we intend to realize this capability by extending OBJ to the object-oriented language FOOPS. The major areas needing further research and/or development within OBJ itself are the user interface (better integration between editing and execution, and better error messages), generalizing module expressions to permit code modification for efficiency, and better optimized object code.

References

Backus, John. Can programming be liberated from the von Neumann style? *Communications of the Association for Computing Machinery* 21(8):613–641 1978.

Balzer, Robert. Transformational implementation: An example. *IEEE Transactions on Software Engineering* SE-7 (1):3–14 1981.

Battiston, E.; F. DeCindio; and Giancarlo Mauri. OBJSA net systems: A class of high-level nets having domains as objects. Tech. rept. draft, University of Milano, 1987.

Beierle, Christoph, and Angelika Voss. Implementation specifications. In *Recent Trends in Data Type Specification*, Hans-Jorg Kreowski, ed., pp. 39–52. Springer-Verlag, 1985.

Bergstra, Jan, and John Tucker. Characterization of computable data types by means of a finite equational specification method. In *Automata, Languages, and Programming*, seventh colloquium, J. W. de Bakker and J. van Leeuwen, eds., pp. 76–90. Springer-Verlag, 1980.

Berry, Gerrard, and Pierre-Luc Currien. Theory and practice of sequential algorithms: The kernel of the applicative language CDS. In *Algebraic Methods in Semantics*, Maurice Nivat and John Reynolds, eds., pp. 35–88. Cambridge University Press, 1985.

Bidoit, M.; Christine Choppy; and F. Voisin. The ASSPEGIQUE specification environment—Motivations and design. In *Recent Trends in Data Type Specification*, Hans-Jorg Kreowski, ed., pp. 54–72. Springer-Verlag, 1985.

Burstall, Rod. Programming with modules as typed functional programming. *Proceedings, International Conference on Fifth Generation Computing Systems*, Tokyo, Japan, 1985.

Burstall, Rod, and John Darlington. A transformation system for developing recursive programs. *Journal of the Association for Computing Machinery* 24, (1):44–67 1977.

Burstall, Rod, and Joseph Goguen. Putting theories together to make specifications. In *Proceedings, Fifth International Joint Conference on Artificial Intelligence*, Raj Reddy, ed., pp. 1045–1058. Department of Computer Science, Carnegie-Mellon University, 1977.

————. The semantics of Clear, a specification language. In *Proceedings of the 1979 Copenhagen Winter School on Abstract Software Specification*, Dines Bjorner, ed., pp. 292–332. Springer-Verlag, 1980.

————. An informal introduction to specifications using Clear. In *The Correctness Problem in Computer Science*, Robert Boyer and J. Moore, eds., pp. 185–213. Academic Press, 1981. (Reprinted in Software Specification Techniques, Narain Gehani and Andrew McGettrick, eds., pp. 363–390. Addison-Wesley, 1985.)

————. Algebras, theories, and freeness: An introduction for computer scientists. In *Theoretical Foundations of Programming Methodology*, Manfred Wirsing and Gunther Schmidt, eds., pp. 329–350. Reidel, 1982.

Burstall, Rod, and Butler Lampson. A kernel language for abstract data types and modules. In *Proceedings, International Symposium on the Semantics of Data Types*, Giles Kahn, David MacQueen, and Gordon Plotkin, eds., pp. 1–50. Springer-Verlag, 1984.

Burstall, Rod; David MacQueen; and Donald Sannella. Hope: An experimental applicative language. In *Proceedings, First LISP Conference*, pp. 136–143. Stanford University, 1980.

Cartmell, John. Formalising the network and hierarchical data models—An application of categorical logic. In *Proceedings, Conference on Category Theory and Computer Programming*, David Pitt, Samson Abramsky, Axel Poigne, and David Rydeheard, eds., pp. 466–492. Springer-Verlag, 1986.

Cavenathi, C.; M. De Zanet; and Giancarlo Mauri. MC-OBJ: A C interpreter for OBJ. Tech. rept. draft, Department of Information Science, University of Milan, 1987.

Cheatham, Thomas, Jr. The introduction of definitional facilities into higher level programming languages. In *Proceedings, AFIPS Fall Joint Computer Conference*, pp. 623–637. Spartan Books, 1966.

Coleman, Derek; Robin Gallimore; and Victoria Stavridou. The design of a rewrite rule interpreter from algebraic specifications. *IEEE Software Engineering Journal* pp. 95–104 July 1987.

Coleman, Derek; Robin Gallimore; and Joseph Goguen. *Experience with OBJ*. Addison-Wesley, 1989. (To appear.)

Colmerauer, Alan; H. Kanoui; and M. van Caneghem. Etude et realisation d'un systeme Prolog. Groupe d'Intelligence Artificielle, U.E.R. de Luminy, Universite d'Aix-Marseille II, 1979.

Duce, David, and E. V. C. Fielding. Formal specification—A comparison of two techniques. Tech. rept. draft, Rutherford Appleton Laboratory, 1987.

Ehrig, Hartmut, and Bernd Mahr. *Fundamentals of Algebraic Specification*. Vol. 1, *Equations and Initial Semantics*. Springer-Verlag, 1985.

Futatsugi, Kokichi; Joseph Goguen; Jean-Pierre Jouannaud; and José Meseguer. Principles of OBJ2. In *Proceedings, Twelfth Symposium on Principles of Programming Languages*, Brian K. Reid, ed., pp. 52–66. Association for Computing Machinery, 1985.

Futatsugi, Kokichi; Joseph Goguen; José Meseguer; and Koji Okada. Parameterized programming in OBJ2. In *Proceedings, Ninth International Conference on Software Engineering*, Robert Balzer, ed., pp. 51–60. IEEE Computer Society Press, 1987.

Gerrard, Christopher Paul. The specification and controlled implementation of a configuration management tool using OBJ and Ada. In *Experience with OBJ*, Derek Coleman, Robin Gallimore, and Joseph Goguen, eds., Addison-Wesley, 1989. (To appear.)

Gogolla, Martin. Partially ordered sorts in algebraic specifications. In *Proceedings, Ninth CAAP (Bordeaux)*, Bruno Courcelle, ed., pp. 139–153. Cambridge University Press, 1984. (Also, Forschungsbericht Nr. 169, Universität Dortmund, Abteilung Informatik, 1983.)

———. A final algebra semantics for errors and exceptions. In *Recent Trends in Data Type Specification*, Hans-Jorg Kreowski, ed., pp. 89–103. Springer-Verlag, 1985.

Goguen, Joseph. Mathematical representation of hierarchically organized systems. In *Global Systems Dynamics*, E. Attinger, ed., pp. 112–128. S. Karger, 1971.

———. Abstract errors for abstract data types. In *Proceedings of First IFIP Working Conference on Formal Description of Programming Concepts*, Peter Neuhold, ed., pp. 21.1–21.32. MIT, 1977. (Also published in *Formal Description of Programming Concepts*, Peter Neuhold, ed., pp. 491–522. North-Holland, 1979.)

———. Order sorted algebra. Semantics and Theory of Computation Report 14. UCLA Computer Science Department, 1978.

———. How to prove algebraic inductive hypotheses without induction, with applications to the correctness of data type representations. In *Proceedings, Fifth Conference on Automated Deduction*, Wolfgang Bibel and Robert Kowalski, eds., pp. 356–373. Springer-Verlag, 1980.

———. Parameterized programming. *Transactions on Software Engineering* SE-10(5): 528–543, September 1984. Early versions in *Proceedings, Workshop on Reusability in Programming*, T. Biggerstaff and T. Cheatham, eds., pp. 138–150. ITT, 1983. Also in report number CSLI-84-9, Center for the Study of Language and Information, Stanford University, September 1984.

———. Reusing and interconnecting software components. *Computer* 19(2):16–28, February 1986a. (Reprinted in *Tutorial: Software Reusability*, Peter Freeman, ed., pp. 251–263. IEEE Computer Society Press, 1987.)

———. One, none, a hundred thousand specification languages. In *Information Processing '86*, H.-J. Kugler, ed., pp. 995–1003. Elsevier, 1986b.

———. Graphical programming by generic example. In *Proceedings, Second International Supercomputing Conference*, vol. 1, Steven and Svetlana Kartashev, eds., pp. 209–216. Van Nostrand, 1987.

———. OBJ as a theorem prover, with application to hardware verification. Tech. rept. SRI-CSL-88-4, SRI Computer Science Lab, April 1988. To appear in *Proceedings of the Second Banff Hardware Verification Workshop*, V. P. Subramanyan, ed., Springer-Verlag, 1989.

Goguen, Joseph, and Rod Burstall. CAT, a system for the structured elaboration of correct programs from structured specifications. Tech. rept. CSL-118, SRI Computer Science Lab, October 1980.

————. Institutions: Abstract model theory for computer science. Tech. rept. number CSLI-85-30, Center for the Study of Language and Information, Stanford University, 1985. (Also submitted for publication; a preliminary version appears in *Proceedings, Logics of Programming Workshop*, Edward Clarke and Dexter Kozen, eds., pp. 221–256. Springer-Verlag, 1984.)

Goguen, Joseph; Jean-Pierre Jouannaud; and José Meseguer. Operational semantics of order-sorted algebra. In *Proceedings, 1985 International Conference on Automata, Languages and Programming*, W. Brauer, ed., Lecture Notes in Computer Science, vol. 194. Springer-Verlag, 1985.

Goguen, Joseph, and José Meseguer. Universal realization, persistent interconnection, and implementation of abstract modules. In *Proceedings, Ninth International Conference on Automata, Languages, and Programming*, M. Nielsen and E. M. Schmidt, eds., pp. 265–281. Springer-Verlag, 1982.

————. Rapid prototyping in the OBJ executable specification language. *Software Engineering Notes* 7(5):75–84, December 1982b.

————. Eqlog: Equality, types, and generic modules for logic programming. In *Logic Programming: Functions, Relations, and Equations*, Douglas DeGroot and Gary Lindstrom, eds., pp. 295–363. Prentice-Hall, 1986. (Earlier versions appear in *Journal of Logic Programming* 1(2):179–210, September 1984, and in *Proceedings, Second International Logic Programming Conference* (Uppsala, Sweden), pp. 115–126, July 1984.)

————. Unifying functional, object-oriented and relational programming with logical semantics. In *Research Directions in Object-Oriented Programming*, Bruce Shriver and Peter Wegner, eds., pp. 417–477. MIT Press, 1987a. (Abstract in *SIGPLAN Notices*, 21(10):153–162, October 1986; also, report number CSLI-87-93, Center for the Study of Language and Information, Stanford University.)

————. Order-sorted algebra solves the constructor-selector, multiple representation, and coercion problems. In *Proceedings, Second Logic in Computer Science Conference*, Albert Meyer, ed., pp. 18–29. IEEE Computer Society Press, 1987b. (Also, report number CSLI-87-92, Center for the Study of Language and Information, Stanford University, March 1987.)

————. Order-sorted algebra I: Equational deduction for multiple inheritance, polymorphism, and partial operations. Tech. rept. to appear, SRI International, Computer Science Lab, 1989.

Goguen, Joseph; José Meseguer; and David Plaisted. Programming with parameterized abstract objects in OBJ. In *Theory and Practice of Software Technology*, Domenico Ferrari, Mario Bolognani, and Joseph Goguen, eds., pp. 163–193. North-Holland, 1983.

Goguen, Joseph, and Kamran Parsaye-Ghomi. Algebraic denotational Semantics using parameterized abstract modules. In *Formalizing Programming Concepts*, J. Diaz and I. Ramos, eds., pp. 292–309. Lecture Notes in Computer Science, vol. 107. Springer-Verlag, 1981.

Goguen, Joseph, and Joseph Tardo. An introduction to OBJ: A language for writing and testing software specifications. In *Specification of Reliable Software*, Marvin Zelkowitz, ed., pp. 170–189. IEEE Press, 1979. (Reprinted in *Software Specification Techniques*, Narain Gehani and Andrew McGettrick, eds., pp. 391–420. Addison-Wesley, 1985.)

Goguen, Joseph; James Thatcher; and Eric Wagner. An initial algebra approach to the specification, correctness, and implementation of abstract data types. Tech. rept. RC 6487, IBM Watson Research Center, October 1976. (Appears in *Current Trends in Programming Methodology*, vol. 4, Raymond Yeh, ed., pp. 80–149. Prentice-Hall, 1978.)

Goguen, Joseph; James Thatcher; Eric Wagner; and Jesse Wright. Abstract data types as initial algebras and the correctness of data representations. In *Computer Graphics, Pattern Recognition, and Data Structure*, Alan Klinger, ed., pp. 89–93. IEEE Press, 1975.

Gordon, Michael; Robin Milner; and Christopher Wadsworth. *Edinburgh LCF*. Lecture Notes in Computer Science, vol. 78. Springer-Verlag, 1979.

Guttag, John. The specification and application to programming of abstract data types. Ph.D. thesis., University of Toronto, Computer Science Department, report CSRG-59, 1975.

Guttag, John; James Horning; and Jeanette Wing. Larch in five easy pieces. Tech. rept. number 5, Digital Equipment Corporation, Systems Research Center, July 1985.

Guttag, John; Ellis Horowitz; and David Musser. Abstract data types and software validation. *Communications of the Association for Computing Machinery* 21(12):1048–1064, 1978.

Harper, Rober; David MacQueen; and Robin Milner. Standard ML. Tech. rept. ECS-LFCS-86-2, Department of Computer Science, University of Edinburgh, 1986.

Hayashi, Susumu, and Hiroshi Nakano. PX: A computational logic. Tech. rept. RIMS-573, Research Institute for Mathematical Sciences, Kyoto, Japan, April 1987.

Hoare, C. A. R. An axiomatic basis for computer programming. *Communications of the Association for Computing Machinery* 12(10):576–580, October 1969.

———. Proof of correctness of data representation. *Acta Informatica* 1:271–281, 1972.

Hoffmann, Christoph, and Michael O'Donnell. Programming with equations. *Transactions on Programming Languages and Systems* 1(4):83–112, 1982.

Hsiang, Jieh. Refutational theorem proving using term rewriting systems. Ph.D. thesis, University of Illinois at Urbana-Champaign, 1981.

Huet, Gerard, and Derek Oppen. Equations and rewrite rules: A survey. In *Formal Language Theory: Perspectives and Open Problems*, Ronald Book, ed., pp. 349–405. Academic Press, 1980

Hughes, John. Why functional programming matters. Tech. rept. 16, Programming Methodology Group, University of Goteborg, November 1984.

Jackson, Michael. *Principles of Program Design*. Academic Press, 1975.

Kaphengst, H., and Horst Reichel. Initial algebraic semantics for non-context-free languages. In *Fundamentals of Computation Theory*, M. Karpinski, ed., pp. 120–126. Lecture Notes in Computer Science, vol. 56. Springer-Verlag, 1977.

Kirchner, Claude; Hélène Kirchner; and José Meseguer. Operational semantics of OBJ3. In preparation, SRI International, 1987.

Knuth, Donald, and P. Bendix. Simple word problems in universal algebra. In *Computational Problems in Abstract Algebra*, J. Leech, ed. Pergamon Press, 1970.

Kowalski, Robert. Logic for problem solving. Tech. rept. DCL memo 75, Department of Artificial Intelligence, University of Edinburgh, 1974. (Also, a book in the Artificial Intelligence Series, North-Holland Press, 1979.)

Latham, John T. Abstract Pascal: A tutorial introduction. Tech. rept. (version 2.1), Department of Computer Science, University of Manchester, 1987.

Leinwand, Sany, and Joseph Goguen. Architectural options for the rewrite rule machine. In *Proceedings, Second International Supercomputing Conference*, vol. 3, Steven Kartashev and Svetlana Kartashev, eds., pp. 63–70. Van Nostrand, 1987.

Lerman, Claus-Werner, and Jacques Loeckx. OBSCURE, a new specification language. In *Recent Trends in Data Type Specification*, Hans-Jörg Kreowski, ed., pp. 28–30. Springer-Verlag, 1985. (Selected papers from the Third Workshop on Theory-and-Applications of Abstract Data Types.)

Levy, Giorgio, and F. Sirovich. TEL: A proof-theoretic language for efficient symbolic expression manipulation. IEI, Nota Interna B77-3, February 1977.

Lucas, Peter, and Tore Risch. Representation of factual information by equations and their evaluation. IBM Research, Yorktown Heights, 1982.

MacQueen, David; Ravi Sethi; and Gordon Plotkin. An ideal model for recursive polymorphic types. *Proceedings, Symposium on Principles of Programming Languages*, pp. 165-174, 1984.

Martin-Löf, Per. Constructive mathematics and computer programming. In *Logic, Methodology, and Philosophy of Science*, vol. 6, pp. 153–175. North-Holland, 1982.

McCarthy, John, Michael Levin, *et al. LISP 1.5 Programmer's Manual.* MIT Press, 1966.

Meseguer, José, and Joseph Goguen. Initiality, induction, and computability. In *Algebraic Methods in Semantics*, Maurice Nivat and John C. Reynolds, eds., pp. 459–541. Cambridge University Press, 1985. (Also SRI Computer Science Lab technical report CSL-140, December 1983.)

Meseguer, José; Joseph Goguen; and Gert Smolka. Order-sorted unification. Tech. rept. CSLI-87-86, Center for the Study of Language and Information, Stanford University, March 1987. (To be submitted for publication.)

Michie, Donald. "Memo" functions and machine learning. *Nature* 218:19–22, April 1968.

Milner, Robin. A theory of type polymorphism in programming. *Journal of Computer and System Sciences* 17(3):348–375, 1978.

Mosses, Peter. Abstract semantic algebras! In *Formal Description of Programming Concepts*, vol. 2, Dines Bjorner, ed., pp. 45–70. IFIP Press, 1983.

———. A basic semantic algebra. In *Proceedings, International Symposium on the Semantics of Data Types*, Giles Kahn, David MacQueen, and Gordon Plotkin, eds., pp. 87–107. Lecture Notes in Computer Science, vol. 173. Springer-Verlag, 1985.

Mycroft, Alan. Abstract interpretation and optimising transformations for applicative programs. Ph.D. thesis, University of Edinburgh, 1981.

Nakagawa, Ataru; Kokichi Futatsugi; S. Tomura; and T. Shimizu. Algebraic specification of Macintosh's QuickDraw using OBJ2. Tech. rept. draft, ElectroTechnical Laboratory, Tsukuba Science City, Japan, 1987. (To appear, *Proceedings, Tenth International Conference on Software Engineering*, Singapore, April 1988.)

O'Donnell, Michael. *Equational Logic as a Programming Language.* MIT Press, 1985.

O'Keefe, Richard. Source level tools for logic programming. In *Symposium on Logic Programming*, pp. 68–72. IEEE, 1985.

Orejas, Fernando. Passing compatibility is almost persistent. In *Recent Trends in Data Type Specification*, Hans-Jorg Kreowski, ed., pp. 196–206. Springer-Verlag, 1985.

(Selected papers from the Third Workshop on Theory and Applications of Abstract Data Types.)

Parnas, David. A technique for software module specification. *Communications of the Association for Computing Machinery* 15:330–336, 1972a.

————. Information distribution aspects of design methodology. *Information Processing '72* 71:339–344, 1972b. (Proceedings of 1972 IFIP Congress.)

Plaisted, David. An initial algebra semantics for error presentations. SRI International, Computer Science Laboratory, 1982.

Poigné, Axel. On semantic algebras: Higher order structures. *Informatik II*, Universität Dortmund, 1983.

Prywes, Noah, and Amir Pnueli. Compilation of nonprocedural specifications into computer programs. *IEEE Transactions on Software Engineering* SE-9(3):267–279, May 1983.

Reynolds, John. Using category theory to design implicit conversions and generic operators. In *Semantics Directed Compiler Generation*, Neal D. Jones, ed., pp. 211–258. Lecture Notes in Computer Science, vol. 94. Springer-Verlag, 1980.

Scherlis, William. Abstract data types, specialization, and program reuse. In *Proceedings, Workshop on Advanced Programming Environments*, Reidar Conradi, Tor Didriksen, and Dag Wanvik, eds., pp. 433–453. Lecture Notes in Computer Science, vol. 244. Springer-Verlag, 1986.

Scherlis, William, and Dana Scott. First steps towards inferential programming. In *Information Processing 83*, R. E. A. Mason, ed., pp. 199–212. Elsevier, North-Holland, 1983.

Scott, Dana, and Christopher Strachey. Towards a mathematical semantics for computer languages. In *Proceedings, 21st Symposium on Computers and Automata*, Polytechnic Institute of Brooklyn, pp. 19–46, 1971. (Also appeared as technical monograph PRG 6, Programming Research Group, Oxford University.)

Seely, R. A. G. Locally Cartesian closed categories and type theory. *Mathematical Proceedings of the Cambridge Philosophical Society* 95:33–48, 1964.

Smolka, Gert; Werner Nutt; Joseph Goguen; and José Meseguer. Order-sorted equational computation. In *Resolution of Equations in Algebraic Structures*, Maurice Nivat and Hassan Ait-Kaci, eds. Academic Press, to appear 1989. (Preliminary version in *Proceedings, Colloquium on the Resolution of Equations in Algebraic Structures*, held in Lakeway, Texas, May 1987.)

Sridhar, S. An implementation of OBJ2: An object-oriented language for abstract program specification. In *Proceedings, Sixth Conference on Foundations of Software Technology and Theoretical Computer Science*, K. V. Nori, ed., pp. 81–95. Lecture Notes in Computer Science. Springer-Verlag, 1986.

Stavridou, Victoria. Specifying in OBJ, verifying in REVE, and some ideas about time. Tech. rept. draft, Department of Computer Science, University of Manchester, 1987.

Sterling, Leon, and Ehud Shapiro. *The Art of Prolog*. MIT Press, 1986.

Stoy, Joseph. *Denotational Semantics of Programming Languages*. MIT Press, 1977.

Strachey, Christopher. Fundamental concepts in programming languages. Lecture notes from International Summer School in Computer Programming, Copenhagen, 1963.

Tardo, Joseph. The design, specification, and implementation of OBJT: A language for writing and testing abstract algebraic program specifications. Ph.D. thesis, Computer Science Department, UCLA, 1981.

Turner, David. Miranda: A non-strict functional language with polymorphic types. In *Functional Programming Languages and Computer Architectures*, Jean-Pierre Jouannaud, ed., pp. 1–16. Lecture Notes in Computer Science, vol. 201. Springer-Verlag, 1985.

United States Department of Defense. Reference manual for the Ada programming language. United States Government report ANSI/MIL-STD-1815 A, 1983.

Wadge, William. Classified algebras. Tech. rept. 46, University of Warwick, October 1982.

Wadler, Philip. Views: A way for pattern matching to cohabit with data abstraction. In *Proceedings, 14th Symposium on Principles of Programming Languages*, Steve Munchnik, ed., pp. 307–312. Association for Computing Machinery, 1987.

Wand, Mitchell. First-order identities as a defining language. *Acta Informatica* 14:337–357, 1980. (Originally report 29, Computer Science Department, Indiana University, 1977.)

Zilles, Steven. Abstract specification of data types. Tech. rept. 119, Computation Structures Group, MIT, 1974.

CHAPTER **8**

Design of Ada Systems Yielding Reusable Components: An Approach Using Structured Algebraic Specification

STEVEN D. LITVINTCHOUK
Mitre Corporation

ALLEN S. MATSUMOTO
Cimflex Teknowledge

8.1 INTRODUCTION

This paper addresses the problem of designing an Ada-based software system [U.S. Dept. of Defense, 1983], for maximum reusability of its component modules within different systems.

Our work on this problem was motivated by original work on the Raytheon HLS (high-level simulator) project [Litvintchouk *et al.*, 1982]. The goal of that project was to design a modeling system having a catalog of reusable Ada modeling components and a means of connecting them into complete models.

We realized that a central part of the problem of designing the catalog was the problem of rigorously specifying the allowable uses of each component, that is, specifying the class of contexts into which a given component could meaningfully fit, and the kinds of components that could fit within a given context.

It is highly desirable that a system be designed as a structured collection of components that can be easily reused either within the current system or within future systems. Such techniques have long existed for languages with a fixed number of allowable data types, such as Fortran. A software system can be implemented in Fortran as a structured collection of subroutines; as each subroutine is implemented, it automatically becomes eligible for future reuse.

Modern strongly typed languages permit the user to define his or her own structures of types and related functions. Components within a system depend upon having these structures available. In order to reuse a component in a different system, it is necessary to understand its dependence upon the structures of types and functions that were present in the original system. We believe that an algebraic specification of those structures, including the semantic properties required, will be necessary for general reuse of components.

Implementation of reusable software components is feasible in Ada, a programming language that provides user-defined types and parameterized modules. However, in order to realize Ada's full potential in this area, a methodology and an integrated set of tools must be developed that directly address the problem of maximizing reusability. Components designed for maximum reusability must be rigorously specified in terms of both their behavior and the class of environments in which they are meaningful. We believe that the application of category theory to the static semantics of systems may provide a formal basis for a rigorous, consistent design methodology capable of attacking these problems.

We assume that the reader of this paper has a working knowledge of semantic issues in modern high-level programming languages and the basic concepts of modern algebra. Adequate introductions to these are given in Chapter 10 of [Wegner, 1979] and in [Lipson, 1981], respectively.

8.2 INTRACOMPONENT SPECIFICATION IN ADA

We believe that two separate formalisms are necessary for the design and management of reusable components because of the differing requirements of intracomponent and intercomponent specification. These are defined as follows:

Intramodule View: Designing the interior structure of the module.

Intermodule View: Expressing and managing the relationships between modules viewed as "black boxes." This concerns only the module behavior as defined by the exterior module specifications.

Consistency between these two viewpoints must be maintained.

The Ada programming language provides for construction of user-defined data types at varying levels of abstraction. Ada's encapsulation mechanism (the *package* construct) aids in defining the external interfaces of software components. Ada's *generic* facility provides for limited (compile-time) definition of parameterized types and functions.

The use of Ada for expressing the intramodule view of specific software components is described in many places, [Downes and Goldsack, 1982], for example. Also, Chase and Gerhardt [1982] advocate the use of Ada for component design. Our concern is to extend these uses to include the development of components that can be reused in multiple applications.

8.3   LIMITATIONS OF ADA FOR INTERCOMPONENT SPECIFICATION

To maximize reusability of components, proven Ada design methodologies must be modified.

Ada Constructs Provided for System Design

The features provided by the Ada language for large-scale software systems seem to support directly only

☐ top-down development of monolithic systems (systems whose components are not reusable), and

☐ bottom-up development of systems from existing reusable components.

In Ada, top-down design may be accomplished by a nested unit specification with the body replaced by a body stub in the parent unit. A subunit representing the body can then be separately compiled. The problem with this is that the separately compiled subunit is meaningfully defined in just that one place; this one place must in fact be specified via the *separate* statement. Therefore such units are not multiply reusable.

Reusability in Ada is supported by context specification (*with*) clauses, by which a program unit references another previously defined unit. Multiple references to a unit are possible. However, the flow of information is only from the referenced unit to the unit that references it. This leads to essentially bottom-up program development.

A general paradigm for development of Ada systems yielding reusable components should not require any particular order of development. In particular, both top-down and bottom-up development should be facilitated. We believe that disciplined use of instantiations of Ada generic program units can provide such a paradigm.

Ada Generic Units

This section summarizes Ada's generic facility. A *generic program unit* is a template for a module. A module created using the template is called an *instance* of the generic unit. A *generic instantiation* is an Ada declaration that creates an instance. *Elaboration* is the process by which Ada declarations (including generic instantiations) achieve their effect. When a generic instantiation is elaborated, the facilities (types, functions, etc.) provided by the generic unit are made visible to the outer enclosing environment starting from the point of the instantiation.

Generic units may be parameterized, that is, they can be written to require the importation of various types and functions that are visible in the outer enclosing environment at the point of the instantiation.

Figure 8.1 shows a generic package E_CLASS_PACKAGE. The user must supply actual parameters for the formal ones, that is, a class of elements, ELEMENT, the binary operator "*," and a BOOLEAN function EQUIV_REL of two ELEMENTs. An instantiation of E_CLASS_PACKAGE provides the caller with the new type, E_CLASS, and operations defined on that type. The triple (ELEMENT, *, EQUIV_REL) is a single (algebraic) structure, and the pair (E_CLASS, *) is another. In Ada, however, we cannot express the semantic meaning of the structures in the (visible) package specification.

This package is intended to supply facilities for equivalence classes of a group. This is, if the class ELEMENT and the function "*" defined a group, and EQUIV_REL was a congruence relation, then the package would provide a quotient group.

The inability to express these intentions in Ada is a severe limitation on the reusability of such packages. If EQUIV_REL were not an equivalence relation, then E_CLASS would not represent equivalence classes and the function "*" on pairs of E_CLASS would not be well defined. If (ELEMENT, *) were not a group, (E_CLASS, *) would not be a group. The issue of the meaningful usage of such a package will be discussed later.

A generic program unit may be thought of as an elaboration-time *data type constructor*; that is, as a function that (at elaboration time) takes the environment existing at the point of instantiation and produces a new, modified environment. For the above example, if an environment includes a group with a congruence relation, then E_CLASS_PACKAGE could be instantiated to provide a new (quotient) group for the environment.

FIGURE 8.1
GENERIC PACKAGE FOR QUOTIENT SET

```
generic

  type ELEMENT is private;
  with function "*" (A, B: ELEMENT) return ELEMENT;
  with function EQUIV_REL (A, B: ELEMENT) return BOOLEAN;

package E_CLASS_PACKAGE is

  type E_CLASS is private;
  function CREATE (A: ELEMENT) return E_CLASS;
  function EQUAL (A, B: E_CLASS) return BOOLEAN;
  function "=" (A, B: E_CLASS) return BOOLEAN
                      rename EQUAL;
  function "*" (A, B: E_CLASS) return E_CLASS;

private
  type E_CLASS is new ELEMENT;
end E_CLASS_PACKAGE;

package body E_CLASS_PACKAGE is

  function CREATE (A: ELEMENT) return E_CLASS is
  begin
   return E_CLASS(A);
  end;

  function EQUAL (A, B: E_CLASS) return BOOLEAN is
  begin
   return EQUIV_REL (ELEMENT(A), ELEMENT(B));
  end;

  function "*" (A, B: E_CLASS) return E_CLASS is
  begin
   return E_CLASS (ELEMENT(A) *ELEMENT(B));
  end;

end E_CLASS_PACKAGE;
```

Controlled Generic Instantiation

We have developed a methodology for top-down development of Ada systems
by means of generic (and therefore reusable in controlled ways) components.
This methodology works by a process of exchange of information between

the component and the outer environment in which it is instantiated. Each component is implemented as a two-level nested generic, so that it must be instantiated twice in order to be used. In the first instantiation, the component and the outer environment exchange the types of interest to each other. In the second instantiation, linking functions relating these types are passed from the outer environment to the component. The component may now meaningfully reference the environment; the facilities intended for export to the outer environment are now well defined and available for use there.

To develop and use such a consistent methodology, reusable components should have standard visible interfaces both for inclusion in outer contexts and for accepting lower-level components. Furthermore, in order to ensure that components can be reused at any level within systems, the design methodology must provide a consistent policy for fitting together the visible interfaces between components at successive levels. This contrasts with the extremes of Pascal-like systems, where components are meaningful only in their original positions (like jigsaw puzzle pieces), and Fortran-like systems, where components are reusable in any subsystem but are of limited expressive power (like bricks that can be used anywhere but only to build brick structures).

Limited Semantics for Generic Parameters

Unfortunately, while Ada does provide the capability to construct parameterized (generic) modules, the ability to define required semantics in Ada for imported types and functions is significantly restricted.

In Ada there is no way to require that a particular generic formal type, say T, be representable by a particular algebraic structure. Generic formal types can be classified as discrete, integer, fixed point, floating point, or private (any type for which equality and assignment exist). Further classification of the algebra that T must represent is impossible. For example, it is not possible to require that T be any numeric type, or be any task type. These are lumped together with all *private* or *limited private* types.

Other aspects of required surrounding context structure are totally semantic-free as viewed from the component. Consider the design of a reusable software component for sorting lists of elements of some generic type T. This requires that a generic total ordering exist over T. The surrounding context for the component thus must contain an algebraic structure satisfying this requirement.

Another example is the E_CLASS_PACKAGE given earlier, where the design of the package body depends on the fact that EQUIV_REL actually defines an equivalence relation. If the implementor of the package cannot require that EQUIV_REL be an equivalence relation, he or she cannot implement functions for working with equivalence classes. Conversely, once this package has been implemented, if the user does not fulfill this requirement, the instantiation of the package will not produce a well-defined quotient set.

However, such requirements are not expressible in Ada. The most that can be accomplished is to write a generic component that requires both a set of types and the signatures of mapping functions among those types, the semantics of which are undefined. The inability to require that the signatures have particular semantic meanings impedes the development of components tailored for signatures with particular semantic definitions. A possible solution is addressed in the following section.

8.4 ALGEBRAIC INTERCOMPONENT SPECIFICATION

There has been increasing interest in the application of category theory to the expression of the static semantics of systems (particularly software systems). Specification languages based on category theory have been developed that appear applicable for expressing the allowable environment class for reusable components. We believe such languages are necessary for designing systems that yield reusable components.

Category Theory and Reusable Components

The environment of a component may be expressed as an algebraic structure consisting of a set of *sorts* (data type identifiers) and related operations [Goguen *et al.*, 1977]. These represent the aspects of the system that the component must have available to perform its function. In a particular system, each component is fixed within a specific local environment. A component can be reused within another context provided that the local environment available there contains a subenvironment that can be mapped into the environment needed by the component.

Modern algebra provides the conceptual basis for classes of algebraic structures, and *category theory* [MacLane, 1971] is the branch of mathematics that deals with classification of algebraic structures. Here we summarize some of the basic concepts of category theory that will be used throughout the remainder of the paper.

Overview of Category Theory.   A *category* is a class of *objects* together with a set of mappings, called *morphisms*, defined for each pair of objects in the category. (The formal definition of category is more general than this, but we only consider categories of objects and mappings.)

For a category C, we denote the class of objects by obj(C) and the class of morphisms by mor(C). Each morphism F in mor(C) has a source $s(F)$ and a target $t(F)$, both in obj(C). Morphisms can be composed whenever the target of one is in the source of another, and the operation of composition is associative whenever it is defined. The identity morphism 1_X exists in mor(C) for each X in obj(C).

Familiar examples of categories are S, V, and G, defined as follows:

☐ S: obj(S) = class of sets; mor(S) = set mappings
☐ V: obj(V) = class of real vector spaces; mor(V) = linear transformations
☐ G: obj(G) = class of groups; mor(G) = group homomorphisms

The standard tool for reasoning about a category C is a *diagram*, a directed graph whose nodes correspond to objects in obj(C) and whose edges correspond to morphisms in mor(C). A diagram is said to *commute* if, for any two nodes (objects) A and B, any two compositions of edges (morphisms) from A to B are equal morphisms.

For later use, we will now introduce the concepts of coproduct, cone, and colimit. For these, we will assume we are working in a fixed category C.

If A and B are in obj(C), their *coproduct* is an element P of obj(C) and morphisms I_A: $A \rightarrow P$ and I_B: $B \rightarrow P$, satisfying the following "universal property": for any Q in obj(C) and morphisms J_A: $A \rightarrow Q$ and J_B: $B \rightarrow Q$, there exists a unique morphism U: $P \rightarrow Q$ such that the diagram in Fig. 8.2 commutes. (Recall that the diagram commutes if $U \circ I_A = J_A$ and $U \circ I_B = J_B$.)

Intuitively, the images of the possible J's in Q are analogs of the types and operations in A and B. Therefore, the images $I(A)$ and $I(B)$ in P must represent the definitive features of A and B together. The notion of definitive features is, of course, relative to the category in use.

Suppose we have a diagram $D = (N, E)$ where N is the set of nodes and E is the set of edges. A *cone* on D consists of an object A and a set of morphisms m_n: $n \rightarrow A$, indexed by the nodes n of D, such that for each edge e (from, say, $n1$ to $n2$) in E, the diagram in Fig. 8.3 commutes.

The *colimit* of $D = (N, E)$ is a cone (A, M) where M consists of m_n: $n \rightarrow A$, indexed by the nodes n of N, which satisfies the following "universal property:" for any cone (B, L) where L consists of l_n: $n \rightarrow B$, there is a *unique* morphism U: $A \rightarrow B$ such that for any edge e (from, say,

FIGURE 8.2
UNIVERSAL PROPERTY OF COPRODUCT

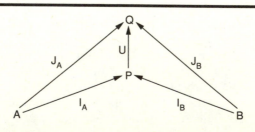

FIGURE 8.3
CONE OVER EDGE OF DIAGRAM

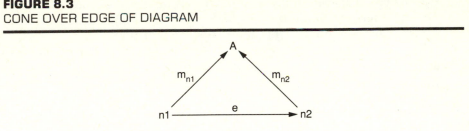

$n1$ to $n2$) the diagram in Fig. 8.4 commutes. That is, the colimit is the cone that is the "nearest" to the diagram.

As in the case of the coproduct, the colimit is intuitively a collection of the definitive features of a diagram. In this case, however, the mappings in the diagram identify aspects of the structures that are represented by a single image in the colimit.

These concepts are used later for describing component environments in a structured manner. We will also need the concept of a functor, a mapping of one category to another that preserves the relationships among the objects.

A *functor* is a mapping from objects and morphisms in one category to objects and morphisms in another such that morphism source, morphism target, and the operations of identity and composition are preserved. Consequently, commuting diagrams map to commuting diagrams, coproducts map to coproducts, and so on.

Examples of functors, using the categories S, V, and G given earlier, include the following:

☐ For a set s in obj(S), construct the free group generated by s (the elements are strings made from elements of s and formal inverses of elements of s, and the operation is concatenation).

FIGURE 8.4
UNIVERSAL PROPERTY OF COLIMIT

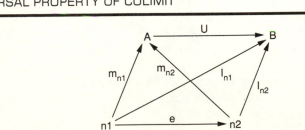

☐ Given a vector space v in obj(V), the underlying group obtained by ignoring scalar multiplication is in obj(G). This is an example of a "forgetful" functor, that is, a functor that discards some structure.

☐ Given a vector space v in obj(V), the underlying set obtained by ignoring addition and scalar multiplication is in obj(S). This is another forgetful functor.

Ada Generic Units as Functors. We now restate in category-theoretic terms the concepts of Ada generic program units.

The class of allowable environments for a component is an isomorphism class of many-sorted algebraic structures. We define the *category of many-sorted algebraic structures*, whose morphisms are mappings that preserve structure; that is, they map sorts to sorts and operation identifiers to operation identifiers. The inclusion of a component into a system may be viewed as a morphism from the environment existing before inclusion to a new environment.

A parameterized data type, or data type constructor, may then be thought of as the embodiment of a functor between categories of algebraic structures having substructures (the actual parameters of the data type) related by isomorphism [Thatcher *et al.*, 1978]. For Ada, such a parameterized data type and its related functions may be implemented (at compile time) via a generic package. When it is instantiated, a new environment is created containing the algebraic structures made available by the generic package specification.

For each such package, there is a class of environments within which the necessary generic parameters are available to legally and meaningfully instantiate the package. As noted earlier, the specification of the environment is, in general, not possible in Ada. The intended environment is (an isomorphism class of) a many-sorted algebraic structure, while Ada can only specify a set of types and the signatures of mappings among them.

An Ada generic package, like all other Ada program units, may be implemented as a module containing instantiations of yet lower level generic packages. An entire Ada system may be implemented as a nested hierarchy of such generic instantiations. Each level of the system may be thought of as the composition of the morphisms corresponding to each generic instantiation at that level. Each level of the system may therefore be represented as a diagram. Each of these morphisms, and their composition, are in turn instances of functors; these *algebraic constructor functors* correspond to components of a (level-independent) layer of the Ada system.

The decomposition of an Ada generic package into a sequence of lower-level generic instantiations is itself a morphism, which we may call a *morphism of decomposition*. Next, consider the category of algebraic constructor functors. The morphisms among these objects are the morphisms of decomposition of the Ada generic packages for which the diagrams representing each level of the system commute.

Intercomponent Languages Based on Category Theory

We believe that a formalism is required for specifying the externally viewed behavior of Ada generic components and that category theory can be used to provide a formal underpinning of the semantics of this specification language.

The languages that appear most promising for intercomponent specification permit the expression of functors defined on algebraic structures. One such language is Clear, developed by Burstall and Goguen [Burstall and Goguen, 1980] for formal, well-structured specification of software components. It provides formalisms for expression of *algebraic theories* (i.e., many-sorted algebraic structures), operators for building new theories from combinations of old theories, and the definition of *theory morphisms* (functors between categories of structured theories), which implement mappings between algebraic theories defined in terms of theory-building expressions. The semantics of Clear are formally defined using category theory.

In this section a short summary of Clear is given, adopted from [Burstall and Goguen, 1977, 1980, 1981]. A specification in Clear defines a *theory* of what a piece of software is supposed to do. A theory is a finite set of sorts and operation symbols (a signature) together with a finite set of axioms. (The signature may be thought of as corresponding to syntax, and the axioms to semantics.)

The axioms can be defined using any underlying logical system which satisfies certain basic conditions as explained in [Burstall and Goguen, 1981]. Such a suitable logical system is called an *institution*. Equational logic is an institution for which the axioms are equations. For the rest of this paper, we shall assume equational logic as the underlying institution to be used with Clear (except as otherwise noted).

In Clear syntax, *theory X . . . endth* denotes a theory X. A theory describes a set of algebras, each of which

- ☐ provides a set of data items corresponding to each sort of the theory;
- ☐ provides a function on those sets corresponding to each operator; and
- ☐ satisfies the axioms of the theory.

Clear provides several theory-building operators for building up new theories from old ones. With these operators, theories can be defined in a structured manner, as a hierarchical collection of theories.

The *combine* operator, signified by infix " + ," creates the coproduct of two theories; $E + E'$ is a theory whose sorts are the union of the sorts of E and E', whose operators are the union of their operators, and whose equations are the union of their equations. The *combine* operator allows theories to share subtheories. For example, if the theories E and E' contain a theory BOOL representing truth values, then $E + E'$ should have only one copy of BOOL, not two. (Category theory is used to make this concept precise in Clear.)

The operation *enrich E by X enden* creates a new theory from *E* by adding some new sorts, operations, and/or equations as specified by *X*. (With this operator we can regard any theory as an enrichment of the "empty theory.") If *X* is prefixed by the option *data*, this indicates that the enriched theory should be interpreted *relative to* the interpretation of *E*; once a model is chosen for *E*, the enriched theory can then specify a particular algebra uniquely (up to isomorphism).

The expression *derive D from E by M: D → E endde* denotes the theory obtained by taking the quotient of theory *D* by the inverse image under *M* of equations of *E*. This operator may be used after building up a theory using *combine* and *enrich*, if the resulting theory contains more than is desired.

The Clear operators +, *enrich*, and *derive* thus permit the construction of new theories in terms of previously defined ones. However, no matter how many times an existing global theory (which may exist in a library of such theories) is referenced in a given theory expression, only one copy of the theory is involved. To properly handle the concept of shared library subtheories, we associate with each theory the names of all globally available (and potentially shareable) subtheories on which the given theory depends. The mapping from these names to the theories they name is called the *base* of the theory, and the theory itself is called a *based theory*. (Note that since a theory is considered global to itself, the base of a theory contains the theory itself.)

We extend the semantics of the Clear operators +, *enrich*, and *derive* to deal with based theories. The base of *X + Y* is the union of the bases of *X* and *Y*. An enrichment of an existing theory has the same base as the existing theory. A derivation from an existing theory also has the same base as the existing theory.

Clear also enables the user to create his or her own (possibly parameterized) theory-building procedures from these primitive theory-building operators. The arguments to such user-defined procedures are theories satisfying a *metasort*, a paradigm for a class of theories (much as a data type defines a set of objects). The procedure is written using the metasort as a formal parameter and can be invoked with an actual theory by associating the sorts and operations of the actual theory with those of the metasort.

As an example, we can specify the **E_CLASS_PACKAGE** example in a pseudo-Clear notation:

```
procedure E_CLASS_PACKAGE (Element: Group_with_
Equiv_Rel)=
   Element enriched by
         data sorts E_CLASS;
         opns _*_:E_CLASS, E_CLASS = > E_CLASS;
         axioms axioms for equivalence classes ;
   enden
```

The metasort Group_with_Equiv_Rel must have been previously defined, and any actual parameter for Element will be in that metasort.

In Clear, the operations are formally defined in category-theoretic terms; for example, enrichments are cones and combinations are coproducts in a suitable category. These operations exist in any category of theories that has colimits of finite diagrams. Therefore, the basic theorem in defining the semantics of Clear is that the category of data theories expressible in Clear is finitely cocomplete, that is, has colimits of all finite diagrams. This establishes the semantic basis for the Clear operations.

8.5 MAPPING SPECIFICATIONS TO IMPLEMENTATION

Ada design methodologies should be developed that enable a system to be designed as a structured collection of components that can be easily reused either within the current system or within future systems. Ada is a strongly typed language permitting components to have user-defined algebraic structures (types and related functions), and new methodologies are needed to control relationships between different algebraic structures defined in different components. Algebraic structures must be passed as parameters between components.

Any methodology for Ada system development should integrate the design and management of reusable components into proven current design techniques. Such methodologies could maintain structure-preserving isomorphisms between levels, guaranteeing that components thus designed are neither level-specific nor order-specific. These methodologies would be integrated with formal specification of Ada systems; in fact, design could be carried out in the specification language, and later translated to Ada for implementation.

We now give an informal treatment of how Clear specifications can be mapped to an Ada implementation. This discussion will necessarily omit a great many details and special cases.

First, the signature of each theory can be implemented as an Ada package specification. (The axioms of a theory, of course, have no Ada equivalent. Ensuring that an Ada component also implements the semantics of the theory will require additional tools in the development environment.) In the following, we will abbreviate "implementing the signature of a theory in Ada" to simply "implementing the theory in Ada."

In Ada, when a library unit is referenced via *with* clauses, only one copy of the library unit is provided, no matter how many units reference it. This is similar to the behavior of based theories in Clear, since you only get one copy of a Clear subtheory, no matter how many theories are based on it. It is therefore logical to use the Ada *with* clause to record the dependence of an Ada implementation of a theory on the implementations of the subtheories

FIGURE 8.5
SIMPLE COMBINE OPERATOR IMPLEMENTED IN ADA

```
[with {base_of_X} ∪ {base_of_y};]
package X_PLUS_Y is

end X_PLUS_Y;
```

named in the base of the theory. The Ada package implementation of a theory *T* should therefore *with* the implementation of all subtheories named in the base of *T* (except *T* itself).

If *X* and *Y* are Clear theories with corresponding Ada package implementations, their combination, *X* + *Y*, may be implemented in a package in which their implementations, as well as the implementations of their subtheories, are all made visible, as in Fig. 8.5.

If theory *E* is implemented by an Ada package with the same name, and *X* is a list of enrichments, then *F* = *enrich E by X enden* may be implemented by an Ada package as in Fig. 8.6.

The *derive* operator, as in *C* = *derive D from E by M endde*, may be implemented as follows. As before, we must make available *E* (and its subtheories). Then the package specification for *C* provides the signature of *D*, the private part of *C* refines the sorts of *D* in terms of the sorts of *E* according to *M*, by using explicit conversion where necessary. See Fig. 8.7.

Theory-building procedures may be implemented as Ada generic packages. For the theory procedure *P(X: R)*, where *R* is the metasort defining the required semantics for formal theory parameter *X*, the corresponding Ada generic package will have the signature of *R* as generic formal parameters. We must be able, therefore, to determine the signature of a given metasort. This is not difficult, but we must be careful to avoid including multiple copies

FIGURE 8.6
ENRICH OPERATOR IMPLEMENTED IN ADA

```
[with {based_theory_list};] --may include library theory E
package F_PACKAGE is

use...                        --optional, for direct visibility

{enrichment X}

end F_PACKAGE;
```

FIGURE 8.7
DERIVE OPERATOR IMPLEMENTED IN ADA

```
[with {base_of_E};]
package C_PACKAGE is

 {signature D; sorts declared limited private}

private
{Mₜ: types(D) -> types(E)}              --implement with derived

                                        --types

end C_PACKAGE;

package body C_PACKAGE is
{Mf: functions(D) -> functions(E)      --use explicit conversion
                                       --between types of D
                                       --and types of E

end C_PACKAGE;
```

of sorts and operations from shared subtheories. (This gets even trickier for a theory procedure with more than one formal argument, each with its own metasort.)

Sannella [1982], as part of his development of a set-theoretic semantic definition of Clear, describes a technique applicable to this problem; it involves tagging each sort and operator with the name of the theory in which it is originally defined and treating the Clear operators as set-theoretic constructions, such as set union. In Sannella's semantics, the combination of theories $X + Y$, for example, really does take the set union of the sorts and operators of theories X and Y. Therefore, if a given sort or operator occurs in both X and Y, we will only include one copy, not two (unless their tags indicate the copies came from different original theories).

8.6 SUPPORT ENVIRONMENT

Software tools will be necessary to provide automated support for the methodologies we have outlined. They should also enforce compliance with the standards imposed by the formalisms and discipline. Such tools must be incorporated into the Ada programming support environment (APSE) [U.S. Dept. of Defense, 1980]. The requirements for some of these tools are given next.

Clear Semantic Analyzer. In order to map out a system as a structured collection of Clear specifications, it will be necessary to reason about the semantics of the relationships between specifications (including such things as how one theory can serve as an actual parameter to a theory-building procedure). We believe that an automated theorem-prover can be developed for Clear that will greatly aid this reasoning. (In fact, Sannella [1982] has already done some work on this.)

Clear-to-Ada Mapper. We have indicated in Section 8.5 the desirability of making systematic the mapping from Clear specifications to their corresponding Ada implementations. As noted, today we can at best map from a Clear specifications to an Ada package skeleton, which, when filled in by the designer, will implement the Clear specification. This process can and should be automated. This will both facilitate the process of design and help ensure consistency between the Ada package and its Clear specification.

Ada Component Verifier. To formally prove consistency between the developed Ada package and its Clear specification, a tool will be needed to develop (or at least check) formal proofs that the Ada design meets its Clear specification. It is not feasible to develop such a tool at this time, given the lack of a formal algebraic definition of Ada. However, for now, less formal approaches to demonstrating correctness, such as testing, are feasible.

Ada Component Library. The library of reusable Ada software components should be structured to reflect the dependencies among the associated theory morphisms. Theory morphisms would also serve as the criteria for selection of components from the library. A candidate representation for such a library is an acyclic graph, whose edges correspond to the components' associated theory morphisms and injections from the source of one morphism into the target of another morphism, where such an injection can be shown to exist. The nodes of the graph would correspond to elements of the source or target of the morphisms.

Such a component library could be implemented using a relational database. A library of reusable components should be usable by users unfamiliar with the mathematical concepts upon which the library structure and retrieval mechanisms are based. We believe that much of this mathematics can be hidden by a user-friendly interface to the library manager and by automated assistance in mathematical reasoning.

8.7 FUTURE CONCERNS

Other issues which we hope to address in the future include the following.

A major unresolved problem at the time of this writing is how to specify the behavior of Ada components whose interfaces involve task types (or composite types containing tasks). It will be necessary to replace the under-lying institution of equational logic with one expressive enough to permit reasoning about multitasking. One logical system which appears promising is *dynamic logic*, a variant of modal logic capable of reasoning about nondeter-minism [Harel, 1979]. We plan to investigate the suitability of dynamic logic as an institution to permit the expression of the semantics of multitasking components using Clear.

The very concept of reusability must be defined more rigorously, in terms of the dependence of a component on enclosing or higher-level environments (probably defined in terms of number and complexity of algebraic structure parameters). It should be possible to develop metrics for such component dependence, enabling quantification of potential reusability.

Such quantification would facilitate serious investigation into program transformations to improve component reusability. Transformations could improve a component's reusability by enlarging its class of allowable enclosing scopes. We have begun preliminary investigation into such transformations for Ada components, but as yet cannot quantify their effect on potential reusability. An Ada dependency manipulation tool, as outlined in the previous section, would help in this investigation.

Finally, the approach outlined thus far can manage Ada software com-ponents according to their externally viewed static semantic behavior, but it cannot distinguish between components with the same static semantic behav-ior that differ in other ways, that is, in levels of performance, reliability, and so on. (We believe that for the foreseeable future, the performance criteria will have to be specified heuristically.) Once the problems of managing com-ponents according to semantic specification have been solved, techniques can be developed to deal with these additional performance criteria.

Components which have the same externally viewed static semantic behavior but differ in various performance criteria can still be grouped together in the component library. In this case, a criterion for retrieval based only on static semantic specification will retrieve from the library a range of possible subsystem configurations, all semantically valid. Then other tech-niques (possibly heuristic search) can be applied to find the configuration that is optimal according to the specified performance criteria. Wymore [1976] gives one possible approach, but its compatibility with our approach to formal semantic component management is uncertain.

8.8 CONCLUSIONS

As a result of our work in developing a methodology and support system for integrated multilevel Ada design, we believe that integration of management of reusable components into proven design techniques is both desirable and feasible for Ada design. This paper shows that using structured algebraic descriptions for environments is a promising approach for specification and implementation of reusable Ada components.

ACKNOWLEDGMENT

We gratefully acknowledge the support we received from the following people. At Raytheon: A. Simmons, our project leader on HLS; P. Felton, our department manager; and M. Gerhardt, for his technical assistance. At SRI International: Dr. J. Goguen, for supplying us with much important information on algebraic semantics of software.

REFERENCES

Burstall, R. M., and J. A. Goguen. Putting theories together to make specifications. *Proc. 5th Int. Joint Conf. Artificial Intell.*, Cambridge, Mass., 1977.

————. The semantics of Clear, a specification language. *Proc. 1979 Copenhagen Winter School on Abstract Software Specification* (Lecture Notes in Computer Science, vol. 86), pp. 292–332. New York: Springer-Verlag, 1980.

————. An informal introduction to specification using Clear. In *The Correctness Problem in Computer Science*, R. S. Boyer and J. S. Moore, eds. New York: Academic, 1981.

Chase, A. I., and M. S. Gerhardt. The case for full Ada as a PDL. *Ada Lett.*, ACM AdaTEC, Nov. 1982.

Downes, V. A., and S. J. Goldsack. *Programming Embedded Systems with Ada*. Englewood Cliffs, N.J.: Prentice-Hall, 1982.

Goguen, J. A.; J. W. Thatcher; and E. G. Wagner. An initial algebra approach to the specification, correctness, and implementation of abstract data types. IBM Thomas J. Watson Research Center, Yorktown Heights, N.Y., res. rep., 1977.

Harel, D. *First-Order Dynamic Logic*. Lecture Notes in Computer Science, vol. 68. New York: Springer-Verlag, 1979.

Lipson, J. D. *Elements of Algebra and Algebraic Computing*. Reading, Mass.: Addison-Wesley, 1981.

Litvintchouk, S.; A. Matsumoto; and A. Simmons. High Level Simulator (HLS) technical specification. Raytheon Co., Portsmouth, R.I., tech. doc. 3122031A, Aug. 1982.

MacLane, S. *Categories for the Working Mathematician*. New York: Springer-Verlag, 1971.

Sannella, D. The semantics and implementation of Clear, a program specification language. Ph.D. dissertation, Univ. Edinburgh, Edinburgh, Scotland, 1982.

Thatcher, J.; E. Wagner; and J. Wright. Data type specification: Parameterization and the power of specification techniques. Presented at the ACM SIGACT 10th Annu. Symp. Theory Comput., 1978.

United States Department of Defense. *Requirements for the Ada Programming Support Environment (STONEMAN)*. Feb. 1980.

————. *Reference Manual for the Ada Programming Language*. ANSI/MIL-STD-1815A, Jan. 1983.

Wegner, P., ed. *Research Directions in Software Technology*. Cambridge, Mass.: MIT Press, 1979.

Wymore, A. W. *Systems Engineering Methodology for Interdisciplinary Teams*. New York: Wiley, 1976.

CHAPTER 9

THE TEMPLATES APPROACH
TO SOFTWARE REUSE

DENNIS M. VOLPANO[*]
Microelectronics and Computer Technology Corporation (MCC)

RICHARD B. KIEBURTZ
Department of Computer Science and Engineering
Oregon Graduate Center

9.1 INTRODUCTION

Conventional, imperative languages usually do not allow programmers to realize algorithms without fully specifying the types and representations of data. For example, specifying a program to sort the elements of a set ordinarily requires committing to a type and representation of the data to be sorted. Clearly, commitments appropriate for one application may not be suitable for another.

This paper describes a programming method that fosters software reuse. In this method, the programming process is factored into two separate activities: algorithm specification and implementation specification. Algorithms

[*]Currently at Cornell University.

are expressed in such a way that only their essential properties are captured, leaving the types and representations of the data on which they operate unspecified. By deferring choices concerning data, an algorithm specification, called a software template, can be reused in those applications that call for the same algorithm but with different types of data. In a sort template, for example, the types of the elements to be sorted can be left unspecified so that the template can be used to sort integers, say, in one application and character strings in another.

Templates are defined over the values of abstract data types. These data types are implemented in an imperative language by a programmer who is an expert at this level, perhaps someone different from the template designer. An implementor produces a library of reusable implementations of data types such as sets, sequences, graphs, and trees—types commonly used in formulating algorithms. A template designer, on the other hand, uses these data types to produce a library of templates for standard algorithms.

To use a template, a programmer chooses implementations of the template's data types from a library. If there is a choice of available implementations then selection is guided by certain user requirements such as program capacity, performance, or function. The template is then automatically translated, or instantiated, to a program tailored to the selected implementations. An algorithm can be implemented in different ways by binding the data types of its template specification to different implementations. This brief overview of the templates method is summarized in Fig. 9.1.

To illustrate, we will define a template called `sort` that sorts the elements of a sequence. `Sort` will insert each member of an input sequence into a

FIGURE 9.1
TEMPLATES METHOD OVERVIEW

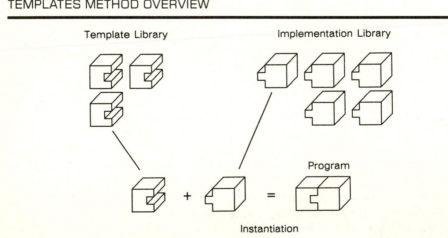

FIGURE 9.2
TEMPLATE SORT

```
sort(nil) = niltree
sort(cons(x,y)) = insert(x, sort(y))

insert(n, niltree) = leaf(n)
insert(n, leaf(m)) =
              if n < m then node (leaf(n), m, niltree)
              else node(niltree, m, leaf(n))
insert(n, node(l, m, r)) =
              if (n < m) then node(insert(n, l), m, r)
              else node(l, m, insert(n, r))
```

binary tree maintaining the property that for any node *n* with left subtree *t*1 and right subtree *t*2, all values contained in *t*1 are "less than" the value at *n* which in turn is "less than or equal" to all values contained in *t*2. Template sort therefore will use an abstract data type called Seq (sequence) and another called Bintree (binary tree).

A value of type Seq is defined to be either the empty sequence nil, or a sequence constructed from a value and another sequence with cons. A Bintree value is defined to be niltree, a leaf node constructed from a value with leaf, or an interior node formed from a value and two subtrees with node. The definition of sort, given in Fig. 9.2, is generic in the type of the elements to be sorted. The operator < is polymorphic, meaning it can be applied to operands of many distinct types, each type defining it differently. In this way, sort is implicitly parameterized on an order relation, an abstraction also expressible in CLU with cluster parameters [Liskov *et al.*, 1977] and in CLEAR [Burstall and Goguen, 1977].

To use template sort, a programmer specifies an instantiation directive in a program, which conveys the implementations selected for the data types Seq and Bintree. Since sort is generic, the directive must also specify a type for the elements that will be sorted. For example, suppose we wish to instantiate sort to a C function that sorts an array of character strings, and that our library contains C implementations of Seq and Bintree called Carray and Ctree. Carray represents a sequence by an array in C. For Carray to be useful in a wide variety of contexts, it must be parameterized on array size. If we select an array size of say 128, then instantiating sort with the directive in Fig. 9.3 will produce the body of the desired function.

The directive indicates that template sort is to be instantiated and that it must obtain its input from x, and bind its result to y. The types of variables x and y are given in the Where clause using the "implemented-by"

FIGURE 9.3
SORT AN ARRAY OF STRINGS IN C

```
Assign(y, sort x) Where
      x : Seq(String)/Carray(128)
      y : Bintree(String)/Ctree
Endwhere
```

FIGURE 9.4
SORT AN ARRAY OF INTEGERS IN PASCAL

```
Assign(y, sort x) Where
      x : Seq(Int)/Pascalarray(128)
      y : Bintree(Int)/Pascaltree
Endwhere
```

symbol /. Variable x denotes a sequence of strings implemented by Carray, and y denotes a binary tree of strings implemented by Ctree.

Template sort can also be used to produce a Pascal procedure that sorts an array of integers. If our library contains Pascal implementations of Seq and Bintree called Pascalarray and Pascaltree, then instantiating sort with the directive in Fig. 9.4 will yield the desired procedure body.

9.2 THE TEMPLATES METHOD

The templates method permits algorithms to be expressed without committing to types and representations of data. This is possible because templates are defined over values of polymorphic abstract data types. An abstract data type is an algebra consisting of a finite set of operators and a carrier, a set of values on which these operators act [Goguen et al., 1977]. An abstract data type has the advantage that the exact representation of the carrier need not be visible to clients of the type, that is, to programs that invoke its operators.

Traditionally, programming languages support abstract data types by allowing programmers to define interfaces for data type implementations that are intended to hide representations. Clients of abstract types must be expressed using these interfaces which usually reveal whether or not abstract operators should be interpreted as statements or expressions. Consequently, in a client, it is not always possible to treat abstract operators as functions in the mathematical sense [Gries and Prins, 1985]. This is where the templates method differs from the traditional use of abstract data types. Abstract operators are always interpreted as functions. Implementations of new functions defined using composition and recursion are derived automatically from implementations of lower-level abstract operators.

9.2.1 Defining Templates

An algorithm specification should possess certain properties. To capture computational complexity or performance, it must be constructive in that it prescribes how to compute. It should be free of side effects since computing by effect is peculiar to a particular model of computation. Finally, it should be amenable to transformation and formal reasoning. In order to achieve these properties, templates are defined in an applicative notation [Henderson, 1980].

A template is a set of typed, first-order function definitions. A first-order function does not take another function as input or produce a function as a result. Moreover, all operators used in a template, except conditional (if-then-else), are interpreted strictly, meaning their operands are fully evaluated when they are applied. Each function definition comprising a template has a type that can be inferred from the function's form and the types of its subexpressions. Template `sort`, for example, has type `Seq(alpha)` → `Bintree (alpha)`, where `alpha` is a universally quantified type variable. Therefore, `sort` can be viewed as a finite representation of an infinite class of monomorphically typed sort functions. This class contains, for instance, functions to sort integers, strings, and so on.

9.2.2 Implementing Abstract Data Types

An implementor's job is to find a data representation for values of an abstract data type, and then use it to implement the type's operators efficiently while ensuring correctness. Data types can be implemented in any imperative language, such as C or Pascal, that has a facility for defining types. Template instantiation, then, is the process of composing a program from the imperative language code segments that implement the various operators of abstract data types [Volpano, 1986].

Values of an abstract data type are represented by concrete values in the implementing language. A declaration for a data representation called `R` of an abstract type `T` has the form `R( ): T [|Tc|]` where `Tc` is a concrete type of the implementing language. The symbols `[|` and `|]` delimit text that will be treated as a macro definition by the instantiator. In this way, the instantiator remains independent of any particular implementing language. For example, consider the declaration:

```
Repint( ):  Int[| integer |]
```

FIGURE 9.5
CTREE DECLARATION

```
Ctree( ) : Bintree(alpha)
[|struct $_tnode {
         alpha val;
         struct $_tnode *lsucc, *rsucc;
};|]
[|  struct $_tnode  *  |]
```

Repint is a representation in which abstract data type Int is represented by concrete type integer of Pascal. If the concrete type specified in a declaration is not predefined in the implementing language then its definition must be given in another block also delimited by [| and |] (see Fig. 9.5).

Polymorphism.   Without the ability to represent polymorphic types, implementation libraries grow very quickly with implementations of monomorphic types. A library, for instance, may contain implementations of Bintree(Int), Bintree(String), and so on. This kind of proliferation can be averted by giving representations for polymorphic types such as Bintree(alpha), where alpha is a type variable.

A representation of a polymorphic type is distinguished from a monomorphic representation by the use of a concrete type scheme, instances of which are created by the template instantiator. If a concrete type is defined using a type variable, then the type becomes a scheme. For example, representation Ctree, declared in Fig. 9.5, is polymorphic as conveyed by concrete type scheme $_tnode, which is defined using type variable alpha.

Since Ctree is polymorphic, instances of it must be generated by the instantiator as needed. But text between [| and |] is not interpreted, and therefore the implementor must use the special symbol $ to indicate where uniquely generated names should be placed to create instances of Ctree.

Operators of an abstract data type are implemented using declared data representations and either expressions or statements of the implementing language. An operator implementation is specified by a declaration of the form pattern = [| l |] where l is a code segment of the implementing language, and pattern conveys the syntactic property of whether l is an expression or a statement. Patterns may contain variables whose declarations determine the data representations admissible in l. For example, in a Pascal implementation of abstract type Int, suppose x and y are variables declared by x, y: Repint. An equality operator can then be implemented by the declaration:

```
eq x y = [| x = y |]
```

The pattern on the left side indicates that eq is implemented by an expression. Like data representations, the implementing code segment on the right side is treated as a macro parameterized on x and y.

An operator can also be implemented by one or more statements that, taken collectively, behave as a single assignment of a value to a variable. In this case, the keyword assign is used in the pattern. For example, suppose t3 is a variable declared by t3: Ctree in a C implementation of Bintree. Then an implementation of node might be declared by the following.

```
assign(t3, node t1 nv t2) = [|
       t3 = (struct $_ tnode *) malloc(sizeof(struct $_ tnode));
       t3 ->lsucc = t1; t3->rsucc = t2;
       assign(t3->val, nv, alpha)
|]
```

The last statement of this code segment is an abstract assignment of nv to t3->val. Such assignments provide an implementor with a way to assign values to variables whose types are unknown. A type variable representing the type of the assignment is given as the third argument. When alpha becomes bound to a type at instantiation time, this assignment will be replaced by a code segment that performs it. The code segment is produced from implementations of assignment that an implementor also specifies. A complete implementation of Bintree is given in Appendix A.

Processing an implementation specification involves inferring a type for each implementation of an operator, reporting any ill-typed patterns, and ensuring that if there is a type variable in a right side then it is a parameter of a type for some variable in the left-side pattern. Other forms of support have been proposed as the result of research aimed at developing a methodology for the efficient implementation of abstract data types in an imperative language [Thomas, 1987].

9.2.3 Instantiating Templates

A template is instantiated relative to an *instantiation directive* in a program. A directive contains the name of a template and one or more variables whose declarations establish a context for the instantiation. Variables are declared with type expressions that capture the implementations desired for abstract types. Examples of instantiation directives were given in Figs. 9.3 and 9.4 for template sort. Note that no implementations are specified for the abstract types Int and String in the declarations of x and y. This is because they are primitive types with standard representations that are selected by default if none are specified. Although these examples do not illustrate it, variables in a directive need not be declared if their types can be inferred from the template.

9.3 SOFTWARE TEMPLATES SYSTEM

Tools have been developed to support programming in the templates paradigm. They include an instantiator for instantiating templates and a tool for processing implementation specifications [Volpano, 1987].

The template type checker has been reconstructed using templates. As expected, this exercise involved more effort than encoding the type checker directly without templates since a separate library of implementations had to be developed. But this library has been useful in many other applications because it gives implementations of general-purpose data types such as sequences, trees, and symbol tables.

9.4 CONCLUSION

With software templates, the programming process is factored into algorithm and implementation specification. A template is automatically instantiated to a program tailored to the implementations of abstract data types selected by a programmer. An evident advantage of this method is that efficient, well-documented algorithms, such as those described by Knuth [1973] for searching, can be encoded as implementations of data types and reused with very little effort.

APPENDIX

Bintree Implementation in C

```
1          Ctree( ) : Bintree(alpha)
2          [|struct $_tnode {
3                  alpha val;
4                  struct $_tnode *lsucc, *rsucc;
5          };|]
6          [|struct $_tnode *|]

7          t3 : Ctree

8          isniltree t3 = [|(t3 == 0)|]
9          isleaf t3 = [|(t3-> lsucc == 0 && t3->rsucc == 0)|]
10         nodeval t3 = [|(t3-> val)|]
11         lchild t3 = [|(t3-> lsucc)|]
12         rchild t3 = [|(t3-> rsucc)|]
13         assign(t3, niltree) = [|t3 = 0;|]
14         assign(t3, leaf nv) = [|
15                 t3 = (struct $_tnode *) malloc(sizeof(struct $_tnode));
16                 t3->lsucc = t3-> rsucc = 0;
17                 assign(t3-> val, nv, alpha)
18         |]
```

```
19              assign(t3, node t1 nv t2) = [|
20                       t3 = (struct $_tnode *) malloc(sizeof(struct $_tnode));
21                       t3->lsucc = t1;  t3->rsucc = t2;
22                       assign(t3->val, nv, alpha)
23              |]

24              assign(t3, t2) = [|t3 = t2;|]
```

References

Burstall, R. M., and Goguen, J. A. Putting theories together to make specifications. *Proc. 5th International Joint Conference on Artificial Intelligence*, Cambridge, Mass., pp. 1045–1058, August 1977.

Goguen, J. A.; Thatcher, J. W.; and Wagner, E. G. An initial algebra approach to the specification, correctness, and implementation of abstract data types. In Yeh, R. (ed.), *Current Trends in Programming Methodology*, pp. 80–149, Prentice Hall, 1977.

Gries, D., and Prins, J. A new notion of encapsulation. *Proceedings ACM SIGPLAN Symposium on Language Issues in Programming Environments*, Seattle, Wash., pp. 131–139, June 1985.

Henderson, P. *Functional Programming Application and Implementation*. Prentice-Hall, 1980.

Knuth, D. E. *Sorting and Searching*, volume 3. Addison-Wesley, 1973.

Liskov, B.; Snyder, A.; Atkinson, R.; and Schaffert, C. Abstraction mechanisms in CLU. *Communications of the ACM* 20(8): 564–576, 1977.

Thomas, M. Implementing algebraically specified abstract data types in an imperative programming language. In Lecture Notes in Computer Science, vol. 250, pp. 197–211, Springer-Verlag, 1987.

Volpano, D. M. Software templates. Ph.D. thesis, Department of Computer Science and Engineering, Oregon Graduate Center, Beaverton, Oregon, 1986.

Volpano, D. M. STS—Software Templates System. MCC technical report STP-257-87, 1987.

CHAPTER 10

PARIS: A System for Reusing Partially Interpreted Schemas

SHMUEL KATZ,[1] **CHARLES A. RICHTER,** *and* **KHE-SING THE***
Microelectronics and Computer Technology Corporation (MCC)

10.1 INTRODUCTION

As the number of large and complicated software systems keeps growing, there is a trend in software development processes towards reusability as applied in other engineering disciplines: A large system consists of a hierarchy of building blocks, and similar components should be reusable once invented. A more concrete objective of reusability in software design is to be able to capture the designer's experience in an artifact, so that in building a software component one doesn't have to start from scratch over and over again.

The reusability issue (see, e.g., [Biggerstaff and Perlis, 1984]) is particularly significant for distributed software because of the difficulty of inventing

From 9th International Conference on Software Engineering, March 30–April 2, 1987, Monterey, California. Copyright 1987, Association for Computing Machinery, Inc. Reprinted by permission.

[1]On leave from the Computer Science Department, The Technion, Haifa, Israel.

*Currently at the Computer Science Department, University of Texas at Austin.

correct distributed algorithms. It is desirable to have a system that can store clever and correct algorithms once they are created, and then retrieve them later when they are needed in a design process. This is the primary motivation for our prototype of a system to formalize and automate the reuse of software components.

The prototype discussed in this paper is a LISP [Wilensky, 1984] implementation of the software reusability concept described in the article "Partially Interpreted Schemas for CSP Programming" by Baruch and Katz [1985]. We named this system PARIS, an acronym for "partially interpreted schemas." The prototype is a partial implementation of the proposed system; it is subject to improvements and refinements before it can serve as a fully practical tool for software designers. Its primary objective is to help us, the implementors, understand some of the difficulties that arise in translating theory to a running system. This is necessary both in order to refine and improve the theory and to identify ways of overcoming its implementation problems.

A *partially interpreted schema* is a program in which some parts remain abstract or undefined. These abstract entities can include both program sections and nonprogram entities such as functions, domains, or variables. For different interpretations of abstract entities in the schema, the results will be different programs performing different functions. In other words, many programs can have an identical program skeleton, even though each program behaves differently, according to the components that are inserted into the skeleton.

Our system maintains a library of partially interpreted schemas, each of which is stored along with assertions about its applicability and results. When a user presents a problem statement (i.e., description of requirements from a program), the system searches through the library for a schema that can potentially satisfy the user's problem statement. If a candidate is found, then its abstract entities can be replaced by concrete entities. The replacement of nonprogram abstract entities can be done two ways, as will be explained in Section 10.2.3. After all abstract entities in the schema have been correctly interpreted, the resulting program is presented to the user.

10.2 THE PARIS SYSTEM

10.2.1 Definitions

A partially interpreted program schema is syntactically a program or independent module in some programming language, but it contains abstract entities such as abstract functions, predicates, constant symbols, unspecified domains, or unrealized program parts, each represented by free variables in the abstract entities set.

Each schema is accompanied by its specification, which includes the following:

1. Applicability conditions, defining the restrictions on and requirements for using the schema. These are all assertions involving the required input to the schema and all other nonprogram abstract entities of the schema (e.g., restrictions on the possible data types, ranges of parameters, and subclasses of functions that can be treated by the schema).
2. Section conditions, which are assertions about the program sections that must be substituted for free variables.
3. Result assertions, indicating what the schema can achieve. The result assertions can be classified as *postassertions*, which define, in terms of the abstract entities and the input, some conditions that hold after execution of the schema; invariant assertions, which define conditions that are true throughout the execution of the schema; and liveness claims, which assert that some events will occur in any program derived from the schema.

The *presentation* of a schema includes the text of the schema, the abstract entities set, a statement in temporal logic of all aspects of the schema specification, and a proof of correctness of the result assertions of the schema, assuming both the applicability conditions and the section conditions.

A *problem statement* consists of *requirements* about the needed computation and *facts* about the input of the concrete task and about the requirements (mathematical properties, etc.). These may have the same forms allowed for schema specifications but will not include free variables or undefined functions, as statements in the schema specification do.

The matching of a problem statement to a schema and its specification involves demonstrating a possible substitution of named entities from the problem statement for each nonprogram abstract entity in the schema and the specification, and showing that (a) the facts of the problem statement imply the schema conditions for that substitution, and (b) when the substitution is made, the result assertions of the schema's specification imply the requirements of the problem statement.

Once the matching has been demonstrated, the *instantiation* of the schema to a solution of a problem statement may occur. This involves first carrying out the above-mentioned substitution, and then supplying program parts that satisfy the appropriate section conditions. Supplying the sections of program can involve a recursive application of the schema methodology, or it can be done directly, when the specification is sufficiently straightforward. The resulting instance of the schema is a program guaranteed to be correct with respect to the problem statement—provided the supplied program parts are correct with respect to the section conditions. The generic proof of the schema can also be instantiated to provide a proof for a specific instance of the schema.

10.2.2 The Implementation Criteria

The schema library is a list of schema entries. As implied by the above definitions, each schema entry has five components: entity list, applicability conditions, result assertions, section conditions, and schema body. We assume that the system and the user agree upon the vocabulary and syntax of schema entries. We have not yet specified exactly which keywords are contained in the vocabulary and what the definition of each keyword is, but the keyword library is extendable and the keywords we have so far defined are sufficient for the examples in the schema library.

The entity list includes all abstract entities used in a schema. The entities will be interpreted based on the problem statement. Restrictions on the concrete entities that may be substituted for nonprogram abstract entities are listed in the applicability conditions. The result of executing the schema (provided that all applicability conditions are satisfied) will satisfy the temporal logic assertions in the result assertions. The section conditions contain specifications for each required program section; the specifications will be presented to the user so he or she can supply the program sections accordingly.

The schema body is a list of strings and atoms: Constant parts of the schema are represented as strings and abstract entities as atoms. Eventually, these atoms will be interpreted; all of them may be replaced with concrete entities, or some of them may be left unspecified. Then all elements of the list are concatenated to form a long string, which is the resulting program.

The most difficult questions for partially interpreted schemas involve the abstract and concrete specifications, as part of the presentation of a schema and of a concrete problem statement. The abstract specification, the problem statement, and the match between them are crucial to the usability of the system. The philosophy adopted here is to be semi-interactive. This means that the user is to be protected as much as we are able from the inner workings, representations, and decision procedures of the system. However, when the automatic tools are inadequate, the user is to be consulted in as clear a manner as possible.

In order to avoid overconsultation, we require that the system interact with a theorem prover. The PARIS system uses the Boyer-Moore theorem prover [Boyer and Moore, 1979] as a subsystem. Potentially, PARIS should "protect" the user from the vagaries of the theorem prover, and much work can be done in this direction.

In the theoretical description of partially interpreted schemas [Baruch and Katz, 1985], any temporal logic assertion can be part of a specification, as well as any quantified predicate as a precondition, postcondition, or invariant. In order to achieve matching, we need to check whether one such assertion implies another. Clearly, the full implications of temporal formulas could not be treated. Even more significantly, quantification is explicitly excluded by the Boyer-Moore system.

As an attempted solution, we use a keyword approach. The hypothesis underlying the approach is that a reasonable number of English words will appear uninterpreted as far as the system is concerned but will be used for matching. Thus no general definitional facility such as algebraic specification is used. So far, keywords from three categories have been identified: domains (or abstract data types), mathematical properties, and specification operators. In the first category are terms such as *domain, integer, real, function, set, programsection, numberofarguments, numberofprocesses,* and *givenvalue*; in the second are terms such as *associative, commutative, nonnegative,* and *nonempty*; while the specification-related terms include *eventually, always, invariant, terminated, forall, forsome, precondition,* and *postcondition.*[2] The way in which these terms can be presented to the theorem prover is explained in [Boyer and Moore, 1979].

In the specifications we have considered, both the quantification and use of temporal operators is very limited, and thus amenable to partial treatment by the theorem prover. Nevertheless, the potential user of the system as presently implemented must present his or her problem statement in a form similar to the abstract specification of the appropriate schema, or rely on the linear shopping list presentation of each schema specification, as explained later. In a full implementation, with a large schema library, it would be reasonable to select classes of relevant schemas by only one or two properties. Although the system has only been demonstrated for CSP [Hoare, 1978] schemas, in fact any language or computational model could be used, and the schemas could be divided into categories such as sequential, functional, parallel shared memory, distributed message passing, CSP, Raddle [Forman, 1986], and so on. Another natural category would be the type of specification (e.g., functional, invariant property, etc.). Use of descriptive names for the schemas (e.g., scheduler, queue, mutual-exclusion) should also help the user select likely candidates. Note that none of these aids in the preliminary matching should replace the eventual check for a true match, which is essential to prevent misunderstandings of the potential applicability of a schema.

An extension in which use of the theorem prover is restricted, called "problem statement by interrogation," could be incorporated into later versions of PARIS. In this mode, once a potential schema had been selected by a few basic criteria, the system would interrogate the user in order to internally construct a problem statement similar in form to the schema specification.

10.2.3 From Abstract Specification to Concrete Program

In this section, we first describe a typical PARIS session of producing a program from a problem statement by interpreting the abstract entities, then we go over the details of its system organization to get an overview about

---

[2]Some of these keywords are modified in PARIS's current version to avoid confusion with the built-in functions of Franz LISP.

how the functionalities are achieved. Here we assume that the schemas have been correctly presented to the schema library, that is, that a generic proof has been (or could be) devised to show that if the abstract entities are correctly instantiated and program sections provided satisfying the section conditions, the result is guaranteed to satisfy the result assertions. Heuristics for developing schemas from specific instances of sequential programs may be found in [Dershowitz, 1985].

To start a PARIS session, the user has to input a problem statement. A problem statement consists of three components: an entity list, applicability conditions, and result assertions. These three components look similar to, and have the same syntax as, the first three components of a schema entry in the library, except that they contain no abstract entities.

After a problem statement has been correctly specified, PARIS searches the schema library to find a possible candidate. If a candidate is found, then the interpretation of abstract entities is initiated. The interpretation is done in two stages: First the nonprogram abstract entities are interpreted and then the abstract program sections are interpreted. The replacement of nonprogram abstract entities can be done either by manual matching or by automated matching, as discussed in the following two paragraphs.

If *manual matching* mode (also called shopping list mode) is selected to interpret the nonprogram abstract entities, then the system will present all possible candidates until the user chooses one or it fails to find another candidate. When a schema is presented, the user will decide whether to take it and supply all matching nonprogram entities or to try another candidate. After all nonprogram abstract entities have been replaced, and before the system prompts for entering program sections, the user has an option to ask the theorem prover to verify whether the choice and matchings satisfy the requirements of the problem statement.

If *automated matching* mode is selected, the system matches each nonprogram abstract entity in the schema with a concrete entity mentioned in the problem statement and invokes the Boyer-Moore theorem prover to carry out the verification. If the system finds a schema that satisfies the problem statement, then it will return a partially substituted schema (with all nonprogram abstract entities automatically replaced with concrete instances) and expect the user to fill in the program sections. On the other hand, if it fails to find one, the user will be informed about this situation.

In both matching modes, the preliminary matching (of nonprogram entities) is considered successful when the system displays section conditions and requires the user to input program sections. This insertion procedure is repeated until all abstract programs have been interpreted. In the current version, the replacement of program section abstract entities is done by having the user manually supply lines of code when the system displays conditions about a particular program section. At least theoretically, by using the window manager the user can suspend the activation and recursively use the PARIS system to satisfy the section conditions from the schema library.

If the user fails to supply a program section, then PARIS will assume that the user can't correctly interpret the abstract program; hence, the schema will be incompletely interpreted and thus aborted; PARIS will then explore another possible candidate. The system displays the resulting program after all program section abstract entities have been correctly interpreted.

The approximately 70 LISP functions of the PARIS system can be grouped into six modules, whose interrelations are informally shown in Fig. 10.1. The six modules can be summarized as follows:

Module 1.   Specifying the problem—representing the user's requirements in a form understood by PARIS. The purpose of this module is to acquire a problem from the user and put it in an internal form understood by the other modules.

FIGURE 10.1
OVERVIEW OF THE PARIS SYSTEM

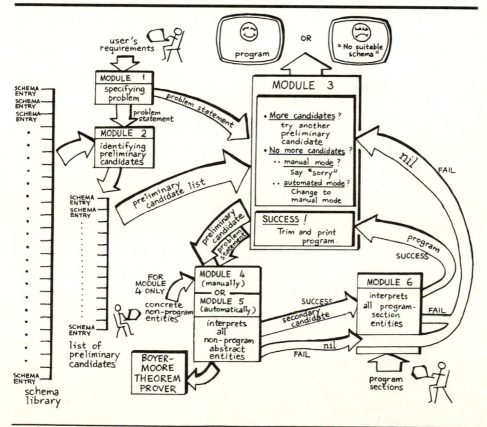

Module 2. Identifying the candidates—narrowing the choice by excluding irrelevant schemas. When the system encounters a problem statement, it builds a corresponding candidate list. Each schema entry (preliminary candidate) in the candidate list will be interpreted until either (a) a preliminary candidate is successfully built up to a program, or (b) there are no more schema entries left in the candidate list. A schema entry in the library is included in this list if the set of entities of the problem statement is a subset of the set of entities of the schema entry, considering the type declarations.

Module 3. Coordinating other modules: Based on the requirements specified in the result of module 1, this module tries to build a program by interpreting candidates in the result of module 2. Interpretation of a candidate consists of two stages: matching of nonprogram abstract entities (using either module 4 for manual mode or module 5 for automated mode) and insertion of program sections (using module 6).

Module 4. Interpreting nonprogram entities, manual mode—interactive communication with the user to interpret nonprogram abstract entities.

After the manual matching is done, the user has the option of having the matchings checked by the Theorem Prover. However, if the Theorem Prover fails, the user can still override its result.

Module 5. Interpreting nonprogram entities, automated mode—permuting the abstract entity list to generate different matching instances of nonprogram entities and invoking the Boyer-Moore theorem prover to verify every matching instance.

When an instance of the permutation is generated, the theorem prover is invoked to determine whether this matching of nonprogram entities will successfully build a secondary candidate. If it returns *true*, then the matching is used to substitute all nonprogram abstract entities, otherwise another instance of the permutation will be generated. The automated matching fails if none of the permutation instances causes the theorem prover to return *true*.

If all of the preliminary candidates fail to go through the automated matching, the user has an option to initiate a manual matching process.

Module 6. Inserting program sections—interactive communication with the user to interpret abstract program sections. This module interacts with the user to insert program sections into a secondary candidate (which was built from a preliminary candidate by having all of its nonprogram abstract entities interpreted). If it detects that the user fails to supply a program section, the current candidate is aborted.

When all program sections in a secondary candidate have been successfully interpreted, the result is the final program.

10.3 EXAMPLES OF SCHEMAS

10.3.1 A Schema for Linked List Insertion

The first example we give illustrates the specifications of a schema by means of a C program that inserts a new list node into a totally ordered linked list. A node in the list contains two fields: *next* and *data*. *Next* is the pointer to the next node and *data* is the value (which might be a complicated data structure) of the current node. The functions *leq*, *equal*, and *f* define a total ordering of the list nodes. The domain of function *f* is the set of possible data of list nodes, and its range is a set of values by which the list is ordered, using the predicate *leq*. To maintain the ordering of the nodes in a list, both the applicability conditions and result assertions state that the list is ordered. The relation *equal* tests whether two elements of the data domain are identical.

The entity list for this schema contains all abstract entities, which will be replaced by concrete entities when the schema is interpreted. The applicability conditions impose some conditions on the functions and the requirement that the linked list should be ordered before an insertion is performed. The result assertions indicate that after the insertion is done, the list is ordered and the new node is inserted in the proper place.

The program section S1 assigns the value of inserted data to the allocated memory space. The assignment operation is abstracted because it may be in different forms based on the data structure. The main program, which is another independent module, should satisfy the invariant that the list is ordered. It is left implicit that after an insertion is done, the list contains all the nodes it had before the insertion was done.

The abstracted schema of the insertion module is shown below. Note that the user of such a schema need not understand the code of the schema body itself, as long as his or her instantiations of the abstract entities satisfy the specifications.

Entity List

> function *f*
> function *leq*
> function *equal*
> domain D1, D2

variable *data* : D1
variable *newdata* : D1
structure *node* : D1 × pointer(*node*)
programsec S1

Applicability Conditions

f : –> D2
leq : D2 × D2 –> boolean
equal : D1 × D1 –> boolean
∀ *n* : *n in node* : *n* –> *next* ≠ NULL ⇒
   leq(*f*(*n* –> *data*), *f*((*n* –> *next*) –> *data*))

Result Assertions

[∃ *n* : *n* ∈ *node* : *equal*(*n* –> *data*, *newdata*)]
[∀ *n* : *n in node* : *n* –> *next* ≠ NULL ⇒
   leq(*f*(*n* –> *data*), *f*((*n* –> *next*) –>data))]

Section Conditions

S1: precondition: *true*
    postcondition: *equal*(*new* –> *date*, *newdata*)

Schema Body

```
struct node {struct node *next;
                    D1 data;}

insert(listhead, newdata)
struct node *listhead;
D1 newdata;
{
     struct     node *p, *q, *new;

     new = malloc (sizeof (struct node));

     /* assign newdata to new->data */
     S1

     if (listhead == NULL)
     {
          listhead = new;
          listhead->next = NULL;
     }
     else if ( leq(f(new),f(listhead)) )
```

```
    {
        new->next = listhead;
        listhead = new;
    }
    else
    {
        p = listhead;
        q = listhead->next;
        while ( !leq(f(new),f(q)) && q != NULL )
        {
            p = q;
            q = q->next;
        }
        p->next = new;
        new->next = q;
    }
}
```

This schema can be easily instantiated to handle different node data types D1. For example, if D1 is integer, then *f* will be the identity function and *leq* and *equal* will be $\leq$ and $==$, respectively; the assignment in S1 will be $=$. If D1 is character string (*char** in C jargon), then the functions *f*, *leq*, and *equal* can be based on the C library string manipulation functions, and the assignment in S1 is simply the C library function *strcpy*. The three functions and the program section can also be custom-made to cope with more complicated data structures as the need arises.

10.3.2 A Distributed Snapshot Schema

We now look at a variant of a schema for the distributed snapshot algorithm of Chandy and Lamport [1985]. In this algorithm, processes cooperate to detect global stable properties—that is, properties that, once they hold, continue to hold. A single communication skeleton will suffice to detect any kind of stable property. Therefore, we want a schema in which the basic communication skeleton is concrete, while the portion that detects the particular stable property is abstract.

We assume asynchronous message passing. To express the schema, we use a notation with nonblocking sends. A send is written *send* (*m*, *i*), meaning send message *m* to process *i* (along the appropriate outgoing channel). Receives are of the form *receive* (*m*, *i*), meaning receive a message in m from process, *i*. We also use guarded commands, denoted by *guard* → *action*. In each process *i*, *channel_ from* (*j*) is true iff *i* has an incoming channel from process *j*, while *channel_ to* (*j*) is true iff *i* has an outgoing channel to *j*. The number of incoming channels of the process is *innumber*. We assume there is at most one channel from any process *i* to another process *j* and that the channels are first-in-first-out.

To simplify this exposition, we assume the designation of an initiator—that is, when the schema is instantiated, one process is designated as the one which will initiate the detection algorithm. A more general (and complicated) schema would permit the dynamic selection of an initiator. We also restrict the algorithm to the detection of boolean conditions; the schema could be expanded to include an abstract domain for the stable property.

The schema given here will set local indicators to reflect a consistent global state. However, in order to actually determine the truth of the global predicate P, the values of the local indicators must be gathered together to a single process, using an additional schema. The global state satisfies *at(begin)* when the schema is initiated, and *at(end)* when the number of markers received equals *innumber* for all the processes.

The entity list must include the abstract parts of the schema, namely:

- [ ] n is the the number of processes;
- [ ] 1 through n are processes;
- [ ] S1, S2, S3, S4, and S5 are program sections;
- [ ] P and P_1 through P_n are predicates; and
- [ ] p_1 through p_n are local variables (called indicators).

The applicability conditions are that

- [ ] we have some global stable property, P;
- [ ] we have local properties P_1 through P_n;
- [ ] if the channels are empty and properties P_1 through P_n all hold in a global state, then P holds; and
- [ ] communication is fair (i.e., any message sent is eventually received).

The result assertions are that

- [ ] if all local indicators p_1 through p_n hold at the end of the algorithm, then P also holds at that time; and
- [ ] if P holds at the beginning of the algorithm, then the local indicators p_1 through p_n all hold at the end of the algorithm.

Our schema for the snapshot algorithm is as follows:

Entity List

    numproc n
    process $1, \ldots, n$
    programsec S1, S2, S3, S4, S5
    predicate $P, P_1, \ldots, P_n$

variable $p_1, \ldots, p_n$: local indicators

Applicability Conditions

global P

stable P

local $P_1 \ldots, P_n$

(empty channels) $\wedge P_1 \wedge \ldots \wedge P_n \Rightarrow P$

$\Box(\forall i, j(send_i(m, j) \Rightarrow \Diamond receive_j(m, i)))$

Result Assertions

$at(end) \wedge p_1 \wedge \ldots \wedge p_n \Rightarrow P$

$at(begin) \wedge P \Rightarrow \Diamond at(end) \wedge p_1 \wedge \ldots \wedge p_n$

Section Conditions

S1: boolean condition that, when it evaluates to true, causes the initiator to initiate the snapshot

S2: boolean expression within each process to detect the local property, P_i, in that process

S3: body of function that, given p, the current value of the local indicator for P_i, and m, a message that was received, determines the new value of local property P_i and assigns it to new_p

S4: the desired action on the receipt of an incoming message (must NOT contain any receives)

S5: the nonreceive code for the process, in the form of $(guard \rightarrow action)*$ (this code must NOT contain any receives)

Schema Body

```
process 1 ::    { the initiator }
      var p: boolean,
          c: integer,
          m: message,
          marker_recd: array [n] of boolean;
      const marker = "marker";  { the value of a marker }

      begin
        S1 -->
            p := S2; {detect whether local property Pi
                      holds}
            forall j (channel_from (j))
                marker_recd [j] := false;
            forall j (channel_to (j)) send (marker, j);
```

```
              c := 0;  { count of markers received }
        receive (marker, j) -->
           { received marker from j }
           if not marker_recd [j] then
              marker_recd [j] := true;
              c := c + 1;
           fi;


        receive (m, j) ^ (m <> marker) -->
           if (c <> 0) ^ not marker_recd [j] then
              p := new_p (p, m);  { compute new value in
                                    terms of old, message }
           fi;
           S4


     S5
  end;


process (i: 2 to n) ::   { the non-initiators }
   var p: boolean,
       c: integer := 0,
       m: message,
       marker_recd : array [n] of boolean;
   const marker = "marker";  { the value of a marker }


   begin
      receive (marker, j) ^ (c = 0) -->
         { received first marker }
         marker_recd [j] := true;
         p := S2;  { detect whether the local property
                     Pi holds }
         forall k (channel_to (k)) send (marker, k);
            { send a marker on all outgoing channels }
         forall k (channel_from (k) ^ (k <> j))
            marker_recd [k] := false;
         c := 1;

      receive (marker, j) ^ (c <> 0) -->
         if not marker_recd [j] then
            marker_recd [j] := true;
            c := c + 1;
         fi;


      receive (m, j) ^ (m <> marker) -->
         if (c <> 0) ^ not marker_recd [j] then
            p := new_p (p, m);  { compute new value in
                                  terms of old, message }
         fi;
         S4
```

```
            S5
        end;

    function new_p (p: boolean, m: message);
        begin
            S3
        end;


    (1 || .. || n)
```

Note that the section conditions for this particular schema are informal, unlike those for the previous example.

Let us consider instantiating the schema to determine whether all tokens in the system have disappeared. In other words, we want to detect the local condition "there are no tokens in this process." Section condition S1 would cause the distinguished process to initiate the snapshot. S2 would be the code in each process to determine whether any tokens resided in that process. S3 would be the body of a function to determine if an incoming message contained a token. S4 and S5 would be the regular code to handle receives and nonreceives, respectively.

This example illustrates one of the problems with PARIS schemas: There is no easy way to deal with schemas when the schema code interleaves with the user-supplied code. In this example, we must prevent the user from adding his or her own receives, as we must intercept all receives along a channel after we take a local snapshot and before we receive a marker along that channel. One of the authors is currently investigating *superimposition*, a means of interleaving code.

10.4 CONCLUDING REMARKS AND FUTURE DEVELOPMENTS

Our experience in building the PARIS prototype indicates that transforming abstract logic expressions into precise implementational definitions is quite difficult. It is not easy to provide a friendly interface to the user and at the same time produce correct and efficient input to the theorem-proving mechanism. Preparing a large schema is also a formidable challenge. As suggested in Section 10.2.2, the practicality of a large-scale schema system depends upon the ability to quickly identify a subclass of schemas that might be relevant to a problem statement. Database techniques using keywords to identify the computational model, language, and intuitive role of the schema should be adequate for this task. Therefore, a larger scale does not seem to pose a fundamental difficulty in itself, but it would require significant resources for its preparation.

In summary, for this prototype to really work in helping software designers, it should be extended in the following directions:

- [ ] Adding more schemas into the library, for a variety of computational models.
- [ ] Classifying all schemas within the library to increase searching efficiency.
- [ ] Defining additional keywords in the system's vocabulary.
- [ ] Developing a user-friendly interface to add more convenience for the user's formulation of a problem statement and to provide more interactive communication during the process of matching and verification. In particular, when the theorem prover fails to prove one of the two implications needed for a successful matching, the user should not have to be an expert in automatic theorem proving in order to understand the reason for the failure.
- [ ] Augmenting the theorem prover with facts in the problem domain of the schemas, especially with facts about temporal logic assertions.

Despite the outlined problems and the remaining obstacles, the system does provide (provably) correct programs, without burdening the average user with the work of proving the correctness. It thus provides a first step towards automated reusability, although it still falls short of program synthesis.

Acknowledgments

The authors would like to thank Les Belady, Ted Biggerstaff, Ira Forman, and Jim Peterson of the MCC Software Technology Program for their comments and suggestions; and also Chua-Huang Huang and Warren Hunt of the Department of Computer Sciences, The University of Texas at Austin, for their efforts to get the authors acquainted with the Boyer-Moore theorem prover.

References

Baruch, O., and S. Katz. Partially interpreted schemas for CSP programming. Computer Science Dept., The Technion, Israel Inst. of Tech., Haifa, Israel, 1985.

Biggerstaff, T. J., and A. J. Perlis, editors. Special issue on software reusability. *IEEE Transactions on Software Engineering*, SE-10; 474–609, Sep. 1984.

Boyer, R. S., and J. S. Moore. *A Computational Logic.* New York: Academic Press, 1979.

Chandy, K. M., and L. Lamport. Distributed snapshots: Determining global states of distributed systems. *ACM Transactions on Computer Systems* 3: 63–75, Feb. 1985.

Dershowitz, N. Program abstraction and instantiation. *ACM Transactions on Programming Languages and Systems* 7: 446–477, July 1985.

Forman, I. On the design of large distributed systems. *Proceedings of the International Conference on Computer Languages*, Miami Beach, Fla., Oct. 1986.

Hoare, C. A. R. Communicating sequential processes. *Communications of the ACM*, 21: 666–677, Aug. 1978.

Wilensky, R. *LISPcraft*. New York: W. W. Norton, 1984.

Generation-Based Systems

Reusability of design for large software systems: An Experiment with the SETL Optimizer

ED DUBINSKY
Department of Mathematics, Clarkson College

STEFAN FREUDENBERGER
Multiflow Computer, Inc.

EDITH SCHONBERG *and* **J. T. SCHWARTZ**
Computer Science Department, New York University

11.1 A BRIEF OVERVIEW OF THE EXPERIMENT

Reusability of design is the ability to convey the overall procedural structure and principal data designs of large complex programs to those who wish to develop the same or similar functions in new environments. This is an important aspect of program reusability overall. Design reuse will frequently be associated with increased efficiency requirements; for example, a programming system designed for a computer of a certain size may have to be redeveloped for a significantly smaller machine, or a program used only occasionally or only during development and testing may be accepted for production use and have to be made more efficient. For these purposes, an appropriate software design tool is a specification language for fully describing all significant abstract features of complex programs, but suppressing as many design-irrelevant details as possible.

This paper reports on a significant experiment in the expression and reuse of a program design. The vehicle used for transmission of design is an executable, procedural, but very high-level language called SETL, developed at New York University [Schwartz *et al.*, 1986; Dewar *et al.*, 1979]. The goal was to significantly improve the efficiency (at least by an order of magnitude) of a large and complex program written in SETL simply by translating it into a lower-level language. The translation methodology aimed for may be described as manual but mechanical; neither the algorithms nor overall program structure were to be changed. The program translated in the experiment is the SETL optimizer, a part of the SETL system itself.

This experiment in two-step program development shows that the high-level specification language provides a good tool not only for experimenting with algorithms, but also for clearly documenting design; the translated version is markedly more efficient, and the code is well organized and clean; the translation process proceeds quickly and accurately, with fewer bugs than if developed from scratch. In short, the postponement of low-level implementation decisions until the end of a large software development project enhances the final product.

SETL, the source language in our experiment, has general finite sets, maps/relations, and tuples as its basic data types. In addition to conventional control structures, it implements more sophisticated operations, such as universal and existential quantification over sets. The language is weakly typed, but optionally a data representation sublanguage (DRSL) can be used to provide information on the desired representation of variables. The DRSL serves both to improve the efficiency of SETL programs and to document the use of variables. We have found that the DRSL plays an important role in the manual translation of SETL; more precisely, it suggests data structure implementations for SETL objects.

The target language was LITTLE, a lower-level language whose semantics lies somewhere between FORTRAN and C. Its basic data type is the bit string, which may be accessed directly and also interpreted as an integer, Boolean, real, or character string. The only available data structure in LITTLE is the one-dimensional static array. Control structures are conventional and comparable to those of Pascal, except that LITTLE does not support recursion. Although LITTLE has no record structures, it has a macro definition facility that is heavily used to improve code readability and enables programmers to emulate records.

The SETL optimizer/analyzer is a sophisticated package that performs global (interprocedural) analysis of SETL programs and, on the basis of this analysis, attempts ambitious code improvements [Freudenberger, 1984;

Freudenberger *et al.*, 1983]. Novel features of the optimizer include complex algorithms for inter- and intraprocedural data flow analysis [Schwartz and Sharir, 1979], automatic variable type detection [Tenenbaum, 1974], and automatic selection of run-time data structures for sets and maps [Schonberg, Schwartz, and Sharir, 1979]. It uses the full expressive power of SETL, including the use of deeply nested sets, maps, and tuples, and complex set-former expressions. The optimizer, developed over a period of four years, consists of about 15,000 lines of SETL code.

Even though the rest of the SETL system is in LITTLE, SETL was chosen as the initial implementation language for the optimizer for a number of reasons. The optimizer served as a research testbed for experimenting with new algorithms; SETL facilitates prototyping and program modification, which are important for algorithm testing. The DRSL enables experimentation with different set representations without modifying any code. The ability to write algorithms in a lucid and concise manner was also valuable, both for joint project work and for inclusion of code in reports.

However, because of its size and slowness, the SETL version can only be used to optimize small programs (about 300 lines in 25 minutes). On the other hand, the optimized results from these small test programs indicated that a production-quality implementation was worth building. Thus the rewrite project had a very practical goal: to improve the optimizer's speed so that it could be applied to large SETL programs, and actually serve as a useful tool for SETL programmers. For another example of the implementation of a large software system from a SETL specification, see [Schonberg and Schields, 1986].

Section 11.2 gives a brief summary of SETL. Section 11.3 presents issues arising in the translation project. Sections 11.4, 11.5, and 11.6 give, in order of increasing complexity, three examples of data structure choices made in LITTLE that were guided by the DRSL declarations in SETL; these examples illustrate how the high-level design is reused. The conclusion, Section 11.7, gives specific performance results and summarizes our viewpoint.

11.2   SETL BASICS

Detailed descriptions of SETL can be found in [Dewar *et al.*, 1979] and [Schwartz *et al.*, 1986]. We limit ourselves here to the most salient features of the language and those features that are most significant in the SETL version of the optimizer.

SETL is an imperative, sequential language with assignment, weak typing, dynamic storage allocation, and the usual atomic types: numeric types, Booleans, strings, and generated atoms. (An atom is simply a token that is distinct from all other atoms; the only operation among atoms is equality comparison.) Declarations are optional: The data representation sublanguage (Section 11.2.2) may be used to facilitate the choice of suitable data structures for SETL objects. The composite types of SETL—*sets*, *tuples*, and *maps*—give the language its expressive power. We proceed to describe these.

11.2.1 The Types of SETL

Sets. Sets in SETL have the standard mathematical properties of sets: They are unordered collections of values of arbitrary types, containing no duplicate values, and the usual operations are defined on these collections: membership, union, intersection, range and domain, power set construction, and so on. Set iterators and constructors are built-in control structures that operate on sets. For example,

```
{x in S | P(x)}
```

denotes a subset of the set S, all of whose members x satisfy the predicate $P(x)$. Quantified expressions over sets use the quantifiers of first-order predicate calculus and describe common search constructs. For example,

```
exists x in S | P(x)
```

is a Boolean-valued expression whose value is **true** if some member of S satisfies the predicate P. As a side effect of its execution, the existentially quantified expression assigns to the bound variable x the value of some member of S that satisfies $P(x)$, if one exists.

A compound statement of the form

```
loop forall x in S | P(x) do
                    statements
            end forall;
```

iterates over all elements x of S that satisfy $P(x)$, and executes *statements* for each iteration.

Tuples. Tuples in SETL are ordered sequences of arbitrary size, indexed by positive integers. As with all SETL composite types, the components of a tuple can be of arbitrary types, so that sets of tuples, tuples of sets, tuples of tuples of sets of integers, and so on, can be constructed. Insertions and deletions from either end allow tuples to be used as stacks and queues; concatenation makes tuples akin to lists for certain purposes. Tuple constructors and iterators are similar to the corresponding constructs for sets. For example:

```
[x: x in [2..100] | not exists y
                        in [2..x-1] | x mod y = 0]
```

constructs (inefficiently) the sequence of primes smaller than 100.

Maps.   Maps in SETL faithfully reproduce the notion of mapping in set theory: A map is a set of ordered pairs, that is, tuples of length 2; the first components of these tuples constitute the *domain*. Both the domain and range of a map can be of arbitrary types. Maps can be used as tabular functions, and the *application* $M(x)$ can be evaluated (a map is an associative structure) or be the target of an assignment. Finally, mappings can be multivalued (relations) or single-valued (functions) and the image set $M\{x\}$ of a value x under the mapping M can also be retrieved and assigned to.

These familiar notions constitute the core of SETL. What distinguishes SETL from purely mathematical discourse is the requirements of executability. To guarantee that all valid SETL constructs are executable, only finite objects can be denoted.

11.2.2 Data Representation Sublanguage

At runtime, every object in SETL has a fixed length specifier that stores its type and, if the object is simple, its value, or, if otherwise, a pointer to its value. The elements of a set S are stored in a hash table referenced by the specifier of S. The elements of a tuple T are stored in an array referenced by the specifier of T. The elements of both sets and tuples are themselves specifiers, and may in turn point to other blocks. Since sets of two-tuples are maps, two-tuples are hashed on their first component to facilitate map retrieval. Operations such as set insertion, deletion, and membership test and map retrieval cost a hash operation. Figure 11.1 shows the default representation for a single-valued map M.

Through optional DRSL declarations, it is possible to obtain more efficient representations for sets and maps. A distinctive feature of the DRSL is that relationships among different variables may be described. The result

FIGURE 11.1
DEFAULT REPRESENTATION FOR MAPS. X AND Z HAVE SAME HASH-CODE

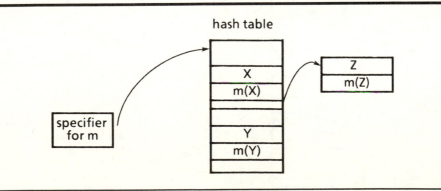

is, for example, that objects may internally store pointers to other objects, subsets may be represented as bit strings, and a form of record structure is supported, thus saving on hashing operations. Next we summarize the more important structures of the sublanguage.

The fundamental domains of a program, for example, sets that are typically the domains and ranges of maps, are declared as *base sets*. A program variable X may then be *based on* a base set. If X is a simple object, then the values assigned to X range over the elements of the base; if X is a set, a map, or a tuple, then the values of the components of X range over the elements of the base. A base set itself is not a program variable, and does not appear explicitly in the executable code; elements are added to the base according to the values that based variables take on. The representation of the based objects depends on how they are declared, as illustrated in the following examples.

In the **repr** statement below, B is declared to be a base set of integers, and variable V to be an *element* of the base B.

```
repr      B:        base (integer);
          V:        elmt B;
       end;
```

When V is assigned a value, the value is added to the base if it is not there already, and V stores a pointer directly to the value's element block.

Sets and maps based on B may be either *local* or *remote*. For locally based objects, component data is stored directly within the element blocks of the base (see Fig. 11.2). More specifically, for a local single-valued map LM with

FIGURE 11.2
BASE *B* AND OBJECTS BASED ON *B*

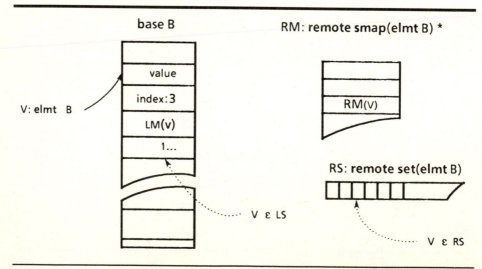

domain *B*, the range value LM(*V*) is stored in the element block of *V*. For a
local set LS declared as a subset of *B*, each element block of *B* has a one-bit
flag indicating whether the element is in LS. Local variables LM and LS are
declared as follows:

```
repr      LM:        local smap (elmt B) integer;
          LS:        local set (elmt B);
end;
```

Local basings therefore provide a means of implementing a record structure
for domains and associated attributes.

Remote objects, on the other hand, are stored in separate sequential data
structures and not in the base itself. Each element in the base does, however,
store a distinct index value, which is used as an object offset for the element
in the remote structure. For example, consider a remote map RM, declared

```
RM:        remote smap (elmt B) integer;
```

The range of RM is stored as an array of integers (see Fig. 11.2). To retrieve
RM(*V*), the index stored in the element block for *V* is used as an array index.
Remote maps may have shorter lifetimes than the base.

A remote set is stored as a bit string. Set union and intersection operations
are particularly efficient on remote sets. The variable RS declared below is a
subset of *B*:

```
RS:        remote set (elmt B);
```

Each bit position in the bit string RS corresponds to an element in *B* and
indicates membership of that element in RS. The index value of the element
specifies the bit position of the element.

A **mode** declaration is provided in DRSL for defining frequently used
types. For example, the following statements are equivalent to the declarations above:

```
repr
                    B:        base (integer);
          mode      el__B:    elmt B;

                    V:        el__B;
                    LM:       local smap (el__B) integer;
                    RM:       remote smap (el__B) integer;
                    LS:       local set (el__B);
                    RS:       remote set (el__B);
          end;
```

Such a set of **repr** declarations profile the types, relationships, and uses of
program variables.

11.3 THE TRANSLATION PROCESS: PROBLEMS AND APPROACHES

The SETL system (Fig. 11.3) includes a front end, which translates SETL source programs into an intermediate quadruple form (called Q1); a code generator, which translates Q1 into interpretable quadruples (called Q2), using DRSL or optimizer-specified information to choose instructions; an interpreter, which executes the Q2 instructions; and a run-time library, which implements SETL objects and operations and manages run-time storage. The optimizer is an optional pass before code generation and consists of 14 separate modules. It inputs and outputs Q1 quadruples. Since analysis is interprocedural, the optimizer must accommodate an entire source program at once.

In addition to various classical optimizations, such as code motion, redundant subexpression elimination, removal of unreachable code, and constant propagation, the optimizer also

1. determines the types of variables, and selects data structure representations for sets and maps, according to the way variables are used;
2. determines which routines are recursive and which temporaries and local variables can be made static; and
3. determines when copies must be made or may be suppressed as part of an instruction. (SETL has value semantics; i.e., objects are logically copied on assignment.)

Some of the initial problems encountered in translating the optimizer are common to all large program translation efforts. The group involved in the translation were not involved in writing the original SETL optimizer. In fact, the rewrite team was split geographically (between New York University and

FIGURE 11.3
STRUCTURE OF THE SETL SYSTEM

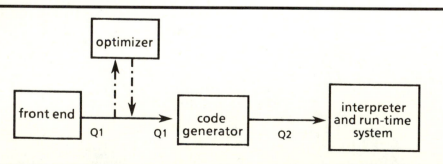

Clarkson College), making communication much harder. Additionally, the optimizer is a highly complex program—not because of poor coding style or lack of documentation, as is often the case, but because it includes intricate and novel algorithms. Finally, the target language LITTLE is awkward at best (its choice being dictated more for historic than good technical reasons). The lack of typing, records, recursion, and separate compilation protection, which are available in other systems languages such as C, Pascal, and Ada, exacerbated the difficulty of the task.

On the other hand, as a high-level specification, the SETL version is lucid and readable. Moreover, since it is an executable specification, it has been subjected to substantial testing and is trustworthy. Debugging the separate passes of the LITTLE version was greatly facilitated because the output could be compared with the output from the SETL version. Finally, the interfaces between modules are clean and well documented, so each module could be redeveloped independently.

The two main translation issues were (a) choosing data structures in LITTLE to implement abstract SETL objects (sets, tuples, maps)—with a suitable data structure interface, actual code transcription is straightforward— and (b) what to do about storage allocation—SETL is fully dynamic and runs in a garbage-collected environment, while LITTLE, like FORTRAN, is completely static.

A significant concern in the design was efficient use of space, in particular because the data for entire source programs is stored all at once and a great deal of information is generated during analysis. Therefore it is important to have both compact representations of objects and the ability to reclaim space no longer in use.

An appealing and seemingly convenient option, which was tried initially and later abandoned, is to reuse the storage management and set manipulation routines already written in LITTLE—namely, the routines in the SETL run-time library itself. The storage manager includes a compacting garbage collector; library routines are available for creating and manipulating SETL objects in various representations (those defined in the DRSL). The advantage of this approach is the possibility of a one-to-one correspondence between sets and tuples in the SETL version and in the LITTLE version and of using the same LITTLE code to implement these corresponding structures; translation would become completely mechanical, and debugging by comparison would be facilitated.

This approach proved too awkward and inefficient for the production quality results that we wanted, for the following reasons.

1. The SETL run-time library itself is very large (100,000 lines).
2. It is hard to use the run-time library interface directly, since it is not designed for an end user, but to be called by an interpreter for operations on single quadruples.

3. It is equally hard to interface directly with a garbage collector. Since the invocation of a garbage collection is unpredictable, pointers can be easily corrupted, unless the whole environment is designed to be protected.
4. Because of their generality, SETL data structures are bulky and wasteful of storage.

Instead, we chose to implement a very simple stack-based allocation scheme, together with a heap manipulated by explicit *allocate* and *free* functions. The SETL object translations were guided very strongly by the DRSL declarations in the SETL version. Section 11.4 describes a straightforward conversion of SETL objects into tables—the vast majority of optimizer structures followed this pattern. Sections 11.5 and 11.6 describe more complex examples of representation choices.

11.4 TABULAR REPRESENTATION OF DATA

The most common paradigm for data in the SETL version of the optimizer is a *domain* of objects with various *attributes* defined on the domain. Domains are represented as sets of atoms. Attributes are represented as maps defined on these sets. In LITTLE, such domains with attributes are conveniently mapped into tables of fixed-length records. Auxiliary tables are needed to accommodate arbitrary-length and multivalued attributes.

Let us consider in more detail one of these domains, *instructions*. Attributes defined on instructions include *opcode*, the operation performed by the instruction, and *arguments*, a variable-length list of arguments. Instructions in each basic block are threaded into a linked list to facilitate ordered iteration and instruction insertion and deletion. There are therefore additional attributes *next_inst*, from instructions to instructions, and *first_inst*, from blocks to instructions.

These maps are declared in **repr** statements as follows:

```
mode instruction:        elmt instructions;
   first_inst:  local smap (block) instruction;
   opcode:      local smap (instruction) elmt opcodes;
   arguments:   local smap (instruction) tuple(elmt symbols);
   next_inst:   local smap (instruction) instruction;
```

In LITTLE, this collection of attributes is grouped into a table of fixed-size records, whose structure is defined as follows. If the range of a single-valued map attribute is of fixed length, the range value is a field in the record. For arbitrary-length range values, an auxiliary table is defined, and the instruction record contains fields storing the offset and length of the attribute (LITTLE does not have pointers) in the auxiliary table. From the **reprs** above, we define, in addition to the instruction table, an auxiliary table, *argument_table*, and the instruction table fields:

opcode:	integer
arguments:	pointer to argument_table
num_arguments:	number of arguments in argument_table
next_inst:	pointer to instructions table

With these definitions, translation of typical code-manipulating global tables is relatively straightforward. For example, SETL code to iterate through all arguments of an instruction is as follows:

```
loop forall a in arguments(i) do
        . . .
end forall;
```

The corresponding LITTLE code is:

```
off = arguments(i);
do j = off + 1 to off + num_arguments(i);
        a = argument_table(j);
            . . .
end do;
```

Tables are allocated from the heap. When a table is full, it is reallocated and copied. Some tables are only needed for certain phases and so can be freed after they are no longer used. There are 33 global tables in all.

11.5 BIT-STRING REPRESENTATION OF DATA-FLOW MAPS

To illustrate more sophisticated uses of SETL, and the use of DRSL to guide translation into LITTLE, we consider the data flow analysis module, which is a general-purpose package called from various phases of the optimizer to solve data flow problems of the bit-vectoring class [Schwartz and Sharir, 1979]. These are the simplest data flow problems that arise in global program optimization, such as live-dead analysis and redundant expression elimination. We first give some background.

11.5.1 Bit-Vector Data Flow Problems

Bit-vector data flow problems are described in a data flow framework (L, F) (cf. [Hecht, 1977; Aho and Ullman, 1977]), for which there exists a finite set

E such that $L = 2^E$, and for each f in F, there exist two subsets S_f and T_f of E such that, for each x in L,

$$f(x) = (S_f \cap x) \cup T_f. \tag{11.1}$$

Heuristically, elements of L represent (Boolean) attribute values (such as availability of expressions, live status of variables, etc.) to be computed at certain program points, and elements of F represent transformations of these values effected by program execution. Elements of F are also called *data flow maps*, and are denoted by tuples $[S_f, T_f]$.

As an example, consider the problem of detecting expression availability. The expressions that are available on exit from a block B are precisely the expressions that are available on entry to B and are not killed in B, plus those expressions that are made available within B itself. Thus we obtain a specific instance of Eq. (11.1):

$$\text{avail}_B(x) = (\text{NOKILL}_{\text{avail}_B} \cap x) \cup \text{GEN}_{\text{avail}_B} \tag{11.2}$$

where x is the set of expressions available on entry to B. These maps must be calculated for all program blocks.

Solving for x, the block entry information, for each basic block involves propagating information globally through the program, in a complex specified manner, which we will not describe more than by the following remarks. Let x_{Bn} denote the information available at entry to block B_n, and x_0 denote the worst-case assumptions upon program entry. Then

$$x_{B0} = x_0 \tag{11.3}$$

where B_0 is the entry block of the program, and

$$x_{Bn} = \cap \{ f_B(x_B) : B \in \text{predecessor blocks of } B_n\} \tag{11.4}$$

for each block B_n. The basic data flow problem is to determine the maximal fixpoint of Eqs. (11.1), (11.3), and (11.4).

SETL procedures from the data flow package implement manipulation of data flow maps in a concise fashion. For example, the procedure *meet* intersects two data flow maps; this operation is used in finding the fixpoint solution to Eqs. (11.3) and (11.4):

```
proc meet(f, g);
return
        if undefined(f) then   g
        elseif undefined(g) then   f
```

```
else
    [f(1) * g(1), f(2) * g(2)]
end;
end proc meet;
```

Here f and g are two-tuples of sets, and the operator "*" is set intersection.

For each particular data flow problem, the data flow solver receives as actual parameter a large map F, which takes each edge (m, n) in the program flow graph into its corresponding data flow map $[f_{m,n}, g_{m,n}]$.

11.5.2 Data Flow Maps in SETL and LITTLE

Elements of L represent Boolean attribute values and so can be represented by bit strings. The data flow maps of the form $[S_f, T_f]$ belonging to F can be represented as pairs of bit strings, and set union and set intersection can be performed using bit-vector *and* and *or* operations. In SETL, a bit-string implementation can be obtained for a set simply by adding DRSL declarations, without modifying any of the body of the code. The LITTLE version follows closely the DRSL formulation but also optimizes the use of space in a way not achievable within SETL.

Let *dom* denote the base domain for the data flow problem, (e.g., expressions, variables, occurrences). The **mode** declarations:

```
mode data_flow_set:  remote set(elmt dom);
mode data_flow_map:  tuple(data_flow_set, data_flow_set);
```

define a data flow set as a bit string, and a data flow map as a two-tuple of bit strings; each bit position in a data flow set corresponds to an element in the base *dom*, and indicates membership of that corresponding element in the data flow set. To represent nodes and edges in the data flow graph, we define the bases

```
base data_flow_nodes:  elmt blocks;
base data_flow_edges:  tuple(elmt data_flow_nodes,
                             elmt data_flow_nodes);
```

Then the map F, passed to the data flow module, is declared as

```
F:  remote smap (elmt data_flow_edges) data_flow_map;
```

that is, a single-valued map from edges to data flow maps. Since it is defined as *remote*, the range of the map is stored as a tuple: in this case a tuple where each entry is a pair of bit strings (Fig. 11.4a).

Using the SETL code as a model, the LITTLE version allocates (and later frees) a single block for F from the heap for each data flow problem. F is an array of data flow map entries, where each entry is a pair of bit strings. The dimension of the array is the number of edges; the size of each entry in F is determined by the size of the domain for the problem. Because the size of the problem is known at time of allocation, we are able to obtain a more compact representation in LITTLE (Fig. 11.4b) than in SETL, where the structure for F has more indirection.

To illustrate the translation, the code below is the LITTLE version of the SETL *meet* procedure. In this subroutine, *andb* and *copyb* are macros that perform bit-string intersect and copy operations on arbitrary-length bit strings, where the length is passed as the last argument. The result is stored in the parameter r. The variable df_map_sz is a global variable that stores the size of the domain of each data flow map for the current data flow problem.

```
subr meet (f, g, r);
              /* f, g are pointers to entries in the array F.
                 r, points to storage for the result data
                 flow map.  */
```

FIGURE 11.4
DATA FLOW MAPS *F*. (A) SETL DATA STRUCTURES (B) LITTLE DATA
STRUCTURES

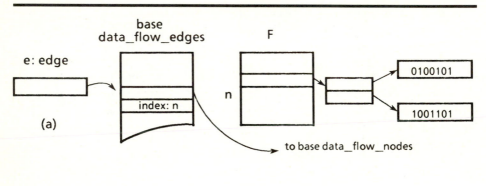

```
if (undefined(f)) then
     copyb(g, r, df__map_sz); /* Copy bit string g
                                   into result r. */

elseif (undefined(g)) then
     copyb(f, r, df__map_sz); /* Copy bit string f
                                   into result r. */
else
   /* Intersect f and g into r by anding
      bit strings f and g. */
   andb(f, g, r, df__map_sz);
end if;

end subr;
```

11.6 REPRESENTATION OF RECURSIVE TYPES

As a final example, we consider the representation of data types in the type finder module. Translation into LITTLE is more difficult here than in the previous examples. There are no **repr** declarations to rely on, since, in fact, the DRSL is not powerful enough to describe the SETL representation of types in a useful way.

The type finder attempts to determine the type of each variable in a SETL source program (see [Tenenbaum, 1974]). Since SETL is weakly typed, a single variable may denote objects of different types at different times. Therefore a type descriptor must be able to represent the union of more than one type (e.g., integer or real). Type descriptors can also be recursive, so they must be able to represent the types of the components of composite objects.

In the SETL optimizer, types are represented by tuples of the form [*type, component_type*]. These descriptors form a lattice, in which vagueness increases towards the top. The basic points on the lattice correspond to the standard types such as integer, real, and Boolean. The set of descriptors with a given basic type form a sublattice. The lattice is infinite; however, by enforcing a nesting limit on descriptors, and by treating all known-length tuples beyond a certain length as unknown-length tuples, we make the lattice finite.

The basic types are somewhere near the bottom of the lattice. Union types are somewhere near the top. The maximal type, called *type_gen*, corresponds to the union of all types. The first component of the *type_gen* descriptor is the set of all other basic types. The minimal type is called *type_zero*.

In SETL, the basic types are represented by the constants *t_om* (undefined), *t_int*, *t_real*, *t_string*, *t_atom*, *t_error*, *t_tuple*, and *t_set*. Common type descriptors are defined in terms of these, as in the following:

1.   Integer descriptor: basic type *integer*, with no components.

```
type_int  =  [ {t_int} ];
```

2.   Set descriptor: basic type *set*, with component type *type_gen*.

```
type_set = [ {t_set}, type_gen];
```

3.   Defined type descriptor: the union of all defined types, with component
type *type_gen*.

```
type_notom = [ {t_int, t_real, t_string, t_atom,
                       t_tuple, t_set}, type_gen];
```

4.   Pair descriptor: a tuple of length 2, with component types defined.

```
type_pair = [{t_tuple}, [type_notom, type_notom]];
```

5.   Map descriptor: a set of pairs.

```
type_map = [ {t_set}, type_pair ];
```

Note that the descriptor for *type_notom* is a union type, and the descriptors
for *type_pair* and *type_map* are nested. There are no **repr** declarations for
such type descriptors because it is not possible in the DRSL to describe a
recursive structure, that is, a composite structure with a component of the
same structure. Similarly, the DRSL does not support union types. This is a
significant deficiency of the current DRSL (see [Weiss and Schonberg, 1986]).

In LITTLE, descriptors are stored in a *type* table and components of
descriptors in an auxiliary *component* table; for known-length tuple types there
may be more than one component per descriptor. Entries in the component
table point back to entries in the type table. The basic type of the descriptor,
which may be a union of several types, is represented by a field of one-bit flags
in a type table record. Basic types can therefore be unioned and intersected
conveniently with bit string *or* and *and* operations.

Fields in the type table include the following:

basic_type	a bit string of (union of) basic types.
component_type	pointer to the component table.
num_components	number of component elements.
is_known_length	flag for known-length tuples.

To avoid generating the same type descriptor more than once, as is
done in the high-level SETL specification when, for example, more than

FIGURE 11.5
LITTLE REPRESENTATION OF *TYPE_MAP*

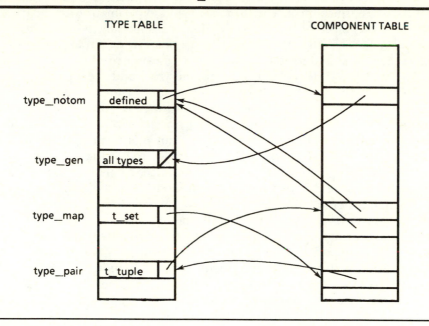

one variable are of the same type, the type table is a hash table. Note that when comparing a new composite type with an existing table entry, it is only necessary to compare nonrecursively the outermost layer of the type (i.e., basic type and component type); components can be compared by pointer comparison because of the uniqueness of type descriptors. Figure 11.5 shows the LITTLE representation of *type_map* as defined earlier.

Translating SETL code of the type finder into LITTLE proved to be more challenging than the previous examples, in part because many of the SETL type finder routines are recursive, and also because the descriptors in LITTLE are harder to manipulate. The result is a significant code expansion. Nonetheless, once appropriate low-level data structures were chosen, the translation proceeded in a stereotyped fashion.

11.7 CONCLUSION

For large software projects, we advocate stepwise refinement, using SETL for high-level prototyping and algorithm specification. Once the algorithms are proved to be effective by experimenting with small examples, the data structure representation language may be used to further experiment with data structures; the DRSL then aids reimplementation in a low-level language. The final product is more reliable than if it were written initially in a low-level language, since it is harder to modify and experiment with the detailed code, and the more abstract specification, substantially tested, provides a scaffolding for structuring the implementation. The SETL algorithms serve as documentation and to communicate new research results.

The translation discussed here took one year, and the LITTLE version is 35,000 lines of code, for a code size expansion factor of 2.3. The largest program optimized is 836 lines of SETL, and it took 162 seconds of execution time. The LITTLE version is faster by a factor of between 10 and 12. Unfortunately, the LITTLE version, while it can analyze programs more than twice as large as the SETL version can, is still limited in the size of programs that it can handle. It is not possible, for instance, to analyze the optimizer. This would require that the algorithms be modified to be able to incrementally analyze programs.

One might argue that if the DRSL and the optimizer were really successful, there would never again be a need for manually translating a SETL program, in that sufficient speedups of SETL programs would be gained via a combination of these tools. Automatic techniques, however, have not yet achieved the efficiency improvements that a programmer can provide. Even the data representation for type descriptors implemented in LITTLE as in Section 11.6 cannot be handled in the current DRSL nor discovered by the optimizer, although this problem has been studied [Weiss *et al.*, 1986]. The need for manual translation will be with us for a long time. The ability to reuse design, as well as actual code, can alleviate this burden.

Acknowledgment

The work of the last three authors has been supported in part by Office of Naval Research Grant N00014-82-K-0381, by grants from the Digital Equipment Corporation and the IBM Corporation, and by National Science Foundation CER Grant No. NSF-DCR-83-20085.

References

Aho, A. V., and Ullman, J. D. *Principles of Compiler Design*. Reading, Mass.: Addison-Wesley, 1977.

Dewar, R.; Grand, A.; Liu, Y.; Schonberg, E.; and Schwartz, J. T. Programming by refinement, as exemplified by the SETL representation sublanguage. *ACM Transactions on Programming Languages and Systems* 1(1): 27, 1979.

Freudenberger, S. M. On the use of global optimization algorithms for the detection of semantics programming errors. Ph.D. thesis, Department of Computer Science, Courant Institute, NYU, 1984.

Freudenberger, S. M.; Schwartz, J. T.; and Sharir, M. Experience with the SETL optimizer. *ACM Transactions on Programming Languages and Systems*, 5(1): 26, 1983.

Hecht, M. S. *Flow Analysis of Computer Programs*. New York: Elsevier North-Holland, 1977.

Schonberg, E.; Schwartz, J. T.; and Sharir, M. Automatic data structure selection in SETL. *Sixth ACM Symposium on Principles of Programming Languages*, Jan. 1979.

Schonberg, E., and Shields, D. From prototype to efficient implementation: A case study using SETL and C. *Proceedings 19th Hawaii International Conference on Systems Sciences*, Honolulu, Jan. 1986.

Schwartz, J. T., and Sharir, M. A design for optimizations of the bitvectoring class. Courant Institute Computer Science Report #NSO-17, 1979.

Schwartz, J. T.; Dewar, R.; Dubinski, E.; and Schonberg, E. *Programming with Sets: An Introduction to SETL*. New York: Springer-Verlag, 1986.

Tenenbaum, A. M. Type determination for very high level languages. Courant Institute Computer Science Report #NSO-3, 1974.

Weiss, G., and Schonberg, E. Typefinding recursive structures: A dataflow analysis in the presence of infinite type sets. *Proceedings IEEE Computer Society International Conference on Computer Languages*, Oct. 1986.

CHAPTER 12

DRACO: A METHOD FOR ENGINEERING REUSABLE SOFTWARE SYSTEMS

JAMES M. NEIGHBORS
System Analysis, Design, and Assessment

12.1 INTRODUCTION

Everyone is looking for an order of magnitude increase in the production of software systems; but, historically, such increases have never been achieved. Certainly such an increase will not be the result of simple extensions of current techniques.

Many factors have contributed to the current "software crisis":

☐ The price/performance ratio of computing hardware has been decreasing about 20 percent per year [Morrissey and Wu, 1979].

☐ The total installed processing capacity is increasing at better than 40 percent per year [Morrissey and Wu, 1979].

This work was supported by the National Science Foundation under grant MCS-81-03718 and by the Air Force Office of Scientific Research (AFOSR). The author's current address is Box 5017, Irvine, CA 92716.

☐ As computers become less expensive, they are used in more application areas, all of which demand software.

☐ The cost of software as a percentage cost of a total computing system has been steadily increasing. The cost of hardware as a percentage cost of a total computing system has been steadily decreasing [Boehm, 1981].

☐ The productivity of the software creation process has increased only 3–8 percent per year for the last 30 years [Morrissey et al., 1979]. This increase in productivity includes all the developments in software engineering and the development of higher-level languages.

☐ There is a shortage of qualified personnel to create software [Lientz and Swanson, 1980].

☐ Larger software systems are increasingly hard to construct.

The software crisis is not a problem of small systems. Adequate methods exist for a single programmer to produce 10k lines of high-level source code or for five programmers to produce 50k lines of high-level source; perhaps finding people who are familiar with the development techniques is difficult, but the methods appear adequate. However, software development becomes a crisis when 20 people attempt to cooperate in the development of a 200k-line system. Systems of this size have murky and ambiguous specifications. The social interactions of the developing team members become a major expense of time.

The interest in reusable software stems from the realization that one way to increase productivity during the production of a particular system is to produce less software for that system while achieving the same fuctionality. This can be done by building the system out of reusable software components and amortizing the cost of developing the general software components over the construction costs of many systems.

The Draco approach to the construction of software from reusable software components deals neither with the organizational interactions of developing team members nor with methods for the complete specification of software systems. Instead we focus only on the constructive aspects of software production (analysis, design, implementation) under the assumption that with such an approach the number of development team members producing a large system could be drastically cut and the specification clarified using a rapid development feedback cycle with the original specifiers.

The first Draco prototype was completed in 1979 [Neighbors, 1980, 1984; Freeman, 1987] and the last major revision of the mechanism was completed in 1983 [Neighbors et al., 1984]. Since that time the instrumental use of the mechanism has been stressed to reveal its limits and pitfalls [Gonzalez, 1981; Sundfor, 1983a, 1983b; Arango et al., 1986]. This paper discusses the Draco approach, including what changes we think will be necessary for the construction of truly large systems. These changes have not been implemented and experimented with on real systems.

12.2 METHODS OF SOFTWARE REUSE

Before we discuss the Draco approach to the problem of software reuse, we will characterize the three basic approaches to the problem. These are extreme points of view, but all approaches contain some aspects of each.

12.2.1 Libraries of Reusable Components

The most obvious approach to the problem of software reuse is to form libraries of software modules. When we consider the reuse of existing programs, we must be careful in describing the goals of the reuse. In some cases a programmer is looking for a program part that can just be plugged in without modification. In other cases the programmer is looking for a program part that can be modified before use. This is an important consideration in the design of a library of reusable program parts. In the first instance only what the program part does needs to be stored, while in the second instance both what the part does and how it does it need to be stored.

The reuse of program parts *without any modification* is extremely successful. An obvious example of this approach is the implementation of compilers by linkage to run-time support routines. The use of classical program libraries supported by linkage editors is another example. This kind of reuse is invisible to the programmers requesting the reuse. The library is kept in an encoded form and thus cannot be changed by the programmer. This approach has been most successful in reusing libraries of mathematical functions, where the data objects being manipulated belong to one of a few different types of number representation.

The reuse of program parts *modified with the aid of a machine* has not been investigated very much. Most of the work in this area is from research on automatic programming, program generators, computer-aided software engineering, and specialized language design. The reuse of program parts modified without the aid of a machine is a major activity of detailed design and coding. Encyclopedic works such as [Knuth, 1968; Sedgewick, 1984; Press *et al.*, 1986] serve as guides supplying information above the level of programming language code that tells the programmer what the part does and how it does it. This "how" information allows the programmer to adapt the part to the system under consideration.

Problems with Software Part Libraries.   If we have the "what" describing the function of each software part in a collection, then one straightforward way of organizing the collection is to put each part into a library of source code. Potential users of the part would search through the "what" descriptions of the parts of the library and select the appropriate part. This is the scheme used by most source program libraries. The problems encountered by this scheme are the following:

— Description language [handwritten annotation]

1. *The classification problem:* What is an appropriate language or scheme for specifying and searching "what" descriptions?

2. *The search problem:* The burden of searching the library is placed on the potential user of a part. Quite often it is easier for a potential user to (re)build a part from scratch than to find a part in a library and understand the constraints on its use and the ramifications of its design.

In addition, if the potential user is looking through the library for a software part that can be modified, the following problems will arise:

Do each to Components? [handwritten annotation]
domain analysis? [handwritten annotation]
variants [handwritten annotation]

1. *The structural specification problem:* What is an appropriate language or scheme for specifying "how" descriptions and constraints of usage between software parts?

2. *The flexibility problem:* Which design and implementation decisions are flexible and which are fixed in each of the software parts in the library?

The Overall Library Problem.   The overall library problem is aggravated by and increases the magnitude of all the other problems. If the parts in the library are to be modified and reused, then they must be small in order to be general, flexible, and understandable. However, if the parts in the library are small, then the number of parts in the library must be very large. These two objectives are always in conflict. If a library contains many small parts, the structural specification and flexibility problems are reduced at the expense of increasing the classification and searching problems. If a library contains a small number of large parts, the classification and searching problems are reduced at the expense of increasing the structural specification and flexibility problems. Some interesting work has dealt with these issues [Prieto-Díaz and Freeman, 1987].

Specialized Languages.   An alternative to program libraries is the use of specialized languages as surface forms to tie together software parts. As a historical example consider FORTRAN, not as a programming language but as a surface description scheme for tying together the software parts that make up the FORTRAN run-time library. Would FORTRAN have been nearly as successful if it had been presented as a library of interesting and useful numeric input, calculation, and output routines with descriptions? If it were just a library, the burden of using it would be placed upon each and every potential user of the library. Having a surface language that ties the library together in restricted ways removes this burden. Fahlman's NETL [Fahlman, 1979], the CCITT protocol description language [CCITT, 1984], and Mallgren's specification of graphics languages [Mallgren, 1983] are all recent examples of this technique in problem domains far removed from FORTRAN. These are problem domain–specific languages.

12.2.2 Narrow-Spectrum Transformational Schemes

In a narrow-spectrum transformational approach a system description is refined through a discrete series of narrow-spectrum languages. The system is held in only one language at a time and goes through stepwise refinement from one language to the next. Each discrete level of language has its own modes of analysis and model of completeness. *The languages for describing the "waterfall" software engineering cycle are narrow-spectrum languages.* Each is concerned with a different aspect of the developing system. The following is a general description of the narrow-spectrum languages that can be applied to the waterfall model.

☐ *Requirements* languages capture the external environment in which the system under consideration must work and the required external operation of the system. It is the interface specification of the proposed system with the rest of the world. Most system requirements are captured in natural language.

☐ *Analysis* languages capture the answer to the questions "What functions are required within the system?" and "What information is produced and consumed by each function?" This information is usually captured in the form of graphical data flow diagrams (DFDs) [Ross, 1977; Gane and Sarson, 1979].

☐ *Architectural design* languages focus on the control flow of the developing system to answer the question "Which of these functions are tightly coupled in data and control flow?" The goal here is to minimize coupling and maximize cohesion. This information is usually captured as graphical control flow hierarchy trees with data-passing and -sharing annotations [Yourdon and Constantine, 1979; Jackson, 1976]. The system is partitioned into modules, collections of tightly coupled functions and procedures.

☐ *Detailed design* or *implementation* languages focus on the control flow within an individual function or procedure, composite data definitions, and the definition of the function or procedure's interface with the rest of the system. The form is usually a pseudocode of control flow constructs and function- or procedure-passed parameter declarations supported by a data dictionary [Yourdon and Constantine, 1979; Caine and Gordon, 1975].

These descriptions are very general and apply to all kinds of systems.[1] *There is no direct relation between the use of the narrow-spectrum transformational approach and a narrow range of systems produced.* However, these general ideas can be tailored to a specific problem domain. Jackson design is an example of such tailoring. *Jackson design* [Jackson, 1976] is a general model of the process of processing input forms, interacting with a database, and producing output reports. The general notations specified above are restricted in Jackson design to producing systems of this form.

Fourth-generation languages (4GLs) are program generators that carry this tailoring process one step further. The process is so domain dependent that

---

[1]With the possible exception of real-time systems, which require time constraints to be added to each of the language levels.

the translation between the narrow-spectrum languages can be carried out by a mechanical agent. However, 4GLs still go through the same narrow-spectrum transformational approach concerned with the same notations as the more general process outlined above.

Problems with the Narrow-Spectrum Transformational Approach.   Since the narrow-spectrum approach captures a view of a developing system above the level of program code, there is some hope that these analysis and design models could be reused. If these models are formed into a library, these libraries will inherit all of the library problems mentioned in the previous section. The more tailored versions of the narrow-spectrum approach, such as 4GLs, reuse analysis and design daily.

The two basic problems specific to the narrow-spectrum approach are these:

☐ How do we make the jump from the narrow-spectrum language that currently describes the system to the next abstraction level down?

☐ Once we have made the jump from one abstraction level to the next, what do we do if we discover that our work in the previous abstraction level was incomplete? Can we back up without undoing all of the work we did to get here?

The top-down rigidity of the software engineering waterfall model of system development demonstrates the second problem. Early proponents of the waterfall model did not intend it as a strictly top-down process without backup [Royce, 1970], but the difficulties developers had in dealing with the second problem caused it to evolve into such a process.

12.2.3 Wide-Spectrum Transformational Schemes

A wide-spectrum transformational approach uses one wide-spectrum language to describe the developing system from its requirements to its final implementation level.[2] The requirements statement is "transformed" (i.e., refined) into lower-level constructs nearer to implementation. At any one time the wide-spectrum statement of the system being refined will include statements from all of the modeling phases of the narrow-spectrum transformational approach (e.g., the statement could contain data flow constraints as well as control flow constraints). Thus the wide-spectrum statement refined to the implementation level contains the complete *refinement history* of the process. The wide-spectrum transformational approach is the predominant approach in knowledge-based automatic programming [Balzer, 1981; Cheatham, 1984; Smith *et al.*, 1985; Waters, 1985; Green, 1976].

---

[2]The final implementation description only contains the control and data description constructs of a conventional high-level language that could be compiled by a conventional compiler.

Problems with the Wide-Spectrum Transformational Approach. The wide-spectrum language must span quite a range of description from the model of the external world in the requirements to the description of indivisible data item operations in the implementation. Prospective users of a wide-spectrum approach should be concerned with the following questions:

☐ How is knowledge about the world encapsulated for reuse using the wide-spectrum language primitives so that we don't end up describing standard high-level constructs like physical matter or low-level constructs like priority queues over and over again during the refinement of many requirements statements?

☐ What encapsulations come already provided?

☐ Can I change these encapsulations if they do not meet my needs?

☐ How can I be assured that the language will not become bloated and thus too complicated to learn as new constructs are perceived to be needed on the many levels of abstraction and in the many problem domains that the language must represent?

In order to capitalize on reuse, wide-spectrum approaches must provide a mechanism for tailoring the general wide-spectrum language to certain problem areas. Otherwise there is nothing to reuse and system descriptions must be stated in terms of first principles each time. The work of providing problem domain—specific customizations of wide-spectrum languages—is under way [Barstow, 1985; Wile, 1986].

12.2.4 Summary

As stated earlier, the viewpoints represented above are extreme, and no system takes entirely one view. The Draco approach borrows from each of the viewpoints. In particular, Draco uses a library of problem domain—specific notations, each of which is narrow-spectrum in scope. These are not arranged in a strict hierarchy for stepwise translation as in the narrow-spectrum approach; instead, a single mechanism spanning the complete wide-spectrum range of abstraction manages refinement using the knowledge specified in all the known domains.

12.3 THE DRACO APPROACH

The Draco approach to the construction of software systems from reusable component parts is strongly influenced by our viewpoint as practicing software engineers. The basic motivation is the frustrating feeling that most of the system you are currently building is the same as the last few systems you have built, but that once again you are building everything from scratch.

(handwritten marginalia: "wisdom / Don't / perfect. / poor / to / flexible / Look / wants / it's")

The current system development is behind schedule and you have no time to figure out what this similarity means.

12.3.1 Purpose and Viewpoint

Our point of view in the analysis and design of Draco is an engineering point of view. We are not trying to advance the state of the art in knowledge representation, language design, parser generation, module interconnection languages, program transformations, or planning. Instead we are attempting to discern which techniques have been successful in these areas, fuse them into an experimental system, and see where the system fails.

As software engineers we are concerned with how Draco would be used by an organization engineering large, real systems. We are attempting to address the software crisis as described above, which is not a crisis in building small systems but a crisis in building large systems.[3]

12.3.2 Organizational Use of Draco

Figure 12.1 shows the flow of information between people in different roles external to Draco. Classically, during the system analysis phase of software construction, a user with a desire for a certain type of system would interact with a systems analyst who would specify *what* the system should do based on the analyst's past experience with these types of systems. This would be passed on to system designers who would specify *how* the system was to perform its function.

With Draco we hypothesize three new major human roles: the application domain analyst, the modeling domain analyst, and the domain designer. The *application domain analyst* examines the needs and requirements of a collection of systems that seem similar. We have found that this work is only successfully done by a person who has built many systems for different clients in the same problem area, or *domain*. Once the domain analyst has described the objects and operations that are germane to an area of interest, then these are given to the *domain designer*, who specifies different implementations for these objects and operations in terms of the other domains already known to Draco. The *modeling domain analyst* performs a function similar to the application domain analyst, but is more concerned with which notations and techniques have been successful in modeling a wide range of applications. The particular information needed to specify a domain is described in the following section.

Once a set of Draco domains has been developed by an organization in their area of software system construction, then new system requirements from users can be considered by the organization's systems analysts in the light of the Draco domains that already exist. If a Draco domain exists that

---

[3] Although historically devices, such as structured programming, developed for use in large systems tend to aid the development of small systems.

FIGURE 12.1
ORGANIZATIONAL CONTEXT OF DRACO

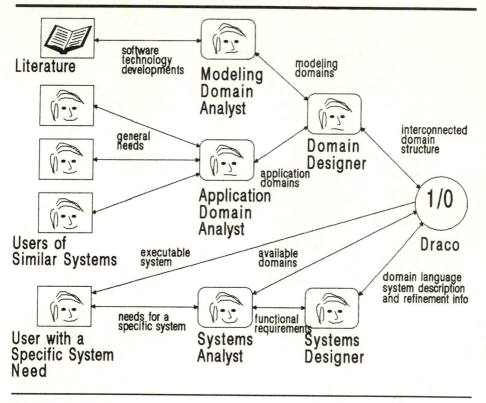

can acceptably describe the objects and operations of a new system, then the systems analyst has a framework on which to hang the new specification. This is the *reuse of analysis information,* and in our opinion it is the most powerful brand of reuse. Once the new system is cast as a domain language notation, then the systems designer interacts with Draco in the refinement of the problem to executable code. In this interaction the systems designer has the ability to decide between different implementations as specified by the domain designers of the Draco domains. This is the *reuse of design information,* and it is the second most powerful brand of reuse.

Thus Draco captures the experience of the old hands of the organization and delivers this experience in problem-specific terms to every systems analyst in the organization for their education and use.

12.3.3 Architectural Design of the Draco Approach

There are three basic points of concern to the different users of the Draco approach: the individual domains, the interrelationships between the existing domains (i.e., the *domain structure*), and how the Draco mechanism controls the refinement of a particular system. We shall deal with these individual points in succeeding sections.

12.4 WHAT COMPRISES A DOMAIN DESCRIPTION

In this section we will describe the results of domain analysis and domain design that must be given to the Draco mechanism to specify a complete domain. There are six parts to a domain description: parser, prettyprinter, optimizations, components, generators, and analyzers.

12.4.1 Parser

The parser description defines the interface between the domain and the mechanism. There are three parts to the parser description:

1. The external syntax of the domain and the internal form of the domain are described in a conventional BNF notation, which is augmented with control mechanisms such as parser error recovery and parser backtracking. The internal form is a tree with an attribute name and data at each node. The internal form is the data actually manipulated by the Draco mechanism.
2. The parser description must define what is a well-formed formula in the domain's internal form. This is a semantic check on the combination of objects and operations in the domain. This subsumes a check on the production and consumption of data by the domain.
3. Finally the parser description must specify the database schema for the information to be maintained by the mechanism for the exclusive use of the agents of the domain.

As Draco manipulates the internal form of a domain, the parser description is the final arbiter of what constitutes a valid notation in the domain both as a fragment of notation and as a complete notation statement. This information can be used to prohibit or trigger the use of other domain definitions by the mechanism. As an example, the refinement of an operation component in the domain may be held up until the semantic checker is convinced that the objects input to the operation are semantically valid types.

12.4.2 Prettyprinter

The prettyprinter description tells Draco how to produce the external syntax of the domain for all possible notation fragments in the internal form of the domain. This is necessary for the mechanism to be able to interact with users in the language of the domain and discuss incomplete parts of the developing system.

Since the prettyprinter is the only agent of the domain that can communicate with the systems designer, it must also be able to present the information gained from the other domain-specific agents described below.

12.4.3 Optimizations

The optimizations[4] represent the rules of exchange between the objects and operations of the domain. Optimizations only work within the domain from which they were specified. They never cross domain boundaries. There are three parts to the optimization specifications:

1. *Source-to-source optimizing rules* are simple source pattern–to–source pattern rewrite rules similar to source-to-source program transformation work [Kibler *et al.*, 1977].

2. *Source-to-source optimizing procedures* are procedures, which may or may not be triggered by a source pattern, that take an instance of the domain's internal form as an argument and produces a new instance of the domain's internal form.

3. *Optimization application scripts* describe possible structured interactions[5] developed by the domain designer that the optimizing rules and procedures can provide to the system designer. These can also be used as an element in refinement planning by the refinement mechanism.

The output domain language fragment of all of the optimizers is subject to the scrutiny of the parser description as the final arbiter of a well-formed notation fragment in the domain. The semantic equivalence of the optimized result is not checked. *The optimizations are guaranteed to be correct independent of any particular implementation (i.e., component refinement) chosen for any object or operation in the domain.* This granularity of meaning is important, and we will see later how it provides us with powerful domain-dependent optimizations.

12.4.4 Components

The software components specify the semantics of the domain. There is one software component for each object or operation in the domain. The software components make implementation decisions. Each component consists of one or more refinements, which represent the different implementations for the object or operation. Each refinement is a restatement of the semantics of the object or operation in terms of one or more domain languages known to

---

[4]Previously these were referred to as transformations in the source-to-source transformation sense. However, since the wide-spectrum approaches refer to transformations as operations that make implementation decisions (i.e., refinement decisions) we decided on a more appropriate name.

[5]Previously these were specific to the mechanism and were called tactics.

Draco. Thus component refinements cross domain boundaries. Conceptually, it is easiest to view each refinement as a macro body[6] for the domain object or operation it represents. The macro body is written in terms of other (perhaps the same but not usually) domain notations.

Components are the only part of a domain description that cross domain boundaries (i.e., components need to know about other domains), and these are patterns, not procedures. We do not use procedures for this function since the wide-spectrum mechanism must be able to analyze the possible interdomain connections made by a component.

12.4.5 Generators

Generators are domain-specific procedures used in circumstances where the knowledge to do domain-specific code generation is algorithmic. They are analogous to program generators. A generator does not do an optimization task, but actually writes new code in the domain. The construction of LR(k) parser tables from a grammar description and the normalization of database schemas are two examples of generation. Like optimizing procedures, generators only operate and produce the internal form of the one domain where they are described. The resulting output notation fragment is checked by the parser description.

12.4.6 Analyzers

Analyzers are domain-specific procedures that gather information about an input instance of domain notation. As with all other procedural specifications in a domain definition, a particular analyzer only works with the specific domain where it was defined. As with all domain-specific procedures, the data produced and consumed by each analyzer is kept under the schema described in the domain parser definition. The actual data is managed by the Draco mechanism, which is described in a later section. Data flow analyzers, execution monitors, theorem provers, and design quality measures are examples of analyzers.

12.4.7 Domain Description Summary

The basis of the Draco work is the use of domain analysis to produce domain languages. Once a statement in a domain language has been parsed into internal form it may be

1.   prettyprinted back into the external syntax of the domain;

---

[6]Simple macro expansion or instantiation in-line with suitable systematic renaming is only one possible alternative for architectural design. The applicative feel of this process, however, makes it a comfortable model.

2. optimized into a statement in the same domain language;
3. taken as input to a program generator that restates the problem in the same domain;
4. analyzed for possible leads for optimization, generation, or refinement; or
5. implemented by software components, each of which contains multiple refinements and which make implementation decisions by restating the problem in other domain languages.

12.5 THE NATURE AND STRUCTURE OF DOMAINS

Since the semantics of the components of one domain are described by translation into the components of other domains, a hierarchy of domains is formed. This structure of domains is a cyclic directed graph.[7] Obviously, if we ever expect to produce executable systems, some of the domains must be the equivalent of some conventional programming language. These are called *executable domains*. We define the *level of abstraction* of a domain with respect to an executable domain to be the longest acyclic path from any of the refinements of the domain's components to the executable domain. The domains with the highest levels of abstraction are called *application domains*, while the domains in the abstraction levels between the application domains and execution domains are called *modeling domains*.

The idea of a hierarchy of domains came from early work on source-to-source program transformations [Standish *et al.*, 1976; Kibler *et al.*, 1977]. In that work we were attempting to perform the specialization of a general high-level language program in its source form so that the programmer could see the modification. As an example, we would refine a general Pascal matrix multiply program under the specialization that one of the matrices was an upper triangular matrix. We would chain together many transformations, some of them specializations and some general compiler-like optimizations, to produce the resulting program. Consider the case of matrix multiplication with the identity matrix: In Pascal the source-to-source transformation system had to work very hard to realize that a matrix multiply becomes a matrix copy; in APL this was a single, trivial transformation. This is because APL performs matrix operations at a higher level of abstraction than Pascal. Clearly, it is important to perform optimizations at the highest level of abstraction possible. We explored domain-specific high-level languages and discovered that not only were significant optimizations easier in these languages, but systems specification and synthesis were also easier since they were free of low-level implementation details.

---

[7]The graph is cyclic because, for instance, in many cases two modeling domains will use each other as modeling domains.

12.5.1 Application Domains

There are two kinds of domain analysts: those that primarily construct modeling domains and those that primarily construct application domains. A database is not a complete application but many applications use its services. It comes as no surprise that an accounting systems expert is not a database expert, but most accounting systems use a database.

From our experience, application domains become a kind of glue that ties existing modeling domains together in a restricted way. An accounting systems application domain would not allow full access to all of a database domain's capabilities. Instead the accounting systems domain would form a model of accounting objects and operations in the notation of the database domain. Accounting objects like journals and ledgers are each a restricted class of general database objects like relations. All journals and ledgers in all systems constructed using a particular accounting systems domain have a certain basic form. Of course, this basic form can be expanded in different ways in constructing different systems, but the core descriptions of the accounting objects never change. Similarly, an accounting operation like posting is a specific type of restricted database operation.

An application domain analyst must be able to view all of the possible modeling domains as relatively simple data flow processes without worrying about all the details. As an example, one model of a database is a process that, when given a schema, a query or fact, and a database, produces a relation. A *relation* is a set of records that can be generated one at a time in a specified order. This is a very simple description of a very complex mechanism. It is not clear what is done during refinement and what is done during execution. The application domain analyst does a data flow analysis model for one particular, familiar domain using the basic building blocks of the modeling domains.

12.5.2 Modeling Domains

Most of the domains known to Draco will be modeling domains. A modeling domain is not a complete application but the encapsulation of the engineering knowledge necessary to produce a significant but well-defined subpart of a complete application [Rowe and Tonge, 1978]. The concept of many domains sets the Draco approach apart from other approaches to software reuse. *A modeling domain is created by partitioning the knowledge needed to construct systems, similar to the way a module is created by partitioning the control and data flow of the system itself.* A system module is a collection of functions, procedures, private definitions, and public definitions that performs a significant, encapsulated function for the system as a whole. Analogously, a modeling domain is a collection of objects, operations, optimizations, and semantic translations that encapsulates the analysis, designs, and implementations of software parts that perform the domain's major function. This does not mean that the refinement of a domain will necessarily map into a module in the final system. As Balzer [Balzer, 1981] has described, "the process of refinement is the spreading of information through the developing system." Initially, however, this information must be in one place.

In the preceeding description of a domain structure we have scrupulously avoided the refinement of one domain into another by a procedure. This is by design since it couples the domains too tightly and makes the knowledge base hard to analyze.[8] The mechanism that manages the refinement must be able to analyze the refinement process. Similarly, programmers who manage the control and data flow in software systems must have modules in order to be able to analyze the control and data flow process.

In our experiments using the Draco method, understanding what is an appropriate modeling domain seems to have been the hardest problem. This is not a surprise. Doing the module decomposition of a single concrete system is hard enough, and partitioning and selection of domains in Draco is not driven by a single specification, but by the domain analyst's experience in the construction of many systems.

12.5.3 Execution Domains

In the beginning we assumed that there could be multiple executable domains, and indeed there can; but building execution domains represents a pitfall for computer scientists. Computer scientists are well trained in general control flow and data structure constructs; thus they are domain experts in this area. Naturally, domain experts like to build and experiment with domains in their area of expertise. The explosive growth in the number of general-purpose languages in the 1960s bears witness to this fact. In our early work we also fell victim to this desire.[9] We now believe that the selection of one executable domain, a *base language*, is the key to keeping the focus on truly domain-specific languages.

Once a base language has been selected, the compiling can be left to the compilers and the truly powerful application-specific domains can be explored. This does not mean that Draco could not be used for the production of a compiler; it is just that the construction of compilers is not the problem precipitating the software crisis. We have learned that the following features are required of the base language.

A Function/Procedure Parameter-Passing Model. As the mechanism keeps track of the system being refined, many architectural design models are

---

[8] An analyzing system would have to understand the refining procedures, and program understanding has not been successful even in simple domains.

[9] Some constructed domains: MC68000 assembly, Intel 8080 assembly, Dec20 assembly, Lisp primitives, stack machine assembly, SIMAL: an Algollike language, and RML: a Pascallike language with modules.

possible. A refinement may be instantiated in-line, or a procedure may be created to save space. Without a model of the process of making a procedure or function and passing information to it, the mechanism becomes very difficult. Consider attempting to handle Lisp's EXPRS, FEXPRS, LEXPRS; Pascal's call by value unless it is a structure; and FORTRAN's ancient call by return value.

A Module, Module Interconnection, and Scoping Model.   As the mechanism constructs new parts of the system, it sometimes needs to create names to call things and to enable only certain other parts of the system to access them. Consider dynamic scoping and lexical scoping. In addition, the mechanism needs the concepts of module and module interconnection for much the same reason that people do, to bound the context of definitions in larger systems.

A Parallel Processing Model.   Many concepts, such as natural language parsing using an augmented transition network (ATN) are naturally described as parallel processes. In fact it is quite a bit of work to remove the parallelism. It should be possible to describe parallel processes in a parallel form that might allow a multiprocessing computer to directly exploit the resulting parallel system.

An Exception-Handling Model.   All of the refinements are based upon the principles of abstract data types, and different exceptions can occur in each different implementation of the objects and operations. Unless there is exception handling in the base language, the Draco approach will produce systems that spend time explicitly looking for exceptions. Exceptions should seldom happen and indicate an interruption in the main control flow processing. The main control flow processing should not be checking for them explicitly all the time.

Standard Control Flow and Data Structure Definitions.   These are of interest if the resulting system is to ever be understood by a regular programmer.

A Compatible Compiler Implementation.   Once something has been refined it should be executable on a collection of machines.

The base language is a high-level model of the computer on which we expect the resulting system to run. The above description is for a von Neumann computer. I would not expect the base language for a massively parallel computer to be the same.

The choice of a base language is not important as long as one is chosen and it meets the above criteria. The problem is the construction of large, reliable, application systems in the base language, not the development of another general-purpose, high-level language.

12.6 THE DRACO MECHANISM

The Draco mechanism interacts with all of the human roles in system development. It must provide support to application domain analysts, modeling domain analysts, and domain designers in their efforts to add to the knowledge base. It must provide support to systems analysts and system designers in their respective functions of specifying and refining a particular system. It maintains the wide-spectrum model of the developing system.

12.6.1 The Basic Refinement Cycle

Once a system description has been cast in the notation of an application domain by a systems analyst, then the systems designer uses the basic cycle of selecting a set of instances of an application or modeling domain in the developing refinement and restricting the refinement focus to only those instances. Within the selected instances the systems designer uses the domain's optimizers, generators, and analyzers before deciding whether to use the domain's components to refine or not.

This *basic refinement cycle* produces the following view of domains during the refinement process. The system is originally described in a single application domain language, but the first refinement will introduce the notations of a modeling domain. Eventually the developing system is described in the notations of many modeling domains at once. Figure 12.2 graphically illustrates the refinement process from a statement in only the application domain (NLRDB) through many modeling domains (ATN and RDB) and into the final executable domain (ADA).

FIGURE 12.2
DOMAINS IN THE REFINEMENT PROCESS

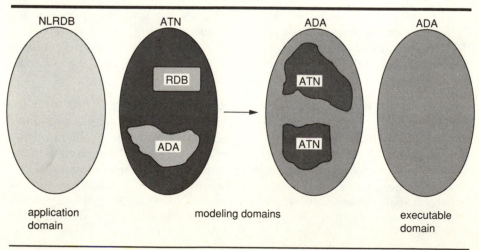

NLRDB   ATN   ADA   ADA

RDB

ATN

ADA

ATN

application   modeling domains   executable
domain   domain

The systems designer works with the refinement mechanism in one domain at a time. In a developing system there probably will be multiple instances of a domain. The refinement mechanism may be directed to work with all instances during refinement or focus on a single one.

The concept of domain supplies a psychological set to the systems designer (i.e., the designer must only consider and think about the objects and operations of one domain at a time). The ability to provide a psychological set is lost if the underlying representation of the developing system is a wide-spectrum language. This applies even in a fully automatic programming system where the systems designer is an automated agent. The selection of domains by the systems designer for refinement provides a method of progressively deepening [Simon, 1969] the system description during the refinement process.

12.6.2 Managing the Refinement Process

As with the refinement of systems by conventional means, the refinement process does not proceed strictly top-down from one modeling domain to another or from modeling domains at one level of abstraction to modeling domains at a lower level of abstraction. Sometimes it is necessary to back up the refinement process to remove an overly restrictive decision. As the process proceeds, a refinement history is recorded, which can supply a top-down derivation for each statement in the resulting executable system. The refinement history tends to be much larger than the resulting program code.[10] There are two uses for this refinement history: to understand the resulting system at different levels of abstraction and to guide the *refinement replay* of the problem if the original specification is changed and a new implementation is needed [Wile, 1983].

In general we have found that design decisions are made as shown in Fig. 12.3.

The number of decisions to be made rises initially, as implementation decisions must be made in the modeling domains, and decreases finally, as the decisions already made constrain the remaining decisions to a few choices. The *intermediate modeling swell* represented by this graph is the largest barrier to refinement.

Refinement Strategies and Tactics.   Refinement strategies deal with the complete problem of how to get an application domain statement refined into an executable system. Refinement tactics deal with the problem of how to refine a set of domain instances under a given set of modeling decisions. Strategies are usually interdomain while tactics are more intradomain.

Refinement strategies must reduce the intermediate modeling swell. One approach is to choose some modeling domain near the application level of abstraction and drive its refinement to near the execution domain level

---

[10]Our best estimate is that the refinement history is about 10 times the size of the resulting source code.

FIGURE 12.3
IMPLEMENTATION DECISIONS PENDING VS. ABSTRACTION LEVEL

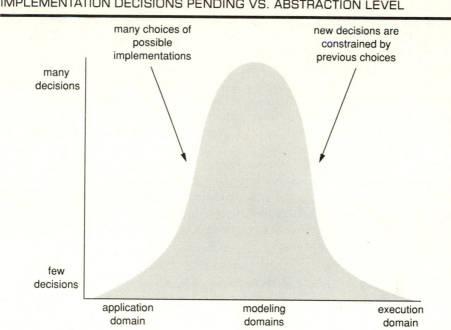

of refinement. During this process many modeling decisions will be made, and these modeling decisions will constrain the choices in other modeling domains.

Once some of the interfaces between modeling domains have been established by the early refinement of one part of the system, then the goal-oriented refinement tactics appropriate to each modeling domain can be invoked [Fickas, 1985; Rich, 1981].

Successful specific strategies must be derived with respect to a specific set of domains. We do not believe that the strategies can be specified by any of the domain analysts or domain designers. The strategies are wide-spectrum in that they encapsulate a view of the entire set of available domains. This means that as the set of domains changes, the strategies must change. To have a chance at automatically deriving strategies, we must limit the expressive power of the domain tactics and domain refinements (components), which are the basic operations within strategies, so that their functions can be analyzed.

12.6.3 The Structure of the Developing System

As the system description undergoes refinement, its architectural design is built up. The architectural design has nothing to do with what the final system does. In building a specific system there are many ways to partition the control flow into functions and procedures. Similarly, there are many ways to partition the data into composite data objects.

While these partitionings do not influence the semantics of the resulting system, they greatly influence the performance, size, and intelligibility of the resulting system. Any aid in the refinement of systems, such as Draco, must be able to deal with the architectural design. Figure 12.4 shows the function and procedure control flow graphs (structure charts) of possible refinements of a single small problem [Neighbors, 1980]. All of these implementations of the same problem were shown to have different space and speed characteristics.

The basic units of architectural design are functions, procedures, in-line instantiations, and partially evaluated functions and procedures. Partial evaluations are functions and procedures where one or more of the usual parameters have been fixed in value. In larger systems, modules, which are collections of functions, procedures, private data types, and private data stores with specific control flow entry points, become the major element of architectural design. In order to build large systems the refinement mechanism must be able to use all of these units.

12.6.4 The Notation of the Refinement Mechanism

To manage the implementation and design decisions made in a developing system the mechanism needs a notation. This notation must capture two kinds of information specific to the particular system being refined: implementation decisions of the different domain parts (detailed design and coding information) and the control and data flow structure of the developing system (architectural design information). The mechanism also needs a notation for

FIGURE 12.4
DIFFERENT ARCHITECTURAL DESIGNS RESULTING FROM THE SAME
PROBLEM

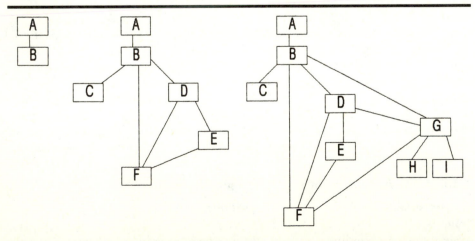

describing and reasoning about the complete set of described domains (domain analysis and design information).

Some useful models for these notations have been *module interconnection languages* (MILs). These were originally proposed for programming in the large [DeRemer and Kron, 1976] as languages for capturing the architectural design of a system built out of functions and procedures written in a programming language. The idea has been extended many ways to include objects described at different levels of abstraction [Prieto-Díaz and Neighbors, 1986; Goguen, 1986].

As a refinement proceeds, the refinement mechanism must use a kind of MIL to keep track of the architectural structure of the developing system and to keep track of what domain objects and operations must be kept compatible. Further, the MIL must be able to deal with notational fragments of each of the domains. Thus implementation consistency checking is an incremental process during refinement.

Even with such a notation correctly managed it is possible to deadlock the refinement. The refinement process is deadlocked when a component that cannot be optimized or generated out of a developing system must be refined but there is no refinement for that component that does not violate the consistency checking of the refinement mechanism. The effects of a refinement deadlock can be far-reaching to the point of requiring the complete refinement process to start over again.

12.6.5 Subsystems as Major Parts

One of the problems with the original implementation of Draco [Neighbors *et al.*, 1984] was that it required each systems designer to refine every statement in a developing system all the way down to the executable domain each time. Even though the system could aid the refinement through the use of tactics so that many tedious decisions did not need to be made, the process was still tedious even for the small (2k–4k line) programs produced. Sundfor was first to realize that large systems would really not be built this way [Sundfor, 1983b], and our recent experience with the structure of large systems reinforces this belief.

The refinement mechanism must be able to use prerefined, large subsystems as part of its reasoning process. These subsystems are nothing more than general implementations of commonly used modeling domains such as database operations and menu operations. The difference between using subsystems and external pieces of program code is that the subsystems were refined by the Draco mechanism. The modeling decisions made during the refinement are related to the domains known to the mechanism, and these modeling decisions are retained. Thus the availability of the refinement history of a subsystem enables the mechanism to reuse it in the development of other systems.

Notice that the use of subsystems meshes quite well with the basic approach of refinement strategies. If a collection of compatible subsystems may be used early in the refinement of a particular system, then they may make implementation and modeling decisions that highly constrain the intermediate modeling swell. Refining a large system using subsystems may be easier than refining a small one without subsystems.

Finally, notice that all systems refined by Draco are candidate subsystems because they all have refinement histories. Some application-specific systems, however, are less likely candidates for reuse than others.

12.7 EXPERIENCE WITH THE DRACO APPROACH

12.7.1 Reuse of Code

The large amount of information in a refinement history is lost to someone attempting to reuse an existing piece of source code. When two existing pieces of executable source code are combined, this information must be recreated to ensure that any exchanged representations are consistent. For this reason we expect the reuse of existing executable source code will be of little long-term benefit where whole systems are built from reusable parts. In the short term, highly controlled source code libraries will provide a quick productivity gain.

In our opinion, significant productivity gains will result only from the reuse of analysis and design information. Since this information is domain specific, only system refinement aids that directly address the problem of domain-specific knowledge will have any significant reuse capability.

12.7.2 Efficiency of Systems Built from Reusable Parts

Systems constructed from reusable parts by the Draco method are not inefficient. The method is capable of refining systems with different implementations and different architectural designs (i.e., modular structures). Each of these have different time-space execution characteristics. In addition, the domain-specific optimizations are far more effective than the well-known optimizations of a general-purpose language compiler. In the state-machine description of a communications protocol, a domain-specific optimization may be able to remove or combine states. There is no analogous optimization in general-purpose compilers (i.e., an execution domain), because the information that enables us to perform the optimization is no longer in the source code. Users attempting to reuse source code without a refinement history will find that their optimization options are limited.

12.7.3 The Problem of Domain Analysis

Domain analysis is knowledge engineering applied to computer science (modeling domains) and computer applications (application domains). The different types of organizations that deal with this knowledge on a daily basis have quite different views of domain analysis.

☐ Academic organizations rightfully view domain analysis as an engineering process. It is not a discovery process where completely new theories are tried out. Instead, it is the process of reviewing previous work and attempting to determine which techniques were successful and which were not. Academic organizations in computer science seem to prefer to work on new theories. However, some of the most successful academic work[11] is a fusion and formalization of successful techniques.

☐ Production organizations are forever caught in a cycle of being focused on the current system under development. A domain analysis must be motivated on the basis of its cost being amortized over the costs of many systems. Furthermore, if the domain analysis is performed by an actual domain expert (as it must be if there is to be any chance of success), then the organization risks failure in the development of the current system by removing the expert from the stream of production during the domain analysis.

☐ Research organizations are caught in the middle between a flood of new theories from computer science, which are untried in practice, and highly filtered information from the streams of software production. To understand what really works in practice, the researchers must build actual systems. However, if the researchers build an actual system, there is a chance that the organization will become a production and support organization.

A production-quality refinement aid would give each of these types of organizations an incentive and framework for domain analysis. In the meantime, the informal process of domain analysis from each type of organization continues in the literature.

12.7.4 Future

After the recent period of experimentation with the current Draco mechanism, we anticipate another period of new mechanism development. This paper represents the analysis of the new mechanism.

For experimentation and explanation purposes, it would be helpful if the mechanism were capable of completely refining itself. In the current implementation [Neighbors *et al.*, 1984] only some of the mechanism (e.g., parsers, prettyprinters, tactics interpreter, refinement library builder) was constructed using the technique. For Draco to refine the Draco mechanism, we must describe an application domain for the class of systems similar to Draco. It is our hope that with the new mechanism such a domain description will be possible.

---

[11]The work by Mallgren on graphics languages [Mallgren, 1983] was a 1982 ACM Distinguished Dissertation.

REFERENCES

Arango, G., I. Baxter, P. Freeman, and C. Pidgeon. TMM: Software maintenance by transformation. *IEEE Software*, pp. 27–39, May 1986.

Balzer, R. Transformational implementation: An example. *IEEE Transactions on Software Engineering*, vol. 7, pp. 3–14, January 1981.

Barstow, D. Domain-specific automatic programming. *IEEE Transactions on Software Engineering*, vol. 11, pp. 1321–1336, November 1985.

Boehm, B. *Software Engineering Economics*. Prentice-Hall, 1981.

Caine, S., and E. K. Gordon. PDL—A tool for software design. In *Proceedings, National Computer Conference*, vol. 44, pp. 271–276. AFIPS Press, 1975.

Cheatham, T. E. Reusability through program transformation. *IEEE Transactions on Software Engineering*, vol. 10, pp. 589–594, September 1984.

Consultative Committee International Telephone and Telegraph. Formal description techniques for data communications, protocols, and services. CCITT recommendation X.250, 1984.

DeRemer, F., and H. Kron. Programming-in-the-large versus programming-in-the-small. *IEEE Transactions on Software Engineering*, vol. 2, pp. 80–86, June 1976.

Fahlman, S. *NETL: A System for Representing and Using Real-World Knowledge*. MIT Press, 1979.

Fickas, S. Automating the transformational development of software. *IEEE Transactions on Software Engineering*, vol. 11, pp. 1268–1277, November 1985.

Freeman, P. Reusable software engineering: Concepts and research directions. In *Proceedings of the ITT Workshop on Reusability in Programming*, ITT, pp. 2–16, September 1983.

Freeman, P. A conceptual analysis of the Draco approach to constructing software systems. *IEEE Transactions on Software Engineering*, vol. 13, pp. 830–844, July 1987.

Gane, C., and T. Sarson. *Structured Systems Analysis: Tools and Techniques*. Prentice-Hall, 1979.

Green, C. The design of the PSI program synthesis system. In *2nd International Conference on Software Engineering*, pp. 4–18, October 1976.

Goguen, J. Reusing and interconnecting software components. *IEEE Computer*, pp. 16–28, February 1986.

Gonzalez, L. A domain language for processing standardized tests. M.S. thesis, University of California, Irvine, ICS Dept., 1981.

Jackson, M. A. Constructive methods of program design. In *Proceedings, 1st Conference of the European Cooperation in Informatics*, vol 44. Springer-Verlag, 1976.

Knuth, D. *The Art of Computer Programming*. Vols. 1–3. Addison-Wesley, 1968–1973.

Kibler, D., J. M. Neighbors, and T. A. Standish. Program manipulation via an efficient production system. *SIGPLAN Notices*, vol. 12, no. 8, pp. 163–173, 1977.

Lientz, B., and E. Swanson. *Software Maintenance Management*. Addison-Wesley, 1980.

Mallgren, W. *Formal Specifications of Interactive Graphics Programming Languages*. MIT Press, 1983.

Morrissey, J., and L. Wu. Software engineering: An economic perspective. In *4th International Conference on Software Engineering*, pp. 412–422, September 1979.

Neighbors, J. M. Software construction using components. Ph.D. thesis and tech. rep. TR-160, University of California, Irvine, ICS Dept., 1980.

Neighbors, J. M.; J. Leite; and G. Arango. Draco 1.3 manual. Tech. rep. RTP003.3, University of California, Irvine, ICS Dept., June 1984.

Neighbors, J. M. The Draco approach to constructing software from reusable components. *IEEE Transactions on Software Engineering*, vol. 10, pp. 564–574, September 1984.

Press, W.; B. Flannery; S. Teukolsky; and W. Vetterling. *Numerical Recipes: The Art of Scientific Computing*. Cambridge University Press, 1986.

Prieto-Díaz, R., and P. Freeman. Classifying software for reusability. *IEEE Software*, pp. 6–16, January 1987.

Prieto-Díaz, R., and J. M. Neighbors. Module interconnection languages. *The Journal of Systems and Software*, vol. 6, pp. 307–334, November 1986.

Rich, C. A formal representation for plans in the programmer's apprentice. In *7th International Joint Conference on Artificial Intelligence*, pp. 1044–1052, August 1981.

Ross, D. Structured analysis (SA): A language for communicating ideas. *IEEE Transactions on Software Engineering*, vol 3, pp. 16–34, January 1977.

Rowe, L., and F. Tonge. Automating the selection of implementation structures. *IEEE Transactions on Software Engineering*, vol. 4, pp. 494–506, November 1978.

Royce, W. Managing the development of large software systems. In *Proceedings, IEEE WESCON*, August 1970. Reprinted in *9th International Conference on Software Engineering*, pp. 328–338, April 1987.

Sedgewick, R. *Algorithms*. Addison-Wesley, 1984.

Simon, H. *The Sciences of the Artificial*. MIT Press, 1969.

Smith, D.; G. Kotik; and S. Westfold. Research on knowledge-based software environments at Kestrel Institute. *IEEE Transactions on Software Engineering*, vol. 11, pp. 1278–1295, November 1985.

Standish, T. A.; D. Harriman; D. Kibler; and J. M. Neighbors. The Irvine program transformation catalogue. Tech. rep., University of California, Irvine, ICS Dept., 1976.

Sundfor, S. Draco domain analysis for a real time application: The analysis. Tech. rep. RTP 015, University of California, Irvine, ICS Dept., 1983a.

Sundfor, S. Draco domain analysis for a real time application: Discussion of the results. Tech. rep. RTP 016, University of California, Irvine, ICS Dept., 1983b.

Waters, R. C. The programmer's apprentice: A session with KBEmacs. *IEEE Transactions on Software Engineering*, vol. 11, pp. 1296–1320, November 1985.

Wile, D. S. Program developments: Formal explanations of implementations. *Communications of the ACM*, vol. 26, pp. 902–911, November 1983.

Wile, D. S. Local formalisms: Widening the spectrum of wide-spectrum languages. In *Conference on Program Specification and Transformation*, IFIP Working Group 2.1, April 1986.

Yourdon, E., and L. Constantine. *Structured Design*. Prentice-Hall, 1979.

CHAPTER **13**

Reusability Through Program Transformations

THOMAS E. CHEATHAM, JR.
Harvard University

13.1 INTRODUCTION

The reuse of programming has a number of obvious payoffs—reduction of costs, increased reliability, increased ease of maintenance and enhancement of software systems, and so on. However, with the exception of a few well-defined mathematical functions and programmers' personal libraries, relatively little programming is actually reused without considerable reworking. And, correctly or not, many programmers perceive that it is better to start afresh than to rework existing programs for some new application.

Some will argue that the fault lies with the structure of most of the existing programming languages, in that programs do not end up sufficiently modularized for parts of them to be readily reused. Indeed, one of the claims for Ada is that through its package and separate compilation mechanisms one will be able to reuse programming in Ada. There are ongoing studies of how to provide for libraries of Ada programming.

We believe that, even with the relatively advanced modularization facilities provided by Ada, the extensive reuse of *concrete* Ada programs is unlikely. The problem is that programs in any concrete high-level programming languages are the result of mapping from some conceptual or abstract specification of what is to be accomplished into very specific data representations and algorithms that provide an *efficient* means for accomplishing the task at hand. Simple abstractions are eliminated in favor of complex but efficient concrete realizations. In this optimization process constructs that are conceptually independent at a sufficiently abstract level tend to become distributed throughout the resulting concrete program, often making it very difficult to change the program, even in minor ways, to be suitable for use in some new setting.

In this paper we will describe a programming methodology and a supporting programming environment that foster the reuse of *abstract* programs through refining a single abstract program to a *family* of distinct concrete programs.

Section 13.2 discusses our approach to developing abstract programs. In Section 13.3 we describe how we derive concrete programs from abstract programs using program transformations. In Section 13.4 we discuss our experience in using our methodology and environment to develop several families of programs. Section 13.5 provides an overview of the programming environments that have evolved to support our methodology. We close with a discussion of some of the future directions our work is expected to take.

13.2 ABSTRACT PROGRAMS

If we are to write abstract programs, we clearly need some programming language in which to write them. A number of very high-level languages (VHLLs) have been proposed for this purpose; SETL [Dewar *et al.*, 1981], GIST [Balzer *et al.*, 1981], and V [Green *et al.*, 1981] are three that have been implemented and used, and several others have been discussed in the literature. Each provides a number of very high-level constructs (for example sets, tuples, bags, and queues, and so on) and operations (for example, generalized iteration, nondeterministic choice with backtracking, and the like). Each also provides means for execution of programs written in the language after some kind of compilation activity, and each provides means for controlling the choice among alternate concrete realizations of the high-level constructs.

We have not been comfortable with accepting a *fixed* programming language in which to write abstract programs. There are two basic reasons for this. First, while a fixed VHLL may offer a wide variety of constructs, it may not provide just the construct that is exactly appropriate for the task at hand—and we believe that the kinds of choices (both explicit and implicit) that are made when we have to "shoehorn" a problem into a fixed language are a good part of the reusability problem. The second reason is that there are often a number of apparently low-level constructs that we may want to realize in nonstandard ways. Examples include constructs like

```
A[i]  ← E

  x.foo
```

if, in the concrete realization, *A* was to be represented by a linked list of sparse array elements, and *x* was to be a binary tree with *x.foo* denoting the leaf named *foo*, to be located, say, by a binary search.

We believe that it is critical that abstract programs be machine representable and that there exist tools to syntactically and semantically analyze them. We would, however, reject a restriction that forced us to use purely functional notation to capture the abstract constructs, employing, say,

```
AssignSparseElement (A, i, E)
      LocateLeaf (x, "foo")
```

to denote the sample fragments above. That is, we believe that form is very important—a designer should be able to choose the notation that is most natural to the problem domain. Also, with procedural abstraction alone it is difficult to realize constructs that include bound variables (for example, iterators) or sets of constructs that need to interact at the concrete level even though they are conceptually orthogonal. An example of the kind of interaction that might be difficult to realize would be process control records that were described as queues in the high-level description of an operating system but that, at the concrete level, needed to be threaded through extra components of the records themselves instead of being handled by the general-purpose queue implementation. This would be difficult to achieve with procedures or type encapsulation facilities alone.

Our method for writing abstract programs is to use the notations provided in a base language (in our case, the EL1 programming language, a high-level language containing a reasonably rich inventory of built-in notations) plus syntactic extensions for various high-level constructs. The programmer can declare the symbols of his choice to act as infix or prefix operators or both, and he may specify precedence and associativity attributes for them. We also have a category of operator pairs called *matchfix* operations. The declaration **Matchfix** ("{", "}"), for instance, adds a new bracketing construct to the language. Subsequent to this declaration, the expression {**x, y** + **2, A[j]**} would be a legal utterance and when evaluated would be equivalent to a call on the left brace operation ({) with the operands shown.

Longer phases, such as the notation supporting the construct

```
WhileExists I In 1. .|A| -1
   SuchThat A[I] > A[I + 1]
        Do Exchange (A[I], A[I + 1]) End
```

are added by analogy with existing ones. Notation appropriate for this example could be introduced by the declaration

```
EquatePhrases ("WhileExists  --In--SuchThat
                              --Do--End",
               "For          --From--To
                             --Repeat--End")
```

This declaration ensures that each terminal symbol of the new phrase will be treated by the parser like the corresponding token from the old phrase. The internal form produced by the parser contains the tokens actually used so that the conversion from internal to external representation (that is, "unparsing" or "prettyprinting") can be done correctly. We would argue that if one understands the meaning of the notation, then it is clear that the given construct defines a correct bubble sort algorithm.

For further elaboration of our argument for such syntactic extension facility we refer the interested reader to [Cheatham *et al.*, 1981].

We argued above that we should be able to analyze abstract programs semantically in addition to analyzing them syntactically. Although we are working on analysis tools that will do a deep analysis of some program constructs (see [Cheatham *et al.*, 1979] for a preliminary account of that work), the analysis tool that we use daily is relatively weak—essentially discovering undefined constructs and propagating (constant) modes. We have used a mechanism called an analogy to extend this analyzer to "understand" new notations for high-level constructs introduced into abstract programs. In essence, an analogy interprets some new construct in terms of more concrete (ultimately, base language) constructs. This (weak) interpretation specifically tells the analysis tool just what it needs to know in order to do its job. Consider this example:

```
WhileExists $i in $r Such That $p Do ? body End <-->
     For $i From $r Repeat $p;?body End
```

This is an analogy with a *subject* and a *target* separated by the "is analogous to" operator (< − >). The prefix dollar ($) and question (?) operators identify match variables; **$i** matches an expression and **?body** matches a list of statements. The interpretation of this analogy is that any program fragment matching the subject is to be treated, by the analyzer, as an occurrence of the target. In EL1 an iteration variable is entered into the environment for the scope of the body of the iteration and then removed. Thus the analogy indicates that the program fragments matching **$p** and **?body** are evaluated in a context in which the variable matching **$i** is defined as a local variable. Considering the bubble-sort fragment discussed above, this is just what we would wish the analyzer to do. As another example,

```
Insert $e Into $q<-> Defined($e, $q)
```

says that a program fragment that inserts **$e** into **$q** is defined if the expressions matching **$e** and **$q** are defined.

13.3 REFINEMENT OF ABSTRACT PROGRAMS TO CONCRETE PROGRAMS

Given that we have developed an abstract program for some application, its refinement to a concrete program that can actually be executed is accomplished using two mechanisms: *definition* and *transformation*. The refinement may be done in several stages, successively deriving a more concrete presentation. By *definition* we mean simply providing a binding (or value) for a procedure, type, data object, or what have you. By *transformation* we mean replacing some high-level construct by a (more) concrete construct that realizes the intended function.

A transformation rule consists of a syntactic pattern part, optionally augmented by a semantic predicate, and a replacement part. The symbol < − > separates the pattern (including any predicate) from the replacement. All three parts may include match variables just as with an analogy. Thus a general transformation rule has the form

```
pattern Where predicate <-> replacement
```

The most common kind of transformation rule that we use carries no semantic predicate and simply serves to implement some abstract notion. For example, the following rule implements notation designating the addition of an element to the end of a queue:

```
Insert $e Into $Q <->
   Begin
   $Q.count<- $Q.count + 1'
   $Q.rear<-
       CreateQueueMember ($e, $Q.rear)
   End
```

Further examples of the kinds of transformations that we have employed are contained in [Cheatham *et al.*, 1981].

We have a transformation tool that is supplied with a collection of (abstract) program entities, a set of transformations, and a sequence of instructions. The instructions direct the tool to apply certain transformations from a set T to a set of program entities P to produce a new set of program entities P':

$$P \times T \rightarrow P'$$

The final concrete program may result from several rounds of transformations. The instructions may be as simple as "apply all applicable transformations to all program entities," or they may specify a sequence of local transformations of particular entities or sets of entities.

13.4 SOME EXPERIENCE WITH REUSING ABSTRACT PROGRAMS

Our reuse of abstract programs is achieved by varying the definitions and transformations that are used to derive a concrete program from its abstract counterpart. There are two different settings in which we have done a number of experiments in varying the transformations in order to derive new implementations; we term these settings *rapid prototyping* and *custom tailoring*.

Rapid Prototyping

We have done a number of experiments in our version of rapid prototyping. Given an abstract program for some application, it is often useful to devise definitions and transformations that enable us to quickly derive a concrete program that has little concern for efficiency but does exhibit the functionality (or, perhaps, a subset of the functionality) desired. There are several reasons for doing this. For one, it enables us to assess whether or not the abstract program actually captures what its user thought she wanted. If it does not, we must, of course, modify the abstract program and try again. In one example that involved devising a user interface using high-resolution graphics and pointing mechanisms, we went through several cycles of respecification. At each stage we produced an operational interface that we explored to expose awkward or unsatisfactory behavior. It would have been difficult, if not impossible, to discover such flaws without being able to actually use the interface.

Another reason for developing a prototype rapidly is to learn what data representations and algorithms will be efficient. That is, with complex programs it may be difficult or impossible to do sufficient formal analysis of the ultimate behavior of the program to ensure good choices—it is much easier to produce a prototype where behavior can actually be observed and measured.

We encountered a third reason for such prototyping while we were developing various tools for the programming support environment that we will discuss in Section 13.5. We often found it very useful to first develop a tool that functioned in a simple testbed that was not integrated into the environment. Only when the testbed version operated satisfactorily did we develop the refinements needed for its integration.

Custom Tailoring

Custom tailoring refers to the development of refinements that permit us to derive from a single abstract program a family of concrete programs, each appropriate for a specific target environment. We have done a number of experiments with custom tailoring; we will discuss two of the larger ones, MSG and ECL.

MSG is a component of the National Software Works (NSW) (see [Massachusetts Comput. Assoc., 1977]) that provides for process-to-process communication between processes operating in the NSW; the processes may be on the same computer or may be on two distinct computers communicating via the ARPANET. Figure 13.1 depicts an instance of MSG; we will not attempt here to discuss MSG in any detail but simply note that it includes a number of queues, I/O with processes and with the network, authentication mechanisms, timeout mechanisms, and so on.

MSG makes a particularly good candidate for custom tailoring. At a sufficiently abstract level, every MSG instance must be identical, while at the concrete level, two MSGs may differ drastically, because they depend upon the particular host computer and operating system. For example, in our experiment two of the target hosts were the PDP-10 under the Tenex operating system and the PDP-11 under Unix; with the PDP-10, communication between MSG and host processes was most efficiently accomplished using shared pages, while with the PDP-11, "pipes" were employed for the same function.

Our MSG experiment involved four target systems: the two aforementioned DEC targets plus an IBM 370/158 and a simulation testbed. The simulation testbed permitted us to test the functionality of MSG with user processes and the network being simulated.

A single abstract MSG program was refined to derive the four distinct target MSGs. There were three stages in the refinement of abstract MSG to each of three actual targets. The first stage of refinement was independent of the eventual target; it introduced a number of constructs that were concerned purely with efficiency. For example, the first refinement provided for a number of threads running through the queue elements to enable efficient access to them. While these were deemed necessary for efficiency reasons, their inclusion in the most abstract model of MSG would have added nothing conceptually; rather, their complexity would have detracted from the model.

FIGURE 13.1
MSG

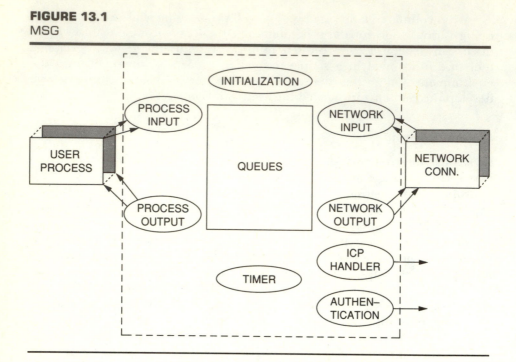

The second stage of refinement was concerned with the overall architecture of the target. For example, the introduction of shared memory as opposed to some kind of channel for communication between MSG and a user process occurred at this stage. The third and final stage of refinement took into account the details of the target, including the specific system calls required to realize the various interfaces.

The MSG experiment produced concrete programs for the four target systems. Because of limited funds and the lack of a compiler producing PDP-11/70 or IBM 370 code, the three MSGs for actual targets were never compiled and tested; the simulation MSG was run satisfactorily. In spite of the fact that we did not produce operational programs, a great deal was learned from the MSG experiment. For example, the experiment demonstrated the feasibility of custom tailoring of a single abstract model to produce widely disparate concrete implementations (see [Holloway *et al.*, 1978] for more details of this). It also showed that developing an abstract model and determining the stages appropriate for refinement were not trivial tasks. Indeed, we went through several iterations before settling on the abstract program and the stages to use in the final refinement.

A second major experiment with custom tailoring is the ECL experiment, which is currently in progress. This experiment involves (re)developing ECL systems for several target computers. An ECL system includes a parser and interpreter for the EL1 programming language plus a rich run-time system including a compactifying garbage collector, an unparser, a hash package, debug facilities, I/O primitives, and so on. For present purposes, let us focus on the EL1 interpreter itself, one of the larger components of the ECL system.

The current ECL system runs on a PDP-10 and was implemented several years ago in a reasonably conventional fashion (that is, the basic interpreter was implemented directly in machine language and most of the run-time facilities were implemented by compiling EL1 representations of them); the compiler itself was bootstrapped by being run interpretively to compile itself.

There are, at present, six target realizations that we wish to derive from an abstract model for an EL1 interpreter. These six are pairs of targets for three different computers: the PDP-10, the Apollo Domain, and the VAX. One member of each pair is a testbed simulation that can be executed interpretively and that provides an implementation in which the basic functionality of the ECL interpreter for the particular target can be validated. The other member of each pair is the stand-alone code that implements the ECL interpreter on that particular target computer. This code is produced by a cross-compiler (running on the PDP-10) that compiles EL1 programs that are constrained from using any part of the ECL run-time system, and it produces text that can be assembled on each of the targets.

The PDP-10 was included as a target in order to provide a benchmark by comparison with the original ECL implementation. The Apollo and VAX targets will enable us to use ECL on those computers as we phase out the PDP-10. Thus the project has the implicit goal of efficient final products—we want the resulting interpreters to compare favorably with hand-coded versions.

The refinement of the abstract EL1 interpreter to one of the six targets is accomplished in two stages. One stage is concerned with refining the high-level constructs that describe the behavior of the interpreter into the constrained subset of EL1 that is handled by the cross-compiler. A second stage introduces refinements that are specific to the particular target computer.

At the present time, the pairs of implementations are operational on the PDP-10 and Apollo computers. The PDP-10 implementations were thoroughly tested prior to attempting the Apollo implementation, with the result that about one week elapsed between the first successful compilation of the Apollo stand-alone code and the Apollo interpreter's becoming operational. Testing of the stand-alone versions of the interpreter was carried out by executing the interpreter on some input and, if it failed, presenting the same input to the testbed simulation and letting it proceed to the same failure point. Since it was running interpretively, all the facilities of the interpreter system were available to explore the reasons for the failure. This was particularly important when testing the Apollo version, since we had no machine-level debug facilities on the Apollo.

It is anticipated that the VAX target will be quite straightforward and involve a very few man-months of work, since a lot of what needs to be done is only replaying what we have done before.

We are going to explore a seventh target at some future date, namely a symbolic interpreter that deals with tokens and formulas rather than values.

13.5 THE PROGRAMMING SUPPORT ENVIRONMENT

The methodology we have been advocating demands a supporting programming environment if it is to be practicable. That is, a "program," in our view, exists at several levels—abstract, concrete, and perhaps several levels in between. In addition, a given abstract program may be the progenitor of a family of custom tailored variants, and each of these may involve several cycles of prototyping before the final result is achieved. Thus for bookkeeping reasons alone we have found it necessary to use the computer to manage the various components of a program and the interrelationships among them. In fact, the environment that we are presently using and will describe briefly below is the result of several evolutionary steps that started in 1975 with a very simple file editor, whose function was to help us keep track of program entities and transformations, and a transform tool that applied the transformations within a file to the program entities in the file.

Our present programming environment is called the *Program Development System* (PDS). It is an integrated programming support environment with three major components: a software database, a user interface, and a collection of tools that can be called via the user interface to manipulate the software modules stored in the software database. We discuss these components in turn.

The Software Database

The elements of the software database are called *modules* and are containers for a collection of *program entities*. Each module has a name, a partition, a version number, a derivation number, and a derivation history. A module name is an identifier, and the partition, if any, is a list of identifiers and/or identifier pairs separated by *is*. The name-partition pair is an extended name in a multidimensional naming space that aids in creating names in a rapid-prototyping and custom-tailoring setting. Here are some examples

Foo
CodeGen (target is Apollo)
M (debug)
M (production)

Modules are either abstract or derived. *Abstract* modules are created by people using the so-called module editor, whereas *derived* modules are created by a tool from one or more *parent* modules. The derivation number of an abstract module is zero, and that of a derived module is the maximum derivation number of its parents plus one. The version number is essentially a time stamp and increases by one each time a module is modified (via the module editor if it is abstract, and via (re)derivation from its parent by some tool otherwise). The derivation history of an abstract module is null, and that of a derived module identifies the tool and parents that were involved in its derivation.

Each program entity within a module has a name and a set of attributes— essentially type-value-version triples. Early on we had only three types of attributes: definitions, transformations, and comments. One of our early evolutionary steps was to generalize the notion of attribute; the present PDS has some 25 distinct attribute types and the set is open-ended. An attribute (type) exists either because there is some tool that can produce it or some tool that can consume it. Attributes now include descriptors, data types, analogies, syntax specification, annotations (the results of analyzing some attribute), and so on. Each attribute bears a version number. When a new module is created from an old module by the module editor, those attributes added or edited receive new version numbers, while those unchanged bear their old version number. The version number of an abstract module is the maximum of the version numbers of the attributes of its entities. If a derivation tool is called to derive some module, it does this by first locating the previous result and then producing a new module whose version number is one greater than that of the previous result; it ascribes this new version number to each attribute it must derive anew (because of changes in the parents) and retains the old version number for each attribute that is unchanged (because the relevant attributes in the parent were unchanged). The derivation tools are actually incremental rederivation tools.

The User Interface

The user interface for the operational PDS essentially offers the user the ability to invoke the various tools, to monitor the progress as some tool does its job, to inspect the current directory of modules and their interrelationships, and to delete modules that are outdated.

The Tool Set

The tool set is open-ended and presently includes the following tools.

☐ *Module editor* permits the user to peruse the entities and attributes of some module and invoke one of several editors (text, structure, and so on) to create or edit some particular attributes.

☐ *Transform* derives a module by collecting a set of attributes and transforming them.

☐ *Merge* derives a module by merging selected parts of existing modules.

☐ *Analyze* derives a module that contains the results of analysis of some given module, citing undefined constructs in various attributes, and so on.

☐ *Package* derives a module in which the attributes are ordered so that an item is defined before use (as a prelude to loading for interpretive execution or for compilation).

☐ *Compile* derives a "load" module by compiling one or more subject modules.

☐ *Fix* provides a "quick fix" by editing one or more abstract entities and rederiving just those concrete entities that depend upon them. Use of this tool avoids the usual patching to repair bugs quickly.

☐ *Aggregate* derives a module that aggregates one or more modules to define a module set. Its major use is to do configuration management.

In addition, there are various utilities to deal with the software database. We commented earlier that the PDS was an *integrated* support environment. The sense in which it is integrated is that there is a set of *policies* that each tool must adhere to. These include the following.

☐ *Version control*: Each tool is responsible for maintaining version control by ensuring that the version number of each attribute of a module derived correctly reflects the changes since the previous derivation.

☐ *Access control*: Each tool deals with the modules it uses or generates via utilities provided in the software database to ensure proper authorization, to maintain correct derivation histories, and the like.

☐ *Common representation*: A small set of representations is provided for modules and attributes contained therein, and a collection of utilities is provided to deal with these. It is possible that some new tool would require the introduction of a new representation tailored to its use, but the general principle is that tools deal with the representations provided.

13.6 CONCLUSIONS AND FUTURE DIRECTIONS

Our experience to date using the methodology we have described to do rapid prototyping and custom tailoring of program families by the reuse of abstract programming has given us considerable confidence in this methodology as a variable alternative to the conventional programming paradigm. We do not propose, however, that at this point we have a "package" ready for widespread use. Rather, we believe that we have concluded a feasibility demonstration and that we have mapped out a course of action that will result in a viable methodology and supporting environment in a few years' time.

Several of the threads that we are following are worth a brief comment.

Documentation.   Our methodology and its supporting systems are poorly documented. We have recently mounted a significant effort to produce the kinds of primers, examples, and the like that will permit the use of the methodology on other than an "apprentice" basis. However, even with excellent documentation of the system, there would still remain the question of teaching people how to develop an abstract program, how to stage the refinements, and so on. It may take a good deal of trial and error before we can produce a guide to abstract programming that will enable *anyone* to use our methodology and system.

A Life Cycle Support System.   We are presently in the early stages of developing a successor to the PDS. Termed LISUS (for LIfe cycle SUpport System), it will augment the PDS to deal with multiple simultaneous users, and it will eventually provide facilities that let us experiment with knowledge-based mechanisms that coordinate ongoing activities and assist in overall project management. In addition, we are replacing the present user interface that uses "dumb" terminals with a new user interface that uses high-resolution graphics terminals, multiple windows, pointing devices, menu-driven interaction, and so on.

Improved Compilation Facilities.   There is a problem with our methodology in terms of getting production quality products if we use conventional compiling techniques. This arises because the concrete programs we produce tend to have large numbers of small and/or sparsely used procedures. The overhead with conventional compilers that use standard calling sequences (which are expensive if the called procedure is small) is too high. Thus we are designing a new compiler that will do quite sophisticated interprocedural analysis in order to generate code tailored to particular uses of procedures and thereby significantly reduce (or eliminate) procedure call overhead.

A Wide-Spectrum Language.   As we noted earlier, we rejected the idea of a fixed VHLL as the language for writing abstract programs.   At the same time we do recognize that the base language we presently use to host high-level constructs and notations would be easier to use if it did provide a collection of very high-level facilities—sets, tuples, bags, and so on—that could be used, say, early on in developing a prototype, when the efficiency of their implementation was not a foremost concern. Our strategy is to develop a two-level language containing a very high-level (VHL) component plus a reasonably conventional base-level component. The whole will enjoy formal semantics and will be interpretable; only the base-level component will be compilable, so that at some point it will be necessary to refine the VHL constructs into equivalent base-level constructs. Even with the VHL constructs available, we will still permit the user to define new constructs and notations that he feels are particularly germane to the problem at hand.

Program analysis. We continue to seek program analysis tools that can do deep analysis of programs and enable other tools to "reason" about various aspects of a program (for example, to find faults, validate the applicability of a transformation, ensure absence of unwanted side effects, and so on). Given our methodology, a concomitant problem is to "extend" the analysis to new high-level constructs introduced by the programmer. It is our hope that some variant of the analogy mechanism now used to "explain" high-level constructs to the present (simple) analyzer can be developed to "explain" them to a more sophisticated analyzer.

About the Author

Thomas E. Cheatham, Jr. received B.S. and M.S. degrees in mathematics from Purdue University, West Lafayette, Indiana, in 1951 and 1953, respectively.

Since 1969 he has been Gordon McKay Professor of Computer Science and director of the Center for Research in Computing Technology at Harvard University, Cambridge, MA. As of 1981 he has been chairman of the board of Software Options, Inc., Cambridge, Massachusetts. His current research interests include symbolic evaluation of programs, mechanical theorem proving for program verification, and the construction of systems for program development and maintenance.

Professor Cheatham is a fellow of the American Academy of Arts and Sciences and a member of Sigma Xi and the Association for Computing Machinery.

References

Balzer, R. M., *et al.* Operational specification as the basis for rapid prototyping. Inform. Sci. Inst., Univ. Southern California, Marina del Rey, 1981.

Cheatham, T. E.; G. H. Holloway; and J. Townley. Symbolic evaluation and the analysis of programs. *IEEE Trans. Software Eng.*, vol. SE-5, pp. 301–317, 1979.

———. Program refinement by transformation. In *Proc. 5th IEEE Int. Conf. Software Eng.*, San Diego, Calif., 1981.

Dewar, R. B. K., *et al.* Higher level languages: Introduction to the use of the set-theoretic programming languages—SETL. Courant Inst. Math. Sci., Dep. Comput. Sci., New York University, New York, N.Y., 1981.

Green, C., *et al*. Research on knowledge-based programming and algorithm design—1981. Kestrel Inst., Palo Alto, Calif., 1981.

Holloway, G. H.; W. R. Bush; and G. H. Mealy. Abstract model of MSG: First phase on an experiment in software development. Center Res. Comput. Technol., Harvard Univ., Cambridge, Mass., tech. rep. 25–78, 1978.

Massachusetts Computer Associates, Inc. MSG design specification. In *Third Semi-Annual Technical Report for the National Software Works*. Wakefield, Mass.: Massachusetts Comput. Assoc., Inc., 1977.

CHAPTER 14

REUSE IN THE CONTEXT OF A TRANSFORMATION-BASED METHODOLOGY

MARTIN S. FEATHER
USC/Information Sciences Institute

14.1 A DEVELOPMENT METHODOLOGY

At ISI we are researching a methodology for assisting software development. It is our firm belief that to make significant progress in this direction we must formalize, record, and manipulate the development process itself. We advocate a methodology of constructing a formal specification expressing desired (functional) behavior and then transforming this into an efficient implementation while preserving functionality.

What differentiates our research from that of others pursuing this trans-formational approach is the nature of our specification language. It has been designed to minimize the distance between informal conceptualizations and formal specifications of tasks. The consequent richness of our specification

From *ITT Proceedings of the Workshop on Reusability in Programming*, Newport, R.I., 1983. Reprinted with permission of the author.

language puts automatic compilation into tolerably efficient programs beyond our present capability (yet to restrict ourselves to only those constructs that we can presently compile would be a grave mistake for any specification language). Hence the transformation from specification to implementation must rely upon human guidance (although it can and should benefit from machine assistance to record and perform the detailed steps).

Within this methodology reuse may occur at two levels:

☐ Reuse at the specification level: Our specification language comprises a small set of powerful constructs, which are used in stylistically recurring ways in specifying a broad range of tasks. Reuse also occurs when a specification is modified, either to make changes inspired by feedback from the implementation or to adapt an existing specification to a similar task.

☐ Reuse at the transformational development level—when instances of the high-level specification constructs have to be transformed into efficient (implementation) constructs: Stylistically similar uses of such constructs involve the same issues in selecting appropriate implementations and in applying transformations to the specifications. When a specification is modified, major portions of the transformational development of the unmodified specification might be reusable in transforming the modified specification.

We stress the importance of performing modification and maintenance on a specification, and then redeveloping the implementation from that, as opposed to tinkering with the implementation directly.

14.2 SPECIFICATION LANGUAGE

Our specification language, Gist, is motivated by the power of natural language descriptions; Gist attempts to capture this power in formal language constructs. Briefly, these capabilities are as follows:

☐ a relational and associative model of data, which captures the logical structure without imposing an access regime;

☐ implicit information, which allows for data to be defined implicitly in terms of other data;

☐ historical reference, the ability to extract information from past states of the process;

☐ constraints, which express restrictions on system behavior via global declarations and pre- or postconditions to statements;

☐ demons, which are constructs for performing a computation whenever some condition occurs; and

☐ closed system specification, the ability to specify a component of a composite system by describing the behaviors required of the entire system and of the other components and thus implicitly defining the behavior required of the component (such components are often referred to as embedded systems).

Gist's constructs encourage a descriptive style of specification, in which desired properties are stated directly (as opposed to a prescriptive style, in which it must be inferred that the specification in fact exhibits these properties). Also, the constructs admit localized expression of desired properties (e.g., an invariant that relates two values can be stated directly; in contrast, a less expressive language or an efficient implementation might require that such an invariant be maintained by pieces of code spread throughout the program).

These aspects make Gist supportive of both initial specification and later modifications to the specification. Gist specifications tend to be *robust* in the sense that a conceptually small modification can often be realized as a small change to the specification. The descriptive and localized aspects make it easy to identify the impact of the modifications on the specification, and easy to perform the appropriate adjustments. In contrast, a less expressive specification language would force the mental conversion of changes at the conceptual level into changes at a lower, more implementation-oriented level. This would be harder (requiring more mental effort with less opportunity for machine support—hence being more error prone) and it would fail to record some of the development process. With less documentation, the process would be less comprehensible, and there would be less support for future change.

14.3 DEVELOPMENT OF IMPLEMENTATION

In the development of an implementation from a Gist specification, Gist's high-level constructs must be eliminated, since their success in the realm of specification is at the expense of efficient use of data representations and algorithms. We perform such development by program *transformation*.

There are two ways we could go about eliminating high-level constructs. One approach is to naively translate all high-level constructs into a kernel of the language (some subset with sufficient expressive power) and thereafter manipulate specifications in that kernel to obtain efficient forms. The other approach is to achieve most of the efficiency by manipulating the high-level constructs into a form (still using high-level constructs) that can be translated directly into efficient lower-level constructs without significant further manipulation. The former approach has the advantage of requiring far fewer transformations, but the disadvantage of discarding clues provided by those expressive high-level constructs. We have chosen to follow the latter approach, reasoning that the extra effort of providing many transformations among high-level constructs will be recouped by easing the transformation process. (This decision parallels other transformation research.)

For each type of construct, our research has been aimed at accumulating the following:

☐ Implementation options: the range of commonly available options for converting an instance of a construct into a more efficient expression of the same behavior, typically in terms of lower-level constructs.

☐ Selection criteria: means for selecting among several implementation options applicable to the same instance.

☐ Mappings: transformations that convert the construct into a lower-level (or alternate) form.

For example, suppose a specification contains a reference to the time-ordered sequence of objects that satisfy some given predicate. One implementation option is to continually maintain that sequence, appending new objects as they come to satisfy the predicate, so that the reference becomes a simple access of that sequence. An alternative would be to retain with each object the information of when it satisfied the predicate and to replace the reference with the appropriate search for, and ordering of, those objects. Selection criteria would compare the cost of continually maintaining the sequence (in the first option) as compared to maintaining the information with objects and performing the more elaborate computation (in the second option). Mappings would provide the transformations for each of these options into lower-level code.

14.4 AN EXAMPLE DOMAIN

We will use examples drawn from the domain of a single problem to illustrate our approach. The problem is to represent a routing system for distributing packages into destination bins. This problem is typical of real-world process control applications. Hommel's study of various programming methodologies used this problem as the comparative example [Hommel, 1980]. For conciseness we consider here a simplified version of the router; our specification of the complete problem can be found in [London and Feather, 1982].

Figure 14.1 illustrates the routing network. It takes the form of a binary tree, whose root is the source station (from which packages are fed one at a time into the network), whose internal nodes are switches, and whose terminal nodes are the destination bins.

Packages appear at the source station, with their destinations set to be one of the bins. No more than one package is at the source station at once.

Packages progress through the network, from the source, through switches, and ultimately into bins. Each switch a package passes through directs the

FIGURE 14.1
THE PACKAGE ROUTER

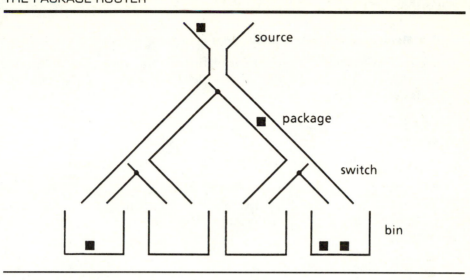

package to the next location according to the switch's current setting. No switch ever holds more than one package at once. A switch setting must not be changed while there is a package in that switch.

The task is to control the setting of switches to direct packages to their correct destination bins. Only a limited amount of information is available to the package router to effect the desired behavior: The presence and destination of a package at the source can be determined, and sensors, placed on the exits of the source and all switches, can detect the passage of packages (but not their identity or destination).

14.5 GIST'S CONSTRUCTS

In this section we focus on Gist's expressive constructs to see how they facilitate reuse of specifications and transformations. The Gist specification of the simplified package router is given in Appendix A, along with some examples of changes to the specification.

In this section, for each of Gist's major constructs, we

☐ informally describe the semantics of the construct, with illustrations from the package router domain;

☐ describe the freedoms the construct provides for specification;

☐ discuss how the construct supports modifications; and

☐ briefly describe some alternative mappings for the construct, together with criteria for choosing among these alternatives.

Throughout these discussions, we give illustrations in terms of the package router described in the previous section.

14.5.1 Relational and Associative Model of Information

We begin the discussion of Gist's major features by focusing on its underlying data model. Information in Gist is modeled simply by typed objects and relations among them.

> The package router domain involves objects of types package, location, switch, and so on. Type hierarchies are possible; for example, a location is always a switch, a bin, or the source.

> The position of a package is modeled by relating a package to its location; similarly, the source is related to the switch to which it feeds packages. Each switch is related to the location to which it is currently set to feed packages.

The collection of objects and relations at any time during the interpretation of a specification comprises what we call a *state*. Change in the domain is modeled by the creation and destruction of objects and by the insertion and deletion of relations. Each change is a transition from the current state into a new state. Multiple changes may occur simultaneously in a single transition from one state to the next.

> The appearance of a package at the source is modeled by creating a new object of type package and setting its position relation to be the source and its destination to be any bin.

> Altering the setting of a switch is modeled by changing the switch-setting relation, that is, deleting the relationship between switch and old setting, and inserting the relationship between switch and new setting.

Specification Freedom.   The relational model of information permits the specifier to use a descriptive reference to an object.

> The bin that is the destination of this package.

> The location into which this switch is set to direct packages.

The relational data model is a very general data representation. The specifier need not be concerned about data access paths, for instance, because any description of an object may be used as a reference to that object. Relations may be used in descriptions of any of the objects that participate in the relationships. In database terminology, this means that the relationships are fully associative (or, equivalently, that the database is fully inverted).

The position relation of a package may be used to refer to the location of a given package; conversely, it may be used to refer to the package (if any) positioned at a given location.

Specification Reuse.   The uniformity of the relational model and the freedom from representation concerns that it provides facilitate the expression of changed specifications.

A refinement to the router to check that packages have sufficient postage stamps to pay for delivery to their respective destinations involves extra information—stamp values on packages and delivery costs for destinations. This extra information is modeled by relating a stamp value with packages and a delivery cost with bins, and introducing the computation of whether a package's stamp value is at least as great as its destination's delivery cost.

Mappings.   The most general way to implement information storage is to support an associative relational database and leave the specification's insertions and retrievals of information unchanged. In most cases, however, a specification does not indiscriminately insert and retrieve data; rather, it displays predictable data access patterns. These can be mapped into appropriate data structures (arrays, hash tables, etc.) to conserve space and time.

If the packages' destination relations are accessed in one direction only, by asking for the bin that is the destination of a package, then it might be efficient to store the destination information as a field of a record structure associated with each package.

Concerns for efficiency of time and space dictate the selection of data structures. Probabilistic expectations of frequency of use are not explicitly described in Gist specifications, but clearly such information will be of importance in making this selection.

Many of the issues relating to the relational data model are similar to those investigated by the SETL group [Dewar *et al.,* 1979; Schonberg *et al.,* 1981] by Rovner [1978], Low [1976], and Barstow [1979], and more recently by the Kestrel group [Smith *et al.,* 1985].

14.5.2 Implicit Information

It is convenient to be able to implicitly define a relation in terms of other data. Within Gist, we need state only the invariant that relates the values of the implicit relationship with other data. That implicitly defined relationship may be queried as any other relationship, and by definition its values will be those that satisfy the invariant.

A switch may be said to be "empty" if there is no package positioned in the switch.

A location may be said to be "somewhere-below" a second location if it is directly below that second location, or is directly below some third location that is in turn *somewhere-below* the second location (i.e., *somewhere-below* is the transitive closure of directly below).

Specification Freedom. The power of this construct comes from the ability to state the invariant in a single place (i.e., this construct exhibits the quality of *locality*). As with nonimplicit relations (whose values are determined by explicit statements in the specification), query of implicit relations is fully associative.

The implicitly defined *somewhere-below* relation may be accessed in either direction; that is, given a location, the relation may be accessed to find either the locations that are *somewhere-below* it or the locations to which the given location is *somewhere-below*.

Specification Reuse. Implicit relations are robust in the face of specification change, both because of their localized nature and because they are defined in terms of the information upon which they depend (i.e., they have the descriptive quality).

Should the structure of the package router network be extended by addition of more switches and bins, the invariants that define the relations *empty* and *somewhere-below* will continue to be valid.

An implicit relation can be redefined by simply changing its invariant.

Mappings. Since no construct corresponding to implicit relations is likely to be available in an implementation language,[1] we must map the implicit relation into explicit data structures and support mechanisms scattered throughout the program. We have a wide range of choices as to how we might do this mapping.

At one extreme, we might simply unfold the invariant that defines the relation's values at each place where a reference to the relation is made. Having done this, we may completely discard the relation and its invariant.

Wherever the specification makes reference to the *empty* relation on a switch, unfold the definition of *empty* to leave in its place an explicit search

---

[1]Many of the Artificial Intelligence programming languages do provide facilities for implementing implicit relations in terms of inference processes. For example, an implementation might be provided in CONNIVER [McDermott and Sussman, 1974] in terms of IF-ADDED or IF-NEEDED methods. However, AI programming languages in which these facilities are present typically do not provide for efficient execution, nor do these facilities provide the precise semantics desired without the inclusion of satisfactory "truth maintenance" capabilities [Doyle, 1979; London, 1978].

through all the packages to determine whether any of them are located at the switch.

This approach is a kind of backward inference, where computation is performed on demand and at the site of the need.

At the other extreme we might retain the relation, but distribute throughout the program the code necessary to explicitly maintain the invariant between the implicit information and the information upon which it depends.

To maintain the relation *empty*, introduce explicit storage (in the form of a nonimplicit relation) to represent this information, and introduce the appropriate maintenance code in the specification wherever packages' positions might change (more precisely, at the places where a package may become positioned at, or cease being positioned at, switches).

This approach is a kind of forward inference, where computation is performed whenever a modification to a relevant predicate occurs and at the site of the change. This mapping must be capable of

1. determining all those locations in the specification at which the value of an implicit relation could possibly be changed, and
2. inserting code to do the recalculation at those locations.

The latter capability can be achieved by either recomputing the implicit relation from scratch or incrementally changing its present value.

To maintain the time-ordered sequence of packages that have entered a bin, when a package enters the bin, concatenate that package onto the end of the maintained sequence.

This is an example of a general technique we call *incremental maintenance*, and is derived from the work of other researchers in set theoretic settings, particularly Paige and Schwartz [1977], who call the technique *formal differentiation*, and Earley [1976], who calls it *iterator inversion*.

The choices among the implementation alternatives involve tradeoffs between storage and computation in the resulting program. Completely unfolding the invariant puts the burden on computation at time of query, whereas maintaining an implicit relation makes for simple queries, but involves storing the relation and updating its stored values whenever they change.

14.5.3 Historical Reference

Historical reference in Gist specifications provides the ability to extract information from any preceding state in the computation history.

Has this package ever been at that switch?
What was the most recent package to have been in this switch?
Was the bin empty when the package entered the network?

Note that the past can only be queried, not changed.

Specification Freedom.   Historical reference allows the specifier to easily and unambiguously describe what information is needed from earlier states without concern for the details of how it might be made available (i.e., like implicit information, this construct has the descriptive quality). Reference to the past has been studied in the database world, where the freedom has been called *memory independence,* and temporal logic has been applied to formally investigate the matter (see, e.g., [Sernadas, 1980]). Implicit relations and historical reference may be mixed, by using implicit relations in expressing a historical reference, and by using historical reference in defining an implicit relation.

Historical reference: "Was this switch ever 'empty'?"
Implicit relation definition: "The sequence of packages to have been located at the source, in their order of appearance there."

This exemplifies one of Gist's strengths, the *orthogonality* of the constructs, that is, their ability to be successfully used in combination.

Specification Reuse.   Historical reference, like implicit relations, is robust as a consequence of its descriptive nature. In this case, the robustness is in the face of modifications that result in changed histories.

Should the topology of the network be modified, say to feed the output of several switches into the same bin, then the descriptive historical reference "the sequence of packages to have reached the bin in their order of arrival" will continue to be valid.

Mappings.   Two generally applicable methods exist for mapping historical reference into a reasonable implementation. These are:

1. Save the information desired in the earlier state, then modify the historical reference to extract it from the saved information.
2. Modify the historical reference to rederive the desired information from the current state.

To use the first method, it is necessary to introduce and maintain auxiliary data structures to store information that might be referenced in a later state, and to modify the historical references to extract the desired information from those introduced structures when needed. The desire for economy of storage in an implementation encourages the implementor to determine just what information need be preserved, to seek a compact representation facilitating both storage and retrieval, and to discard the information once it is no longer useful.

> To be prepared to answer the query, "What was the destination of the last package to have passed through this switch?" we could choose to remember the time-ordered sequence of packages to have been in the switch, or more efficiently, to remember only the destination of the immediately preceding package. The latter case would require storage space for the identity of only a single bin; upon arrival of a new package, the identity of its destination would be remembered in that space, overwriting the old information.

The second method for implementing historical reference is to rederive the desired information in terms of information available in the current state (without having to retain extra information from past states).

> The sequence of switches through which a package has already passed can be determined by tracing back the sequence of switches from that package's current position to the source of the router.

We suspect that complete rederivation is rarely an available option; the information desired is often not derivable from current available information. Rather, some mixture of remembered information and rederivation will usually be necessary. When alternative mixes are possible, they present the classic store/recompute tradeoffs. An implementor must compare the cost of the derivation with the cost of storage of information from past states.

Idiomatic Uses of Historical Reference. Certain patterns of historical reference recur frequently in Gist specifications, for example, evaluating *<expression>* as of *<event>* (as in "What was the setting of the switch at the time the package entered the network?"). For an idiom like this we can construct special-purpose mappings,[2] reducing the effort that would be required during implementation development if a general-purpose mapping technique were applied. A general-purpose mapping technique would require further simplifications to tailor the result for the special case.

Other idioms that we deal with include

☐ the latest object to satisfy a given predicate,

☐ a sequence of objects ordered by their time of creation or the time at which they satisfied a given predicate, and

☐ whether event 1 took place before event 2.

---

[2]This idiom is mapped into an explicit relation between the objects that parameterize the event and the expression, together with code to maintain this relation, namely to insert the relation whenever the event occurs and there exists an object denoted by the *<expression>*.

14.5.4 Nondeterminism and Constraints

Nondeterminism within Gist arises in two ways: when use is made of a descriptive reference that denotes more than one object,

> Set the package's destination to be any bin.

or when some specifically nondeterministic control structure is used.

> Choose between "Set switch" and "Move package."

A nondeterministic Gist specification denotes a set of behaviors; a valid implementation must exhibit those, or some (nonempty!) subset[3] of those behaviors.

Constraints within Gist provide a means of stating integrity conditions that must always remain satisfied.

> No more than one package can be in a switch at once.
> A switch must be empty in order to change its setting.
> A package must never reach a bin other than its destination.

Within Gist, constraints are more than merely redundant checks that the specification always generates valid behaviors; they serve to *rule out* those behaviors that would be invalid.

> The nondeterminism of switch setting, in conjunction with the constraint on packages reaching correct bins, denotes only behaviors that route the packages to their proper destination bins.

Specification Freedom.   The constructs described in earlier sections provided freedoms related to information; nondeterminism and constraints provide freedoms related to control.

Where there are several equally acceptable alternatives in the resolution of a data reference or a control structure choice, nondeterminism makes it easy to express them all. Where there are integrity conditions that must be satisfied, constraints provide a concise (i.e., localized) means of stating them. Such integrity conditions may serve as descriptions of the environment in which the portion to be implemented is to operate (e.g., the limitation on there being no more than one package in any switch at once is a property of the physical routing mechanism). Other integrity conditions serve as require-

---

[3]That is, there may be behaviors denoted by the specification not displayed by the implementation. Conversely, however, any behavior displayed by the implementation must be one of the behaviors denoted by the specification.

ments on the behavior of the entire system, implying that the implementation must cooperate with the environment so as to satisfy those conditions (e.g., that packages not reach the wrong bins).

The conjunction of nondeterminism and constraints proves to be an extremely powerful specification technique; a specification denotes those and only those behaviors that do not violate constraints. In contrast, an implementation is characterized by a cunning encoding guaranteed to result in only valid behaviors.

Specification Reuse.   Constraints provide robustness because by their very nature they guarantee that all the behaviors (old or new) denoted by a changed specification must abide by all the constraints that remain in, or have been added to, the specification.

> The constraint that a switch be empty in order to change its setting assures us that no matter how the topology of the network might be modified, no new behavior will result in which a switch setting changes while some package is present in that switch.

Constraints themselves are readily modified to reflect changing criteria.

> To further restrict when a switch setting may be changed, say to only those occasions when both the switch and its preceding location (switch or source that feeds into the switch) are empty, we simply modify the constraint accordingly—a single modification at only one place in the specification.

Mapping Away Constraints and Nondeterminism.   A general mapping technique to eliminate constraints is to make each nondeterministic activity into a choice point and to unfold global constraints so as to provide tests at all points in the program where the constraint might possibly be violated. When a violation is detected, a "failure" results; this causes backtracking to the most recent choice point with an alternative choice.

> To place eight queens on a chess board under the constraint that no queen may attack any other queen, place all the queens on the board simultaneously (64^8 nondeterministic choices!) and then check to see whether the no-capture constraint is violated—if so, try the next choice of placements.

This mapping requires

1. determining all locations in the specification at which the constraint—a predicate—could possibly be false, and
2. inserting code at those points to backtrack if it is false.

Our research suggests that it is possible to intermix Gist's nondeterminism and constraints with explicit backtracking, permitting the incremental mapping of individual nondeterministic choice points and of the constraints that impinge upon them (as opposed to having to map away all the nondeterminism and constraints at once). The task of building the backtracking mechanism itself is trivial if our intended target language supports backtracking (as does, for example, PROLOG [Clocksin and Mellish, 1981]).

Backtracking, however, presupposes the ability to undo actions that have been executed since the last choice point. Since this is often not possible, strict backtracking is not always an option for mapping to an implementation of nondeterminism.

> In controlling the switches in the routing network, we are constrained to ensure that the packages do not reach wrong destinations. Backtracking presupposes that we have the ability to return the packages to the switching points after an error is detected, and then send them in different directions. Obviously, in the case of a package router whose package movement mechanism is not under our control, this is not an available option.

An alternative technique to mapping nondeterminism into backtracking is a *predictive* solution. Here the global constraints are unfolded into *point constraints* rather than into calls on a backtracking failure mechanism. These point constraints are then pushed back to be incorporated into the choice points, becoming filters that propose only those choices that guarantee no constraints will be violated. Pushing a point constraint backwards over a statement is a matter of reformulating the constraint into the weakest precondition to that statement that guarantees execution of the statement will not violate the constraint. When the constraint is pushed all the way back to a choice point, it is incorporated as a filter on the choices.

> When choosing how to set an empty switch, if there is a package approaching from above, set the switch to lead toward that package's destination.

Compromise between these two extremes is possible; we may employ a backtracking algorithm, but push some of the unfolded constraints into the choice generators.

> In the eight-queens problem, split the nondeterminism into several successive choices (place the first queen, place the second queen and check for capture, etc.), and incorporate some of the no-capture constraint into the placement (by not attempting to place a subsequent queen on a row already occupied by a queen). See [Balzer, 1981] for a detailed development illustrating this.

The choice between a backtracking implementation and a predictive implementation is determined very much by the domain of the specification. The control the implementation portion may exert, the amount of information available for making decisions, and the desired amount of precomputation all affect the choice of algorithm.

14.5.5 Demons

Demons are Gist's mechanism for data-directed invocation of processes. A demon has two components: a predicate serving as its trigger and a statement. Whenever a demon's trigger predicate is true, its statement is begun.

> Whenever a package reaches a bin, send a signal.

Specification Freedom. Demons are convenient for stating that some computation should begin whenever some condition occurs. To get the same effect without the demon construct we would have to insert tests into all the places where the condition could possibly become true, causing the computation to be performed if the test is positive. Since the demon's trigger is a predicate, it may, of course, be stated using implicit and historical information; thus the demon construct is enhanced by the power of those other constructs.

Specification Reuse. The descriptive nature of demons—that is, the description of the condition on which some activity is to be started—provides robustness. Should modifications to the specification change the behaviors that may occur, the demons will continue to be triggered when and only when their triggering conditions are met.

> Should the topology of the router network be modified so that several switches lead to the same output bin (i.e., the network is no longer a tree), then the demon that signals arrivals of packages at that bin will continue to do its signaling regardless of which switch they happen to emerge from.

Mapping Away Demons. Mapping away a demon involves identifying all places in the program where the demon's trigger predicate could possibly be true, and then inserting code at those places to evaluate that predicate and perform the demon's response when necessary.

> To map away a demon that sends a signal every time a package reaches a bin, introduce code into the places where package movement occurs to check to see whether that package has moved into a bin; in such a case, perform the signaling.

14.5.6 Closed System Style

For specification purposes it is convenient to describe the behavior required of an entire system and to build that description in terms of information throughout the system. How that entire system is to be decomposed into components, the restrictions on the control that components may exert over one another, and the access that components may have to each other's information may be described separately from the overall system behavior description.

> In the package router, we describe the behavior required of the overall system, namely the routing of packages. This description is expressed in terms of package positions and destinations. Separately, we describe how the system comprises several components:
>
> ☐ a physical routing mechanism (the binary tree of source, switches, and bins),
> ☐ a mechanism to move packages,
> ☐ the appearance of packages at the source to be routed, and
> ☐ the switch controller, which changes switch settings.
>
> Our development task is to implement the switch controller's interaction with the other components in such a way as to cause the desired routing of packages. The switch controller has only limited control of and access to the other components. The only occasion upon which the controller mechanism may read the destination of a package is when that package is at the source. The only information available to the controller about packages in the router is the indication of passage of individual packages past sensors (which includes neither the identity nor the destination of those packages).

Specification Freedom.   Closed system description provides the freedom to describe the behavior required of the whole system and to give this description in terms of system-wide information. The decomposition of the system into components is specified separately. The behaviors of these components are thus implicitly defined to be those that in conjunction will achieve the required system-wide behavior while complying with the limitations on control and information passing between components. The developer may choose any of these implicitly defined behaviors for the components to be implemented.

Specification Reuse.   Since system-wide behavior is specified directly, modifications to that behavior are easy to incorporate. Modifications to the environment (within which the implemented portion resides) may also be readily expressed while the system-wide specification of required behavior remains unchanged.

If the movement mechanism is adjusted to move packages at constant speeds, this extra property may simply be added to the specification of the environment. The implementor might be able to take advantage of this extra information in rederiving an implementation (e.g., one could find the earliest package to have entered the network but not yet reached its bin by simply looking for the package lowest in the network of switches).

Having the decomposition stated separately from system behavior—indeed, having it explicitly stated at all—supports modifications to the decomposition.

If the sensors throughout the package router network are enhanced to report not only the passage of a package, but also the destination of the passing package, then this enhancement may be incorporated into the specification of the decomposition, permitting the implementor of the router mechanism to make use of the extra information (which should result in a reduction in the amount of storage space required by the implementation).

Mapping Away Reliance on System-wide Control and Information. The general problem of mapping away reliance on system-wide information is quite difficult. Mostow calls this aspect of development *operationalization,* and has investigated heuristic means for dealing with it [Mostow, 1981].

For some simple cases of reliance on system-wide information, techniques similar to those used for mapping away historical references might prove appropriate—introduce and maintain auxiliary data structures to store information when it is made available in order to be able to supply it when it is needed, or look for ways to derive the required information from other information that is available.

14.6 SUMMARY AND FUTURE WORK

Gist's combination of constructs makes for a good specification language, and we anticipate that it will support reuse at the specification level. We attribute Gist's success to its purposeful design—modeled on the power of natural language descriptions, brought together into a coherent formal framework.

The development methodology we advocate is one of transformation of specifications to obtain implementations. The success or failure of this methodology for supporting reuse will rest upon our ability to reperform the transformational development upon a modified specification. This is a crucial outstanding research issue.

It has been recognized that transformational developments must be reusable objects in their own right, so that they may be appropriately modified to be applied to modified specifications [Darlington and Feather, 1980]. The language for recording such developments must be rich enough to capture the implementor's goal structure, motivations, and design decisions, [Sintzoff, 1980; Wile, 1983]. The system that applies such developments must deal with this goal structure, methods for achieving goals, and selection criteria for choosing among competing methods. For the foreseeable future, such systems will not be fully automatic and so must rely upon interaction with a skilled implementor. See [Fickas, 1982] for a first cut at such a system.

Acknowledgments

This research was supported by Defense Advanced Research Projects Agency contract MDA 903 81 C 0335. Views and conclusions contained in this document are those of the author and should not be interpreted as representing the official opinion or policy of DARPA, the U.S. Government, or any other person or agency connected with them. I would like to thank the other members (past and present) of the ISI Transformational Implementation group: Bob Balzer, Don Cohen, Steve Fickas, Neil Goldman, Lewis Johnson, Phil London, Jack Mostow, Bill Swartout, Dave Wile, and Kai Yue.

Appendix: Gist Specifications

Here we present some actual Gist specifications to illustrate the nature of our formal representations.

The Simplified Package Router

```
{ static singleton type source with
  { static singleton relation Source-outlet(switch) }
```

The source, of which there is precisely one instance, has its own static relation called *Source-outlet,* which relates it to (precisely one) switch.

```
demon Create-package
  when true
    do choose { [ ] , create package with { Position := (the source),
                                             Destination := (any bin) } }
```

The source has a demon which, in every state, chooses between doing nothing, [ ], and creating a package whose *Position* relation is set to the source and whose *Destination* relation is set to some (nondeterministically chosen) bin.

```
    }

    static type switch with
    { static relation Switch-outlets( s-o | switch union bin )

        singleton relation Switch-setting( s-s | switch union bin)

        constraint (the switch):Switch-setting =
            (any location || (the switch):Switch-outlets = location))
```

Each switch has a *Switch-outlets* relation (the next locations to which the switch may be set to direct packages) and a *Switch-setting* relation, constrained to be one of its *Switch-outlets*.

```
    }

    static type bin

    static type location supertype of (source union switch union bin) with
    { implicit relation Next-location(next | location)
        iff (location = (the source) and next = location:Source-outlet) or
            (location = (a switch)   and next = location:Switch-setting)
```

Type location is either the source, a switch, or a bin. A location may be related to another location via its *Next-location* relation; if it is the source, that next location will be the source outlet; if it is a switch, that next location will be the current setting of the switch (which may change); if it is a bin, it doesn't have a next location.

```
    type package with
    { singleton relation Position(location),
      static singleton relation Destination(bin) }
```

Each package has a *Position* relation relating it to a single location, and a static *Destination* relation relating it to a single bin.

```
    constraint count(any package || package:Position=(the source)) =< 1 and
             all switch || count(any package || package:Position = switch) =< 1
```

At most one package may be positioned at the source, and, for every switch, at most one package may be positioned at that switch.

```
    demon SET-SWITCH[switch]
      when true
      do choose { [ ] ,
                  precondition Empty(switch) to
                      update switch:Switch-setting to switch:Switch-outlets }
```

In every state, every switch nondeterministically does nothing, or, provided it is empty, updates its setting to any one of its outlets.

```
implicit relation Empty(location)
  iff not exists package || package:Position = location

demon Move-Package(package)
  when true
  do choose { [ ] , update package:Position to
                      package:Position:Next-location }
```

In every state, every package is either left unmoved or moved to the next location from its current position.

```
constraint all p|package ||
  ( p:Position = (a bin) => p:Position = p:Destination )
```

No package may reach a bin other than its destination.

```
}
```

The following information is available to the router mechanism:

```
{ implicit relation Destination-of-package-at-source(bin)
    iff exists package || package:Position = (the source) and
                          package:Destination = bin

  implicit relation Package-has-reached-location(location)
    iff exists package || start package:Position = location
}
```

Examples of Modifications to the Specification

Shown here are some of the hypothetical modifications to the router specification described in Section 14.5.

Refining the router to compute whether packages have sufficient postage stamps to pay for delivery to their respective destinations:

```
type package with
{ singleton relation Position(location),
  static singleton relation Destination(bin),
  static singleton relation Postage(number) }
...
  static type bin with
{ static singleton relation Delivery-cost(number) }
```

. . .

```
implicit relation Underpaid-Packages(package)
  iff package:Postage < package:Destination:Delivery-cost
```

Whenever a package reaches a bin, send a signal:

```
demon Package-reached-bin(bin)
  when exists package || start package:Position = bin
  do Send-signal[ ]
```

Example of Part of the Implementation of the Specification

In an implementation of the router that uses only the available information, we would have to keep track of the destination bins of packages that are within the router. We add a relation *Destination* on locations to hold this information, and we maintain *Destination* by watching for the arrival of a package at a location; if the location is the source, it is a new package, and its destination is queried and inserted into the *Destination* relation of the source; otherwise, the destination is removed from the previous location's *Destination* relation and added to the new location's *Destination* relation.

```
type location with { relation Destination(bin) ... }

demon Update-destinations(location)
  when Package-has-reached-location(location)
  do if location = the source
     then insert location:Destination = Destination-of-package-at-source(?)
     else atomic { delete location:Previous:Destination = bin ,
                   insert location:Destination = bin }
       where bin = location:Previous:Destination
```

We can use this to rewrite the SET-SWITCH demon to set the switch whenever the switch is empty, there is a package in the previous location to that switch, and the switch lies on the route toward the package's destination:

```
demon SET-SWITCH[switch]
  when Empty(switch) and
       (exists bin || switch:Previous:Destination = bin and
                      Somewhere-below(bin,switch)
  do update switch:Switch-setting to
            (the outlet || outlet = switch:Switch-outlet and
                           Somewhere-below(bin,switch-outlet))
```

presuming that *Somewhere-below* is defined to hold between a bin and a switch if and only if the switch is on route to the bin.

This last version is well on the way to an algorithm to explicitly set switches when necessary, rather than rely upon the interaction between nondeterminism and constraints to implicitly denote appropriate switch setting. Note that the expression of when and which way to set switches is quite intricate, reflecting the mix of a number of implementation concerns (notably realizing a predictive-style algorithm and using only available information).

References

Balzer, R. Transformational implementation: An example. *IEEE Transactions on Software Engineering* SE-7(1):3, 1981.

Barstow, D. R. *Knowledge-Based Program Construction*. New York: Elsevier North-Holland, 1979.

Clocksin, W. F., and Mellish, C. S. *Programming in Prolog*. Berlin: Springer-Verlag, 1981.

Darlington, J., and Feather, M. S. A transformational approach to program modification. Department of Computing and Control, Imperial College, London, technical report 80/3, 1980.

Dewar, R. B. K.; Grand, A.; Liu, S-C.; and Schwartz, J. T. Programming by refinement, as exemplified by the SETL representation sublanguage. *ACM Transactions on Programming Languages and Systems* 1(1):27, 1979.

Doyle, J. A truth maintenance system. *Artificial Intelligence* 12(3):231, 1979.

Earley, J. High level iterators and a method for automatically designing data structure representation. *Computer Languages* 1(4):321, 1976.

Fickas, S. F. Automating the transformational development of software. Ph.D. thesis, University of California, Irvine, 1982.

Hommel, G. Vergleich verschiedener Spezifikationsverfahren am Beispiel einer Paketverteilanlage. Kernforschungszentrum Karlsruhe, technical report, August 1980.

London, P. A dependency-based modelling mechanism for problem solving. *AFIPS Conference Proceedings* 47:263, 1978.

London, P. E., and Feather, M. S. Implementing specification freedoms. *Science of Computer Programming* 2:91, 1982.

Low, J. R. *Interdisciplinary Systems Research*. Vol. 16: *Automatic Coding: Choice of Data Structures*. Basel and Stuttgart: Birkhauser Verlag, 1976.

McDermott, D., and Sussman, G. J. The CONNIVER reference manual. MIT, technical report memo 259a, 1974.

Mostow, D. J. Mechanical transformation of task heuristics into operational procedures. Ph.D. thesis, Computer Science Department, Carnegie-Mellon University, 1981.

Paige, R., and Schwartz, J. Expression continuity and the formal differentiation of algorithms. *Proceedings, 4th ACM POPL Symposium,* Los Angeles, p. 58, 1977.

Rovner, P. Automatic representation selection for associative data structures. *Proceedings, AFIPS National Computer Conference,* Anaheim, California, p. 691, 1978.

Schonberg, E.; Schwartz, J. T.; and Sharir, M. An automatic technique for selection of data representations in SETL programs. *ACM Transactions on Programming Languages and Systems* 3(2):126, 1981.

Sernadas, A. Temporal aspects of logical procedure definition. *Information Systems* 5(3):167, 1980.

Sintzoff, M. Suggestions for composing and specifying program design decisions. *4th International Symposium on Programming*, Paris, 1980.

Smith, D. R.; Kotik, G. B.; and Westfold, S. J. Research on knowledge-based software environments at Kestrel Institute. *IEEE Transactions on Software Engineering* SE-11(11): 1278, 1985.

Wile, D. S. Program developments: Formal explanations of implementations. *Communications of the ACM* 26(11):902, 1983

CHAPTER # 15

ABSTRACT PROGRAMMING AND PROGRAM TRANSFORMATION— AN APPROACH TO REUSING PROGRAMS

JAMES M. BOYLE
Mathematics and Computer Science Division
Argonne National Laboratory

15.1 INTRODUCTION

"I'd like to use that linear algebra package Jean spent a year developing, but it won't work with my packed matrices."

"I need to move my program to the new vector supercomputer we just got. Do you think it will vectorize?"

This work was supported by the Applied Mathematical Sciences subprogram (KC-04-02) of the Office of Energy Research of the U.S. Department of Energy under Contract W-31-109-Eng-38.

"I need to use this Lisp program with one written in Fortran. How can I combine them?"

"I wrote this program using what I thought was a good data structure, but now I've discovered a better one. I'd like to use it, but I would have to change almost the *whole* program!"

"We just got a new parallel computer with 16 processors. Damn! I wish I had known about it when I wrote this program."

"This program doesn't run as fast as it should. If only I could tell the compiler how to optimize tensors. . . ."

Laments such as these point to the central dilemma of program reuse. Each of us would like to reuse programs to save time, money, and debugging—especially debugging! All too often, however, some seemingly minor glitch prevents us from doing so. Perhaps the program was written for the wrong machine, or in the wrong language, or for the wrong type of data. Perhaps the program (but not the algorithm it implements) is not efficient enough for the new application.

Is there an approach to program design and implementation that avoids these problems? I believe that abstract programming, supported by automated program transformation, is such an approach. To substantiate this claim, I discuss in this paper an "industrial strength" example of the use of abstract programming and program transformation.

The program that I have been able to reuse is a moderately large Lisp program comprising 3100 lines and 51 functions. It is highly recursive. It is thoroughly debugged and has been in use for several years. To be practical, it must run compiled, not interpreted. Using the methodology described here, I have been able to move it to many different machines, including shared-memory parallel machines.

How was I able to reuse this program? Three ingredients were essential:

☐ I had available a relatively high-level specification of the program, written in pure Lisp.

☐ I was able to devise a strategy for deriving efficient implementations of the pure Lisp program in a commonly available programming language.

☐ I had available an automated program transformation system that could automatically carry out derivations according to this strategy to produce programs tuned to different computer architectures.

In 1981, when the project began, I decided that the implementation language giving the widest possible portability was Fortran. Although there is a Lisp interpreter available in Fortran, the LISP F3 system [Nordstrom, 1978], I knew of no Lisp-to-Fortran compiler. So I faced the problem of converting the Lisp program to Fortran.

Reimplementing the program by hand using Fortran was the most obvious possibility. This approach had several serious drawbacks, however.

I would have to contend with Fortran's lack of support (if not outright antagonism) for recursion and for the list data type. These shortcomings of Fortran were the reasons I had written the program in Lisp in the first place. Worse yet, I would have to debug the program again, and for this type of program, Fortran's lack of support for lists and recursion would make debugging all the more difficult.

Moreover, I would have these problems in spades when trying to implement the program in parallel Fortran. I would have to rewrite virtually the whole program yet again. Worse, I would have to debug both this rewrite of the basic algorithm and the details of the parallel implementation at the same time! Finally, if I made a fundamental mistake in the design of the parallel implementation, I would face further complete rewrites.

To get a feel for the difficulties of reimplementing the program by hand, look at the example program in Fig. 15.1. Can you figure out what it computes? (Only the names have been changed to protect the innocent!)

An alternative to rewriting the Lisp program by hand was to transform it into Fortran by some automatic means. I asked myself, "Could I use program transformations—rules that repeatedly rewrite small fragments of the

FIGURE 15.1
A RECURSIVE LISP PROGRAM IMPLEMENTED IN FORTRAN

```
      subroutine wxyz
      integer plus,diff
      mjp = jp
      mjp = mjp - 5
      if (mjp .le. ip) call stkerx
      jp = mjp
         stack(mjp) = mknum(2)
         stack(mjp+1) = mknum(1)
         stack(mjp+2) = mknum(0)
         stack(mjp+3) = mknum(25)
         stack(ip+1) = 1
         go to 20
10    continue
   stack(mjp+4) = stack(jp-1)
   mjp = mjp + 5
   jp = mjp
   return
20    continue
         ip = ip + 1
         jp = jp - 1
         if (jp .le. ip) call stkerx
      stack(jp-2) = stack(mjp+3)
            stack(ip+1) = 1
            go to 40
```

FIGURE 15.1 *(Cont.)*

```
30      continue
     stack(jp) = stack(jp-1)
     stack(jp-2) = stack(jp)
     call print
     stack(jp) = stack(jp-1)
     jp = jp + 1
     irlab = stack(ip)
     ip = ip - 1
     go to 10
40   continue
     ip = ip + 1
     jp = jp - 3
     if (jp .le. ip) call stkerx
     if (stack(jp+1) .ne. stack(mjp+2)) go to 50
         stack(jp+2) = stack(mjp+1)
     go to 90
50   continue
     if (stack(jp+1) .ne. stack(mjp+1)) go to 60
         stack(jp+2) = stack(mjp+1)
     go to 90
60   continue
         stack(jp-2) = diff(stack(jp+1),stack(mjp+1))
             stack(ip+1) = 2
             go to 40
70           continue
         stack(jp+2) = stack(jp-1)
         stack(jp-2) = diff(stack(jp+1),stack(mjp))
             stack(ip+1) = 3
             go to 40
80           continue
         stack(jp) = stack(jp-1)
         stack(jp+2) = plus(stack(jp+2),stack(jp))
90   continue
     jp = jp + 3
     irlab = stack(ip)
     ip = ip - 1
     if (irlab .eq. 1) go to 30
     irlab = irlab - 1
     if (irlab .eq. 1) go to 70
     go to 80
  end
```

program—for this task?" I had the tool I needed, the TAMPR program transformation system [Boyle and Matz, 1976; Boyle, 1970], at hand. In fact, the transformer component of this system was the very program I wished to reuse. The program transformation approach would be a bootstrapping one—TAMPR (running in Lisp) would transform itself from Lisp into Fortran. This approach would reuse the Lisp program for the transformer by deriving the Fortran version from it.

15.1.1 Why Use Program Transformation?

Why is transforming the program into Fortran attractive when reimplementing it by hand in Fortran is not? Even when using transformations, the problems of implementing both recursion (or parallel function evaluation) and the list data type, mentioned above, still remain.

There are at least three answers to this question. Perhaps the most important is that transforming from Lisp to Fortran is an automatic process rather than a manual one. If one rewrote the program in Fortran by hand using the existing Lisp program as a guide, errors would almost certainly creep in. On the other hand, if one used sound correctness-preserving transformations to rewrite the Lisp automatically, the transformed program would retain all the reliability of the original one. The TAMPR system's transformer program is thoroughly tested. Over the years that it has been in use, it has correctly applied millions of transformations and has been used to produce widely used software, including the programs in the LINPACK package [Dongarra *et. al.*, 1979] for solving systems of linear equations. I did not wish to throw such reliability away lightly.

The second answer is that program transformations help in overcoming the problems posed by Fortran's lack of support for recursion (or parallelism) and for the list data type. In the Fortran version of the program, the implementation of these two features must be explicit. Their implementation is also global—it pervades the entire program. Virtually every statement contains details of implementing lists or recursion, and most statements contain a mixture of both. The difficulty with rewriting the program by hand is that one must deal with both of these kinds of detail simultaneously. In contrast, the tasks of writing the transformations that implement lists and those that implement recursion can be completely separated. This separation enables one to think about each of these implementations in isolation, significantly increasing the likelihood that one will implement each correctly.

The third answer is that, by using transformations to rewrite the program from Lisp into Fortran, one can at the same time optimize the resulting program to improve its performance. When reimplementing the program in Fortran by hand, one might be reluctant to attempt optimizations because the task of implementing recursion and lists is already very demanding intellectually. But the transformations that perform optimization are completely distinct from those that implement lists and recursion, and, as before, this separation enhances the possibility of formulating them correctly.

15.1.2 Structure of This Paper

In the remainder of this paper I discuss how my colleagues (K. W. Dritz, M. N. Muralidharan, and R. Taylor) and I used program transformations to reuse the Lisp program for the TAMPR transformer in Fortran, not just on ordinary sequential computers, but also on global-memory parallel processors. This paper integrates research results reported in two earlier papers [Boyle, 1984, 1987].

The two main threads in this discussion are abstract programming and program transformation. *Abstract programming* is writing a program using a high-level programming model, a model as divorced as possible from considerations of computer architecture. Unless written using such a model, a program is neither adaptable nor portable—hence it is not even *potentially* reusable. *Program transformation* is a tool for automating the derivation of a concrete program from an abstract one. Without such a tool, an abstract program is difficult to convert to an executable one—hence it is not *actually* reusable.

Closely related to these threads are three others: transformation strategy, intermediate programming models, and local formal notations. *Transformation strategy* guides the design of the program transformations that derive one or more concrete programs from an abstract one; it is absolutely necessary if transformation is to be carried out automatically. *Intermediate programming models* support transformation and strategy by providing a basis for expressing programs at an intermediate level of abstraction between abstract and concrete. Intermediate models also support proofs of correctness for the steps in a derivation and hence for the derived concrete program. They can be thought of as reapplying the abstract programming approach at intermediate stages of the derivation. *Local formal notations* support transformation by providing a syntax for programs that use intermediate programming models. A local formal notation is a kind of catalyst—it is used to express an intermediate form of the program but not to express the initial abstract nor the final concrete program.

To explain how to achieve program reusability through abstract programming and program transformation, I must explain a little about each of these threads. Like real threads, they must be interwoven to be useful, so I shall revisit each a number of times. I begin with discussion of abstract programming and why the Lisp program for the TAMPR transformer can be considered an abstract program.

15.2 THE LISP PROGRAM AS AN ABSTRACT PROGRAM

The Lisp program for the TAMPR transformer is not, perhaps, a typical one. It is written (with the exception of a top-level function that performs input/output) in pure applicative Lisp (PAL). It does not use such Lisp constructs as *prog, setq, rplaca,* and *rplacd,* and it makes only very limited use of *read, print,* and *gensym.* Functions written in PAL cannot have side effects. They thus correspond to the mathematical idea of a function—if two calls to a function have the same arguments, they produce the same value.

If the function definitions constituting a specification are further restricted to use abstract data types exhaustively, the usual strong connection between Lisp and list processing disappears. One is left with a universal specification language that has an interesting minimalist character—the only language constructs are:

- [ ] lambda-binding (definition and application of unnamed functions),
- [ ] conditional evaluation of expressions, and
- [ ] recursion (recursive function definition and application).

A specification written in abstract pure Lisp is a *functional program,* and it has a declarative, nonprocedural interpretation based on the mathematics of the lambda-calculus and recursive function theory. (Of course, it also has the advantage of being an executable specification, if a Lisp system and definitions of the abstract data types in terms of Lisp primitives are at hand.)

From the point of view of program transformation, the clean mathematical properties of abstract pure Lisp offer two important advantages. One is that for such a language, transformations do not need access to complicated data flow analyses to determine what value a particular use of a variable represents. Each use of a variable is simply a shorthand for the value of the expression to which it is bound, a property that is sometimes called *referential transparency.*

Formally speaking, when a program has the pure applicative property, the rules of Church's lambda-calculus [Church, 1941] can be used as the basis for transformations that manipulate it. That is, the transformation rules can freely (except for taking care to avoid name clashes) replace instances of an evaluation of a function by instances of a lambda-variable, after binding that lambda-variable to the result of evaluating the function. Similarly they can replace instances of a lambda-variable by instances of the function evaluation to which it is bound.

The second advantage of abstract pure Lisp is that its declarative nature helps to avoid overspecifying a problem. Specifically, it helps to avoid unnecessary sequentiality in a specification, which in turn facilitates introduction of parallelism. (I have discussed the relationship between abstraction and transformation further in [Boyle, 1980a, 1980b].)

15.2.1 Origin of the Pure Lisp Specification for the TAMPR Transformer

Since it is not often that Lisp programmers choose to avoid the use of *prog* and *setq,* you may wonder how I happen to have written the TAMPR transformer in pure applicative Lisp. Therein lies a tale.

At the time I wrote the transformer program, I was a graduate student performing my Ph.D. research at Argonne. John Reynolds was my Argonne adviser—an even greater good fortune than I realized at the time—and I described to him in general terms the behavior that I wanted the transformer program to have. He told me that the program I was describing was doing list processing, and suggested that I learn Lisp. He added quietly, "And by the way, forget about the functions *prog* and *setq*—don't bring me a program that uses them."

Naively, I replied, "OK."

In the coming weeks, as I struggled to write the program—How can I write a program without assignment? I muttered over and over to myself—I often rued my quick agreement. But it was probably the best piece of programming advice I ever received, for it helped me to write a correct and highly adaptable program.

15.2.2 A Simple Example in Pure Lisp

The TAMPR transformer itself is too long and too complex to serve as an example in this discussion. Instead, I use a simple program written in pure Lisp—one that is trivial to understand but still illustrates the key points about transformation to both sequential and parallel Fortran. This abstract program, from which the sequential Fortran program in Fig. 15.1 was derived, is shown in Fig. 15.2.

The function *fib*, as you might guess, computes the Fibonacci numbers; in Figs. 15.1 and 15.2 it is accompanied by a driver function that calls it to compute *fib*(25).

Of course, it would be naive to actually compute Fibonacci numbers by the double recursion in this specification. A concrete implementation of Fibonacci should return both the requested Fibonacci number and its prede-

FIGURE 15.2

RECURSIVE LISP PROGRAM CORRESPONDING TO THE FORTRAN PROGRAM IN FIGURE 15.1

```
(defun fibd (lambda ( )
    (print (fib 25))
))

(defun fib (lambda (n)
    (cond
        ((eq n 0) 1)
        ((eq n 1) 1)
        (t (plus (fib (difference n 1)) (fib (difference n 2)))))
    )
))
```

cessor, thereby avoiding the double recursion. In fact, Burstall and Darlington [1977] have shown how to use program transformations to eliminate this
double recursion. Nevertheless, the Fibonacci program is a useful example
because it is simple, illustrates recursion, and contains latent parallelism. In
fact, the parallelism shown here closely models one of the principal sources
of parallelism in the TAMPR transformer. In the transformer, however, the
two arguments evaluated in parallel do not involve calls to the same function,
and so the Burstall and Darlington optimization does not apply.

I shall return to the thread of how to take advantage of the abstractness
of a pure applicative Lisp program in the discussion of strategies for transformation in Sections 15.3.2 and 15.3.5. First, however, I discuss what I mean
by program transformation.

15.3 PROGRAM TRANSFORMATION

When I speak of program transformation, I mean a process of making a large
number of relatively small alterations to a program—alterations that do not
destroy the meaning of the program. The derived program thus *evolves* from
the original. In contrast to monolithic processes such as compilation, program
transformation permits access to the program at any intermediate step of its
evolution. This access helps one to see that the derivation is being performed
correctly. Moreover, as you will see, potential optimizations can be discovered
by examining the intermediate steps.

In most applications of program transformation, evolution is from the
more abstract form of the program to the more concrete. That is, an individual transformation or set of transformations incorporates a particular
implementation decision into the program. Implementation decisions involve
choosing some more concrete implementation for an abstraction or simplifying part of the program based on earlier implementation decisions. Each of
the small alterations that such transformations make to a program is a refinement step—it moves the program a step closer to a concrete implementation.

Thus the complete derivation of a concrete program from an abstract one
occurs by *stepwise refinement.* Wirth discusses manual stepwise refinements in
[Wirth, 1971]. Here, of course, I emphasize using transformations to carry
out refinements automatically.

15.3.1 Structuring an Automated Stepwise Refinement

How does one go about creating sets of transformations to carry out a substantial refinement, such as the one from Lisp to Fortran? At the heart of this
process is identification of a sequence of implementation decisions that leads
in a logical and consistent manner from the abstract program to the desired
concrete one. Some of these decisions obviously need to be made, such as
how lists are to be represented or how a parameter of a function is to be

accessed. Others are more subtle—the need for them emerges only after considering the consequences of other implementation decisions. Simplifications and optimizations are in this latter class. The sequence of implementation decisions is the basis for the transformation strategy that I discuss in the next section.

Once the implementation decisions have been made, one or more transformations can be written that incorporate each into a program. The guiding principle for writing each transformation (or small group of transformations) is that it be *correctness preserving*—that any property that can be proved about the program before the transformation applies still be provable about the program after it applies. This requirement is useful even when no properties have been proved about the original program, because it at least guarantees that applying such transformations yields a program that executes just as correctly as the original one.

15.3.2 Strategy for Transformation to Sequential Fortran

I can now discuss how to organize the transformational refinement of a program from Lisp into Fortran. The process starts from the Lisp program written in terms of lists and recursion and refines it by steps into a Fortran program written in terms of arrays, indices, and *go-to* statements. The idea of proceeding by small changes encourages one to break the transformation problem, which may appear virtually impossible at first, into a sequence of steps. This approach is an example of the "divide and conquer" metastrategy.

For the transformation to sequential Fortran, the first major insight is a division of the problem into two steps:

☐ converting the Lisp program to recursive Fortran, and
☐ converting the recursive Fortran to executable Fortran 66 or 77.

The second of these steps turns out to be relatively straightforward. Implementing recursion in Fortran has been discussed by Larmouth [Larmouth, 1973a, 1973b]. I chose a similar approach, which can be described as follows:

1. Replace each local variable in a function subprogram by a reference to a position in an array used as a stack.
2. Replace each formal parameter of a function by a reference to a position in the stack.
3. Replace each actual parameter that appears in a call to a function by a statement that places its value on the stack.
4. Return the result produced by the function on the stack.
5. Replace the use of the value of a function by a reference to the result of the function on the stack.

At this point, the program is expressed in a subset of recursive Fortran that permits only recursive, parameterless subroutines—recursive functions, parameters, and local variables have been transformed away.

After these steps, the program is very near the goal of executable Fortran 66 or 77. The remaining steps are these:

6. Combine the code for all of the functions into a single program unit, beginning the code for each function with a label and ending it with a computed *go-to* statement whose labels are those of the statements that follow the calls to that function.

7. Replace each call to a function with two statements: one that stacks an index (for a computed *go-to* statement) specifying the label following that call and one that transfers to the label of the function body.

Each of these steps corresponds roughly to a step in the transformational derivation—to one or two sets of transformations.

Interestingly, the particular approach chosen to implement recursive Fortran induces requirements on the steps leading up to recursive Fortran. These requirements provide guidance on how to divide and conquer the first major step of the strategy, transforming Lisp to recursive Fortran. For example, in the implementation produced by these substeps, each function call in the recursive Fortran program will be replaced by a sequence of several Fortran statements. But sequences of statements cannot be directly substituted for function calls in Fortran, since function calls are operands of expressions. In order for replacement of a function call by a sequence of statements to be convenient, the recursive Fortran program should have at most one nontrivial function call per statement. (By nontrivial function I mean a function other than the Lisp primitives, such as *car* and *cdr*.) In the following paragraphs, I discuss how this requirement can be met.

Transformation to Prepared PAL.   How can one manipulate the program to accommodate the implementation decision to have only one function call per statement? Fortunately, one can find an antecedent for this idea in the lambda-calculus, in binding the result of a function evaluation to the lambda-variable of a lambda-expression. To see why creating a lambda-expression is useful, consider the Lisp subexpression in Fig. 15.3, in which one of the arguments of the function f is a nontrivial function evaluation of the function g.

FIGURE 15.3
LISP EXPRESSION WITH EMBEDDED FUNCTION EVALUATION

```
...(f (g a b) c)...
```

FIGURE 15.4

EMBEDDED FUNCTION EVALUATION BOUND TO LAMBDA-VARIABLE

```
...((lambda (lv1) (f lv1 c)) (g a b))...
```

An equivalent subexpression in the lambda-calculus is shown in Fig. 15.4, in which the result of evaluating the function *g* is bound to a lambda-variable, *lv1*. Such a subexpression has the straightforward translation into Fortran (assuming that the name of the lambda-variable is unique) shown in Fig. 15.5. Of course, if the expression in Fig. 15.3 were translated directly into Fortran, the call to *g* would be nested within the call to *f* in a single statement. Figures 15.4 and 15.5 thus illustrate how a lambda-binding can reduce the nesting of function calls in a program.

It is not sufficient to simply *reduce* the number of function calls per statement, however. One must guarantee that there will be *at most one* function call per statement. Here two ideas central to program transformation methodology, the idea of making only small, correctness-preserving changes and that of using canonical forms, come to the rescue. Instead of going directly from the expression of Fig. 15.3 to that of Fig. 15.4, I use several steps, each as small as possible.

The first of the small steps uses a trick analogous to one sometimes used in mathematical proofs. Remember how your mathematics professor used to say, "Now we multiply on the right by the identity element, and then we replace it by $a \times a^{-1}, \ldots$"? In this case, one uses a transformation that introduces an identity lambda-expression. It simply replaces each nontrivial function evaluation that is an argument to another function evaluation by the equivalent lambda-expression, with that function evaluation bound to the lambda-variable. As the example in Figs. 15.3–15.5 suggests, introducing these lambda-expressions ultimately leads to a form of the program with at most one function call per statement. The result of this rather pointless-appearing—but nevertheless correct—transformation applied to the program fragment in Fig. 15.3 is shown in Fig. 15.6.

Why is this transformation correct? It is based on an identity of the lambda-calculus, which is shown in Fig. 15.7.

FIGURE 15.5

FORTRAN TRANSLATION OF LAMBDA-EXPRESSION IN FIGURE 15.4

```
lv1 = g(a,b)
...f(lv1,c)...
```

FIGURE 15.6
START OF TRANSFORMATION OF EXPRESSION OF FIGURE 15.3

```
...(f ((lambda (lv1) lv1) (g a b)) c)...
```

To carry out the remaining small steps that lead to the one-function-call-per-statement form of the program, one writes other transformations that enlarge the scope of the introduced lambda-expressions (as necessary) by distributing them out of the outer function evaluation in order to obtain, for this example, the expression of Fig. 15.4. The correctness of these transformations is also based on identities of the lambda-calculus, namely, distributive laws for lambda-expressions and function evaluation.

Inserting lambda-expressions in the Lisp program to prepare for removing recursion at the Fortran level is useful because the lambda-expressions can be inserted with complete reliability at the applicative language level. That is, the transformations that manipulate the lambda-expressions can be shown to be correct because they implement identities in the lambda-calculus, and appealing to the lambda-calculus is in turn justified by the requirement that the program being transformed be written in pure applicative Lisp.

(The preceding is, of course, a purist's view. In practice, these particular transformations could be justified on the basis of somewhat more relaxed assumptions, akin to those made by typical Lisp compilers. Such assumptions would enable one to apply the transformations to Lisp programs that use such nonapplicative constructs as *prog* and *setq*. I have extended the transformations that produce sequential Fortran to handle some nonapplicative constructs. As you will see, however, the assumption of pure applicative Lisp is much more important in the transformations that produce parallel Fortran.)

I call this language level, in which all nontrivial function evaluations have been bound to lambda-variables, *prepared pure applicative Lisp*, or *prepared PAL*.

Transformation to Canonicalized PAL. Transforming directly from PAL to prepared PAL is still a fairly big step, however. Having at least one intermediate language level is useful. I call this level *canonicalized pure applicative*

FIGURE 15.7
A LAMBDA-CALCULUS IDENTITY

```
e ≡ ((lambda (z) z) e)
```

FIGURE 15.8
LISP CONDITIONAL EXPRESSION

```
(cond (p₁ e₁) (p₂ e₂) (t e₃))
```

Lisp because it is a canonical form (albeit a weak one) for Lisp programs. The motivation for introducing it is to simplify many of the subsequent transformations by reducing the number of special cases with which they must cope. Some of the canonicalizations are as follows:

1. generating a Fortran function header for each Lisp function definition and assigning the Lisp expression in the function body to the Fortran function identifier;
2. expanding Lisp nlambda functions—those with a variable number of arguments, such as *list*, *and*, and *or*—into their definitions in terms of repeated application of Lisp functions;
3. renaming duplicate lambda-variables so that the name of every lambda-variable is unique within a function;
4. converting multiple-variable lambda-expressions into nested single-variable ones;
5. converting Lisp conditional expressions such as the one shown in Fig. 15.8 into nested TAMPR extended-Fortran conditional expressions such as the one shown in Fig. 15.9.

The first of these canonicalizations paves the way for the ultimate translation to recursive Fortran, by introducing into each function a single Fortran assignment statement, which will be transformed as discussed in Section 15.3.4. The second, fourth, and fifth reduce the variety of Lisp constructs in the program by defining some in terms of others.

The third canonicalization is perhaps the most important, for it permits later transformations to enlarge the scope of lambda-expressions freely. Several transformations, including those that transform to prepared PAL, change the scope of lambda-expressions. Without the third canonicalization, each such transformation would have to check whether changing the scope causes a name clash and, if so, change one of the clashing names. It is simpler

FIGURE 15.9
TAMPR EXTENDED-FORTRAN CONDITIONAL EXPRESSION

```
use (e₁) if (p₁) otherwise
    use (e₂) if (p₂) otherwise (e₃)
```

to place the program in a canonical form that guarantees that name clashes cannot occur. (Of course, later transformations must be written so that they do not destroy the canonicalization. Thus a transformation that introduces new lambda-expressions must maintain this property by, for example, generating lambda-variable names that differ from all other names in the program, using a service built into TAMPR.)

Implementation decisions cost something. Every time one makes an implementation decision—applies a transformation that makes the program more concrete—one eliminates some possible versions, or *realizations,* of the program. In this respect, the implementation decision to convert multiple-variable lambda-expressions to nested single-variable ones is interesting to consider.

In Lisp, the order of evaluating the arguments of a multiple-variable lambda-expression is not defined. Therefore, when pure Lisp is implemented in parallel Fortran, such lambda-expressions are a source of parallelism, because their arguments can be evaluated simultaneously. On the other hand, if a multiple-variable lambda-expression is converted to a nest of single-variable ones, an order of evaluation is fixed, and it is no longer easy to take advantage of the parallelism originally present.

For the implementation of pure Lisp in sequential Fortran, transforming to a nest of single-variable lambda-expressions is useful because it is a canonicalization that simplifies later transformations. The decision is not without cost, however, because it sacrifices parallelism in the program.

Transformations that introduce implementation decisions have another interesting property—they preserve correctness, but not equivalence. This statement is an obvious consequence of the fact that choosing one from many possible implementations cuts off the others.

For example, consider the transformation that converts multiple-variable lambda-expressions to nested single-variable ones. Like all the transformations I discuss here, this transformation preserves the correctness of the original program; that is, any property that one can prove about the original program can still be proved about the transformed program. But the converse of this statement—that any property that one can prove about the transformed program can be proved about the original program—is not true. Thus the transformed program, while as correct as the original, is not equivalent to it.

In general, a program that has been transformed contains additional information, which is why some properties can be proved about the transformed program that cannot be proved (or even stated) about the original one. In the case of the canonicalization transformation, the transformed program specifies a particular order for the evaluation of the lambda-arguments, which was not specified in the original program. Thus properties that depend on that order can be proved after transformation but not before. Of course, if I were working with absolutely pure functional Lisp, no such properties would exist, but I have to admit the impure functions *read, print,* and *gensym.*

FIGURE 15.10

LISP EXPRESSION WITH ORDER OF EVALUATION UNSPECIFIED

```
((lambda (x y)
   (cons x (cons y nil))
)
   (read) (read)
)
```

Consider the multiple-variable lambda-expression in Fig. 15.10 and its corresponding single-variable canonical form in Fig. 15.11. For the second version
of the program (Fig. 15.11), one can prove that, if it is given as input the list
(*a*) followed by the list (*b*), then it will produce the list ((*a*) (*b*)). However, one
can prove no such property for the program in Fig. 15.10—one can prove
only that it will produce either the list ((*a*) (*b*)) or the list ((*b*) (*a*)).

This situation of being able to state and prove more properties about a
program after transformation than before is typical. In fact, the ability of
transformations to add information representing implementation decisions is
the reason I say that the transformed program is more concrete than the
original. In addition, this ability explains how an abstract program in which
many things are incompletely specified can be transformed into a concrete
one in which virtually everything is fully specified. Finally, the ability to add
information transformationally makes it possible to derive several different
concrete programs from a single abstract one. For every transformation that
represents an implementation decision, others could be written that reflect
alternative decisions.

Transformations that embody implementation decisions, such as the one
to canonicalize lambda-expressions, tend to be irreversible. Perhaps *irreversible*
is too strong a word, but often the information they add to the program
cannot readily be removed, because proving that it is nonessential may be

FIGURE 15.11

LISP EXPRESSION WITH ORDER OF EVALUATION SPECIFIED

```
((lambda (x)
   ((lambda (y)
      (cons x (cons y nil))
   )
      (read)
   )
)
   (read)
)
```

difficult. For example, given a program using nested single-variable lambda-expressions (as in Fig. 15.11), it is impossible to tell from the program alone whether the fixed order of the evaluation of the lambda-expressions has been used to prove any properties about the program. (One must know something about the specification for the program to answer such questions.) Therefore it is necessary to assume that the order of evaluation has been used and that transforming the program back to multiple-variable lambda-expression form (as in Fig. 15.10) would not preserve its correctness.

Most computer programs—the ones written every day to solve scientific and commercial problems—are concrete ones. As such, each embodies literally thousands of implementation decisions that are not dictated in any way by the specification of the problem to be solved. The fact that concrete programs have a plethora of such *possibly*, but not *provably*, irrelevant properties makes them difficult to modify, extend, adapt, and transport. On the other hand, abstract programs contain (almost by definition) only such information as is necessary to show that they solve the problem for which they were written. Therefore, modifying, extending, adapting, and transporting them is much easier than it is for concrete programs. These issues, and especially their implications for the reuse of programs on different machines, are discussed further in [Boyle, 1980a, 1980c], while the role of abstract programming in raising the level of proofs about computer programs is discussed in Chapter 12 of [Wos *et al.*, 1984].

Preparing the Lisp Program for Transformation.   One step in the conversion of Lisp to recursive Fortran remains to be mentioned—the initial step of the process, in which an editor script is used to convert the Lisp program into a single large expression in the TAMPR extended-Fortran language. This conversion consists primarily of moving opening parentheses to the right over function names and inserting commas between function arguments. Such changes convert the function notation of Lisp into a form that is parsable in the TAMPR extended-Fortran grammar, so that the process of applying transformations can begin. The effect of this editing on the function *fib* in Fig. 15.2 is illustrated in Fig. 15.13 in Section 15.3.3.

Language Levels.   As I have tried to show throughout the preceding discussion of strategy, the process of transforming Lisp to Fortran can be thought of as moving the program through a sequence of levels of decreasing abstractness until a concrete, executable Fortran program is obtained. Each of these levels of abstraction is characterized by a particular programming model and the collection of notations that it uses, beginning with the notations of pure applicative Lisp and ending with those of executable Fortran. In an excellent paper on the role of these notations in transformational derivations, Wile [1987] coins the term *locally formal notations* for them and describes their relationship to the concept of *wide-spectrum language*, a term coined by Bauer [1976].

Simply put, a locally formal notation is some notation introduced into a derivation by one or more sets of transformations and removed by one or more later sets of transformations. Such a notation may be spatially local in a program (that is, have some restricted scope), but, more important, it is temporally local to particular stages of the derivation. It thus plays the role of a catalyst in the derivation, permitting the expression of intermediate levels, while not becoming part of the final product.

Wide-spectrum languages and locally formal notations are both attempts to solve a problem that arises in formulating stepwise refinements: Some parts of the program must be expressed at one level of abstraction at the same time as others are expressed at a different level. For example, as discussed earlier (and as illustrated by the program in Figs. 15.14 and 15.15 in Section 15.3.3), when the program is at the canonicalized pure applicative Lisp level, part of each function body is in assignment form and part is in lambda-expression form.

Wide-spectrum languages encompass many levels of abstraction, from the descriptive to the imperative, simultaneously. Bauer briefly discusses the role of wide-spectrum languages in program transformation in [Bauer, 1976]. Further discussion can be found in [Bauer *et al.*, 1981].

A serious problem with wide-spectrum languages is that they require many diverse language constructs to be defined simultaneously and consistently. Locally formal notations address this problem by extending the base language in ways whose scope and use are limited. These extensions can be chosen independently to support a particular derivation. They can convey information needed for optimization from one stage of the derivation to the next, just as can the notations available in a wide-spectrum language. But not all extensions required for all problems need be defined simultaneously and consistently.

Locally formal notations can be introduced easily into a base language. Typically, one simply appropriates part of the notation in the base language for a special purpose in a portion of the derivation, as in the derivation of parallel Fortran from pure Lisp (see Fig. 15.27 in Section 15.3.5). The locally formal notation is defined by the transformations that implement it in terms of other (lower-level) locally formal notations or constructs in the base language.

Sequential Strategy Summary.   In this section I have discussed the overall strategy that I employ to transform a program in pure applicative Lisp into one in Fortran. The most important point is that to carry out any program derivation, one must break up the problem into a sequence of intellectually manageable steps—steps that one can hope to implement correctly. Once the derivation is so structured, the writing of the transformations to carry out the derivation is straightforward.

The language levels identified in the discussion of strategy are summarized in Fig. 15.12. In practice, several of these levels are split—that is, refined—into two or more levels. The levels depicted in Fig. 15.12 are the conceptually important ones, however.

FIGURE 15.12
LANGUAGE LEVELS BETWEEN LISP AND FORTRAN

Pure applicative Lisp program
↓
Pure applicative Lisp, expressed in
extended-Fortran syntax
↓
Canonicalized pure applicative Lisp
↓
Prepared pure applicative Lisp
↓
Recursive Fortran, one function call
per statement
↓
Recursive Fortran, no dynamic local
variables (local variables stacked)
↓
Recursive Fortran, no parameters
(parameters stacked)
↓
Nonrecursive Fortran, executable

15.3.3 An Example Derivation

What happens to the Fibonacci program of Fig. 15.2 as it passes through
the various stages in the derivation? For the sake of brevity, consider just
the definition of the Fibonacci function itself, the second *defun* in the Lisp
program in Fig. 15.2. The first step is to edit the program to convert it to the
TAMPR extended-Fortran syntax. The edited form of the Fibonacci function
is shown in Fig. 15.13.

The result of transforming this program to canonicalized PAL is shown
in Fig. 15.14. Recall that at this stage, Fortran function headers and the

FIGURE 15.13
EDITED, TAMPR EXTENDED-FORTRAN PROGRAM

```
expressions
function (fib, body (args (n),
 cond (cc (eq (n, 0), 1),
  cc (eq (n, 1), 1),
   cc (true (dummy), plus (fib (difference (n, 1)), fib (difference (n, 2))))
 )
))
;
end;
```

FIGURE 15.14
PURE APPLICATIVE LISP, CANONICALIZED

```
integer function fib(n);
preamble declare integer n;
   enddeclare;
endpreamble
fib = use m00007 if(eq(n,m00006)) otherwise
   use m00007 if(eq(n,m00007)) otherwise
      plus(fib(difference(n,m00007)),fib(difference (n,m00008)));
return;
end;
```

assignment of the body expression to the function identifier are introduced, and Lisp conditional expressions are converted to TAMPR extended-Fortran conditional expressions. (In addition, the constants in the Fibonacci specification have been replaced by named constants whose values incorporate the special representation for integers used in LISP F3.)

In the next step, this program is transformed to prepared PAL, as shown in Fig. 15.15. These transformations create expressions for nontrivial function evaluations and introduce notation for functional composition and application.

The program next passes through an intermediate level not shown in Fig. 15.12. At this level, conditional statements and assignments with local declarations of variables have been introduced, but the local declarations have not yet been moved to the beginning of the function. (The lambda-variable *p00010* disappears because an optimizing transformation recognizes that the

FIGURE 15.15
PURE APPLICATIVE LISP, PREPARED

```
integer function fib(n);
preamble declare integer n;
   enddeclare;
endpreamble
fib =
   use m00007 if(eq(n,m00006)) otherwise
   use m00007 if(eq(n,m00007)) otherwise
      lambda(body(args(p00010),
         lambda(body(args(p00011),
            plus(p00010,p00011)),
         apply(compose(fib), toargs(difference(n,m00008)))))),
      apply(compose(fib), toargs(difference(n,m00007))));
return;
end;
```

function identifier is available for use as a temporary variable in its stead.) The program at this level is illustrated in Fig. 15.16.

Two sets of transformations complete the transition to the recursive Fortran level listed next in Fig. 15.12. One is a set of library transformations. It merges declarations that occur in parallel blocks and moves them to the specification part of the Fortran function definition. The other is a set of transformations that introduces Fortran equivalents for the basic Lisp predicates (*null, atom,* etc.). At this level, the program would be executable in an implementation of Fortran that supported recursion (provided such things as *if-then-else* statements were converted to Fortran *if* statements and *go-to* statements, and provided the *apply-compose* notation were replaced by function calls). The program at the recursive Fortran level is shown in Fig. 15.17.

The remaining stages of the transformation to standard Fortran are concerned with recursion removal. The transformations that carry them out embody implementation decisions about how recursion will be represented, as discussed at the beginning of Section 15.3.2.

The transformations of the first stage place local variables of functions in a stack frame and place the stack frame on a stack. Figure 15.18 shows the program at this level, which can be thought of as permitting recursive calls only to functions that do not use local variables.

FIGURE 15.16
PREPARED PAL, LAMBDA- AND CONDITIONAL EXPRESSIONS CODED

```
integer function fib(n);
preamble declare integer n;
    enddeclare;
endpreamble
if(n .eq. m00006)then;
    fib = m00007;
end else
    if(n .eq. m00007)then;
        fib = m00007;
    end else
        fib = apply(compose(fib), toargs(difference(n,m00007)));
        block;
            declare integer p00011;
            enddeclare;
            p00011 = apply(compose(fib), toargs(difference(n,m00008)));
            fib = plus(fib,p00011);
        end;
    end;
end;
return;
end;
```

FIGURE 15.17
RECURSIVE FORTRAN, ONE FUNCTION CALL PER STATEMENT

```
integer function fib(n);
preamble declare integer n;
      integer p00011;
   enddeclare;
endpreamble
if(n .eq. m00006)then;
   fib = m00007;
end else
   if(n .eq. m00007)then;
      fib = m00007;
   end else
      fib = apply(compose(fib), toargs(difference(n,m00007)));
      p00011 = apply(compose(fib), toargs(difference(n,m00008)));
      fib = plus(fib,p00011);
   end;
end;
return;
end;
```

FIGURE 15.18
RECURSIVE FORTRAN, NO DYNAMIC LOCAL VARIABLES

```
integer function fib(n);
preamble declare integer n;
   enddeclare;
endpreamble
assert(stackref(stack(jp)));
jp = jp - 1;
if(jp .le. ip)call stkerx;
if(n .eq. stack(mjp + 2)) then;
   fib = stack(mjp + 1);
end else
   if(n .eq. stack(mjp + 1)) then;
      fib = stack(mjp + 1);
   end else
      fib = apply(compose(fib), toargs(difference(n,stack(mjp + 1))));
      stack(jp)= apply(compose(fib), toargs(difference(n,stack(mjp))));
      fib = plus(fib,stack(jp));
   end;
end;
jp = jp + 1;
return;
end;
```

As a result, the local variable *p00011* of Fig. 15.17 has been replaced by a reference to *stack(jp)*.

At the next level, the subset of the language used by the program permits only recursive calls to parameterless subroutines—all aspects of recursion have been implemented except the stacking of return points from recursive calls. The transformations to this level place the parameters and returned function values into the stack frame (with the local variables), both in function definitions and function calls. Then they convert function definitions to subroutine definitions and replace function calls by parameterless subroutine calls. The resulting program is shown in Fig. 15.19.

The transition to the final level, executable nonrecursive Fortran, is a fully global process, requiring a transformation that applies to the entire list of function definitions. The implementation decision embodied in this set of transformations is to use *go-to* statements to implement recursive calls and computed *go-to* statements to implement recursive returns. In order to do so, all the subroutine definitions must be merged into a single monolithic subroutine because, in the semantics of Fortran, labels are local to the subroutine in which they occur. As the transformations fold each individual subroutine into the monolithic one, they generate a label for the first statement of its body and labels for all points of return from calls to it. The label on the body

FIGURE 15.19
RECURSIVE FORTRAN, NO PARAMETERS

```
subroutine fib;
jp = jp - 3;
if(jp .le. ip)call stkerx;
if(stack(jp + 1).eq. stack(mjp + 2)) then;
   stack(jp + 2)= stack(mjp + 1);
end else
   if(stack(jp + 1).eq. stack(mjp + 1)) then;
      stack(jp + 2)= stack(mjp + 1);
   end else
      stack(jp - 2)= difference(stack(jp + 1), stack(mjp + 1));
      call fib;
      stack(jp + 2)= stack(jp - 1);
      stack(jp - 2)= difference(stack(jp + 1), stack(mjp));
      call fib;
      stack(jp)= stack(jp - 1);
      stack(jp + 2)= plus(stack(jp + 2), stack(jp));
   end;
end;
jp = jp + 3;
return;
end;
```

is used in the *go-to* statement that replaces each call to that subroutine. All the return point labels for the subroutine are collected in a list that is used in the computed *go-to* statement that replaces its return statement. This list is also used to generate an index for the label of each point of return; this index is stacked just prior to the call. (The return index is stacked at the opposite end of the stack from the variable and argument frame, in order to maintain compatibility with the LISP F3 system [Nordstrom, 1978], whose list and atom representation, garbage collector, and read and print routines are used to provide list-processing support for the executable Fortran program.)

These transformations produce the program shown in Fig. 15.1. This program is shown in executable, rather than structured, Fortran form, and it includes the code resulting from both of the functions in the original Lisp program in Fig. 15.2. (The code generated from the definition of *fib* extends from label 40 to the end of the program.) TAMPR generates the executable Fortran form of a program from the structured form by applying transformations and a set of formatting instructions that convert constructs such as *if-then-else* statements and *do-while* loops to their representations in terms of logical-*if* and *go-to* statements. (The program in Fig. 15.1 is written in Fortran 66 except for the use of subscripted variables as subscripts, which is permitted in Fortran 77 but not in Fortran 66. If a Fortran 66 program is desired, the transformations can be modified to assign such subscripts to temporary variables.)

It is interesting to compare the strategy and stages for the derivation of sequential programs from pure Lisp with those for the derivation of parallel ones, as discussed in Section 15.3.5. First, however, I show how transformations can be used to implement the transition from one language level to another.

15.3.4 Some Representative Transformations

In the preceding sections, I have discussed a general strategy for transforming pure applicative Lisp into Fortran and have illustrated its application to a simple example program. Now I consider how to write some of the transformations that enable the TAMPR system to carry out the manipulations dictated by the strategy.

As you follow the progress of the example program through the levels depicted in Figs. 15.13–15.19 and Fig. 15.1, you will notice that in the early levels it looks basically like a Lisp program—more correctly, like a Fortran function with a Lisp expression for its body. In the later stages—from the recursive Fortran level to the executable Fortran level—it looks much like a typical Fortran program. A dramatic change occurs, however, in passing from the prepared pure applicative Lisp level (Fig. 15.15) to the recursive Fortran level (Fig. 15.17). It is in this transition that the program leaves the functional, expression-oriented domain of Lisp and enters the imperative, statement-oriented one of Fortran.

Coding Transformations.   The set of transformations that effect the first part of the transition from the program in Fig. 15.15 to that in Fig. 15.16 is an interesting one to study in more detail. Moreover, it is representative of the sets of transformations that are used at other levels.

The coding of lambda-expressions and conditional expressions at the prepared pure applicative Lisp level involves implementing such expressions in terms of Fortran assignment and conditional statements. The TAMPR transformation for coding lambda-expressions is shown in Fig. 15.20. This rewrite rule describes how to code an assignment statement in which the right-hand side is a lambda-expression. It consists of a *pattern*—the part between .sd. and the arrow (= = >)—and a *replacement*—the part between the arrow and .sc. The pattern matches any assignment statement that has a variable on the left (as do all assignments) and a lambda-expression on the right. When the pattern matches such an assignment, the replacement describes how to assemble a statement to substitute for it. The replacement of this transformation assembles an extended-Fortran block that declares the lambda-variable (<var>"2") and assigns to it the value of the actual argument expression (<expr>"2") in the original lambda-expression; it follows this assignment by one that assigns the lambda-body expression to the original left-hand-side variable. For example, given the program fragment shown in Fig. 15.21, the transformation in Fig. 15.20 applies to it and produces the program fragment shown in Fig. 15.22.

Of course, either or both of the assignment statements created by the replacement of this transformation may now be of the form described by the pattern of this rule or one of the other rules discussed later. TAMPR uses an exhaustive postorder sequencing rule, which ensures that it applies trans-

FIGURE 15.20
LAMBDA-EXPRESSION CODING TRANSFORMATION

```
.sd.
        <var>"1"  =
            lambda ( body
                ( args ( <var>"2" ) ,
                    <expr>"1" ) ,
                <expr>"2" ) ;
    ==>
        block ;
            declare
                integer <var>"2" ;
            enddeclare ;
            <var>"2" = <expr>"2" ;
            <var>"1" = <expr>"1" ;
        end ;
    .sc.
```

FIGURE 15.21
A LAMBDA-EXPRESSION

```
h = lambda(body(args(lv1),f(lv1,c)),g(a,b));
```

FIGURE 15.22
TRANSFORMED LAMBDA-EXPRESSION

```
block;
    declare integer lv1;
    enddeclare;
    lv1 = g(a,b);
    h = f(lv1,c);
end;
```

formations such as this one until no more matching instances remain in the program. That is, when a new instance of the pattern of some transformation is created in a replacement, the exhaustive postorder sequencing rule ensures that eventually the appropriate transformation will be applied to the new instance.

A transformation similar to the one for coding lambda-expressions codes assignment statements in which the right-hand side is a TAMPR extended-Fortran conditional expression. This transformation is shown in Fig. 15.23.

The set of transformations for coding lambda-expressions and conditional expressions also contains two similar transformations that code such expressions when they occur in the test of an *if* statement. These four rules are

FIGURE 15.23
CONDITIONAL EXPRESSION CODING TRANSFORMATION

```
.sd.
    <var>"1" =
        use <var>"2"
        if ( <expr>"1" )
        otherwise <var>"3" ;
==>
    if ( <expr>"1" ) then ;
        <var>"1" = <var>"2" ;
    end else
        <var>"1" = <var>"3" ;
    end ;
.sc.
```

sufficient to describe the coding at this level. However, the coding transformations used in practice are more complicated; they perform certain optimizations, including reusing temporary variables when possible, as discussed
in conjunction with Fig. 15.16.

The set of transformations just described brings the program from prepared PAL to the level depicted in Fig. 15.16. The remainder of the transformation to the recursive Fortran level is accomplished by two sets of
transformations. One codes Lisp predicates (for example, *null(l)*) as Fortran relations *(l.eq.nil)*. These transformations, of course, depend on the
particular data representation chosen for lists. The other set of transformations (originally developed for use in another context) moves the
local declarations introduced by the coding transformations to the head of
the function definition. In the process, it merges variables declared with disjoint scope in order to minimize the number of temporary variables. (These
merging transformations illustrate that not just programs, but also transformations, can be reused.)

Coding as Canonicalization.   Although at first glance you may not realize
it, the set of transformations that code lambda-expressions and conditional
expressions is actually manipulating the program into a new canonical form.
The effect of these transformations is to distribute assignment over the
lambda-operator and the conditional operator.

You can understand the canonical form produced by these transformations
by analogy. Think of assignment as multiplication, the lambda-operator as
addition, and the conditional operator as subtraction. Then these transformations carry out the analog of converting algebraic expressions to fully
multiplied-out form. Thus what happens to the assignment to *fib* in the
transformation from Fig. 15.15 to Fig. 15.16 is analogous to what happens
to multiplication by *fib* in rewriting the expression *fib* $\times$ ($-m7 - m7 + plus$) as
$- fib \times m7 - fib \times m7 + fib \times plus$.

The strong connection between sets of transformations and canonical
forms is an interesting topic for further investigation. From this point of view,
the problem of transforming Lisp to Fortran can be solved by converting the
program from one canonical form to another, just as some algebraic problems
can be solved, for example, by multiplying out a factored expression and then
factoring it in a different way. Based on this observation, the problem of
developing a strategy for a program derivation can be seen as the problem of
choosing and defining a sequence of canonical forms linking the initial form
of the program with the desired form.

It appears to me that any process of program transformation, including
traditional language compilation, can be viewed as involving canonical forms.
This point of view is of important practical interest, for it can be used to guide
the demonstration of the correctness of such processes. My colleague Peter
Schütz and I describe an initial step in this direction in [Boyle and Schütz,
1988].

15.3.5 Strategy for Transformation to Parallel Fortran

The most important question to be answered in regard to transforming pure Lisp to parallel Fortran is whether there is any parallelism latent in a pure Lisp specification.

Of course, there is *potential* parallelism: Because each function is a mathematical function, its value depends only upon the values of its arguments and not upon the order in which those arguments are evaluated. (In a declarative, mathematical view of pure Lisp, it is not even meaningful to talk about order of evaluation.) Thus, whenever two or more functions appear as actual arguments to a function or lambda-expression, they can be evaluated in the derived program in any order, or even in parallel. For example, returning to Fig. 15.2, the two calls to *fib* that are arguments to *plus* can be evaluated in parallel. The rapidly multiplying possibilities for parallel evaluation in Fibonacci are illustrated in Fig. 15.24. (Not every pure Lisp specification has parallelism, however. For example, the usual definition of the factorial function has none.)

Having noted that there may be parallelism latent in a pure Lisp speci-

FIGURE 15.24
PARALLEL EXECUTION TREE FOR *FIB*(6)

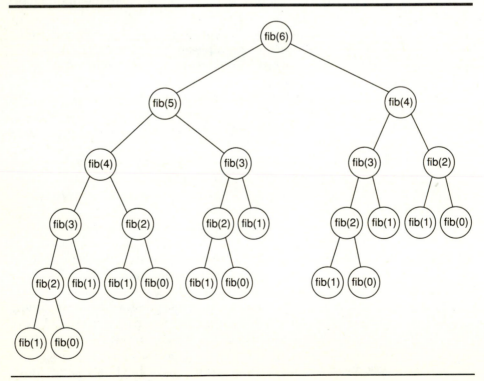

fication, how can one take advantage of it to derive a parallel program? The
first step is to identify an intermediate language level that corresponds to
recursive Fortran in the sequential case. (Of course, one of my goals was to
reuse as many of the transformations from the sequential case as possible,
either directly or with only minor modifications. Hence I wished the strategy
for the parallel case to be as similar as possible to that for the sequential
one.)

Most parallel hardware systems, and even multitasking software on
sequential machines, provide mechanisms for creating and destroying tasks,
or processes. When a process is created, it receives its own copy of local
storage, and if the global-memory paradigm is being used, access to global
storage. This behavior is exactly what one needs to implement recursion. So,
implementation of pure Lisp is simple: For each call to a function in the pure
Lisp program, simply create a process to evaluate the function, and make the
current process wait for the result.

Unfortunately, process creation and destruction on most hardware and
software systems is time-consuming. Even more unfortunately, usually only a
limited number, say 100, of such processes can exist simultaneously. To compute *fib*(25) in parallel requires a few hundred thousand processes, with at
least a few hundred existing simultaneously. Nevertheless, the abstract programming paradigm tells one to take an "ivory tower" approach, ignore efficiency, and assume one can easily create and destroy an unbounded number
of processes.

The unbounded-number-of-processes level of abstraction is shown at the
middle of Fig. 15.25. It defines the boundary between the first and second
parts of the parallel derivation.

The first part of the parallel derivation is similar to the first part of
the sequential derivation, with one major exception. The parallel case must
not include canonicalizing toward single-variable lambda-expressions, because
doing so destroys parallelism.

The goal of the first part of the parallel derivation is to manipulate the
program to cause as many function evaluations as possible to be actual arguments to multiple-variable lambda-expressions. The transformations introduce a special class of lambda-expression, plambda-expressions (a locally
formal notation), when the pure Lisp is prepared for conversion to parallel Fortran. These plambda-expressions represent lambda-bindings created
for function calls. When independent plambda-expressions are nested inside
one another, the transformations manipulate the plambda-expressions to create a single, multiple-variable plambda-expression, whose actual arguments
can be evaluated in parallel. This approach extracts the parallelism inher-
ent in the pure Lisp specification very cheaply. Moreover, it permits any
remaining lambda-expressions to be canonicalized to single-variable form (as
in the sequential derivation), simplifying reuse of certain of the sequential
transformations. The Fibonacci program at this stage is shown in Fig. 15.26.

FIGURE 15.25

LANGUAGE LEVELS BETWEEN PURE LISP AND PARALLEL FORTRAN

Pure applicative Lisp program
↓
Pure applicative Lisp, expressed in
    extended Fortran syntax
↓
Pure applicative Lisp, canonicalized
↓
Pure applicative Lisp, prepared
↓
Pure applicative Lisp, multiple-variable
    plambda-expressions collected
↓
Parallel Fortran, unbounded number of
    processes
↓
Parallel Fortran, unbounded number of
    chores, finite number of servers
↓
Parallel Fortran, unbounded number of
    chores, finite number of servers,
    only unblocked chores queued

FIGURE 15.26

PLAMBDA-EXPRESSION FORM OF THE FIBONACCI SPECIFICATION FOR
PARALLEL MACHINES

```
integer function fib(n);
preamble declare integer n;
    enddeclare;
endpreamble
fib =
    use m00007 if(eq(n,m00006)) otherwise
    use m00007 if(eq(n,m00007)) otherwise
        plambda(body(args(f00012,f00013),
            plus(f00012,f00013)),
        apply(compose(fib),toargs(difference(n,m00007)))
        apply(compose(fib),toargs(difference(n,m00008))));
return;
end;
```

A language level that permits an unbounded number of processes to be created corresponds to an *abstract machine*. Using such an abstract machine as the target for these transformations has two important advantages:

☐ It separates the detection of parallelism from its actual implementation.
☐ It facilitates showing the correctness of the parallel implementation.

For example, it makes it easy to demonstrate that the parallel form of the program terminates if the sequential one does. Further discussion of the utility of the unbounded-number-of-processors model can be found in [Moitra and Iyengar, 1984].

At the end of the first part of the derivation of the parallel realization, the program is in parallel Fortran, assuming an unbounded number of processes. Fig. 15.27 shows the Fibonacci function from Fig. 15.2 at this stage; this corresponds to Fig. 15.17 in the sequential derivation. Near the end of *fib*, the program creates two child processes that evaluate *fib*(n − 1) and *fib*(n − 2) in parallel and assign the results to the local variables *fib* and *f00013*, respectively. The parent process then waits until both results are available and, when they are, adds them to produce its result. (For syntactic convenience, I use subroutine calls as notation for these intermediate-level abstractions for parallelism, without regard to the appropriateness of the semantics of subroutine calls in Fortran. This use of *call* with *initwait*, *pcreate*,

FIGURE 15.27
INTERMEDIATE PARALLEL FORTRAN REALIZATION OF THE FIBONACCI
SPECIFICATION FOR PARALLEL MACHINES

```
integer function fib(n);
preamble declare integer n;
        integer f00013;
    enddeclare;
endpreamble
if (n .eq. m00006) then;
    fib = m00007;
end or else;
if (n .eq. m00007) then;
    fib = m00007;
end else;
    call initwait(fib,f00013);
    call pcreate(fib,fib(difference(n,m00007)));
    call pcreate(f00013,fib(difference(n,m00008)));
    call awaitresult(fib,f00013);
    fib = plus(fib,f00013);
end;
return;
end;
```

and *awaitresult* is an example of a locally formal notation, as discussed in [Wile, 1987]. Such calls will be completely removed by later transformations, which define their special semantics.)

The program in Fig. 15.27 is still an abstract program for a virtual machine. Thus further transformational refinement is required to obtain a program that is executable, let alone efficiently executable. There are two efficiency problems with the virtual implementation: It uses an unbounded number of processes, and at any given time most processes will be idle, waiting for results from their subprocesses.

How can one implement an abstract machine with an unbounded number of processes using only a small finite number of real processes? The answer is to generalize what is done to implement recursion in the sequential case. There, one uses an unbounded number of data structures (on a stack) to represent the unbounded recursive function evaluation in the problem, with a single process to carry out the actual evaluation. In the parallel case, one can again use an unbounded number of data structures, but now with several processes to carry out the actual evaluation.

To avoid confusion, my colleague Ken Dritz suggested calling the abstract process created for each function evaluation a *chore* and the real processes that evaluate chores *servers*. Chores and servers are implemented in such a way that, when an abstract process must wait for the results from its subprocesses to become available, its corresponding chore waits, but its server is available to serve another chore. This approach solves both efficiency problems mentioned earlier.

The data structure representing a chore is a *frame*, analogous to a stack frame in the sequential case. However, in the parallel case the creation and freeing of frames does not follow a stack discipline, and a frame "heap" must be used. The frame for a function contains the local storage for that function and storage for some control information.

The implementation of chores and servers requires one further structure, a chore queue that holds the chores currently awaiting service.

There is a close kinship between the implementations of recursive function calls in the parallel and sequential cases. The sequential implementation using a stack of frames is simply an optimization of the parallel one using a heap of frames. The stack optimization becomes possible under the condition that only one server be used. With that hypothesis, and with a judicious choice of the order of creating processes and queuing and dequeuing chores, one can prove that frames are created and destroyed in last-in-first-out order. This relationship suggests that the parallel-process-creation view of implementing recursive functions is more abstract than the traditional stack view, since additional information—an additional design decision—is needed to obtain the stack view from the process-creation view.

Both the creation and freeing of frames and the queuing and dequeuing of chores must be synchronized, of course, since several servers can attempt to perform these operations simultaneously. The concept of *monitor* [Hansen, 1977; Hoare, 1974] in the form discussed in [Lusk and Overbeek, 1983, 1984] can be used to encapsulate the synchronization. A monitor can be thought of as an abstract data type with synchronization. Thus the frame monitor comprises two externally available functions, *crfram* and *frfram*, and the data structures to support them. By definition, only one parallel process (server) can be executing a function from a given monitor at any one time. This property greatly facilitates designing and thinking about parallel programs. In this implementation, it enables one to show that the lower-level abstraction of chores and servers implements the higher-level abstraction of an unbounded number of processes without introducing deadlock.

Once the program has been transformed to the level of chores and servers, it is executable on real parallel processors. However, it would be rather inefficient, because resources would be devoted to evaluating the *await-result* subroutine. The remaining step consists of optimizing the program to eliminate this waste of resources. Observe that results can become available to satisfy an *awaitresult* only when a function evaluation terminates. This observation suggests using the idea of *code motion* from compiler-optimization theory to move detection and signaling of the condition "all results available" to the end of each function evaluation. To support this implementation, the frame for a function contains a count of the number of results needed. As each child process terminates, it reduces this count (using a monitor). The child process that reduces the count to zero places the frame of the parent function back on the unblocked-chore queue.

This optimization leads to the executable form of the program shown in Figs. 15.28 and 15.29, in which the only chores queued for execution by the servers are unblocked (nonwaiting) chores. This version of the concrete program can be run on global-memory parallel computers such as the Denelcor HEP, Sequent Balance 8000, Encore Multimax, and Alliant FX/8 with only

FIGURE 15.28
REALIZATION OF THE FIBONACCI SPECIFICATION FOR GLOBAL-MEMORY
MULTIPLE-INSTRUCTION STREAM, MULTIPLE-DATA STREAM (MIMD)
PARALLEL MACHINES, PART 1

```
subroutine fibd(strtfl)
logical strtfl
integer fp,tfp,plus,diff
integer crfram,gubkcr
if (.not.strtfl) go to 20
    fp = crfram(1)
    frames(fp-4) = 1
    tfp = crfram(6)
    frames(tfp-3) = fp
    frames(tfp+6-1) = fp
    frames(tfp-5) = 7
    frames(fp-5) = 7 + 1
    fp = tfp
    go to 40
```

FIGURE 15.28   *(Cont.)*

```
   10 continue
      tfp = crfram(1)
      frames(tfp-5) = 7 + 1
      call qchore(tfp)
      call frfram(fp,1)
      return
   20 continue
   30 continue
      fp = gubkcr(0)
   40 continue
      irespt = frames(fp-5)
      go to (170,160,130,100,90,60,50,10), irespt
   50 continue
c     assert (framesz(fibd) .eq. 6)
      mfp = fp
         frames(mfp)   = mknum(2)
         frames(mfp+1) = mknum(1)
         frames(mfp+2) = mknum(0)
         frames(mfp+3) = mknum(25)
      frames(mfp-4) = 1
      tfp = crfram(1)
      frames(tfp-3) = mfp
      frames(tfp+1-1) = (mfp + 4)
      frames(tfp-5) = 5
      frames(mfp-5) = 6
      fp = tfp
      go to 40
   60 continue
      frames(frames(mfp+5)) = frames(mfp+4)
      itmppp = frames(mfp-3)
      call plock(frames(itmppp-6))
      itmpct = frames(itmppp-4) - 1
      frames(itmppp-4) = itmpct
      call punlock(frames(itmppp-6))
      if (itmpct .ne. 0) go to 70
         tfp = mfp
         fp = frames(mfp-3)
         call frfram(tfp,6)
      go to 80
   70 continue
         call frfram(mfp,6)
         go to 30
```

FIGURE 15.29
REALIZATION OF THE FIBONACCI SPECIFICATION FOR GLOBAL-MEMORY
MIMD PARALLEL MACHINES, PART 2

```
      80  continue
          go to 40
      90  continue
          ...
          go to 40
     130  continue
c         assert (framesz(fib) .eq. 3)
          if (frames(fp+1) .ne. frames(mfp+2)) go to 140
              frames(frames(fp+2)) = frames(mfp+1)
          go to 180
     140  continue
          if (frames(fp+1) .ne. frames(mfp+1)) go to 150
              frames(frames(fp+2)) = frames(mfp+1)
          go to 180
     150  continue
              frames(fp-4) = 2
              tfp = crfram(3)
              frames(tfp-3) = fp
              frames(tfp+3-2) = diff(frames(fp+1),frames(mfp+1))
              frames(tfp+3-1) = frames(fp+2)
              frames(tfp-5) = 3
              frames(fp-5) = 2
              call qchore(fp)
              fp = tfp
              go to 40
     160      continue
              tfp = crfram(3)
              frames(tfp-3) = fp
              frames(tfp+3-2) = diff(frames(fp+1),frames(mfp))
              frames(tfp+3-1) = fp
              frames(tfp-5) = 3
              frames(fp-5) = 1
              fp = tfp
              go to 40
     170      continue
              frames(frames(fp+2)) =
                  plus(frames(frames(fp+2)),frames(fp))
     180  continue
          itmppp = frames(fp-3)
          call plock(frames(itmppp-6))
          itmpct = frames(itmppp-4) - 1
          frames(itmppp-4) = itmpct
          call punlock(frames(itmppp-6))
          if (itmpct .ne. 0) go to 190
```

FIGURE 15.29 (*Cont.*)

```
        tfp =    fp
        fp = frames(fp-3)
        call frfram(tfp,3)
     go to 200
190 continue
        call frfram(fp,3)
        go to 30
200 continue
     go to 40
     end
```

slight modification. (The code for the calls to *print* and to *fib*(25) is omitted to save space. The code generated from the definition of *fib* begins after the comment "assert (framesz(fib) .eq. 3)" at the top of Fig. 15.29.)

The program in Figs. 15.28 and 15.29 becomes executable after it is combined with fixed (specification-independent) routines for initialization, reading, and printing and with parallel support routines to create and free frames (*crfram* and *frfram*), to queue and dequeue chores (*qchore* and *gubkcr*), and to set and clear hardware locks (*plock* and *punlock*).

My colleague Ken Dritz has prepared an excellent discussion of the details of the concrete implementation of the parallel programs derived from pure Lisp and the accompanying parallel support routines [Dritz and Boyle, 1987]. In addition, he discusses optimizations that reduce contention for access to the monitors when the number of servers is large.

One of the design goals for the parallel strategy was to reuse as many transformations as possible from the sequential case. In the first part of the parallel derivation, many were reused directly. In the second part, very few of the sequential transformations could be reused unchanged, because of the necessary differences between the stack and heap models for frames. However, the transformations that implement chore frames in the parallel case were readily obtained by modifying the ones that implement stack frames in the sequential case. In total, about 60 percent of the transformations used in the parallel derivation are identical to those for the sequential derivation, another 20 percent are systematic modifications of the sequential ones (for example, to handle the frame heap), and the remaining 20 percent are newly written.

15.3.6 Practical Results

Sequential Results.   The strategy for transforming pure applicative Lisp programs into Fortran, discussed in Section 15.3.2 and illustrated in Section

15.3.3, is implemented by 90 major correctness-preserving transformation rules of the type discussed in Section 15.3.4. The transformations are grouped into 20 independent transformation sets.

These transformations have been used to convert several programs written in pure Lisp to Fortran. The largest of these is the 3100-line, 51-function Lisp program for the TAMPR transformer. To convert itself to Fortran, TAMPR applies the transformations 28,000 times to produce a Fortran program of about 4600 lines. Applying the transformations requires no manual assistance (interaction); the entire process is automatic.

The Fortran program produced by the transformations executed correctly (after circumventing some Fortran compiler bugs) the first time it was run, producing output identical to the Lisp version. This Fortran program runs 25 percent faster on a DEC VAX 11/780 than it does in compiled Franz Lisp (opus 38.26) on that machine. A number of well-understood optimizations that are made by the Franz Lisp compiler (for example, removal of tail recursion) have not yet been implemented as part of the Lisp-to-Fortran transformations. I expect that further modest improvements in execution speed will result from implementing these optimizations.

The transformation process itself, however, is not particularly efficient. TAMPR requires about 4 hours running in compiled Franz Lisp on a VAX 11/780 to convert a 1300-line subset of its transformer, or about 1.4 seconds per transformation applied. (This subset implements all the major functionality of the transformer except for the generation of new program identifiers.) The longest single step (about 1.3 hours) is the last transition of Fig. 15.12—the transition that implements calls to recursive parameterless subroutines. This process is fully global, since throughout the program, calls to each function must be replaced by *go-to* statements and labels. I did not write the transformations for this step to be efficient. For clarity, I wrote them in a way (described in Section 15.3.3) that makes m passes over the program, where m is the number of functions in the original Lisp program. Since m is roughly proportional to the length of the program, this set of transformations is effectively $O(n^2)$ in a measure n of the length of the program; it could be written to be $O(n)$ by generating and collecting return-point labels for all functions in a single pass.

The total time for all the steps of recursion removal is 2.5 hours. Of the remaining 1.4 hours, the transformations spend 0.5 hour collecting Lisp quoted constants (another global process not discussed here) and 0.5 hour performing the refinement from canonicalized pure applicative lisp to prepared pure applicative lisp. In contrast, applying the set of coding transformations discussed in Section 15.3.4 (including the optimization discussed in Section 15.4)—in which the individual transformations are not global—requires only 0.1 hour.

I regard the time of 4 hours to transform this program from Lisp to Fortran as slow but not impossibly so. It is certainly fast—and inexpensive—compared to carrying out the task by hand.

Parallel Results.   The parallel version of the program shown in Figs. 15.28 and 15.29 (or suitable variations thereof) has been run on the Denelcor HEP, the Sequent Balance 8000, the Encore Multimax, and Alliant FX/8 computers. It was initially tested on a one-PEM (eight-processor) Denelcor HEP. The derived parallel version of Fibonacci ran the first time it was compiled and produced a speedup of 6.25 (relative to the one-process parallel version) for the computation of $fib(25) = 121,393$. This speedup is good but not spectacular.

There are two possible causes of poor speedup in a parallel program. One possibility that is widely discussed is insufficient parallelism. If even a small percentage of the program must be executed sequentially, speedup for large numbers of processes is severely limited. The other possibility is too much time spent in critical regions—*critical region conflict*. In the implementation discussed here, all critical regions occur in monitors: the frame, queue, and await-result monitors. (The functions of the await-result monitor happen to be unfolded in-line, but it is a monitor nonetheless.)

Lack of parallelism is not an issue for *fib*. As illustrated in Fig. 15.24, processes that can run in parallel are created immediately and exist until the last few moments of execution. However, critical region conflict in the monitors is a potential problem. The frame monitor is the most frequently executed monitor, since a *crfram* and a *frfram* call are done for each function call.

My colleague Ken Dritz instrumented the program to gather statistics on the factors limiting performance [Dritz and Boyle, 1987]. These statistics confirmed that, as he had conjectured, the speedup is limited by competition for access to the critical regions in the frame monitor. After applying a number of optimizations (described in more detail in [Boyle *et al.*, 1987]) to the monitors to reduce critical region conflict, we obtained a speedup of 14.33 for 23 processes (servers) running on the eight-processor Denelcor HEP. A speedup greater than 14 on such a machine is excellent. (Speedups greater than the number of hardware processors were possible on the HEP because the hardware contained special features for queuing waiting processes and for rapid context switching. See [Boyle *et al.*, 1987] for a brief discussion of these features.)

Computing speedups relative to the performance of a single process running the parallel version of the program gives a good indication of how effectively parallel processing is being used. However, as can be seen by comparing Fig. 15.1 with Figs. 15.28 and 15.29, the parallel version of the program is more complicated than the sequential one. Might not the parallel code require so much more time to execute that no benefit is obtained from parallel processing?

In this case, the answer is no. The speedup of 14.33 corresponds to a speedup of 10.57 relative to the version derived by the sequential transformations. There is thus some penalty incurred in order to be able to execute the program in parallel, but it is still definitely worthwhile to do so. In terms of execution time, the sequential version of the program on the

HEP required 82.216 seconds, the 1-process version required 111 seconds, and the 23-process version required 7.781 seconds. The ratio of 111 to 82 can be taken to be the essential cost of the parallel implementation. It consists primarily of the increased cost of managing the frame heap over managing a frame stack, and of entering additional control information in each frame in the parallel case.

All of the experiments on the Denelcor HEP used a central frame queue and chore queue. Dritz later conducted experiments on the Encore Multimax with versions of Fibonacci using distributed chore and frame queues (see [Dritz and Boyle, 1987]). In these versions, there is no contention for the frame queue (each server has its local frame queue), and contention for the chore queue occurs only when some server is out of work. Dritz eventually obtained speedups (relative to the one-process parallel version) of better than 15.5 for 16 servers (processes) on the Encore Multimax.

The Fibonacci program is, of course, not interesting as an example of what improvements in execution parallelism can be expected to make for practical problems. Obviously, if Burstall and Darlington's optimization were applied, a sequential processor could compute $fib(25)$ in a few milliseconds or less! Thus no one would ever run this parallel program in practice. Even apart from its inefficiency, the naive Fibonacci computation is special in that it always makes ample parallelism available.

What level of performance can be achieved for practical list-processing problems? Table 15.1 shows speedups (relative to the parallel version running with one process) for the TAMPR transformer on four shared-memory parallel machines. The transformations used as data for this run were taken from those that produce the parallel realization of pure Lisp specifications.

TABLE 15.1

SPEEDUPS FOR TAMPR TRANSFORMER, OPTIMIZED MONITORS, LOCAL TRANSFORMATION

Machine	Number of Processes	Time (sec.)	Speedup
Denelcor HEP	1	45.188	
	8	6.173	7.32
	16	3.510	12.87
Encore Multimax	1	78.394	
	8	10.886	7.20
	16	6.248	12.55
Sequent B8000	1	74.690	
	8	13.160	5.68
Alliant FX/8	1	12.850	
	8	1.980	6.49

Unlike Fibonacci, for which ample parallelism is available at all times, the parallelism available in the TAMPR transformer depends on the data it is given—specifically, on the properties of the transformations it must apply. The data presented in Table 15.1 are representative of speedups that the program can achieve under good conditions, when the transformations are local, that is, when they apply independently to individual statements, expressions, or variables in a program. When the transformations being applied by the parallel version of the TAMPR transformer are global (for example, when they apply only to an entire subroutine or function body, or to an entire program), the speedups are much smaller. In the worst case, they are about 2.5 for 16 processors.

Generality of the Results.   Could the techniques and transformations discussed here be used for Lisp programs that are not written in pure applicative Lisp? For the sequential derivation the strategy and transformations make only weak use of the pure applicative property—a use that does not differ significantly from that made by a typical Lisp compiler. For example, none of the transformations replaces multiple instances of a function evaluation (common subexpressions) by a single lambda-variable, which would represent a strong use. However, the transformations do create lambda-expressions with a single use of the lambda-variable and then enlarge their scope. Such manipulations can change the order of evaluation of functions, and hence could change the behavior of a program in which side effects of functions were permitted. However, these changes would be no worse than those made by some existing Lisp compilers, in which the order of evaluation of the actual arguments of multiple-variable expressions (and also of the arguments of functions) is different in compiled code from that in interpreted code.

I have prepared a version of the sequential transformations that implements *progs* with local variables and *setq*. Implementations for global variables and even lexically scoped nonlocal variables could be added fairly easily. Thus it seems clear that the sequential transformations could be extended to a complete compiler for Lisp.

Of course, the parallel version of the transformation makes extensive use of the pure Lisp property to permit arguments to be evaluated in parallel. Nevertheless, it is possible to find circumstances under which the pure Lisp requirement could be relaxed. The parallel transformations do not change the number of evaluations of a function, only the order. Thus functions that have side effects but that perform commutative and associative operations can be accommodated correctly. For example, the TAMPR transformer keeps a count of the number of transformations applied. Since incrementing the count is commutative and associative, this function can be implemented correctly in the parallel version of the program simply by making the increment function into a monitor, thereby guaranteeing processes exclusive access to the shared variable.

An interesting area for further research would be to use the algebraic aspect of the transformation approach to study other circumstances under which the pure Lisp requirement could be relaxed. Such work might make it possible to use pure Lisp to specify the high-level control aspects of, say, a large numerical application, while still using existing Fortran library routines to carry out the computations.

15.4 ADVANTAGES OF PROGRAM TRANSFORMATION

The program transformation approach to reusing abstract programs offers a number of advantages, some of which I summarize and illustrate in this section. For each I give an aphorism as a mnemonic aid.

Transformations work best when you use them to make large numbers of small changes. This fact should strongly encourage you to divide the problem to be solved by transformations into a sequence of small, intellectually manageable subproblems. It is much easier to demonstrate the correctness of small steps than it is that of large ones. In turn, because the small steps can be done correctly, you can show that the program produced by the entire set of transformations is correct. Examples of this advantage are woven throughout the preceding sections. *Small is beautiful.*

Using transformations exposes design decisions that you otherwise might make without realizing it. Once these decisions are exposed, you can examine their consequences, as well as the consequences of their alternatives. *Look before you leap.*

Organizing implementation decisions by codifying them in transformations, with the result that they are incorporated sequentially into the program, exposes opportunities for optimization that you might otherwise overlook. For example, if you use the lambda-expression coding transformation given in Fig. 15.20, it produces, at the recursive Fortran level, fragments of code that look like that shown in Fig. 15.30. This example uses three temporary variables, $lv1$, $lv2$, and $lv3$, where obviously one would suffice. Because you can examine the code after this set of transformations applies, it is easy

FIGURE 15.30
MULTIPLE TEMPORARY VARIABLES

```
lv1 = p(a,b,c);
if (lv1 .eq. nil) then;
    lv2 = nil;
else;
    lv2 = f(x,y,a);
end;
lv3 = g(x,y,lv2);
```

FIGURE 15.31
REUSE OF A TEMPORARY VARIABLE

```
lv1 = p(a,b,c);
if (lv1 .eq. nil) then;
    lv1 = nil;
else;
    lv1 = f(x,y,a);
end;
lv1 = g(x,y,lv1);
```

to consider an alternative implementation decision: to reuse program variables wherever possible when coding lambda-expressions. A set of transformations that implement this decision (such as the set used to produce the examples in Section 15.3.3) produces the program of Fig. 15.31 instead of that of Fig. 15.30. The optimizing transformations are written to recognize and reuse an available variable.

What is interesting is that this optimization is not possible at earlier stages in the derivation, because it acts on properties of assignment statements that cannot be reflected in the scope of lambda-expressions. Hence it cannot be done earlier: *Haste makes waste*. Similarly, if the transformations do not make the optimization as they introduce the assignment statements (by recording the earliest assignment to a variable), the optimization becomes difficult to make, because flow analysis is required. Hence this optimization should not be done later: *Opportunity knocks but once*. To summarize these two aphorisms: *To everything there is a season*.

This example also illustrates that making one optimization frequently enables others. It is silly to assign the value *nil* to *lv1* in Fig. 15.31, for *lv1* has just been tested and is known to have that value. It is clear that you should not assign a variable a value it already has. The necessary transformation is trivial to write, and using it ultimately produces the fragment shown in Fig. 15.32. This fragment saves one assignment and reduces the size of the program. The important point here is that this optimization is not possi-

FIGURE 15.32
REUSE OF A TEMPORARY VARIABLE, SIMPLIFIED CODE

```
lv1 = p(a,b,c);
if (lv1 .ne. nil) then;
    lv1 = f(x,y,a);
end;
lv1 = g(x,y,lv1);
```

ble until the implementation decision to reuse variables has been taken. *Optimization begets optimization.*

15.5 RELATED WORK

The ideas of abstract programming and program transformation can be traced to the use of macro processors to raise the level of abstraction in assembly language programs. Later, macro processors were used with higher-level languages and the abstract machine concept. However, typical macro processors do not understand higher-level programming languages—they operate on a program in such a language as if it were an unstructured string of characters. Thus macro processors offer little assistance in implementing transformations of programs correctly; in fact, macro implementations tend to be difficult to design and debug.

True program transformation systems understand syntactic constructions in higher-level languages—identifiers, variables, expressions, statements and the like—and manipulate them reliably. They permit only well-formed constructs of the same syntactic type to be substituted for one another; thus they assist in writing transformations that are at least syntactically correct. I implemented the first such program transformation system in 1970 for the Algol 60 programming language [Boyle, 1970]. It is a direct ancestor of the TAMPR system discussed here.

15.5.1 Other Program Transformation Systems

Several other projects emphasize abstract programming and production of efficient programs by transformation. One is Project CIP at the Technical University of Munich. An early discussion of this work can be found in [Bauer, 1976], while a recent example appears in [Broy and Pepper, 1982]; there are also numerous technical reports available from the university. Project CIP has emphasized the development of a wide-spectrum language, CIP-L, for abstract programming as well as a transformation system. An important feature of CIP-L is its precise formal definition, which is based on the algebraic theory of abstract data types. Another program transformation project is the GIST project at the Information Sciences Institute. Descriptions of this project can be found in [Balzer, Goldman, and Wile, 1976; Balzer *et al.*, 1983; Wile, 1983]. The project has emphasized the development of a very high-level specification language, GIST, that accommodates problem-oriented notations implemented transformationally. An interesting part of the project is the development of a program that automatically paraphrases GIST specifications in English.

Burstall and his colleagues at the University of Edinburgh have studied transformations of recursion equations and recursive programs extensively

[Burstall and Darlington, 1977; Feather, 1982]. Darlington is continuing this work. Program transformation and abstract programming also play an important role in the extensible programming language ECL developed at Harvard; an early reference is [Cheatham and Wegbreit, 1972]. From this work has evolved the current Harvard Program Development System (PDS) [Cheatham, Holloway, and Townley, 1981]. Other implemented transformation systems include that of Arsac [1979] and the MENTOR system [Donzeau-Gouge *et al.*, 1975]. The original version of MENTOR was designed to transform Pascal programs. It has now been implemented with table-driven components so that it can, like TAMPR, be configured to operate on any language. MENTOR is currently being commercialized. The MIT Programmer's Apprentice project of Rich and Waters [Waters, 1982] uses a generalized notion of transformation applied to plans to perform program synthesis.

Information on the current status of several of these systems can be found in the proceedings of workshops on program transformation held recently in Munich [Pepper, 1984] and in Bad Tölz [Meertens, 1987]. Both of these proceedings contain an extensive record of the participants' discussion of current issues in program transformation. A recent survey article [Partsch and Steinbrueggen, 1983] contains an excellent and extensive (193-entry) bibliography on program transformation topics. Finally, Koster, Meertens, Partsch, and Swierstra have just initiated a project on Specification and Transformation Of Programs (project STOP) in the Netherlands [Partsch *et al.*, 1988]. This project held a workshop in March 1988.

15.5.2 Transformation and Optimization

A number of papers mention the important connection between abstraction, transformation, and optimization. Two early examples are catalogs of correctness-preserving program optimization transformations, the Irvine Program Transformation Catalog [Standish *et al.*, 1976] and the catalog of Loveman [1977]. In Loveman's catalog there is also an interesting example of the use of transformations to optimize the implementation of a moderately abstract (approximately Pascal-level) program. Some of the transformations in Loveman's catalog have been implemented in automatic optimizers, but in hardcoded rather than rewrite-rule form.

At a somewhat higher level of abstraction are transformations of Lisp programs. These have long been used in Lisp compilers to optimize programs before compilation, most notably for recursion removal but also for other optimizations as well. A good discussion of such transformations appears in [Brooks, Gabriel, and Steele, 1982]. A Lisp transformation system that "explains" the nature or purpose of the transformations it applies is discussed by Steele [1980]. It is an outgrowth of a Lisp transformation system constructed to optimize the implementation of abstract data types in the TAMPR transformer.

Paige and Koenig [1982] discuss a particularly elegant class of transformations for highly abstract programs that go beyond optimization and contribute to the implementation of algorithms. These transformations extend the classical mathematical idea of computing numerical functions by finite differencing to optimizing the implementation of set-theoretic abstractions in programs written in the SETL language.

Cheatham, Holloway, and Townley [1981] also discuss specifying the implementation and optimization of abstract algorithms by means of transformations. They stress that when the developer of an algorithm specifies new abstractions (abstract data types and abstract control structures), he or she must also be able to specify optimizations for them. Even when a sophisticated optimizing compiler is available, there are always optimizations that the programmer is aware of but that such an automatic compiler cannot discover. I strongly concur with this observation. The ability to specify *problem-domain-dependent* optimizations and implementations of abstractions simultaneously is one of the major advantages of using program transformations. Moreover, as I have pointed out in Section 15.4, there is usually a point in the transition from abstract program to concrete implementation at which each such optimization is particularly simple to apply. Thus, even if an optimizing compiler were to discover such optimizations, it would have to expend significant additional resources to apply them.

15.5.3 Automated versus Interactive Transformation

Program transformation systems and catalogs of transformations are frequently used as interactive program development tools. In that mode, they rely on the user to select which transformation to apply, to confirm whether an automatically selected transformation should be applied, or to confirm an applicability condition for a transformation. Even when applying a transformation that does not have applicability conditions, they may ask the user to determine whether applying that transformation at a particular point in the program is a good idea. In such systems, the transformations themselves do not incorporate a strategy for achieving a goal.

Interactive transformation systems appear attractive when a particular implementation or optimization decision is to be applied only at selected places in a program. However, systems that require interaction for each application of a transformation (or a small group of transformations) have an obvious disadvantage: They are cumbersome to use, especially for tasks of the Lisp-to-Fortran type, which require thousands of such applications.

To overcome this disadvantage, some systems provide elaborate control languages in which to express detailed specifications of the order and place of application of transformations in the program tree. Typical of such control specifications are instructions to move up or down in the tree from the point of application of a particular transformation, and instructions to try certain transformations next after a particular one applies. These systems suffer from a less obvious, but more serious, disadvantage than interactive ones: What if the instructions for a program are incorrect or incomplete? This question manifests itself as a difficulty in demonstrating the correctness of sets of transformations and control instructions in such systems.

In contrast, the TAMPR system offers automated operation without an elaborate control language. Interaction is limited to the initial selection of which sets of transformations to apply. These selections correspond directly to the programmer's design decisions about the target realization. Of course, the programmer must accept that they will be applied throughout the program, or else must write a set of transformations that selectively introduces some marker at the points where he or she wishes the general transformations to apply. In place of explicit control, TAMPR uses control that is largely implicit, governed by the exhaustive postorder (bottom-up) sequencing rule. This implicit sequencing leaves the order of application of transformations primarily under the control of the program being transformed. Implicit sequencing, coupled with the use of transformations that individually (or in small groups) preserve correctness, makes it easy to see that a set of transformations operates correctly for all admissible programs.

In my experience, automated operation with implicit sequencing is a very satisfactory mode of operation. (See [Boyle, 1984] for a brief description of applications of TAMPR in addition to the Lisp-to-Fortran transformation described here.) Experience with another automated transformation system, the Harvard PDS [Cheatham, Holloway, and Townley, 1981], corroborates this observation. The PDS uses an implicit sequencing rule—exhaustive preorder (top-down)—similar to that used in TAMPR. This rule is presumably more efficient than the TAMPR exhaustive postorder rule, but it does not permit the use of the transformational induction rule for canonical forms, as the TAMPR rule does.

The PDS also provides a notation for limiting the scope of transformations. Limited-scope transformations are useful, for example, for expressing optimizations that are valid only within the scope of some optimization or implementation expressed by an earlier transformation. An analogous facility is provided by the notation for subtransformations in TAMPR (see [Boyle and Matz, 1976]).

(I remark that the TAMPR exhaustive postorder sequencing rule is the same as that used for the equality-rewriting process called *demodulation* in automated reasoning systems; see [Wos *et al.*, 1984].)

There are other program transformation systems that emphasize automated transformations. One is the RAPTS system [Paige, 1984, 1983] used by Paige to apply the finite-differencing transformations discussed earlier. RAPTS uses either rewrite rules or hard-coded rules with built-in guidance, depending on the application. An interesting and powerful feature of RAPTS is that it transforms not only the program, but also measures of the program's complexity and various invariants, all at the same time. The complexity measures and invariants are used to guide the transformation of an abstract program into a concrete one. The primary interaction required with RAPTS is to make a few implementation decisions early in the transformation process, although RAPTS can ask the user to confirm applicability conditions if necessary.

Automated program transformation also plays an important role in the program synthesis systems of Green, for example, in the PSI system discussed in [Green, 1976]. This system contains an elaborate component to help evaluate alternative implementations for abstract constructs (for example, sets) and to select the ones most efficient for a particular program.

15.5.4 Rewrite-Rule versus Hard-coded Transformations

An automated transformation system for conventional languages (the example implementation is for Pascal) that is not rewrite rule based is the GRAMPS system [Cameron and Ito, 1984]. Instead of syntactic pattern matching, it uses a procedural language, or metaprogramming language, to describe transformations. Cameron and Ito state that the metaprogramming approach has decided advantages over approaches employing rewrite rules, especially for expressing complex transformations. However, to me these metaprograms seem more cumbersome and less clear than rewrite rules, specifically in regard to showing that the transformations they carry out are correct. In fact, Cameron and Ito present most of the transformations in their paper first in terms of rewrite rules and then give the metaprogram for them. (The examples given in [Myers and Osterweil, 1981] provide further illustrations of the potential incomprehensibility of nonrewrite-rule transformations.) I answer some of Cameron and Ito's specific criticisms of the rewrite-rule approach in [Boyle *et al.*, 1987].

Based on my experience, I favor using rewrite rules to express nearly all aspects of program transformation. Doing so avoids the complication of using different means for different tasks. And it fosters writing correct transformations, because determining whether a rewrite rule preserves correctness is easier than determining whether a metaprogram does.

15.5.5 Abstract Programming

A number of authors have discussed abstract programming without reference to a specific transformation system. An early (and continuing) advocate of an abstract programming methodology for writing business programs is Jackson. The transformations needed to realize efficient concrete programs in the methodology of [Jackson, 1975] are to be carried out manually. Knuth discusses abstract programming in relation to the disciplined use of the *go-to* statement in [Knuth, 1974]. Gerhart discusses the role of abstraction in simplifying proofs of program correctness in [Gerhart, 1975] (see also [Wos *et al.*, 1984]). Scherlis and Scott give an elegant philosophical discussion of the potential of abstract programming in [Scherlis and Scott, 1983] (see also [Scherlis, 1984]). Finally, further references on abstract programming can be found in [Partsch and Steinbrueggen, 1983].

15.6 CONCLUSIONS

Program specification at a moderately abstract level, when accompanied by program transformation, can be used to produce efficient programs reliably. As a demonstration, I have presented an "industrial strength" example, showing the use of program transformations to derive two programs from a pure Lisp specification. One derived program is tuned for efficient execution on conventional sequential computers. The other is tuned for execution on shared-memory parallel computers. The sequential program runs 25 percent faster in Fortran than in compiled Franz Lisp, while the parallel version has achieved speedups of 12.5 on practical problems.

Approaching such tasks by means of program transformation encourages organizing them in a modular fashion. The general approach is the following:

- ☐ Develop a strategy for solving the problem, by breaking it up into intellectually manageable steps and corresponding language levels and locally formal notations.
- ☐ Implement each of the steps as one or more sets of correctness-preserving program transformations that move the program from one language level to the next by implementing the locally formal notations.
- ☐ Apply the transformations to produce a correct program.
- ☐ Examine this program at intermediate levels to determine whether further optimizations could be made.

It is worth summarizing the advantages of the transformation methodology:

Clearly, deriving the programs by transformation has the potential for saving effort over writing them by hand. For the example in this paper, it is not clear whether the sequential version of the program was produced more cheaply by using program transformations than it would have been by hand; however, the transformations developed have the potential for reuse. I reapplied them to derive a new Fortran version of the TAMPR transformer when I modified the pure Lisp specification to add new functionality. The transformations can also be applied to other pure Lisp specifications to derive sequential programs. In both of these cases, the saving is enormous.

For the parallel case, it was certainly quicker and cheaper to write transformations to derive the program than to write the program by hand. Starting with the experience gained in the sequential case, it took only about three man-months of effort and just two months of elapsed time to produce the parallel program. Most of this time was spent formulating and examining (desk-checking) the levels of abstraction in the strategy. Modifying some of the sequential transformations and writing the few new ones required took only about three man-weeks. Thus, *if several programs are to be derived, program transformation is economic*.

In porting the program to four different parallel machines, a few transformations were modified to tailor the program to each machine. The modifications required perhaps 10 minutes for each machine. To obtain the code for a new machine, it was necessary only to rerun the transformations. Had the program been written by hand, a few hours would have been required to incorporate the same modifications, and the possibility of making errors would have been introduced. This situation illustrates an important property of abstraction and its implementation by transformations—*information that is distributed globally in the program is localized in the transformations, making it easy to change*.

In assessing whether the cost of writing the transformations has been recouped, it is also important to consider the potential savings in writing the specification. Writing a pure Lisp specification for the programs I have considered is certainly easier, more natural, and more amenable to verification than writing the Fortran version directly. I conclude that *pure Lisp specifications are easier to write than concrete programs; moreover, they can be tested, since they are executable*. In addition, should pure Lisp prove an unsuitable specification language for some problem, one can choose a more suitable language and write the transformations that implement it.

Using an abstract-specification, program-transformation approach forces one to think about design decisions. It enables one to consider alternatives, even before the program has been run. One need not fear that months will have been spent writing a concrete program, only to find that some design decision is fundamentally wrong. Thus *use of transformations increases the intellectual manageability of large programming tasks*.

Perhaps the most important advantage of using transformations is that once the specification has been tested and validated, debugging is a thing of the past. This claim may sound extravagant. Here is the experience on which it is based:

In the case of the transformations from Lisp to sequential Fortran, the programs produced by the transformations worked correctly the first time they were run. A few errors were made in the sequential strategy, primarily in accessing elements of the stack frame, but they were caught during the writing of the transformations, by desk-checking and performing thought experiments, before attempting to execute the derived programs.

For the parallel case, the first program derived by the transformations, *fib*, ran correctly the first time it was executed. When I ran the code for the TAMPR transformer, I did encounter two bugs—in 3500 lines of code. One bug resulted from a typographical error in writing a transformation, which caused reversal of the order of the arguments of a function when a plambda-expression was created. Since the function *plus* is commutative, the error did not show up in running *fib!*

The other error was more serious. Interestingly, it followed a pattern common to many programming errors, but at the meta level. I wrote a transformation to expand the scope of a lambda-expression, and I optimized it on the fly, omitting the applicability condition that an expression being moved outside the scope of a lambda-variable must not depend upon that lambda-variable, because I knew (I thought) that that circumstance couldn't arise in this particular situation. In fact, the circumstance did arise (through subsequent changes to other transformations), producing references to uninitialized variables in the transformed code. Thus *using transformations does not completely eliminate bugs, but it does greatly reduce them.*

Finally, I have discussed a number of ways in which transformations illuminate the underlying principles of programming. This increased understanding of computer programming—a process exposed here as largely a science, not an art—is perhaps the greatest benefit of the transformational approach to program reusability.

Acknowledgments

Over the years a number of people have contributed to the development of the TAMPR system and the transformations discussed in this paper. A version of the recursion removal transformations for recursive numeric programs was written by Diane Smith Dick. The set of transformations that merge declarations, which was reused in this application, was written by Karen Wieckert. Terry Harmer, David Henderson, and Bruce Char worked on the TAMPR recognizer. The TAMPR formatter was developed by Ken Dritz with the assistance of Carl Hauser. Kevin Hopkins, Charlotte Metzger, Pete Newton, Marilyn Matz, Barbara Kerns Steele, Brian Smith, Steve Hague, Wendy Barth, Genell Davis, and Barbara Bonar have written transformations for applications of TAMPR. John Darlington and Manfred Broy discussed models for the parallel implementation of pure Lisp and possible ways to refine them. Members of IFIP WG2.1 have listened to early reports on this work and asked questions that have improved its presentation. Larry Wos provided comments on a draft of this paper. Finally, I wish to acknowledge Paul Messina, former director of the Mathematics and Computer Science Division at Argonne, for his support of this work.

References

Arsac, J. J. Syntactic source to source transformation and program manipulation. *Communications of the ACM* 22(1): 43–54, Jan. 1979.

Balzer, R.; Cohen, D.; Feather, M. S.; Goldman, N. M.; Swartout, W.; and Wile, D. S. Operational specification as the basis for specification validation. pp. 21–49 in

Theory and Practice of Software Technology, ed. D. Ferrari, M. Bolognani, and J. Goguen. Amsterdam: North-Holland, 1983.

Balzer, R.; Goldman, N.; and Wile, D. On the transformational implementation approach to programming. *Proceedings of the 2nd International Conference on Software Engineering*, pp. 337–344. San Francisco, 1976.

Bauer, F. L. Programming as an evolutionary process. *Proceedings of the 2nd International Conference on Software Engineering*, pp. 223–234. San Francisco, 1976.

Bauer, F. L.; Broy, M.; Partsch, H.; and Pepper, P. Report on a wide spectrum language for program specification and development. Technical report TUM-18104, Technical University, Munich, May 1981.

Boyle, J. M. A transformational component for programming language grammar. Technical report ANL-7690, Argonne National Laboratory, Argonne, Ill., July 1970.

Boyle, J. M. Towards automatic synthesis of linear algebra programs. pp. 223–245 in *Production and Assessment of Numerical Software*, ed. M. A. Hennell and L. M. Delves. New York: Academic Press, 1980a.

Boyle, J. M. Program adaptation and program transformation. pp. 3–20 in *Practice in Software Adaptation and Maintenance*, ed. R. Ebert, J. Lueger, and L. Goecke. Amsterdam: North-Holland, 1980b.

Boyle, J. M. Software adaptability and program transformation. pp. 75–94 in *Software Engineering*, ed. H. Freeman and P. M. Lewis II. New York: Academic Press, 1980c.

Boyle, James M. Lisp to Fortran—Program transformation applied. pp. 291–298 in *Program Transformation and Programming Environments*, ed. Peter Pepper. NATO ASI Series, vol. F8. New York: Springer-Verlag, 1984.

Boyle, J. M.; Dritz, K. W.; Muralidharan, M. N.; and Taylor, R. Deriving sequential and parallel programs from pure LISP specifications by program transformation. In *Program Specification and Transformation*, ed. L. G. L. T. Meertens. Amsterdam: North-Holland, 1987.

Boyle, J. M., and Matz, M. Automating multiple program realizations. *Proceedings of the MRI Symposium, XXIV: Computer Software Engineering*, pp. 421–456. Polytechnic Press, Brooklyn, 1976.

Boyle, J. M., and Muralidharan, M. N. Program reusability through program transformation. *IEEE Transactions on Software Engineering* SE-10(5): 574–588, Sept. 1984.

Boyle, J. M., and Schütz, C. Peter. Unpublished information, 1988.

Brooks, R. A.; Gabriel, R. P.; and Steele, G. L., Jr. An optimizing compiler for lexically scoped LISP. *ACM SIGPLAN Notices* 17(6): 261–275, June 1982.

Broy, M., and Pepper, P. Combining algebraic and algorithmic reasoning: An approach to the Schorr-Waite algorithm. *ACM Transactions on Programming Languages and Systems* 4(3): 362–381 July 1982.

Burstall, R. M., and Darlington, J. A. A transformation system for developing recursive programs. *Journal of the ACM* 24(1): 44–67, Jan. 1977.

Cameron, Robert D., and Ito, M. Robert. Grammar-based definition of metaprogramming systems. *ACM Transactions on Programming Languages and Systems (TOPLAS)* 6(1): 20–54, Jan. 1984.

Cheatham, Thomas E., Jr.; Holloway, Glenn H.; and Townley, Judy A. Program refinement by transformation. *Proceedings of the 5th International Conference on Software Engineering*, pp. 430–437. San Diego, 1981.

Cheatham, T. E., and Wegbreit, B. A laboratory for the study of automatic programming. *AFIPS Conference Proceedings, SJCC* vol. 40, pp. 11–21, 1972.

Church, A. *The Calculi of Lambda Conversion*. Princeton, N.J.: Princeton University Press, 1941.

Dongarra, J. J.; Moler, C. B.; Bunch, J. R.; and Stewart, G. W. *LINPACK User's Guide*. Philadelphia: SIAM (Society of Industrial and Applied Mathematics), 1979.

Donzeau-Gouge, V.; Huet, G.; Kahn, G.; Lang, B.; and Levy, J. J. A structure-oriented program editor: A first step towards computer-assisted programming. *International Computing Symposium*, pp. 113–120, 1975.

Dritz, K. W., and Boyle, J. M. Beyond "speedup": Performance analysis of parallel programs. Technical report ANL-87-7, Argonne National Laboratory, Argonne, Ill., February 1987.

Feather, M. S. A system for assisting program transformation. *ACM Transactions on Programming Languages and Systems (TOPLAS)* 4(1): 1–20, Jan. 1982.

Gerhart, S. L. Knowledge about programs: A model and case study. *Proceedings of the International Conference on Reliable Software*, pp. 88–95. Los Angeles, April 21–23, 1975.

Green, C. C. The design of the PSI program synthesis system. *Proceedings of the 2nd International Conference on Software Engineering*, pp. 4–18. San Francisco, 1976.

Hansen, Per Brinch. *The Architecture of Concurrent Programs*. Englewood Cliffs, N.J.: Prentice-Hall, 1977.

Hoare, C. A. R. Monitors: An operating system structuring concept. *Communications of the ACM*, pp. 549–557, October 1974.

Jackson, Michael A. *Principles of Program Design*. London: Academic Press, 1975.

Knuth, D. E. Structured programming with GOTO statements. *ACM Computing Surveys* 6(4): 261–301, Dec. 1974.

Larmouth, J. Serious FORTRAN. *Software Practice and Experience* 3(2): 87–107, 1973a.

Larmouth, J. Serious FORTRAN—Part 2. *Software Practice and Experience* 3(3): 197–225, 1973b.

Loveman, D. B. Program improvement by source to source transformation. *Journal of the ACM* 24(1): 121–145, Jan. 1977.

Lusk, E., and Overbeek, R. A. Use of monitors in FORTRAN: A tutorial on the barrier, self-scheduling DO-loop, and askfor monitors. Technical report ANL-84-51, Argonne National Laboratory, Argonne, Ill., July 1984.

Lusk, Ewing L., and Overbeek, Ross A. Implementation of monitors with macros: A programming aid for the HEP and other parallel processors. Technical report ANL-83-97, Argonne National Laboratory, Argonne, Ill., Dec. 1983.

Meertens, L. G. L. T., ed. *Program Specification and Transformation*, Amsterdam: North-Holland, 1987.

Moitra, Abha, and Iyengar, S. Sitharama. Derivation of a maximally parallel algorithm for balancing binary search trees. Technical report TR 84-638, Department of Computer Science, Cornell University, Sept. 1984.

Myers, Eugene W., Jr., and Osterweil, Leon J. BIGMAC II: A FORTRAN language augmentation tool. *Proceedings of the 5th International Conference on Software Engineering*, pp. 410–421. San Diego, 1981.

Nordstrom, M. *LISP F3 Users Guide.* Datalogilaboratoriet, Uppsala University, Uppsala, Sweden, June 1978.

Paige, Robert. Transformational programming—Applications to algorithms and systems. *Proceedings of the 10th ACM Symposium on Principles of Programming Languages*, pp. 73–87, Jan. 1983.

Paige, Robert. Supercompilers—Extended abstract. pp. 331–340 in *Program Transformation and Programming Environments*, ed. Peter Pepper. NATO ASI Series, vol. F8. New York: Springer-Verlag, 1984.

Paige, Robert, and Koenig, Shaye. Finite differencing of computable expressions. *ACM Transactions on Programming Languages and Systems (TOPLAS)* 4(3): 402–454, July 1982.

Partsch, H. A.; Koster, C. H. A.; Meertens, L. G. L. T.; and Swierstra, S. D. Private communication, 1988.

Partsch, H., and Steinbrueggen, R. Program transformation systems. *ACM Computing Surveys* 15(3): 199–236, Sept. 1983.

Pepper, Peter, ed. *Program Transformation and Programming Environments*. NATO ASI Series, vol. F8. New York: Springer-Verlag, 1984.

Scherlis, William L. Software development and inferential programming. pp. 341–346 in *Program Transformation and Programming Environments*, ed. Peter Pepper. NATO ASI Series, vol. F8. New York: Springer-Verlag, 1984.

Scherlis, William L., and Scott, Dana S. First steps towards inferential programming. Technical report CMU-CS-83-142, Computer Science Department, Carnegie-Mellon University, Pittsburgh, July 1983. Also in *Proceedings of the IFIP Congress 83*.

Standish, T. A.; Harriman, D. C.; Kibler, D. F.; and Neighbors, J. M. The Irvine program transformation catalog. University of California at Irvine, Irvine, Calif., Jan. 1976.

Steele, Barbara Kerns. An accountable source-to-source transformation system. Master's thesis, Dept. of Electrical Engineering and Computer Science, Massachusetts Institute of Technology, Cambridge, Mass., July 1980.

Waters, R. C. The programmer's apprentice: Knowledge based program editing. *IEEE Transactions on Software Engineering* 8(1): 1–12, Jan. 1982.

Wile, D. S. Program developments: Formal explanations of implementations. *Communications of the ACM* 26(11): 902–911, Nov. 1983.

Wile, David S. Local formalisms: Widening the spectrum of wide-spectrum languages. In *Program Specification and Transformation*, ed. L. G. L. T. Meertens. Amsterdam: North-Holland, 1987.

Wirth, N. Program development through stepwise refinement. *Communications of the ACM* 14(4): 221–227, April, 1971.

Wos, L.; Overbeek, R.; Lusk, E.; and Boyle, J. *Automated Reasoning: Introduction and Applications*. Englewood Cliffs, N.J.: Prentice-Hall, 1984.

INDEX